Dahla Ayoun

SYNTAX
Volume I

SYNTAX

A FUNCTIONAL-TYPOLOGICAL INTRODUCTION

Volume I

T. GIVÓN
Linguistics Department
University of Oregon, Eugene
and
Ute Language Program
Southern Ute Tribe
Ignacio, Colorado

JOHN BENJAMINS PUBLISHING COMPANY
Amsterdam/Philadelphia

1984

Library of Congress Cataloging in Publication Data

Givón, Talmy, 1936-
Syntax: a functional-typological introduction.

Bibliography: p. 437.
Includes index.
1. Grammar, Comparative and general -- Syntax. 2. Typology (Linguistics)
3. Functionalism (Linguistics) I. Title.
P291.G5   1984   415   84-6195
ISBN 0-915027-07-0 (U.S. hb., v. 1)
ISBN 0-915027-08-9 (U.S. pb., v. 1)
ISBN 90-272-3013-7 (European hb., v. 1)
ISBN 90-272-3012-9 (European pb., v. 1)

To Linda, for her help, patience, perspective and,
above all, grace.

PREFACE

After *On Understanding Grammar* came out, I began to receive letters or even reviews of roughly the following sort: "...terrific, but where are the nuts and bolts, the full detail...?". It took a while to convince myself that the time was ripe for filling in the details. I kept resisting the idea, until I finally realized that "the" definitive work could never be written, but only progressively refined and contingently assembled, like everything else in science. Granting this, the book is nonetheless an attempt to give an explicit, systematic and comprehensive picture of syntax, semantics and pragmatics as a unified whole. Whether the attempt is as successful as I intended it to be is a matter that only time and added perspective may resolve. All I can say now is that a book of this scope, orientation and above all *hutzpa* does not yet exist. By making it now available to others, especially to beginners, I hope to rescue them from the many detours, dead ends, blind alleys and *cul-de-sacs* through which I myself was left to meander during my own early days in linguistics.

Working in relative isolation has both its advantages and pitfalls. One of the latter is, often, neglecting to give credit where credit is due. While the particular way in which I have attempted to integrate the study of grammar, meaning and function is peculiarly my own, it feeds upon the work of many others, most particularly the people I have been fortunate to associate with during the past ten years. While their works are not always cited at the exact point where they should have been, their knowledge — and generosity in sharing it — will always hover over this book. I have always considered human languages and their speakers my true teachers in linguistics, but it has been a rare privilege to travel through human language in such stimulating company. I take this opportunity to thank you all, Andy Anderson, Peter Becker, Derek Bickerton, Dwight Bolinger, Sandy Chung, Bernard Comrie, Colette Craig, Scott DeLancey, Bob Dixon, Erica García, Joe Goguen, Joseph Greenberg, John Haiman, Robert Hetzron, John Hinds, Paul Hopper, Ed Keenan, Margaret Langdon, Ron Langacker, Win Lehmann, Charles Li, Bob Longacre, Jim Matisoff, Pam Munro, Johanna Nichols, Eli Ochs, Charlie Osgood, Andy Pawley, Haj Ross, Gillian Sankoff, Tim Shopen, Dan Slobin, Len Talmy, Sandy Thompson, Alan Timberlake, Russ Tomlin, John Verhaar.

Ignacio, Colorado
May, 1983

CONTENTS

1 | BACKGROUND

1.1. THE STUDY OF LANGUAGE AND THE STUDY OF SYNTAX

1.1.1. Interconnections

As any observant student of history — human or otherwise — should know, there is nothing mysteriously objective about selecting a historical context for a phenomenon under scrutiny. This must be so because historical contexts are themselves embedded within the wider context of one's intellectual goals, philosophical premises and methodological choices. The setting of this book's approach to language and syntax within its proper historical perspective is therefore not exempt from the vagaries of its own context. This is a hazard an author, especially a pragmatist, must accept — indeed welcome — with grace. While in a firmly held and conveniently fixed context some phenomena may indeed seem stable and firm, the choice of context — any context — is in principle arbitrary.

My own context for doing linguistics and, within it, syntax/semantics/pragmatics, is heterogeneous. First comes **biology**, which views the human organism, its socio-cultural organization and its cognitive-intellectual-communicative tools from a functional, evolutionary perspective. The functions may be described as various strategies or sub-strategies by which the organism attempts to cope with the perceived imperatives of environment and survival. At higher evolutionary levels, survival tasks are perceived as being increasingly complex, and coping strategies are devised at increasingly abstract levels. Cognition and communication in the human organism evolved in the context of a certain socio-cultural organization and the need to cooperate for mutual survival. More complex cultural patterns impose more complex tasks, and these in turn require a more intricate communicative code — which then loops back to facilitate a more elaborate culture. And to top it all, the whole enterprise is not now — and has never been — a deterministic automaton of blind neurons and rigid genes. Rather, coping and survival must have always been a matter of making intelligent choices, given the level of information available to the organism at the time.

Next comes **philosophy**, queen of science and often its nemesis, arbiter of method and often of its demise. Within it, the Western epistemological tradition from Plato onward has been oscillating between two extreme biases, empiricist and rationalist. The first proclaims the primacy of environment and external stimuli, while trivializing the analytic, conceptual, willful role of the organism's mind. The second elevates an idealized mind to virtual independence of outside stimulation. Both are locked by choice into an unhealthy dualism equally extreme, seemingly leaving no *Lebensraum* between Carnap's forbidding determinism and Wittgenstein's contextualized mush.[1] But a compromise solution has been available for some time, following Kant and Peirce. Within that tradition one stresses the interactive, mutually-dependent nature of percepts and concepts, environment and organism, input and analyzer, World and Mind. This pragmatic, non-dualist resolution of the artificial historical cleavage between empiricist and rationalist imposes upon its practitioner a number of heavy burdens. For one, the seductive categorial clarity of extreme formulations à la Skinner or Chomsky must be resisted, in favor of less elegant, complex, hybrid and open-ended systems. For another, a much richer, diverse and yet somehow integrated data-base must be addressed and accounted for, in order to sketch out the pragmatist's hybrid solution. Such a solution must allow for enough categorial discreteness and stability, without discarding the fine shades and gradations of context sensitivity. These are burdens one must learn to embrace gladly, if one wishes the study of language to become a viable empirical enterprise.

Next comes **anthropology**, which anchors the study of language and cognition within the matrix of social structure/function and cultural world view. The role of language and communication within this matrix, and the way different language communities solve the task of coding and communicating knowledge, shed light on the balance between cultural and cognitive universals, on one hand, and culture-specific codes of behavior, cognition and communication on the other. Here once again one must navigate between the extreme shallows of Whorfian cultural relativism and Chomsky's Euro-centric 'universalism'. And while such a feat of seamanship is hard indeed, it must

---

1) It is of course curious that both of these relatively late exponents of Western dualist extremes considered themselves true empiricists.

again be embraced gladly if one is ever to strike — on firm empirical foundations and without a priori bias — the right balance between language universality and language specificity.

Last but not least is **psychology**, the empirical rock from which many linguistic expeditions have been launched and upon which many have crashed.
Here, once again, one must negotiate a middle ground between equally un-
tenable extremes. On the one hand is the Chomskian extreme, insisting on the
Cartesian uniqueness of the human *faculté de langage*, on its separability from
and inexplicability in terms of so-called general cognitive capacities. On the
other hand one may find Skinner's propensity for trivializing both language
and cognition by viewing them through the reductionist glasses of stimulus-re-
sponse. But one also finds there perennial tendencies of cognitive psychologists to underestimate the unique organization of human language. The middle grounds that must be struck again should retain both common sense and
empirical accountability. As in other cases of extreme reductionism,[2] one
strongly suspects that the Chomsky-Piaget debate is in large measure artificial.[3] It has been engendered, I believe, by one side's insistence on placing
strict limitations on the data-base relevant to the investigation. A realistic account of the complex inter-relationship between language and cognition
could only be obtained if artificial a priori constraints on the relevant evidence
were removed, and the data-base then allowed to exert its therapeutic force —
and may the chips fall where they may.

We come at last to linguistics and its convoluted history.

1.1.2. Historical threads

The post-Socratic Greek tradition may again be used as the point of departure for the history of linguistics. It mingled in equal measures extreme
versions of both **universalism** and **mentalism**. The first was only implicit, given
the classical Greek's disdain for the Barbarians' culture, language and
thought. As to the second, Aristotelian **syllogisms** and **rhetoric** were clearly
conceived of as both rules of human Language and modes of human Thought.
Through them the Greek language was implicitly viewed — without much attention paid to its syntax — as a human-universal norm.

The same implicit assumptions of both universality and mentalism re-

---

2) See, for example, Quine's (1953) illuminating discussion on "Two dogmas of empiricism".

3) While artificial in origin, it is nonetheless extremely stimulating. For the gory details see Piattelli-Palmarini (ed., 1980).

mained the hallmark of the Latin-bound medieval **Modistae** tradition,[4] and of the French **Port Royal** tradition of **Grammaire Générale et Raisonnée**.[5] Only the "ideal" language had changed. The concept of "grammar" remained logi-cal-rhetorical, no attention was paid to syntactic structure, nor to cross-lan-guage diversity.

One could count the **Neo-Grammarian** movement of the early 19th Cen-tury, and the various strands reaching from it all the way to the present, as the first systematic attempt within the Western tradition to deal with language structure and language diversity[6] in both **phonology** and **morpho-syntax**. In a marked — and probably deliberate — departure from the logical grammar tradition preceding them, the Neo-Grammarians paid relatively little atten-tion to semantic, logical or rhetorical structure; although their pursuit of etymologies and historical change in meaning is marked by considerable sophistication in the area of lexical semantics. Perhaps the direct descendants in linguistics of the scientific revolution and the Enlightenment, the Neo-Grammarians mistrusted earlier mentalist traditions. As heirs to the Euro-centric tradition of the West, they continued to indulge in its implicit and myopic universalism, making narrow value judgments concerning "ideal" language-types. Such judgments were of course reminiscent of earlier pro-ponents of Greek, Latin and French as "ideal" languages. In spite of their typological narrowness, the Neo-Grammarians were responsible for the birth of linguistic **typology**, **comparative linguistics** and **historical reconstruction**. Their impact on linguistics in the latter part of the 19th Century and the first half of the 20th remained immense.

The late 19th Century brought with it a number of elaborations on the great advances of the Neo-Grammarian movements. One of the 'waves' that can be singled out is that of **German Romaticism**, with illustrious exponents such as Schleicher[7] and his peculiar Darwinian ideas on language evolution,

4) Some illustrious names within that tradition are Ockam, Boethius, Aquinas, Abelard, An-selm, Peter of Spain. For some discussion see Henry (1964).

5) Leading exponents were Arnauld (1662), Beauzée (1767), Cordemoy (1666), Du Marsais (1729, 1769), Lancelot and Arnauld (1660), among others. For discussion see Chomsky (1966).

6) Some representatives are Bopp (1833), Brugmann (1902-04), Delbrück (1901), Grimm (1819-37), *inter alia*. For discussion see Bloomfield (1933). The Sanskrit grammarians were perhaps the earliest exponents of descriptive structural linguistics. The Arab grammarians of the Middle Ages represent another early non-Western tradition.

7) See e.g. Schleicher (1961).

intermingled with a hint of racism. Another illustrious name is von Humboldt,[8] responsible for extending the cross-linguistic typological data-base to the Americas and the Pacific, as well as for a bold mentalism that equated language comprehension with cognitive processing ('intellectual activity'), and for a certain measure of typologically-based universalism. The same mentalism and universalism is also discernible in the writings of Herman Paul.[9] And many similar themes in the transition from 19th to 20th Century linguistics are echoed in the works of Schuhardt.[10] This is also the era where linguistics crosses the Atlantic, beginning the serious investigation of Amerindian languages, as in the works of Whitney.[11] The late 19th Century and its elaborations on Neo-Grammarian themes thus represented both consolidation and opening, in extending the data-base for typology and in deserting the implicit anti-mentalism of the early Neo-Grammarians.

The 20th Century, beginning with Saussure,[12] marks the ascent of **Structuralism** in linguistics. Its early, Saussurean version had a number of distinct flavors. First and foremost was the separation of *langue* — the "system" — from *parole* — its actual "expression" or "use" in everyday speech. Such separation was the first step towards idealizing — and abstracting — the linguistic data-base. Following closely was the separation between language *synchrony* — the "steady state" that is again somewhat abstracted — and *diachrony* — the elusive continuum of "change". Last and fully compatible was the rise of the concept of *structure*, an idealized, discrete and somewhat abstract entity, reassuringly removed from messy change, sloppy facts of usage and hard-to-define communicative *function*, be it semantic or rhetorical. The history of linguistics from that point onward reveals the haphazard but philosophically consistent path through which budding **American structuralism** gradually acquired its intellectual baggage. The central figure, L. Bloomfield, went from early mentalism to Saussurean structuralism, grafting upon it the pseudo-scientific jargon of early **Behaviorism**[13] and **logical positivism**.[14] The study of lan-

---

8) Humboldt (1836-39), Humboldt (1836/1971).

9) Paul (1880), (1916-20).

10) Schuhardt (1900), (1914).

11) Whitney (1867), (1874).

12) Saussure (1915).

13) Presumably under the influence of Weiss (1929).

14) Probably implicitly via Russell (1905, 1919), though without direct acknowledgements.

guage meaning, use and function were soon relegated to the realm of other —
natural and social — sciences.[15] And linguistics was then left free to describe
"the way people talk", i.e. sounds and structures.

Bloomfield's linguistic separatism was next fortified by a heavy dose of
anti-universalism, for which one may suggest two separate sources. First, the
retreat from mentalism signaled in fact a retreat from the best *prima-facie* evidence for cross-language universality, meaning translation. If meaning was irrelevant to the study of language, as Bloomfield asserted, then the baffling variety of surface structures encountered in the expanded cross-language data-
base surely suggested extreme language specificity. To this was grafted
Whorf's misguided **cultural-linguistic relativism**, a mentalist approach that re-
lied on the superficial analysis of some semantic aspects of a few languages.[16]
The pendulum had thus swung all the way from the universalist-mentalist extreme of earlier traditions that paid no attention to syntactic structure and language diversity, to an extreme anti-universalist and anti-mentalist structuralism that wallowed in language diversity.

The restrictive dogma that came out of the Bloomfieldian amalgam
lasted into the mid 1950's. Occasional islands of common sense in the **Traditional Grammar** vein of Jespersen,[17] such as Sapir's mentalism-cum-typol-
ogy,[18] the functionalism of the **Prague School**[19] and Bolinger,[20] Greenberg's
cross-language typological universalism with a diachronic twist,[21] or Pike's
cross-disciplinary vision of relevance,[22] remained isolated in the calm ocean of
post-Bloomfieldian smugness. Linguistics was on its way to exhaustively describe its subject matter, so it seemed.

The **transformational-generative** revolution of the late 1950's represented a vigorous shaking up of the linguistic crucible, yielding a blend of
disparate philosophical and methodological features culled from many

---

15) Bloomfield (1922, 1924, 1926, 1933).

16) This is normally referred to as The Sapir-Whorf Hypothesis on Language and Culture. See
Whorf (1956).

17) Jespersen (1909), (1924).

18) Sapir (1921).

19) See collections in Vachek (ed., 1966) and Daneš (ed., 1974).

20) As in Bolinger (1952).

21) As in Greenberg (1966).

22) As in Pike (1954).

acknowledged and unacknowledged antecedents. Whether the particular mix and its coherence or lack thereof were the product of design or accident is still a matter of debate. The components may be summarized as follows:

a. *Structure and function*: Language — and syntax — were conceived of as structure, existing and understandable independently of meaning or function. "Autonomous syntax" then constituted its own explanation even within linguistics, thus essentially following Saussure and Bloomfield while vigorously protesting to the contrary.[23]

b. *Innateness*: Descartes' extreme Rationalism was belatedly adopted,[24] with a formal-structural emphasis contrasting with the notional-mentalist original. For the original explanatory power of The Divine, genetic-neural structure was substituted. But the latter was conceived of as "explanatory" without reference to functional, ecological and evolutionary mediation.

c. *Language and cognition*: A curious notion of "mentalism" was adopted, whereby it is the *formal* properties of language — i.e. structure — that lay claim to mental reality. At the same time, any attempt to explain language in terms of general cognitive capacities and processes was rejected.[25]

d. *Formalization*: While protesting vigorously to the contrary, Chomsky in fact borrowed the Logical-Positivist assumption that language may be described as a formal, deductive, closed and complete system. Its categories were viewed as essentially discrete and Platonic,[26] its "rules of grammar" exceptionless. Shades, degrees and gradations were discarded. The grammar of "competence" became essentially a deterministic automaton, making structural "grammaticality" choices — rather than an instrument for carrying on communication.[27] Finally, the methodological, convenient, heuristic role of formal description was re-interpreted as a theoretical constraint on the "form of grammars" and the "mind of the

23) Cf. Chomsky (1957, 1965).

24) Cf. Chomsky (1966, 1968).

25) See Piattelli-Palmarini (ed., 1980), *inter alia*.

26) As for example in Katz and Fodor (1963).

27) See Chomsky (1961), *inter alia*.

speaker/hearer".

e. *Empirical integrity of the data-base*: Following Saussure's distinc-
    tion between *langue* and *parole*, Chomsky introduced a similar em-
    pirical escape-hatch via the distinction between "competence" and
    "performance", respectively. Rather than being a methodologi-
    cally useful preliminary, this distinction was elevated to high
    theoretical status. Descriptive linguistics thus culminated in con-
    structing models of "competence", liberated from language use,
    speaker's and hearer's behavior, and the general messiness, inde-
    terminancy and fuzzy edges that normally arise from honest in-
    teraction with a complex data-base in the biological and behavioral
    sciences. An abstract theory of "language" thus arose in a hermeti-
    cally-sealed empirical vacuum.

f. *Cross-language variability*: The transformational-generative re-
    volution represents, essentially, a return to the pre-Neo-Gramma-
    rian tradition of utter disregard for the nature and significance of
    cross-language typological variability. The Euro-centric tradition
    now switched from Greek-Latin-French to English, whose syntax
    then served as the basis for making sweeping assumptions about
    typological-syntactic universals. And the "deep-structure typol-
    ogy" that did surface from within the generative tradition rep-
    resented considerable abuse of the observable facts of "surface"
    syntax.[28]

g. *Language development, change and evolution*: Chomsky ab-
    sorbed, without explicit discussion, Saussure's and Bloomfield's
    separation of synchronic from diachronic studies, as well as the as-
    sumption that it was indeed possible — and somehow desirable —
    to formulate universals of language, whatever their nature, on a
    purely synchronic basis. Coupled to this bias was an ambivalent ap-
    proach to child language acquisition. On the one hand, Chomsky
    extolled the role of language acquisition as a major arbiter of his
    Cartesian-Rationalist approach. On the other, the actual facts of
    language acquisition were not approached with even a hint of em-
    pirical integrity. It was assumed from the start that input — linguis-
    tic, functional, pragmatic — played a minimal role in the emergent

---

28) As in, e.g. Bach (1970), McCawley (1970), Ross (1970), Sanders and Thai (1972), *inter alia*.
These are only the early precursors of a burgeoning industry of "deep" typology".

language system. Equally, communicative function was disregarded as a variable in language acquisition, as were the socio-cultural-pragmatic context[29] and "generalized cognitive capacities".[30] What remained was an impoverished caricature of the acquisition of "formal structures" guided deterministically by an in-built genetic-neural structure referred to as "universal grammar". Finally, without a shred of empirical evidence, Descartes' anti-evolutionary bias was transported into the latter part of the 20th Century, via Chomsky's assertion that the human communicative system was unique and that — unlike anatomy, physiology, neurology, cognition, social structure and "general" behavior — it could not be understood in evolutionary terms.[31]

h.   *Social and cultural context*: The separation of "competence" from "performance" also allowed the detaching of linguistics from language as a socio-cultural phenomenon, expression and instrument. The end result was indeed a compatible though perhaps unintended amalgam of pre-Whorfian logical universalism, Saussurean anti-variationism, Positivist formalism and Bloomfieldian structuralism and anti-mentalism.

The approach to the study of syntax adopted in this book developed gradually as a rejection of all the tenets of the transformational-generative tradition as listed above. It feeds on the functionalism inherent in Jespersen, Bolinger and the Prague School. It draws from Greenberg's typological approach to the study of structural and functional universals. It embraces a more Piagetian mentalism which views language and communication as part and parcel of cognition. It is inherently developmentalist in recognizing the determinative role of language acquisition, language change and language evolution in shaping extant language, culture and cognition. It is pragmatically-based and rejects formalism for formalism's sake, recognizing instead the open-ended, contingent and less-than-categorial nature of language, behavior and cognition. It strives to establish an empirically-motivated balance between the relative roles of input and innards — or percepts and concepts — in language acquisition and communicative behavior, stressing pragmatic,

29) See e.g. Chomsky (1965, 1968).

30) See in Piattelli-Palmarini (ed., 1980).

31) Chomsky (1968).

constructivist interaction between environment and mind.[32] It views language
in its biological-social-cultural context, refusing to artificially adjudicate between these three function-laden spheres. Finally, it is a determinedly empirical approach, rejecting Chomsky's "competence" as anything except a useful
preliminary/methodological heuristic in approaching a complex data-base. It
views data of language use, variation, development, behavior, discourse processing and experimental cognitive psychology as part and parcel of one empirical complex. Within this complex, the study of sentences/structures in isolation certainly plays an important and methodologically prior role, but by no
means the prime role, in understanding the vast network of phenomena called
human language. All these philosophical and methodological preferences are
hereby acknowledged in full.[33]

1.2. GRAMMAR, DISCOURSE AND COGNITION: SYNTAX
     AS SCIENCE

The traditional methodology employed by linguists in their study of syntax has been confined, almost exclusively, to the study of meaning and structure of isolated sentences, detached from speaker, hearer and communicative
context. There are many reasons why such an approach is only a necessary
preliminary method, and why if practiced to the exclusion of other methods,
such an approach is bound to yield unsatisfactory results. To begin with,
human communication is **multi-propositional**, where both the immediate discourse context and overall thematic context control the choice and use of most
grammatical devices. While the study of sentences in isolation is a necessary
preliminary step in identifying the inventory of coding devices which make
morpho-syntactic structure, the goal of the investigation is to elucidate how
those devices are used in coding and **communicating knowledge**.

While practicing sentence-level description, one must be aware of certain
dangers of *misrepresentation and misinterpretation* inherent in this otherwise
necessary methodology. It tends to warp our notion of the semantic-func-
tional correlates of syntactic structure. And such potential warping can only
be corrected by proceeding, in due course, onto the next stage of syntactic investigation — the study of texts, and the study of the functional distribution of

---

32) The philosophical antecedence of pragmatism and constructivism derives from Kant,
through Peirce (1955) and onward to — among others — Bateson (1979).

33) For considerable discussion see several sections directly below, the whole of Chapter 2, as
well as Givón (1979a, Chapter 1 in particular).

various morpho-syntactic structures within the text. Such an investigation, which often must involve quantification and statistical/probabilistic analysis, is the *sine qua non* for discovering the communicative conditions under which various syntactic structures — or "rules" — apply. The first stage, of sentence-level analysis, only tells the linguist that some structures are possible, may occur. It reveals nothing about the context and purpose of their occurrence, or how often they occur in comparison with other constructions that seemingly perform "the same" or similar function(s). Finally, the systematic and quantified study of syntax in discourse serves as a necessary and natural transition towards linking language and communication with cognition.

We will continue to assume here that language and its notional/functional and structural organization is intimately bound up with and motivated by the structure of human cognition, perception and neuro-psychology. Studying the use of syntactic structure in its communicative setting eventually makes it possible to come up with hypotheses about the necessary ('iconic') correlations between function and structure in human language, and how such correlations may be systematically motivated by what is known about human cognition, perception and neurology. Once such hypotheses arise out of the linguist's work, the way is clear for the linguist to participate in cooperative research with the cognitive psychologist, adopting more rigorous methods of experimental design, data collection, quantification and statistical analysis. This is the stage where interesting hypotheses about language and cognition are tested, reformulated or discarded. This is where the artificial division between linguistics and psychology begins to break down.

Within this three-step program of studying grammar, discourse and processing, the linguist is uniquely equipped to contribute to the first and second steps, but must cooperate with — or learn from — the cognitive psychologist in carrying out the third step of the investigation. This book summarizes much of the information derived from the first step, supports it wherever possible with information generated from the second step, and attempts to project, whenever possible, likely openings toward the third.

1.3. ON THE NOTION "RULE OF GRAMMAR":[34] CATEGORIES, NORMS AND PROTOTYPES

1.3.1. Platonic categories and exceptionless rules

In his then-celebrated article "On the notion "rule of grammar"",

---

34) With obvious indebtedness to Chomsky (1961).

Chomsky (1961) defined grammar — and language — as a purely formal device whose categories are clean and discrete, and whose rules are deductively decidable and exceptionless, much like the "laws" of physics. To quote:

"...the theory of grammar should meet requirements of the following kind. It should make available:

(1)   (a) a class of possible grammars G_1, G_2,...

        (b) a class of possible sentences S_1, S_2,...

        (c) a function f such that $f(i, j)$ is the set of structural descriptions of the sentences S_i that are provided by the grammar G_j,

        (d) a function $m(i)$ which evaluates G_i,

        (e) a function g such that $g(i, n)$ is the description of a finite automaton that takes sentences of (b) as input and gives structural descriptions assigned to these sentences by G_i (i.e. various, perhaps all members of $f(i, j)$) as output..."

[pp. 6-7]

This type of fully categorial, formal, deductive algorithm is of course *a* possible "grammar". However, its applicability to the description of *natural* language depends on taking liberal advantage of the empirical escape-hatch provided by Chomsky's notion of "competence", as well as on eliminating from consideration all data of semantic and pragmatic function as performed in real communicative context. Unfortunately, such an easy escape-hatch is not available to linguists interested in studying the use of syntax in communication. When one investigates a more realistic data-base of language structure-*cum*-use, one finds that both semantic/grammatical categories and "rules of grammar" exhibit only *partial* categoriality: Categories conform to their basic definitions *in the majority of cases*, and rules obey their strict description *more likely than not*. But there is always a certain amount of messy residue left, one that does not seem to fit into the category/rule in the strictest sense of their definition. This is an old dilemma with cognizing and perceiving organisms, having to do with how to process input categorially while allowing for fuzzy edges. It is best to begin by surveying the history of this problem within the Western philosophical tradition.

1.3.2. Discrete categories, fuzzy-edged continuum and prototypes

One extremist approach to looking at semantic/cognitive/functional space within the Western tradition is the **Platonic** point of view. Within it, "categories of the understanding" are discrete, absolute and pristine, be they God-given as Plato or Descartes would have it; neuro-genetically 'wired in' as

Chomsky (1966, 1968) or Bickerton (1981) would have it; representing the stable features of The Real World as Russell (1905, 1919), Carnap (1947, 1959) and other positivists would have it; or made out of atomic units of perception as the classical empiricists would have it. The age-old argument between empiricist and rationalist concerning the source of such categories in no way impinges upon accepting them as discrete. Membership of such categories/ groups is defined by possession or non-possession of **criterial properties** (necessary and sufficient properties), and this may be represented through set-inclusion diagrams as:

(1)

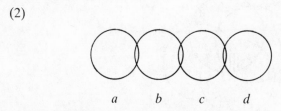

where A is the criterial property determining categorial membership, B is a member possessing such a criterial property, and C is a non-member not possessing such a criterial property.

The other extremist approach within the Western tradition is best represented by the "late" **Wittgenstein** (1953). It holds that, first, categories are not discrete and absolute but rather fuzzy-edged and **contingent** — upon the context/purpose of their use; and second, that a **family resemblance** relation may often hold between the various members of the same category — or between the various categories within a supra-ordinate meta-category — so that while member a may resemble ('share properties with') b, b may resemble c, c may resemble d etc., members a and d may not resemble each other at all (i.e. 'share no properties'). This may be represented through the following set-intersection diagram:

(2)

A family-resemblance set such as diagrammed in (2), Wittgenstein would contend, nonetheless represents a possible natural category within which a, b, *c, d* are equally members.

Each of the two extreme positions, Plato's and Wittgenstein's, indeed represents one important facet of language, cognition and behavior. There is indeed *a great measure* of categoriality in human language. Lexical items, morphemes, syntactic constructions and the rules that govern their appropriate use in communication represent a huge body of *prima facie* evidence in support of the existence of categoriality. But equally well, the very same rules also furnish a wealth of evidence in support of non-discreteness, fuzzy-edges, continua and contingent definitions and applications. If one is then to be empirically responsible — and philosophically honest — one could not subscribe to either extreme point of view as a model for language, cognition and behavior. Rather, one must opt for a **hybrid solution**, a compromise.

In recent years, a non-extremist compromise solution to the representation of notional/functional/cognitive space has indeed been articulated, beginning with the works of cognitive psychologists such as Posner and Keele (1968), Rosch (1973, 1975) and Rosch and Lloyd (eds., 1978). It has been picked up by several anthropologists (Berlin and Kay, 1969; Kay and McDaniel, 1978; Coleman and Kay, 1981), and more recently by linguists (Lakoff, 1973, 1977, 1982; Lakoff and Johnson, 1980; Ross, 1972, 1973, 1974; Givón, 1982; *inter alia*). This compromise position has been called **Prototype Theory**. Like Wittgenstein's, it allows for a non-discrete continuum space within as well as between categories. Like Wittgenstein's again, it concedes that natural cognitive and linguistic categories are not always — and perhaps are seldom — defined in terms of a single or a few, criterial ('sufficient and necessary') properties. Rather, categories within the continuum-space are formed at *intersections* of a number of — sometimes many — "characteristic" or "typical" features/properties, properties that *tend* to coincide statistically/probabilistically, but do not always coincide absolutely. This may be represented through a clustering intersection diagram, as in:

(3)

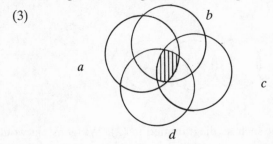

The shaded area in (3) represents members which display all four "characteristic" properties. They are "the most typical" members of the category, its **prototype**. But areas where three out of four properties intersect are still "fairly" typical, certainly more so than those where only two — or none — intersect. Further, the prototype member of a category also possesses the greatest number of *important* characteristic properties. The categorial continuum may thus be characterized by two distinct gradations:

(a)   All features/properties are weighted in terms of their *importance*; and

(b)   All members of a category are ranked in terms of the *number* of characteristic properties they possess.

An overall *degree of prototypicality* measure can thus be derived.

So far our description of the prototype approach has not diverged much from Wittgenstein's extreme position. What makes it truly a compromise view, are the following empirically-verifiable postulates concerning the **clustering** of the members of natural — biological, cognitive and behavioral — categories along the categorial space, within a certain distance from the categorial mean or prototype. The Wittgensteinean approach to "family resemblance" could easily predict a **uniform** distribution of all members of the category along the categorial space, a distribution schematically illustrated in (4) below:

(4)   *Uniform ('Wittgensteinean') distribution*

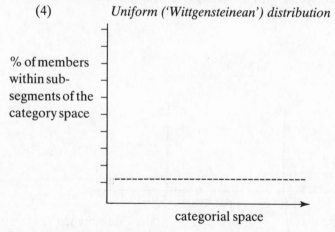

In contrast, the Platonic view would have all members of each category concentrated at a single categorial point on the continuum, as in (5) below:

(5)   *Absolute ('Platonic') categorial distribution*

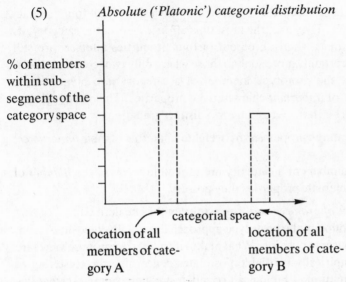

In contrast to both extremes, prototype theory would predict a **prototype clustering** distribution around the prototype/mean, whereby the *majority* — however large —[35] of the membership can be found within a reasonable, well-defined distance. Such distribution may be illustrated in (6) below:

(6)   *Prototypical ('flexible') categorial distribution*

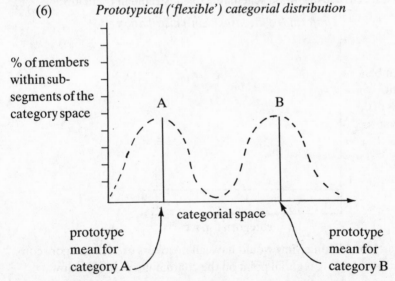

35) The exact size of the majority probably depends on saliency relations within the particular pragmatic context for a category, and cannot — in principle — be determined by deductive means.

A number of details concerning prototype clustering remain open. First, the shape of the curve may or may not conform to the bell-shaped standard distribution curve where 67% of the membership is distributed within one standard deviation from the categorial mean. The curve is probably sharper, displaying more salient *categorial peaks*. It is also most likely that in different biological, cognitive and pragmatic contexts the shape of prototype distribution curves, the separation of categorial peaks within them and the degree of partial overlap between categories may vary, depending most likely on the requisite *saliency* for particular tasks of inter-categorial discrimination.[36] Prototype clustering and category peaks must be *distinct enough* for the organism, at the appropriate level, to associate some majority of the membership with the categorial prototype.

1.3.3. Prototypes and metaphoric extension

The most prototypical member of a category, i.e. the one displaying the greatest number of the most important characteristic properties/features, presumably defines our notion of "the prototype". All other members may then be ranked according to their degree of similarity to the prototype (or 'distance from the prototype-peak').[37] The notion of *resemblance/similarity* is thus crucial for forming natural categories. And it is also crucial for defining the process via which category membership — and eventually also the prototype itself — is extended. This process is called **metaphor** or **analogy**.[38]

1.3.3.1. Metaphoric induction into a prototype

There is nothing logically necessary or discrete about the notion "resemble", "be like", "be similar". Anything can, in principle, be like anything else, given the appropriate context/purpose for defining the criterial properties for "likeness". Metaphor and analogy are thus, in principle, context-dependent,

---

36) For an illuminating discussion of some of these issues, as reflected in the neuro-physiology of color perception and the semantics of color terms in human language, see Kay and McDaniel (1978). For an extensive discussion of the role of context, purpose and saliency in constructing and retaining classificatory categories, see Medin and Schaffer (1978). The hybrid solution of prototypes is defined there in terms of accommodating both *analytic* and *analogical* learning i.e. Platonic & Wittgensteinean, respectively.

37) See discussion in Medin and Schaffer (1978).

38) These two names for the same phenomenon come into linguistics from two separate traditions. The **metaphor** term comes from the literary-poetic tradition, the **analogy** term from the philosophical tradition, most recently via Kant and Peirce. For discussion see Lakoff and Johnson (1980) and Anttila (1977), respectively.

contingent, pragmatic.[39] The extension of category membership to new members is one of the most pervasive facts of human categorization, at the sensory, cognitive, or linguistic levels. It is the fuzzy-edged nature of prototype categories that allows such extension, by which less-typical members may join, given the right context/purpose/ perspective. Instances of such behavior are discussed throughout this book, so that at this point only a few illustrative examples will be cited.[40]

Suppose one says:

(7)   George built a wall around himself

If (7) is interpreted metaphorically, then from the speaker's *point of view* something in George's behavior *resembles* the literal, prototype meaning of "build a wall around". In this particular case, the apt analogy is likely to center on two pragmatic *inferences* concerning the goals and consequences of building a wall around an object:

(8)   a. *Goal*: Walls are built as protection from outside threat.
       b. *Consequence*: Wall-building often results in isolation and lack of contact with the outside.

The metaphoric extension of the membership of "build a wall around" thus allows "defensive/isolating behavior" to join the category — under the right circumstances.

There is nothing logically necessary, however, in selecting inferences (8a,b) as the *important* ones, out of the infinite numbers of possible inferences of "build a wall around". It is the context, purpose or point of view which determine such selection. Some contexts are more general, frequent, obvious and thus "stable". Others are rare, specialized, less obvious and thus "temporary". Inferences (8a,b) are not necessarily the most central ones for the literal, physical meaning of "build a wall around". But they are *sine qua non* for its metaphoric extension. In this particular case, the metaphoric extension to "defensiveness" and "isolation" is a rather obvious one, given the normal context for building walls. But suppose walls — the very same ones — were built for the purpose of, say, climbing to higher locations. A more obvious, general, stable metaphor for (7) would then be "reaching up", "ambition", "self-improvement", "intellectual growth" etc.

39) See discussion in Givón (1982c).

40) For a wealth of examples, see Lakoff and Johnson (1980).

1.3.3.2. Metaphoric extension of the prototype

The flexible manner of constructing prototypes also allows eventual change of the prototype itself, due to repeated metaphoric induction of new members into the category. Such changes involve the *re-definition* of the characteristic properties and their relative ranking, and is the major venue of diachronic change in lexicon, morphology and grammar/syntax. Let us illustrate lexical-semantic change first.

The English words "know" and "can" came initially from the same root, with the meaning 'know' being older. The extension of 'know' to 'be able' arose from a non-central pragmatic inference of 'know', something like:[41]

(9)   '*knowledge* how to do X' ⊃ 'better *ability* to do X'

"Ability", however, involves not only "knowing how" but other, more central ingredients, in particular "power to act". And when "can" eventually split from "know" completely, including its phonological differentiation,[42] "power to act" became a more central characteristic property for its definition, and "knowledge how" was downgraded. Further, "can" soon also developed a *deontic* meaning, that of permission, presumably by the pragmatic inferences:

(10)   a.   'having *power* to act' ⊃ '*not* being *restrained* by outside inter-
             diction'

         b.   '*not* being *restrained*' ⊃ 'being *permitted*'

Finally, "can" has also developed an epistemic/probabilistic sense, presumably through the pragmatic inference:

(11)   'being *able* to act' ⊃ 'increased *probability* of acting'

Each new sense of "know/can" is thus a re-defined prototype, arrived at by the slow process of extending membership in the old prototype to less-similar members/usages which nevertheless "are still similar".

Metaphoric change of prototypes is also the essence of **grammaticaliza-
tion**, the process by which grammatical morphology develops out of lexical items. This may be illustrated by a very common process, where the spatial meaning of "go" — "move toward a target location" — becomes the [future]

41)   None of the inferences involved in analogical/metaphoric extension are deductively necessary. They are all probabilistic, inductive or abductive, and will be referred to here as "pragmatic". See discussion in Givón (1982c).

42)   For further details, due to Anttila (in personal communication), see Givón (1982c).

marker. This is essentially an analogical/metaphoric extension from spatial to temporal movement, most likely as in:[43]

(12) 'going *to a place* where one *will* do X' ⊃ 'moving *to a time* when one *will* do X'

In grammar, the important notion of **transitivity** which describes the properties of prototypical events (see Chapters 4, 5 below) hinges upon — among others — two strong prototypical conditions:

(13) a. The presence of a visible, volitional, controlling **cause/agent**; and
      b. The presence of a clearly visible result- registering **effect/patient**.

Prototypical transitive events are, for example:

(14) a. Mary cut the meat
      b. John destroyed the house
      c. They killed the goat
      d. She broke the chair

Many objects are less-than-prototypical, in that they register a *less-salient* effect, either in terms of physical-perceptual modality or in terms of rate of change. They might be — "objectively" speaking — not patients at all. But metaphorically, from a different point of view, they are *construed* "like patients". Thus, consider the following pairs of expressions:

(15)   *semantically literal*   *viewed as metaphoric patient*

      a. He rode *on* the horse   He rode the horse
          ⊃ [horse is *location*]   ⊃ [horse is *patient*]
          ⊃ [horse is *less controlled*]   ⊃ [horse is *more controlled*]
          ⊃ [horse is *less affected*]   ⊃ [horse is *more affected*]

      b. They took the money *from* him   They robbed him *of* his money
          ⊃ [he is *source*]   ⊃ [he is *patient/victim/affected*]

Promoting an object to "direct object" status is indeed a change in point of view, making that object *more important* and thus making whatever change it undergoes *more salient* — and therefore more discernible.

  The opposite process is also possible in the grammar of transitivity, that of taking a prototypically transitive event which "normally" involves a pro-

---

43) A similar extension is found in all Creole languages, Romance, Germanic, Hebrew, Arabic and others. See details in Givón (1973a, 1982a) and some general discussion in Traugott (1974).

totypical patient-object, and *demoting* that object by various means. As illustrations of this consider:

(16)   *prototypically transitive*   *metaphorically demoted patient*

    a. He ate *the fish*   He ate (regularly)
    b. We hunted *the deer*   We went deer-hunting
    c. He drank *the beer*   He drank (a lot)
    d. He collected *the garbage*   He is a garbage-collector

In many languages, the "demoted" examples in (16) will be coded as intransitive — objectless — constructions. They have one thing in common: While an object may have logically/physically existed, its *specific identity* did not matter in the communication/discourse. Presumably, then, there exists a pragmatic inference which suppresses the coding of transitivity under such conditions, perhaps something like:[44]

(17)   "If the specific identity of the patient/object which registers the change/effect in the event *does not matter* in the communication, then one *pays less attention* to it.
And changes/events to which one pays less attention are *less visible/discernible*".

Non-prototypical subjects/agents may be construed as metaphorically "agent-like", as in:

(18)   a. He saw the mountain
    b. She knew the answer
    c. He heard the song
    d. She feared him

In all of these instances, the "event" is mental, internal and non-volitional, involving neither decision nor action on the part of the subject. But the construction is nonetheless marked as a transitive one, with an object that is also less-than-typical.

Finally, prototypical transitive events may be construed — by changing the point of view — as intransitive by downgrading/demoting the importance or specific identity of the agent. Passive and impersonal constructions are the means by which most languages code such modified points of view, as in:

44) See further discussion in Chapters 4,5 and in particular 11.

(19) a. *They* saw him drunk on the beach.
  b. *Someone* broke the window
  c. The window broke
  d. The window was broken (*by John*)
  e. Spanish is spoken here
  f. He got killed last night

By whatever means, languages tend to code such expressions as closer to the intransitive prototype, and they often mean **resulting states** rather than events.[45] The pragmatic inference that governs such a metaphoric change from transitive to intransitive presumably is similar to (18) above.

1.3.4. The functional significance of prototypes

We have suggested above that what makes linguistic categories and "rules of grammar" categorial and/or rule-governed is neither absolute categoriality nor exceptionless applicability — or predictability. Rather, they are categories or rules by their high **preponderance/frequency**, thus high-enough predictability. Decision-making within the organism, at biological, cognitive and linguistic levels, seems to proceed well with such high-but-not-perfect predictability. But the margin of unpredictability and fuzzy-edges is just as important from a functional point of view. It allows the organism to exercise context-sensitive, contingent, subtle and flexible judgment in matters of relative importance, perspective changes, shades of emphasis and fine gradations along phenomenological continua. Both the use of language and its change and evolution — and acquisition — in response to the challenge of environment, contingency and context, be they personal, social, cultural, communicative or biological, would be impossible without the **flexibility** attached to prototype-like extension of categories and rules. The only real alternative to such flexibility would be to assign a new category to every new context. But there are good reasons why such a solution cannot — in principle — be instituted within an organism:

  a. The number of different contexts is — in principle — potentially *infinite*. Given the uni-directionality of time, no situation is ever *completely* like any other situation.[46]
  b. But the *memory* and *storage* capacity of the organism are finite,

---

45) See further discussion in Givón (1981b).

46) With indebtedness to Heraclitus, *panta rei*.

however large they may be. A non-prototype categorial system will always outstrip such capacities.

c. Similarly, *search procedures* by which one could decide the applicability of a huge inventory of discrete categories (presumably involving some matching with contexts to determine whether they correspond to some existing category) would be in principle impossible to institute.

d. Finally, the acquisition and integration of *new knowledge/information* would be impossible, since this could only be done by analogy/similarity to at least *some* old knowledge which "resembles" the new.[47]

The prototype solution to information processing in biology, cognition and language is thus in some sense both an optimal and necessary solution, allowing organisms to make gross, category-like decisions within finite time while retaining flexibility, context-sensitivity and extendability of the system whenever context/environment demands such flexibility.[48]

1.4. TYPOLOGICAL UNIVERSALS AND "LAWS" OF SCIENCE

One serious consequence of viewing "rules of grammar" as exceptionless "laws" is the rise of the wrong metaphor for grammar, that of the laws of physics. In addition to the reasons already outlined above, and in spite of the *prima facie* categoriality of words, morphemes and syntactic constructions, there are other considerations militating against the view of rules of grammar as exceptionless laws:

(a) Rules of grammar are used by decision-making individuals, whose context-dependent communicative choices must be made on the basis of *incomplete information* culled from divergent sources, some factual and witnessed, some memorized and retrieved, or estimated, guessed, divined etc. Such a system could not be completely deductive, but is probabilistic/inductive/pragmatic at least in part.

(b) The individual himself changes perspective ('point of view') within

47) See extensive discussion in Chapter 7, below. For a review of the psychology of learning literature, see Medin and Schaffer (1978).

48) See further discussion in Givón (1982c).

a certain range, either from one communicative transaction to another or even within the same transaction. Such change in perspective/context results in different metaphoric/analogical extensions of the "same" category or rule.

(c) Finally, "rules of grammar" pertain to communication among individuals within a *population*. And like all biological populations, the human speech community exhibits a range of *individual variability*. Such variability is bound to be revealed in the numerous parameters relevant to the structure and use of language.

The idealized "grammar user" envisioned by Chomsky is indeed a deterministic automaton. Neither the facts of human language, nor those of psychology, nor those of neurology support such a simple-minded model.[49] And the so-called facts of "linguistic competence" support such a model only by accepting an enormous loss in the empirical integrity of the data-base.

One argument frequently cited against typological cross-language generalizations is that they are "tendencies" rather than exceptionless laws. There are two aspects to this question. First, as noted above, one should not expect cognitive/linguistic categories and processes to be *absolutely* categorial, but only *sufficiently* so. Second, typological universals are conditional statements, most commonly expressing *conditional probabilities* in a complex, *multi-variant* empirical environment. Neither categories nor rules-of-grammar operate in a vacuum, but rather in the close proximity of related, interdependent semantic and pragmatic functional domains. The degree of predictability of typological universals thus correlates to our ability to discover as many of the related, co-varying domains as possible. One must discover the manner of their interaction and the extent of their mutual dependencies. For a phenomenon as complex as human language and its use in communication, this is an immense empirical task. For this reason, many typological universals will remain, for a long time, probabilistic in nature. And a number of seeming exceptions from various languages will for a while remain unexplained. But in admitting this, one merely admits that linguistics is just as complex and frustrating a science as is, say, biology. And biology is a much more realistic metaphor for linguistics than is physics.

---

49) It is perhaps no accident that Chomsky's notion of "linguistic creativity" and our ability to produce and interpret novel utterances turns out to be the trivial mechanical device of optional recursivity within the same finite automaton. Such "creativity" has little to do with the organism's ability to absorb new information by metaphoric/analogic extension of extant prototypes in diverging contexts.

1.5. SCOPE AND USES OF THIS BOOK

This book integrates the typological and functional approaches to the study of syntax. It is crammed with facts at the nuts-and-bolts level, but does not shy away from generalizations and explanations. It is also of necessity incomplete, because much of the work of gathering cross-language facts, correlating them in an illuminating fashion and finally explaining them is yet to be done. I have been accused in the past of not presenting a "complete framework" for syntactic description, and this is perhaps as good an opportunity as one could find to say something about the subject. "Framework", "format", "theory" and "Grammar" are words that have been much maligned in the past three decades in linguistics. Ever since the Bloomfieldians, such labels have meant, more likely than not, the closing of one's horizons and the wedding of oneself to a restrictive, counter-empirical and anti-explanatory formalism. Such formalisms foster the illusion of science by downgrading its open-ended, tentative and ongoing nature. My own bias has been, for many years, that such premature closure, completeness, consistency and formalization are both unnecessary and unwise. To begin with, it is in principle impossible, if one pays heed to Goedel's proof. Even within the most restricted, fact-free system of formal logic such closure and consistency were "achieved" only by throwing out the fundamental human-cognitive process of "crossing meta-levels" or changing one's point-of-view, as Russell (1905) did in outlawing self-inclusion paradoxes.[50] From an *empirical* point of view, such closure is unnecessary because biological/cognitive/linguistic systems are unavoidably open-ended and incomplete. It is also *methodologically* unwise, since premature closure and formalization bias one's perception of new facts and freeze one's explanatory intuition. The history of American Linguistics since the 1920's is strewn with the carcasses of "formats", "frameworks", "theories", "Grammars" and assorted formalisms.

In spite of what I have just said, this book outlines as much of a coherent *approach* to language and syntax as is warranted by the available facts. When the data-base is incomplete, as it always is in real science, waiting for "enough" data means waiting forever. In this sense, the scientist is just like the biological organism, bound to act on less-than-complete information and to

---

50) Russell's set-theoretic definition of the paradox took the form of contemplating "the set of all sets that don't include themselves", then asking whether that set "did or didn't include itself". The traditional liar's paradox — "I never tell the truth" — is a reflection of the same problem.

use liberal amounts of inductive/abductive/probabilistic intuition.[51] This book thus represents a similar practical compromise between facts and intuition, and I myself find it neither threatening to my integrity as a scientist nor to my ego as a perfectionist. In this connection, I invite the reader to ponder the following words by which Sir Francis Crick, co-solver of the structure of DNA, referred to the way he and Watson approached a similar predicament in their work just prior to settling on the double helix model:

> "...the sport would be to see how little data they could make do with and still get the structure right... "...You must remember we were trying to solve it with the fewest possible assumptions... there's a perfectly sound reason why you should use the *minimum* of experimental data..." ..."[52]

The two volumes of this book present an integrated though still incomplete outline of syntax, spanning three major functional realms: **Lexical Semantics**, **Propositional Semantics** and **Discourse Pragmatics**. The book starts from the basics and proceeds rapidly and intensively. It presupposes one course of Introduction to Linguistics. However, neither the style nor the level of the discussion are deliberately geared down to the lowest common denominator, an omission motivated by both choice and necessity. The choice is a rebellion against the over-digested nature of "programmed" introductory texts, which to my mind insult both author and reader. The necessity is a frank admission that it is fundamentally impossible to ever start at the *very* beginning, that everything has *some* explicatory background, *ad infinitum*.[53]

This book may be used at a number of levels — and for a number of purposes — of study and/or instruction:

(i)   As an introduction to the substantive (as against 'formal') study of **syntax**, with only an Introduction to Linguistics as prerequisite;

(ii)   As a textbook for **Field Methods** (excluding phonology);

(iii) As a textbook for **Syntactic Typology** and functional-typological universals of language;

(iv)   As a sourcebook and guide in the study and **writing of grammars** (again excluding phonology).

---

51) See extensive discussion in Givón (1982b, 1982c).

52) H.F. Judson (1978), part II, Dec. 4, p.156.

53) It is indeed, to paraphrase an old joke of pragmatics, turtles all the way down.

A problem that must be reckoned with in using — and writing — this book is that of sequence. It arises from the great amount of inter-connection between various parts of the grammar. And it makes it necessary quite often to present some topics in a preliminary fashion, before enough background related to other topics is established — and then to go back and treat them comprehensively. There is no elegant and/or principled way by which this problem can be eliminated completely. One extreme solution may employ costly and boring repetition. Another extreme solution would risk over-terseness and inaccessibility. I have shied away from both extremes, hoping to strike a realistic compromise between economy and accessibility. Such a compromise requires numerous citations, both forward and backward, within and across both volumes. For the certain amount of stylistic infelicity arising from such a compromise, I beg the reader's indulgence.

In spite of the numerous bibliographical citations throughout the book, this work is bibliographically neither exhaustive nor authoritative. My citations are again a compromise between a number of competing requirements. The great bulk of the works cited fall into two categories:

(a) Sources from which *language-data* have been cited; or
(b) Sources where further discussion of *specific topics* is to be found.

Omissions, in the second category in particular, should not be construed as deliberate exclusions based on judgment of relevance or centrality. My citations are personal acknowledgements, they chart my own personal access to data or topics, a path often unpredictable and less than systematic. While the citations are not haphazard, neither are they in any way comprehensive—and were never meant to be so.

1.6. ORGANIZATION OF VOLUME I

The sequencing of the material in the two volumes follows, to the extent possible, my own assumptions about the degree of dependency among various domains in language and syntax.

Chapter 2 deals with methodological preliminaries to the functional-typological approach to syntax, having dispensed with the philosophical and historical preliminaries in Chapter 1.

Chapter 3 presents a sketch of lexical categories ('word classes') and is also implicitly a treatment of lexical semantics, albeit brief and partial.

Chapters 4, 5 and 6 deal separately with three fundamental aspects of Propositional Semantics and syntactic organization of so-called "simple" clauses:

(i)   Semantic structure of propositions, predications and case-roles;
(ii)   Morpho-syntactic typology of case-marking systems; and
(iii)   Word-order typology.

Chapter 7 outlines necessary prerequisites and basic information-theory concepts for the study of discourse-pragmatics, including propositional modalities.

Chapter 8 amplifies propositional modalities further, treating tense-aspect-modality systems from semantic, pragmatic and morpho-syntactic points of view.

Chapter 9 is about negation and its semantics, pragmatics and morpho-syntax.

Chapter 10 deals with pronouns, demonstratives and grammatical agreement, covering primarily semantics and morpho-syntax, with only a preliminary sketch of the pragmatics.

Chapter 11 deals with nominal modalities such as reference and definiteness, semantically, pragmatically and morpho-syntactically.

| 2 | **METHODOLOGICAL PREMILINARIES:**
Communicative Function and Syntactic Structure |

2.1. INTRODUCTION: THE BIOLOGICAL ANALOGY

Syntax is the study of a unique and complex *coding system*. 'Coding' is a binary expression designating two entities holding a peculiar *semiotic* relation, at least as far as language is concerned:

(a)   *The coded entity*: Meaning, message, function
(b)   *The coding entity*: Sign, code, structure

There are many systems in our universe within which the phenomenon of coding does not properly arise. The inorganic physical universe is one such example, where it is not very clear what the "hidden meaning" is that is coded by its peculiar structure.[1] On the other hand, whenever one endeavors to describe the physical structure of biological systems, the duality of structure and function immediately manifests itself. Thus, consider the description of various skeletal support systems. A biologist as a matter of course would describe them *in relation to* the two major functions they are likely to perform in the organism:

(i)   The maintenance of fixed spatial relations of the various organs within the organism in order to insure the discharge of their individual — as well as correlated/cooperative — functions; and
(ii)   The anchoring of the musculature responsible for ambulation.

A biologist would then study the various *types* of skeletal systems, dividing them first into two major types: *exo*-skeleton (external to the body) and *endo*-skeleton (internal to the body). He would proceed toward a more detailed *typology* (or *taxonomy*) of these two major types, differentiating between the

---

1) A mystic might wish to argue here that the physical universe stands in a "coding relation" to the metaphysical or spiritual universe. While this may indeed be intuitively appealing, it is not clear that it is open to scientific investigation.

vertebrate endo-skeleton type and that displayed by coelenterates or squids. He would in the same vein differentiate between the insect exo-skeleton type and that of many mollusks. But this work of typology or taxonomy is only a preliminary to a more profound endeavor whereby the biologist proceeds to note how the various *structural types* of skeletons perform their similar function(s). The biologist thus strives for a systematic understanding of the relation between structure and function in living organisms.[2] In the course of such an investigation, the biologist soon develops an understanding of general principles of biological design. By analogy, one may wish to call these **iconicity** principles, or "principles which govern natural form-function correlations." Ultimately, the biologist is bound to ponder some more fundamental questions, such as the functional, adaptive, or evolutionary reasons for the seeming paucity of diverse types of structures performing the same or similar functions, or the seeming restrictions upon the typological variety of entire organisms.

In a broad way, the study of syntax is rather similar to the study of anatomy-cum-physiology. By insisting on the joint study of function and the typology of structures which code it, one opens the door to a serious investigation of how – and ultimately why – particular structures perform their assigned functions.

2.2. MAJOR FUNCTIONAL REALMS CODED BY HUMAN LANGUAGE

If, for the moment, one sets aside the admittedly important socio-cultural, psycho-emotive and aesthetic functions of language,[3] it is possible to recognize three major **functional realms** which receive systematic and distinct coding in human language:

(a)   Lexical semantics
(b)   Propositional semantics
(c)   Discourse pragmatics

2) In a standard anatomy textbook, Crouch (1978) writes: "...anatomy is the science that deals with the structure of the body... physiology is defined as the science of function. Anatomy and physiology have more meaning when studied together..." [pp. 9-10].

3) Such a setting aside is obviously only a methodological convenience. It may very well be that ultimately one could find systematic correlations between these more tangential functions of language and the core functional realms more central to linguistics.

The functional realm of **lexical semantics** pertains primarily to the storage of **generic**, culturally-shared knowledge largely embodied in the lexicon. This knowledge pertains to relatively stable phenomena, concepts or points of reference which constitute an intricate network that is part and parcel of our cognitive map of the phenomenological universe. This functional realm is coded primarily by linearly sequenced *sounds*, and although it is not totally devoid of iconicity, the degree of arbitrariness found in the relationship between lexical meaning and the sound code is perhaps greatest among all functional realms.[4] While syntax is not primarily the coding instrument for this functional realm, lexical semantics intersects with syntax at a number of points, some of which will be dealt with in chapters 3 and 4, below.

The functional realm of **propositional semantics** pertains to specific *information* couched in *propositions*, which are coded syntactically as *sentences*. This involves primarily two aspects of the proposition:

(i)   Its characterization as *state*, *event*, or *action*; and
(ii)   The characterization of the *participants* ('arguments', 'case-roles') in the proposition as to their **semantic roles** vis-à-vis the predicate.

Roughly, (i) and (ii) combined tell us "who did what to whom, when, where, why, how, etc." — provided that the lexical-semantic information is also available. If the lexical-semantic information is abstracted, the state/event/action is characterized only as *type*, and one may refer to that characterization as **propositional frame**, which is the subject of Chapter 4. In terms of coding, propositional semantics is *jointly coded* with discourse pragmatics via syntax ('syntactic structure'). As we shall see throughout, this joint coding has profound consequences for the structure of human language.

The functional realm of **discourse pragmatics** involves the sequencing or placing of atomic propositions within a wider communicative context, i.e. in discourse. The context within which any proposition is communicated is a large and open-ended complex. A large part of it consists of the generically-shared body of stable knowledge as coded in the lexicon carried by all members of a speech community or *culture*. If one sets aside this cultural common

---

4) By observing that the degree of arbitrariness in the lexical realm is the highest among the three coded functional realms, one does not rule out iconicity in the human lexicon. In fact, there are grounds for suspecting that a rather general "iconicity imperative" — i.e. the assumption that a rough correlation does exist between form and function, striving toward though never reaching the idealized one-to-one relation — repeatedly manifests itself in the speaker's search for lexical iconicity in morphology, onomatopoeia, sound symbolism, rhyme or alliteration.

denominator for the moment, it is possible to divide the bulk of the *specific* context at any point in the discourse into three major components:

(i)   *Speaker's goals*: The speech-act values (information, question, command, etc.) as well as other communicative and pragmatic goals of the speaker;

(ii) *Interaction*: The social relation between speaker and hearer, what they owe each other, what they know of each other's knowledge, goals, and predispositions;

(iii) *Discourse context*: What information was processed in the preceding discourse, what can be taken for granted, what is likely to be challenged, what is important vs. ancillary information, what is the **foreground** of new information as against what is **background**.

In terms of coding, as suggested above, discourse pragmatics is jointly coded with propositional semantics via syntax. When one studies the syntactic structure of sentences, then, one can to some extent separate the aspects of structure that are primarily responsible for coding propositional-semantic information from those whose primary role is to code discourse-pragmatic function.

In a very definite sense, the three functional realms outlined above are concentrically hierarchized. One may refer to them in an abbreviated way as, respectively, *meaning, information*, and *function*. Words ("lexical items") have meaning but carry no information by themselves — unless they are embedded within propositions. It is possible to characterize the meaning of words without reference to either specific propositions or specific discourses in which they are embedded. *Propositions* carry information once words are plugged into them, but they do not carry any specific discourse function unless embedded within discourse. And it is possible to characterize the information carried in a proposition without reference to discourse context. Finally, only within a specific *discourse* context do propositions carry discourse function. Conversely, it is impossible to characterize discourse function without reference to propositional-semantic information. And it is impossible to characterize propositional-semantic information without reference to lexical-semantic meaning. This hierarchic organization may be schematized as:

(1)
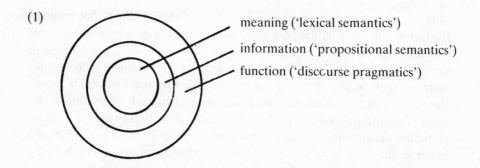

meaning ('lexical semantics')

information ('propositional semantics')

function ('discourse pragmatics')

2.3. FUNCTIONAL DOMAINS CODED BY SYNTAX

The two functional realms coded jointly by syntax, propositional semantics and discourse pragmatics, may be sub-divided into smaller and more concrete **functional domains**. Propositional semantics itself is one coherent functional domain, and discourse pragmatics is comprised of many functional domains of varying complexity. Each sentence in discourse context is thus the
joint expression of the propositional-semantic information plus at least some
discourse-pragmatic function.

There are two traditional ways of discovering and describing functional
domains coded by syntax. First, one may discover them via *structural* means,
by relying on structural/syntactic similarities, either within the same language
or cross-linguistically. This method is implicit in the structuralist tradition in
linguistics, be it represented by Saussure (1915), Bloomfield (1933), or
Chomsky (1957). Still, the notion of 'function' played no explicit role in structuralist descriptions of language structure. What is implicit in this method,
however, is one fundamental assumption concerning **iconicity** or the non-arbitrary nature of the correlation between code and message:

(2)   "It is only because the coding relation between structure and func-
        tion in syntax is *non-arbitrary*, or in some sense *iconic*,[5] that one
        could proceed to infer common function from common structure".

There are certain pitfalls associated with employing the structural path as the

---

5) Whether 'non-arbitrary', 'predictable' or 'natural' in all cases also means 'iconic' is open to
both methodological and factual debate. Haiman (forthcoming) is rather stringent in allowing a
non-arbitrary coding relation to be termed iconic. My own view (Givón, forthcoming) is that to the
extent than an *isomorphism* can be demonstrated between code and message, one is entitled to call
the coding relation iconic.

only means for determining function (or functional domains). One involves the fact that the correlation between structure and function in language is not absolute, but rather an approximation. In particular, *diachronic change* in syntax often removes a particular structure from its original functional domain — while at least initially leaving the structure itself relatively intact. Going by structure alone may lead the linguist, on such occasions, to the wrong definition of a functional domain. Traditionally, structuralists—and in particular the more recent transformational-generative school—have tended to ignore the cross-linguistic *typological diversity* of structure types that may code the same functional domain. This has led, characteristically, to a too narrow or excessively language-specific definition of domains.

Alternatively, one may discover and describe functional domains within the realm of discourse pragmatics — which constitutes the bulk of what is coded by syntax — by studying discourse *function* just as rigorously and exhaustively as one studies structure. This involves the detailed study of texts, conversations and actual communicative interactions, i.e. the study of discourse and the discourse context within which sentences/propositions are embedded. The strength of this method is obvious. One major pitfall associated with it is that functional domains are often related to each other in graded, small-increment steps, along *continua* that are probably grounded in psychological-cognitive space. This is certainly true *within* functional domains, but also *across* domains. In other words, in some fundamental way we are probably dealing here with a *continuous, multi-dimensional* space. By employing only functional considerations without reference to structure, one may on occasion arrive at an overly mushy view of functions and their relative ranking. The obvious solution is to employ both methods, thus combining their strengths and neutralizing their weaknesses. In this way, the discreteness of structure helps constrain the potential mushiness of function, while the substantiality of function helps constrain the occasional vacuity of structure. In methodological terms, then, this is the essence of combining the functionalist and typological approaches to syntax.

The functional domain of propositional semantics is relatively coherent and will be dealt with in Chapters 4, 5, and 6 below. Both in terms of its semantic characterization and the typology of its syntactic coding, it has traditionally been worked out in much more detail.[6] On the other hand, an exhaustive

6) The tradition of propositional logic or predicate calculus is an attempt, albeit deficient, to deal with this functional domain. The traditional typology of case systems, voicing and 'basic' word-order is primarily the typology of the syntactic structures which code this domain.

treatment of the various functional domains falling under discourse pragmatics has yet to be attempted. The bulk of the chapters in these two volumes deal with these. Among others, these functional domains deal with the following major areas of information processing in discourse:

(a) *Referential tracing:* The presentation, identification, and tracing of the various participants ('arguments') in the story/narrative/discourse/conversation, tracking them and keeping them apart.

(b) *Action sequencing:* The presentation and relative sequencing of the events/actions in coherent temporal order, or of states in coherent thematic order, thus tracing the main line or backbone of the discourse.

(c) *Background information:* The presentation, at the appropriate junctures, of propositions carrying background, ancillary, supportive information, necessary for the hearer's proper appreciation of the foreground/backbone/main line.

(d) *Purposive-interactive functions:* Signaling the functions related to the speech-act, the speaker's communicative or pragmatic goals and the interaction between speaker and hearer that is relevant for interpreting the communication.

(e) *Expectations and counter-expectations:* Identifying propositions as either being predictable/expected (to the hearer) or being in various degrees less predictable, unpredictable, or contradictory.

(f) *Larger thematic organization:* Signaling various levels of the higher overall thematic organization of the discourse, in ways that transcend either individual participants or smaller chunks of sequenced information.

2.4. THE NOTION OF STRUCTURE: CODING DEVICES IN SYNTAX

There exists a certain parallelism between the increasing degree of abstractness as we move from lexical *meaning*, to propositional *information* and on to discourse *function*, and the degree of abstractness of the coding devices corresponding to these three realms. At the more concrete end, lexical meaning is indeed more accessible or 'concrete,' much like the sound code is more accessible and concrete. At the other end, the notion of "function" is just as abstract as the notion of "structure."[7] Structure is thus a *second-order*

---

7) Once again one could discern here an *iconic* relation, an *isomorphism* whereby the scale of increasing abstractness in function is matched by the scale of increasing abstraction in code.

construct rather than a first-order phenomenon. This does not mean that structure is not made out of some reasonably concrete and accessible nuts-and-bolts.

The nuts-and-bolts which make up syntactic structure consist of four elements, three of them rather concrete:

(a)   Word order
(b)   Grammatical/inflectional morphology
(c)   Intonational contours

In coding any particular functional domain, different languages make differential use of these three coding devices, sometimes assigning a larger **functional load** to one than to the other(s). In addition to these three rather concrete elements of syntactic structure, one must also deal with a more abstract but ever-present component:

(d)   Constraints

These are conditions on applicability or identifiability of structures or grammatical/communicative devices, most commonly pertaining to identity, co-reference, sequential ordering, shared background knowledge or assumed purpose. We will refer to them repeatedly at the appropriate junctures.

2.5. DISCRETE SYNTACTIC CODING OF NON-DISCRETE FUNCTIONAL DOMAINS

As already mentioned above, there are two aspects to the potential complexity of functional domains coded by syntax:

(a)   *Multi-dimensionality:* Many functional domains are multi-dimensional rather than uni-dimensional; and
(b)   *Scalarity:* Almost all functional domains exhibit some facet of non-discrete, continuous space.

On the other hand structure and its component elements are characteristically discrete entities: A certain word-order is either attested or unattested certain morpheme is either present or absent, and if present it is either prefix or suffix. An intonation contour is either there or not there, a rising intonation is not a falling intonation. And co-reference or shared knowledge constraints, while less concrete, are often just as rigid. There are two distinct problems that arise as a result of the need to code an essentially multi-dimensional and non-discrete entity such as function with an essentially discrete entity such as syntactic structure. The first arises from the multi-dimensionality of functional domains, and may be raised as the question:

(3) "Can one match some elements of a syntactic structure with some dimension of the functional domain coded by it, while similarly matching other elements of the code/structure with other dimensions of the complex domain?"

In other words, can one elaborate *sub-elements* of iconicity in syntactic coding? The answer is, tentatively, that one probably can, and at relevant points in the text these possibilities will be discussed and illustrated.

The second problem is a classical one in cognition and may again be characterized as a question:

(4) "How to match discrete coding units to a non-discrete notional/functional continuum?"

This is indeed a fundamental problem in the coding and analysis of experience, at both the physiological/sensory level of the organism as well as at the fundamentally similar level of the science.[8] The solution adopted by human language in both lexicon and syntax seems to be an interesting compromise, whereby each coding unit is indeed discrete, but a certain flexibility is nonetheless maintained via the following two features:

(a) A series of structural **coding points** are distributed along a scalar functional domain, so that each one of them matches, more or less, a section of the domain; and

(b) While the *relative order* of the coding points along the scalar domain is rigid, the actual *boundaries* between them are to some extent *fuzzy*, so that either in terms of diachronic change, individual creativity or dialect variation, adjacent coding points along a section of the domain retain a certain amount of flexibility as to their exact boundary.

Schematically, this solution may be represented as:

(5)

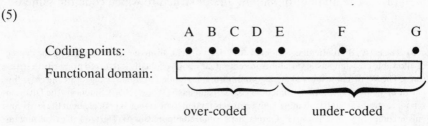

8) For an extensive discussion of these issues, see Givón (1982b, 1982c).

Within the same language, one may look at a certain functional domain in terms of **coding density**. Thus, in (5) above, the left-hand portion of the domain is **over-coded** relative to the right-hand portion, which is **under-coded**. As we shall see further below, the same conceptual framework is also useful in comparing the syntactic coding of the same functional domain in different languages.

2.6. CROSS-LANGUAGE DIVERSITY AND SYNTACTIC TYPOLOGY

In one manner or another, either explicitly or implicitly, most current schools of linguistics have accepted the proposition that the notional-functional base of language and communication is universal. In terms of our terminology of functional domains, this means roughly that there is a limited and cross-linguistically highly comparable inventory of functional domains coded by syntax.[9] On the other hand, even the most cursory cross-linguistic comparison would reveal that the very same functional domain quite often is coded in different languages by different *types* of structures. Such an observation is the beginning of a systematic inquiry into **syntactic typology**, performed initially for every well-identified functional domain. In a fundamental way, syntactic typology of structures is not a viable proposition without a firm definition of universal and cross-linguistically comparable functional domains. Without a firm notion of function, it would be impossible to group structures for comparison.

When one does a syntactic typology of structures which code, across all languages, a particular functional domain, one finds rather quickly that the typological variety within any particular functional domain is severely limited. This limitation may be expressed in two different ways:

(a)   The number of *major types* of structure which code the same do-

---

9) The early, Bloomfieldian School of American structuralism tended to exaggerate the degree of allowable cross-linguistic variability in general, although explicitly it referred primarily to structures. The Whorfian school of language and culture has tended to equally exaggerate the cross-linguistic diversity of the notional-functional base of language (Whorf, 1956). Similarly, the Diverian school centered around Columbia University has tended to be rather skeptical about the cross-linguistic comparison of function (E. García, in personal communication). The area of lexical-semantics, where much of the cross-cultural diversity is reposited, obviously exhibits a lower degree of cross-linguistic comparability than either propositional semantics or discourse pragmatics.

main is rather limited, very seldom more than 5-7 types;[10] and

(b) Cross-linguistically, coding points that are structurally similar also tend to occupy similar sub-sections along a functional domain, and their relative ordering cross-linguistically is just as rigid as it is within a single language.

Point (b) above may be schematically illustrated by a variation on the coding diagram in (5) above:

(6)

	A	B	C	D		E		H
Coding points (Lg. A):	●	●	●	●		●		●
Functional domain:								
Coding points (Lg. B):	●			●		●	●	● ●
	A			D		E	F	G H

In diagram (6) above, we compare schematically the coding of the same scalar domain in two different languages. In Lg. A the left-hand portion of the domain is over-coded, the right-hand under-coded. The reverse is true for Lg. B. The identification of the letter labels of coding points in Lg. A with corresponding ones in Lg. B is meant to illustrate point (b) above, i.e. the claim that they are more likely to be *structurally similar*, though not necessarily identical. Point (b) is also illustrated by the retention of relative order among the coding points in Lg. A and B, regardless of the specific coding density along the domain. This retention of the relative distribution of coding points along a domain — regardless of coding density — is a fundamental fact which allows us to probe the principles of non-arbitrary coding — or iconicity — in syntax.

2.7. CODING PRINCIPLES, ICONICITY AND EXPLANATION IN SYNTAX

The next task for the linguist, once the raw typological facts have been systematically established in an exhaustive cross-linguistic study of functional

---

10) The perennial problem of all taxonomies also rears its ugly head here, namely "how to distinguish between a major type and a minor sub-type", or ultimately how to distinguish between a difference in kind and a difference in degree. There is no field of inquiry where this problem could be solved in a principled way. It is the *pragmatics* of the task that normally dictates the depth of a taxonomy.

domains and the types of syntactic structures which code them, is to proceed toward formulating explanations of the seeming paucity and limited diversity in both the number and type of possible structures which may code any particular domain. In general, there are three types of functionally-grounded explanations that the linguist must seek:

(a) *Language-universal functional explanations*: These will presumably be couched in terms of various *iconicity principles*, which will illuminate and explicate the non-arbitrary relation between form and function or code and message in human language. Throughout the two volumes of this book we will attempt to identify as many of these general principles as current knowledge allows.

(b) *Language specific cross-functional explanations*: The entire grammar is not a mere unordered list of unrelated functional domains. Rather, it seems to be internally structured much like an organism, within which some sub-systems are more closely related to each other — in function as well as in structure — than others. Resorting again to a biological analogy one would expect that in terms of anatomy (structure) and physiology (function), the circulatory, pulmonary, digestive and eliminative systems of the body would exhibit more intimate interaction and *mutual constraints* upon each other, given their interlinked functions in the general realm of *metabolism*, as compared with the mutual constraints each one of them may exert upon, say, the reproductive system or the skeletal support system. Similarly, one would expect the skeletal and muscular systems to interact more closely with each other and exert more stringent reciprocal constraints on each other than either would upon, say, the digestive system. This is so because they share a major functional realm, that of spatial orientation and ambulation. While the hierarchic organization of sub-systems is not neat and unambiguous in either biology or language, there are grounds for believing that the functional sub-systems in language and communication display a similar, complex hierarchic organization. Cross-functional explanation of typological facts thus involves the specific inventory of structures which a language uses to code related functional domains — or sub-sections of one domain — and the way in which they interact with each other and constrain each other, in terms of the *availability* of coding means, the functional and/or structural *proximity* of available coding means, and the *functional load* put upon particular coding points [or its converse, the *coding density* within a domain or sub-domain].

(c)   *Diachronic explanations*: While this book is concerned primarily with the elucidation and understanding of **synchronic** (extant) syntax, it is a fundamental point in the functional-typological approach to language that language change — through **history, ontogeny** (individual maturation) or **phylogeny** (species evolution) is a major — if not the main — mediating force in affecting the non-arbitrary pairing of structure and function. As we will suggest further below, quite often the naturalness or non-arbitrariness of a particular pairing of structure with function is derived from the particular history of the pairing, rather than from synchronic functional explanations. And while diachronic change in syntax is most commonly motivated by functional considerations as well, to some extent what was originally natural for diachronic change may ultimately wind up being less natural in terms of synchronic pairing of function and structure.[11]

2.8. THE FUNCTIONAL BIND IN SYNTACTIC CODING: SIMPLE VS. COMPLEX SENTENCES

As suggested above, syntax jointly codes two distinct functional realms:

(a)   Propositional semantics
(b)   Discourse pragmatics

The division between these two realms echoes, broadly, the generative-transformational division between 'kernel' or **simple sentences** and 'transformed' or **complex sentences**, respectively. This division has been implicit in grammatical analysis since time immemorial, singling out the *main*, *declarative*, *affirmative*, *active* clause-type as in some sense the 'basic' sentence type, a 'point of reference' in the grammatical description of all other types. A major contribution of Harris (1956) and Chomsky (1957) was to make this old intuitive division explicit, and to justify it — at least on **formal** grounds, invoking primarily considerations of simplicity/economy. One thing that this book will attempt to do is justify this formal division on more **substantive** grounds.

---

11) See extensive discussion of these issues in Givón (1979a, Chapter 6).

The first thing one may wish to say about simple sentences — i.e. sentences that would presumably carry only propositional semantic information but no discourse pragmatic function — is that they don't really exist in live communication. Only when linguists artificially isolate them from their discourse context, could they possibly appear to be that pristine. Thus, main, declarative, affirmative active sentences when found in actual discourse, do already perform some distinct discourse function. However, that function is closely related to their propositional-semantic contents: They are the major conduit of *new*, *foreground*, *backbone*, *main-line* information in discourse. With this in mind, one may nonetheless define this discourse function of simple sentences as the **neutral** case, and then proceed to look at all other discourse functions — and syntactic structures which code them — in terms of their variation or *distance* from that neutral case.

The fact that all sentences in discourse carry a dual function, semantic as well as pragmatic, has far-reaching consequences for syntax. While the propositional-semantic contents of a sentence may remain fixed, its discourse-pragmatic function can be modified enormously, and this is associated with radical changes in its syntactic structure — in terms of word-order, morphology and intonation. This may be illustrated in the following group of examples.

(7) (a) John killed the lion   [information, affirmative, active]
     (b) Did John kill the lion?   [yes/no question]
     (c) What did John kill?   [object WH question]
     (d) John didn't kill the lion   [information, negative]
     (e) The lion was killed by John   [information, affirmative, passive]
     (f) John killed the **lion**   [information, affirmative, active, emphatic]

Throughout all the variant sentences in (7), the propositional-semantic content most succintly given in (7a) itself, i.e. in the 'neutral' or 'simple' sentence type, remains virtually constant.[12] But the discourse-pragmatic function varies, and with it syntactic structure is *readjusted*. And some of these readjustments tamper with the original clues — in (7a) — which code the semantic case-role and the transitivity value ('state', 'action', 'event') of the proposition. For example, English is typically a SUBJECT-VERB-OBJECT lan-

12) Sentence (7c) deviates slightly from this generalization, since the actual identity of the object ('lion') is not given in it, but rather requested. But otherwise the rest of the sentences in (7) share the basic information about who did what to whom.

guage in terms of word-order. But in sentence (7b) a verbal element — *did* — precedes the subject, and in (7c) an element corresponding to the object — *what* — precedes the subject, in both cases disrupting the normal, 'neutral' coding strategy. In the same vein, the normal way of coding active events ('actions') in English is by marking the *agent* of the action as subject, the *patient* as object, and the verb in the active form. But in (7e) the patient occupies the subject position, the agent is marked as instrumental-object, and the verb is marked with a stative, adjectival form (the auxiliary 'be', the participial suffix). Thus, because syntax has to *simultaneously* code propositional semantic information and discourse-pragmatic function, it creates a **functional bind**, whereby the execution of one coding function tampers with the execution of the other. What one finds in the syntax of complex sentences, most often, is a series of **recoverability strategies** ('compensatory strategies') specific to particular types of complex sentences. These are structural clues — in word-order, morphology or intonation — which compensate for the disruption in the original set of clues that code propositional-semantic information in the 'neutral', 'simple' pattern. Thus, for example, in the neutral sentence (7a) the coding of the case-roles 'subject' and 'object' is achieved via word-order — the subject preceding the verb, the object following it. But in the WH question (7c) both object and subject precede the verb. This is compensated by marking the object with a WH-word 'what' that is more specifically an object-referring word (the corresponding subject-referring word would have been 'who'), thus compensating by morphological means for the loss of the original word-order strategy. Similarly, the roles of 'agent' and 'patient' in the neutral pattern (7a) are marked by the SUBJECT-VERB-OBJECT word-order strategy, with the agent being subject and the patient being object. But in the passive variant (7e) the patient — 'the lion' — is made the subject, thus tampering with the normal coding strategy. The compensation in this case is two-fold in English:

(a) The verb is coded as a stative/adjectival verb, with the auxiliary 'be' and the participial suffix; this clues the hearer for the subject being a patient rather than an agent; and

(b) The agent — though in the typical object position — is specially marked by the instrumental preposition 'by', thus tagging it as the agent in a passive construction.

In the syntax of complex sentences, one may thus distinguish between structural clues pertaining specifically to the coding of propositional-semantic information, structural clues that specifically code discourse-pragmatic function, and structural clues that are compensatory, i.e. re-code propositional-semantic information following the disruption caused by the need to also code discourse-pragmatic function. And in the study of cross-linguistic syntactic typology, all three types of coding constitute the major parameters via which the typology — especially of complex sentences — is constructed.

In a fundamental way, then, one may view syntax as a **communicative compromise**, a compromise between the need to code propositional-semantic information and the need to code — simultaneously and by the same structure — discourse pragmatic function.

2.9. DEVELOPMENTAL DETERMINATION OF SYNTACTIC STRUCTURE

There is a certain tradition in structuralist linguistics, commencing with Saussure (1915) and continuing with Bloomfield (1933) and implicitly in Chomsky (1957) and the various offshoots of transformational-generative linguistics, of rigorously separating the study of language change — through history (diachrony), child development (ontogeny) and species evolution (phylogeny) — from the study of language as it is (synchrony). This tradition, one suspects from reading F. de Saussure (1915), may have been due initially to a methodological convenience.[13] In American structuralism, this reasonable methodological procedure was elevated to the status of a theoretically significant anti-developmentalist dogma. There are reasons to believe that this instance of granting a theoretical status to a methodological convenience is ultimately a serious mistake. True, in this book we shall concern ourselves primarily with what one finds in the syntax of human languages at a particular point in time. It is hard to describe what changes into what, how and why without first describing the admittedly somewhat fictional steady state. Nonetheless, we must remind ourselves periodically that language never rests, it is *always* in the middle of change, in pronunciation, in lexicon and in syntax. So

---

13) Saussure (1915) writes: "...In practice a language-state is not a point but rather a certain span of time during which the sum of the modifications that have supervened is minimal... Studying a language-state means in practice disregarding changes of little importance... In static linguistics, as in most sciences, no course of reasoning is possible without the usual simplification of the data..." [pp. 101-102]. It is this 'simplification' or 'abstraction' *in practice* that one would assume to be that methodological convenience. The same pragmatism also seems to prevail in Bloomfield's approach: "...We can study linguistic change only by comparing related languages or different historical stages of the same language..." [1933, pp. 16-17]. Bloomfield of course disregards here the method of internal reconstruction and the study of variation within a language community or the speech of a single individual. The methodological fiction of "synchronic state" is nevertheless a *useful* fiction, just as necessary in dealing with the non-discreteness of time as syntax is necessary in the organism's dealing with the non-discreteness of notional/functional space.

that often, in order to really understand why syntax is the way it is and how it performs its complex coding functions, one must investigate the ways in which syntax — through childhood, history or evolution — came to be what it is. This is simply a word of caution, to warn the reader that many fundamental problems in understanding and explaining syntax will not be treated in full in this book, although at appropriate points we will allude to them.

The last point to be raised here, again without elaborating it in much detail either here or throughout the book, is the following: Language change, through childhood, history or evolution, has been shown to be motivated primarily by functional-adaptive requirements of task-oriented organisms. In this way the realm of human language and cognition is fundamentally part and parcel of other function-bound sub-systems of the organism. As in other areas of biology, in language too the non-arbitrary correlation between structure and function is mediated overwhelmingly by developmental processes. These are the venues through which correlations between functions and their coding structures constantly adjust themselves. Thus, for example, in studying the evolution of syntax in the growing child (ontogeny), we find that structures tend to spread their coding range from function to a closely-related function, rather than leap over large functional gaps. The organism thus strives to maintain some semblance of one-to-one iconic correlation between form and function. The same is also true in syntactic change and spread-of-change over the lifetime of a population (diachrony).[14] And there is no reason to assume that the evolution of syntax over the history of the species (phylogeny) is motivated in any radically different way.[15] Ultimately, therefore, the study of syntax from a functional-typological perspective cannot become fully systematic without being closely integrated with the study of linguistic evolution.[16]

14) See discussion in Slobin (1977) concerning the fundamental parallelism between language change in childhood and in history.

15) See discussion in Givón (1979a, Chapters 5, 6, 7) concerning the relation between language diachrony, ontogeny and phylogeny.

16) Here once again one could suggest an analogy from Biology. There is nothing functionally/synchronically necessary about the histological closeness of the skin and the epithelicm lining the digestive tract. Over millions of years, they have each adapted to completely different functions — and have consequently evolved strikingly different histological structures. Nevertheless, they retain some residual similarities which could only be explained by their phylogenetic (and embryological) history, both being descendent from the same ancient embryonic *ectoderm* of the *blastula* stage, before its folding had produced the digestive cavity. At the time the blastula-like organism developed its internal cavity, however, both structurally and functionally the two tissue types were much more closely related, and the evolution from one to the other was a more transparent step-by-step process, which is still recapitulated, in a rough way, in embryonic ontogenesis.

3 | WORD CLASSES

3.1. INTRODUCTION: MEANING AND INFORMATION

As suggested in Chapter 2, above, the basic unit of information in human language is the proposition. When the proposition is coded via syntactic structure, we call it a *sentence* or *clause*. Propositions most commonly carry specific information that a certain hearer wants to communicate to a certain speaker in a certain *context*. But that specific information may either be about *specific* events/actions/states (i.e. those occurring at a particular time and place and involving particular participants), or else it may be *generic* information, about the way things are in general (i.e. true either for all times, for all places or for all persons/things under discussion). Interpersonal discourse tends to carry largely specific information. On the other hand, academic or instructional discourse tends to be largely of a generic nature, thus perhaps functioning to augment the culturally-shared pool of knowledge.

The bulk of the generic ('permanent') cultural knowledge stored by speakers/hearers is coded in their **lexicon**, which is in fact more like an *encyclopedia*. For the purpose of the discussion here, it will be assumed that the lexicon is a list — probably ordered and cross-filed in a complex way that is beyond the scope of this work — of *words* ('lexical items'), where for each item two things are listed:

(a) The **code** unit, i.e. a sequence of sounds; and
(b) The **meaning** unit(s), i.e. a configuration/cluster of "meanings".

Lexicographers and linguists have known for a long time that "meanings" of words are not atomic, but are rather structured in the human lexicon in two distinct senses:

(i) *Internally* they are made out of sub-units ('semantic features') that contribute to the total meaning of the word in some aggregate fashion, and stand in some internal relationship to each other; and

(ii)   *Externally* lexical items are related to each other through *shared* sub-units of meaning, with the degree and manner of such sharing again being highly specific to particular lexical items.

Aspects (i) and (ii) above of lexical structure, which may be termed-*micro*- and *macro*-structure, respectively, are not precise, closed logical systems. But in some rough fashion they do exist as synchronic *filing-and-retrieval* systems in the minds of language users.

The words in the lexicon and their time-stable, generically-shared *meanings* are used as the building blocks of sentences in which specific *information* is communicated. The admittedly flexible boundary between 'meaning' and 'information'[1] thus represents the boundary between two entities that are in a hierarchic, inclusion relation, whereby generic knowledge/meaning units ('words') are used to make up sentences which impart propositional information. These are two of the functional realms discussed in Ch. 2, above: Lexical semantics and propositional semantics.

3.2. LEXICAL VS. GRAMMATICAL VOCABULARY

One may divide the vocabulary of human language, i.e. the stored/ memorized sound:meaning paired expressions in the lexicon, into two general types:

(a)   Lexical words
(b)   Grammatical morphemes

The differences between these two types are summarized in Table 1., below.[2] Grammatical morphemes, in addition, are divided into two types:

(i)   Inflectional morphemes
(ii)   Derivational morphemes

1) The meaning of a lexical item is understood in terms of sets of *propositions* which relate it to the meaning of other lexical items. Thus, for example:
(i) A horse is a quadruped *mammal* used for riding or freight
(ii) A mammal is a *vertebrate* animal that breast-feeds its young
(iii) A vertebrate is an *animal* with a rigid backbone
etc. All of these propositons embody stable, generic knowledge. But as we have suggested above, information may also be of this type.

2) While the differences are clear and define the *prototypes*, one must keep in mind that grammatical morphemes eventually arise out of lexical words, by a parallel process of *semantic bleaching* and *phonological reduction*. Fo extensive discussion see Givón (1971a, 1973a, 1975a, 1979a [Ch.5], 1979b).

Derivational morphemes will not be discussed in this volume in any detail, since their connection with syntax is mostly marginal. Our discussion of grammatical morphemes ('grammatical vocabulary') will thus pertain largely to inflectional morphology.[3]

TABLE 1: LEXICAL VS. GRAMMATICAL VOCABULARY

	LEXICAL WORDS	*INFLECTIONAL MORPHEMES*
phonological size	large	small
stress:	stressed	unstressed
semantic size:	large	small
semantic detail:	specific ('enriched')	generic, classificatory ('bleached')
class size:	large	small
class membership:	open	closed
morphemic status:	free	bound
function:	code generic knowledge (lexical *meaning*)	code propositional *information* or discourse *function*

a. *Phonological size*: Lexical words tend to be larger, in terms of number of phonemes. Inflectional morphemes tend to be smaller, seldom larger than one syllable.

b. *Stress*: Lexical words tend to carry stress. Inflectional morphemes tend to be unstressed.

c. *Semantic size*: Lexical words tend to carry more complex, bigger chunks of semantic baggage. Inflectional morphemes tend to carry a smaller semantic weight.

d. *Semantic specificity*: Lexical words tend to carry highly specific features, down to the *lowest nodes* of the hierarchy. They are thus

3) There are a number of areas in the grammar where the distinction between inflectional and derivational morphology becomes somewhat blurred, due primarily to diachronic change from inflection to derivational function. Thus, for example, passive or de-transitivizing morphology may over a period of time become a largely *lexical* process via which intransitive verbs are derived from erstwhile transitive-active stems. Similarly, causative verbs/morphemes may become over time primarily a lexical process via which transitive-active verbs are derived from intransitive verb stems. The same is true for reciprocal and reflexive-marking morphemes. The converse diachronic change is also possible. Thus, for example, nominal or adjectival derivational morphemes may turn into tense-aspect or even detransitivizing inflections.

semantically 'rich'. Inflectional morphemes tend to be more generic or classificatory, pertaining to the *higher nodes* of hierarchies. They are thus semantically 'bleached'.[4]

e. *Class size*: Classes of words are large. Classes of inflectional morphemes are small.

f. *Class membership*: Lexical classes are open-ended, the culture constantly adds more items to these classes as need arises and the world-view slowly changes. Classes of inflectional morphemes are closed, or new members are admitted only infrequently.[5]

g. *Morphemic status*: Lexical words tend to be independent stems, although often they must carry some obligatory inflections characteristic of the word-class. Inflectional morphemes, while initially independent (and derived from lexical words), tend to become *bound* and then *cliticize* ('cluster') upon stems of lexical words.

h. *Function*: As suggested earlier, lexical words carry primarily lexical meaning that codes our culturally-shared generic knowledge or world-view. On the other hand, inflectional morphemes are part of the structural code of sytax — coding jointly propositional *information* and discourse *function*.

3.3. MORPHOTACTICS AND FUNCTION

In this chapter the treatment of inflectional morphology will be confined to:

(a) Identifying major classes

(b) Identifying their most common classificatory-semantic features

(c) Commenting on their most likely **morphotactics**, by which we mean "the lexical stem-types on which they are most likely to operate/cliticize".

The most complex aspect of inflectional morphology, namely:

---

4) Since both inflectional and derivational morphemes arise historically from erstwhile lexical morphemes, phonological and semantic reduction or bleaching is part and parcel of their diachronic rise. One could single this out as one more *iconic* phenomenon in language, whereby "a larger chunk of meaning/message tends to be coded by a larger chunk of coding material".

5) Grammatical change eventually introduces new inflectional morphemes into existing classes, or restructures the classes and their function. But this is a much slower, more gradual process than the introduction of new lexical vocabulary.

(d)　　Its use in syntactic structure for the signaling of propositional semantic information and discourse pragmatic function

will not be discussed here. It will be treated in detail in subsequent chapters pertaining to specific domains.

3.4. THE TIME-STABILITY SCALE OF LEXICAL CLASSES

We most commonly find four major lexical classes ('word classes') in languages:

(a)　　Nouns
(b)　　Verbs
(c)　　Adjectives
(d)　　Adverbs

Of these four, the class "adverb" is a mixed one, in terms of semantic, morphological/inflectional and syntactic criteria used to characterize word classes. One finds less cross-language generalization in the treatment of adverbs. On the other hand, nouns, adjectives and verbs distribute rather systematically along one coherent semantic dimension, one which is of great interest to linguists, psychologists and philosophers. We will call this the **time-stability scale**.[6]

Experiences — or phenomenological clusters — which stay relatively **stable** over time, i.e. those which over repeated scans appear to be roughly "the same", tend to be lexicalized in human language as **nouns**. The most prototypical nouns are those denoting **concrete**, **physical**, **compact** entities made out of durable, solid matter, such as 'rock', 'tree', 'dog', 'person' etc. Their time-stability is obviously a matter of degree, since animates such as 'dog' or 'person' obviously are born, grow slowly, grow old and then die and cease to be. And they obviously change faster than 'tree', and 'tree' changes faster than 'rock'. But, relative to the ability of the human organism to perceive very subtle changes, and given scanning frequencies of every second, every minute, every hour or every day, such concrete entities obviously appear to remain "the

---

6) For the initial formulation of this topic, see Givón (1979a, Ch. 8). The greater semantic coherence of nouns, adjectives and verbs also corresponds to their greater morphological and syntactic coherence. Here once again a *meta-iconicity* principle is manifesting itself, i.e.: "The more coherent the message level is, the more likely is the coding level to mirror that coherence".

same" over time.[7]

At the other extreme of the lexical-phenomenological scale, one finds experiential clusters denoting **rapid changes** in the state of the universe. These are protoypically *events* or *actions*, and languages tend to lexicalize them as verbs. Members of this lexical category are much more abstract than nouns, although in this respect they may be graded on a scale. Thus, for example, 'break' is much more concrete than 'grieve', and 'grieve' is in turn more concrete than 'speculate'. Further, within the verb category, members may be graded by their degree of time-stability. Thus, 'hit', 'shoot' or 'kick' are **instantaneous** verbs, denoting an extremely rapid change. 'Sing', 'work', 'eat' or 'read' may denote a much slower process of change, and are characteristically **activity/process** verbs. Finally, 'know', 'understand' or 'like' tend to denote long-lasting **states**, coding either no change or very slow change in the phenomenological universe.

The classes of noun and verb, the two prototypical extremes on our time-stability scale, are attested in the lexicon of all languages. On the other hand, the class 'adjective' is a bit problematic. In languages such as English, which has this class (with its characteristic semantics, morphology and syntactic distribution), adjectives occupy the middle of the time-stability scale. They may overlap with the *least* time-stable nouns, such as 'youth', 'adult', 'child', 'divorcee', 'infant'. Most commonly they embrace at least the time-stable physical properties such as size, shape, color, texture, smell or taste. Finally, they may overlap, at the other end of the scale, with the *most* time-stable adjectives/verbs, such as those expressed in English by the following adjectives: 'sad', 'angry', 'hot', 'cold', 'happy', 'ill' etc.

In many languages, such as English, the class of adjectives is greatly augmented via lexical derivation from verbs or nouns. Some of these derivations are fairly stable cross-linguistically. Thus, for example, the following three derivations of adjectives from verbs are fairly common:

(a) *Completed result*: 'broken', 'burnt', 'finished', 'painted', 'shaven';
(b) *Ongoing process*: 'eating', 'burning', 'living', 'running', 'dying';
(c) *Potentiality*: 'breakable', 'edible', 'readable', doable', 'bendable'.

---

7) Both perceptual discrimination and the average frequency of repeated scanning are biologically constrained for a species, within some reasonable bounds that have much to do with environmental adaptability and survival. Thus, presumably for an organism that scans more frequently and observes more detail, our prototypical nouns may seem rapidly changing, unstable, flighty phenomena.

When adjectives are derived from nouns, they then tend to code more time-stable meanings than those coded by verb-derived adjectives. Thus in English, common noun-to-adjective derivation patterns are:[8]

(d) *Noun-to-adjective*: 'circular', 'spherical', 'median', 'colorful', 'brainless'.

There is a small group of underived, 'original' adjectives in English. Diachronically most of them seem to have been derived from nouns.[9] Synchronically they pertain to the most protoypical adjectival qualities, those of stable physical qualities such as size, shape, texture, color, taste or smell.[10]

There are languages where no class 'adjective' exists, and where most adjectival qualities/states which lexicalize in English as adjectives are lexicalized instead as verbs. As an example consider Toposa, a Nilotic language from the Southern Sudan:[11]

(1)

verb		'adjective'	
à-lóz-ī	'I go'	à-pólōt	'I am big'
ì-lóz-ī	'you go'	ì-pólōt	'you are big'
è-lòz-ī	'he/she goes'	è-pòlót	'he/she is big'
kì-lóz-ī	'we go'	kì-pólōq	'we are big'
ì-lóz-étè	'y'all go'	ì-pólōq	'y'all are big'
ē-lōz-ētē	'they go'	è-pólōq	'they are big'

The subject agreement paradigm for verbs and adjectives in this language is identical. Further, 'big' above does not require the verb 'be' which syntactically characterizes the class of adjective predicates in English. Toposa has such a verb, which is used as copula with nominal predicates, or as a locative verb. Thus consider:

(2) a. à-yáì (àyòŋ) qàyī
         I-be (I)   room
         'I am in the room'

8) See discussion in Givón (1970a).

9) See Givón (1970a).

10) See Dixon (1972a).

11) For further detail see Givón (1976a). The data is originally due to Angelo Lobale Lokoro Loirria (in personal communication).

    b. à-yáì (àyòŋ) nyé-kìlé
       I-be (I)   PREF-man
       'I am a man'

In core-Bantu languages, the class 'adjective' is historically derived from 'noun', as the common morphology still attests. Older reconstructible Proto-Bantu adjectives, such as 'male, 'female', 'new' etc. reconstruct back to nominal roots such as 'man', 'woman' and 'child', respectively. In many Bantu languages to this day less-durable states fall into the *verb* class. Thus, consider the following examples from Bemba:[12]

  (3) a. *Active verb*: n-à-soma   icitabo
                   I-PAST-read book
                   'I read a book'

       b. *Stative verb*: n-à-ishiba   umuuntu
                   I-PAST-know person
                   'I knew the guy'

       c. *'Adjective'*: n-à-shipa 'I am brave'
                   I-PAST-brave
                   'I am brave' ('I have become brave')

                   n-à-buuta
                   I-PAST-white
                   'I am white'

                   n-à-fina
                   I-PAST-heavy
                   'I am heavy'

                   n-à-shyuuka
                   I-PAST-lucky
                   'I am lucky'

The small class of 'true' adjectives in Bemba displays noun morphology, as in:[13]

---

12) For details see Givón (1972, Chapters 1,3).

13) This situation prevails in all noun classes in related languages such as Swahili. In Bemba itself, in many noun classes the erstwhile noun prefixes of adjectives have undergone a change, thus differentiating themselves morphologically from nouns. For further discussion, see Givón (1979a, Ch. 6).

(4) a. *Noun*:   Yohani a-à-li   muu-buyi
                    John   he-PAST-be PREF-thief
                    'John was a thief'

     b. *Adjective*: Yohani a-à-li   muu-suma
                    John   he-PAST-be PREF-good
                    'John was good'

Finally, one may note that in languages such as English, where the class adjective does exist, many time-stable adjectives often have an alternative expression as nouns, as in the alternations *young/youth, old/geezer, mature/adult*. At the upper end of the adjective range, many transitory-state adjectives have an alternative expression as verbs, as in *be aware/know, be sick/ail, be afraid/fear, be angry/seethe, be enamoured/love, be in accord/agree*. In adjective/verb pairs of this type, most commonly the adjective denotes a more stable state than the verb. While with the adjective/noun pairs, the adjective most commonly denotes a less stable condition than the noun.

The time-stability scale may be summarized as follows:

(5) NOUNS -------------- ADJECTIVES ---------- VERBS

---

     most time-stable   intermediate states   rapid change

One last note concerns the difference between nouns and the most prototypical adjectives, those denoting the most stable qualities such as *color, shape, size, texture, smell* or *taste*. On the face of it, these are precisely the categories which also classify the most prototypical, most time-stable nouns. So that it seems that these adjectives are at the same point on our time-stability scale as nouns. The difference between the two is, however, that of semantic complexity ('thickness'): A noun such as, say, 'horse' has typical color, shape, size, texture, smell etc. If one of those changes by itself, the others which do not change still suffice to endow 'horse' with sufficiently *prototypical* 'horseness'. It is thus the *cluster effect* of time-stable properties — adjectival properties — which produces the greater time-stability of prototypical nouns. On the other hand, prototypical adjectives involve only a single property/quality. Thus, a change from white to black in a horse — easily possible with age or season — changes the adjective but not the noun 'horse' as a whole. The same is true for change of size with age, or change of fur texture with season. In fact, the notion of prototype of *semantically-rich* concepts is dependent upon this clustering effect, whereby each single property is not necessarily criterial but the cluster of *most* of them taken together always is.[14]

3.5. NOUNS

3.5.1. Semantic characterization

As suggested above, nouns tend to be the most time-stable phenomena coded in the lexicon. The full study of the semantics of nouns should be undertaken within the realm of lexical semantics, and thus will not be attempted here. Rather, we will concern ourselves here only with the most generic features of the noun classificatory hierarchy, those that tend to have **coding consequences** in either morphology or syntax.

Probably the most general set of hierarchically arrayed features used by humans to classify nouns is:

(6) ENTITY>TEMPORAL>CONCRETE>ANIMATE>HUMAN

Entity means 'that which exists',[15] **temporal** 'exists at a particular time'; **concrete** 'exists in both time and place'; **animate** adds to all the above the feature 'living organism', and **human** also adds the feature 'be human'. This hierarchy is thus one of **increased marking** ('markedness'), whereby if an entity has one feature of this hierarchy, it automatically also has all the features to the left on the hierarchy.

When a noun is only "entity", without further specification, it is most commonly referred to as an *abstract* noun, such as 'freedom' or 'dignity'. A 'temporal' noun is often referred to as *semi-abstract*, and examples are 'July', 'day', 'Sunday', 'birthday' etc. Concrete (but inanimate) nouns have spatial dimensions (and other concrete qualities associated with physical objects). They are nouns such as 'house', 'chair', 'tree' etc. Animates (but non-humans) are nouns such as 'horse', 'bee', 'fish' etc. And humans are nouns such

14) Three logically-independent aspects may be discerned in approaching the notion of "prototype" in semantics. One of them is Wittgenstein's (1953) concept of *family resemblance*, whereby A resembles B, B resembles C, C resembles D, etc., though A and Z may share little. Nevertheless, A and Z may be members of a 'class'. The second involves the *cluster-of-properties* notion, whereby no single property is criterial for class membership, but a large enough bunch suffices to define the prototype (Coleman and Kay 1981). Finally, the third aspect involves the matter of *degree* of displaying a certain scalar property, whereby a strong enough degree qualifies for membership in the class (Rosch, 1975). It can be shown that aspects two and three are formally the same.

15) The universe of discourse in which entities exist does not completely overlap with the "real world". Thus, abstract "entities" do not obviously have scientifically verifiable existence in the same sense as 'chair' or 'child'. Further, lexical items are *class names*, not necessarily referring to any specific individual which actually exists, but only outlining its properties in case it did exist.

as 'teacher', 'banker', 'governor' (without further gender specification) or 'man', 'woman', 'ballerina' (with obligatory gender).

Another rather common sub-classification of nouns, primarily pertaining to concrete nouns, involves their properties of *size*, *shape* and *manipulability*, and manifests itself most commonly (at least initially) in quantifying expressions, as in:

(7) a. 'a *grain* of salt'
 b. 'a *cup* of tea'
 c. 'three *sticks* of dynamite'
 d. 'two *sheets* of paper'
 e. 'five *head* of cattle'
 f. 'a *flock* of birds'
 g. 'three *bunches* of grapes'

In many languages such a system, originating in quantifying phrases, eventually develops into an inflectional/morphological classification of nouns (see below). Part of this system also involves the properties of **countability** (i.e. the contrast between countable vs. mass nouns).

Another common classification system involves **handlability** as object, i.e. properties such as 'brittleness', 'softness', 'smoothness' etc. A number of languages base their morphological classification of nouns at least in part on such properties.

A further sub-classification of nouns, with less likely morphological manifestations, refers to other properties, some inherent and time stable (color), others less concrete and more contingent upon *behavior* in various contexts, *interaction* with other nouns, typical *objecthood* to various verbs, etc.

3.5.2. Morphological characterization

In this section we will deal with the most typical grammatical/inflectional morphemes that tend to cluster around — or cliticize to — noun stems. Some of them cluster to nouns already in their lexical **citation form**. Others cluster to them only in sentence or discourse context. The fact that all these morphemes cluster around nouns is not an arbitrary morphotactic phenomenon. Rather, they either pertain to the lexical-semantic features of nouns, or to their propositional-semantic role, or to some aspect of their discourse-pragmatic function. One may thus enunciate a broad **iconicity principle** for inflectional morphology (indeed all morphology):

(8) "Semantic, propositional and/or discourse-pragmatic features that are closely associated with each other also tend to **co-lexicalize**".

3.5.2.1. Noun-class markers

Noun-class markers, at least initially, tend to express the most generic semantic features of nouns (see section 3.5.1., above). Over long periods of historical change in both morphology and meaning, they often lose some — and sometimes all — semantic correlates. Consider, for example, the following noun-class system found in Bantu languages, where features of 'class' and 'number' intersect to give separate singular and plural forms of the same *semantic* class. The semantic basis for the classification is synchronically obscure, though a coherent system based on the size/shape/countability features discussed above (section 3.5.1.) can still be reconstructed.[16] Synchronically, only the feature [human] correlates consistently to a particular class.[17]

(9)   MORPHOLOGICALLY-MARKED NOUN-CLASSES IN
BEMBA (BANTU)

class	singular	plural	older semantic value
1/2	umu-ana 'child'	aba-ana 'children'	humans (extant)
3/4	umu-kate 'bread'	imi-kate 'breads'	plants
5/6	i-sabi 'fish'	ama-sabi 'fish'	fruits
6		ama-inshi 'water'	mass/liquid
7/8	ici-ti 'stick'	ifi-ti 'sticks'	small objects, inanimates
9/10	in-koko 'chicken'	in-koko 'chicken'	animates
11/10	ulu-imbi 'song	iny-imbi 'songs'	elongated objects, inanimate
12/13	aka-pili 'hill'	utu-pili 'hills'	small objects
14		ubu-ushi 'honey'	mass/liquid
15/16	uku-twi 'ear'	ama-twi 'ears'	paired body parts

In the examples above, the classifier morphology was prefixal. But it may also be suffixal, as in the following example from Ute (Uto-Aztecan), where again only the feature [animate] exhibits any regular correspondence to the morphology:[18]

---

16) See details in Denny and Creider (1976) as well as discussion in Givón (1971b).

17) The data here are from Bemba (Givón, 1972).

18) See Givón (1980a).

(10) MORPHOLOGICALLY-MARKED NOUN-CLASSES IN
UTE (UTO-AZTECAN)

suffix	example	semantic class
-ci	mamá-ci 'woman'	animate, strong correlation
-vi	sináą-vi 'wolf'	animate, weak correlation
-pi	wa'á-pi 'penis'	body part, weak correlation
-vụ	'úukụ-vụ 'collar bone'	inanimates
-pụ	tụvú-pụ 'earth'	inanimates
-tụ	pǫ'ǫmi-tụ 'writer'	agent of action, derived
-rụ	nýa-rụ 'wind'	subject of state, derived

Unlike the Bantu example (9), in Ute plurality is not involved in the morphological classification of nouns.

Semitic languages have, typically a gender and number classification, as
in the following example from Hebrew:

(11) MORPHOLOGICALLY-MARKED NOUN-CLASSES IN
HEBREW (SEMITIC)

	singular	plural
masculine	yéled 'boy'	yelad-ím 'boys'
feminine	yald-á 'girl'	yelad-ót 'girls'

In Nilotic languages the system involves three genders, masculine,
feminine and neuter/diminutive. Thus consider the following example from
Toposa:[19]

(12) MORPHOLOGICALLY-MARKED NOUN-CLASSES IN
TOPOSA (NILOTIC)

	singular	plural
masculine	nye-moŋ 'ox'	ŋi-moŋ-in 'oxen'
feminine	nya-beru 'woman'	ŋa-beřřǔ 'women'
neuter	nyi-toon 'person'	ŋi-tuŋ-a 'persons'

The synchronically-regular morphological marking of the three classes and
their singulars/plurals is by prefixes. But the traces of an older suffixal system
of — at least — pluralization can still be discerned.[20]

19) See Givón (1976a).

20) See discussion in Givón (1971b).

In some languages, noun-classifying morphemes do not cliticize around the noun itself, but rather are associated with quantifying/numeral modifiers or with pronouns/articles. Examples of these will be discussed in Chapters 10 and 11 below as well as in Chapter 13, vol. II.

3.5.2.2. Number

Morphemes indicating singularity or, more commonly, plurality[21], very often become cliticized on nouns. Most commonly, the simple form ('stem') of the noun is taken to be the singular form, and a plural form is then added. Thus, consider the following examples from Spanish:

(13)   singular   plural

	singular	plural
masculine	hombre 'man'	hombre-s 'men'
feminine	casa 'house'	casa-s 'houses'
neuter	amor 'love'	amor-es 'loves'

We have already seen in section 3.5.2.1. above a number of examples where pluralization was not affected by a single morpheme, but rather by morphemes specific to various noun-classes. Further, we have already seen there (examples (9) and (12)) situations where both singularity and plurality are morphologically marked by alternating affixes.

One may also find, on occasion, stem-internal morphological alternation marking the singular/plural distinction. English has a number of marginal 'irregular' pairs of this type, as in:

(14)   man/men, foot/feet, mouse/mice etc.

A trace of such an alternation combined with diachronically-younger suffixes may be seen in Hebrew (example (11), section 3.5.2.1., above).

In most languages mass nouns tend to take the form characteristic of singulars, as in the English words 'water', 'blood', 'love', 'sand' etc. In such cases if pluralization can be applied, it usually denotes different instances/batches of the mass. The Bantu data in section 3.5.2.1., example (9), above, illustrate another possibility, whereby class [6] is typically a plural class (for both [5] and [15], as well as occasionally for [14]), but is also the most typical mass-noun class in Bantu.

---

21) The protoypical noun is countable, perceptually large enough to be taken as a separate entity, and thus singular. Morphemically-added pluralization is thus the most common case, although the Bantu or Nilotic situation described above, whereby singular and plural prefixes replace each other and the stem is neutral with respect to this distinction, does occur.

3.5.2.3. Articles

A more extensive treatment of demonstratives and pronouns will be given in Chapter 10, and a more extensive treatment of definite/indefinite articles and the referential/non-referential distinction will be given in Chapter 11, below. At this point one must note that the morphemes marking these distinctions cliticize most commonly on the noun.[22] This is not surprising, given the function of these morphemes in supplying existential, temporal or spatial reference to nouns. As an example of the cliticization of articles to the noun consider the following from Israeli Hebrew:

(15) a. *Definite*: **ha**-ísh 'the man'
      b. *Referential-indefinite*: ísh-**xad** 'a man'
      c. *Non-referential*: 'ísh 'man'

As an example of cliticization of the morphemes marking the referential/non-referential distinction on the noun, consider the following from Bemba (Bantu):[23]

(16) a. *Referential*:   n-dée-fwaaya **ici**-tabo
                              I-PROG-want REF-book
                              'I want a/the (particular) book'

      b. *Non-referential*: n-dée-fwaaya **ci**-tabo
                              I-PROG-want NREF-book
                              'I want some book (be it any)'

3.5.2.4. Case-role markers

In Chapter 4, below, we will deal in greater detail with the semantic basis for case-roles of nouns. In Chapter 5 we will describe in detail the morpho-syntax of case-marking systems. At this point we will deal with, primarily, the morphotactics of case-role markers, and more specifically with the fact that they most commonly cliticize on the nouns whose function they signal. As a typical and clear-cut suffixal marking of case-roles, consider the case markers of Japanese, as in:[24]

---

22) Occasionally one finds definitizing morphemes cliticizing on the *verb*. Most commonly these are object-definitizers, and most commonly they are historically derived from pronominal object agreement. For discussion see Givón (1976b).

23) For further detail see Givón (1972, Ch. 1).

24) For the data I am indebted to Katsue Akiba (in personal communication).

(17) otoka-**wa**   onna-**ni**   tegami-**o**   kaita
      man-SUBJ   woman-DAT letter-ACC wrote
      'The man wrote a letter to the woman'

In this example, SUBJ (subject), DAT (dative-recipient) and ACC (accusative-patient) are marked by transparent suffixes. But they may be marked in other languages by prefixes, as in Bikol (Philippine):[25]

(18) nag-ta'ó   **'ang**-laláke **ning**-líbro **sa**-babáye
      ACT-give SUBJ-man   ACC-book DAT-woman
      'The man gave a book to the woman'

In some languages, most notably many Indo-European ones, the morphemes marking case-roles have fused, via protracted diachronic change, with the morphemes indicating noun-class ('declension') and plurality. As an example of this, consider the following from Classical Greek:[26]

(19)   *first declension masculine*   *first declension feminine*

SINGULAR
subject (NOM)   tamí-ās 'steward'   xórā 'land'
object (ACC)   tamí-ān 'steward'   xórā-n 'land'
recipient (DAT) tamí-ą 'to a steward'   xórą 'to a land'
possessor (GEN) tamí-ou 'of a steward'   xórā-s 'of a land'

PLURAL
subject (NOM)   tamí-ai 'stewards'   xôra-i 'lands'
object (ACC)   tamí-ās 'stewards'   xóra-s 'lands'
recipient (DAT) tamí-ais 'to stewards'   xóra-is 'to lands'
possessor (GEN) tamí-ôn 'of stewards'   xor-ôn 'of lands'

3.5.2.5. Possessor pronouns

It is very common in language for pronouns referring to the possessor of the noun to be cliticized as a prefix or suffix on the noun. As an example of possessive suffixes, consider the following from (Biblical) Hebrew:

25) For the data I am indebted to Manuel Factora (in personal communication).

26) From Goodwin (1898), transcription adjusted.

(20) beyt-í   'my house'
      beyt-xá   'your house' (m.)
      beyt-éx   'your house' (f.)
      beyt-ó   'his house'
      beyt-á   'her house'
      beyt-énu   'our house'
      beyt-xém   'your house' (m.)
      beyt-xén   'your house' (f.)
      bey-ám   'their house' (m.)
      beyt-án   'their house' (f.)

As an example of possessive prefixes, consider the following from Toposa (Nilotic), where the possessive pronoun precedes the possessed-noun stem but follows the noun gender/number prefix:[27]

(21) nyē-qāā-mòŋ   nyē-yōq-mòŋ
      PREF-my-ox   PREF-our-ox
      'my ox'   'our ox' (excl.)

      nyē-qōnɨ-mòŋ   nyē-qōsɨ-mòŋ
      PREF-you-ox   PREF-our-ox
      'your ox'   'our ox' (incl.)

      nyē-qēē-mòŋ   nyē-kūs-mòŋ
      PREF-his-ox   PREF-your-ox
      'his/her ox'   'your-pl. ox'

                          nyē-kēc-mòŋ
                          PREF-their-ox
                          'their ox'

3.5.3. Syntactic/distributional characterization

Nouns tend to distribute in sentences to fill the roles of subject/agent, object/patient, dative/recipient, benefactive, location, time, manner or instrument. All these roles will be discussed in greater detail in Chapters 4 and 5, below. Nouns also occupy the role of one type of predicate, the nominal predicate. In addition, they are more likely to be the **topics** or **participants** in the sentence — rather than the **predicate**. We may demonstrate all these facts informally with the following examples from English:

---

27) See further detail in Givón (1976a).

(22) a. *subject/agent*: *The farmer* died
     b. *nominal predicate*: He is *a farmer*
     c. *object/patient*: She milked *the cow*
     d. *dative/recipient*: He gave a book *to the woman*
     e. *benefactive*: She did it *for her father*
     f. *location*: He went *to the village*
     g. *time*: She returned *the next day*
     h. *manner*: He roared *like a lion*
     i. *instrument*: He cut the meat *with a knife*

In each example in (22) above, a noun forms the core of a **noun phrase** which occupies a particular role — and syntactic position — within the sentence. While the syntactic position of noun phrases in various roles may vary according to the characteristic word-order of a language (see Chapter 6), the fact that nouns typically occupy these roles is true for all languages.

3.6. VERBS

3.6.1. Semantic characterization

As mentioned earlier, verbs tend to code less time-stable experiences, primarily transitory states, events or actions. We have already noted that verbs may code either extremely rapid changes, or processes that may have a certain duration, or even relatively more stable states. In other words, they cover a certain range from one extreme end of the time-stability scale.

The more detailed semantic classification of verbs, the one which has syntactic consequences, is made in terms of the case-roles of the various nouns that must participate in sentences formed out of these verbs, as subjects, objects, datives, instruments, locations etc. The whole of Chapter 4, below, deals with this classification.

3.6.2. Morphological characterization

The major inflectional sub-systems that cluster around the verb will be dealt with in detail in a number of subsequent chapters: Tense-aspect-modality (Chapter 8), negatives (Chapter 9) and pronominal ('grammatical') agreement (Chapter 10). In addition, transitivizing and de-transitivizing morphology of various kinds will be discussed in the appropriate chapters covering these grammatical processes in Volume II. Less common but nonetheless attested in some languages is the cliticization of some case-role markers or definite markers on the verb (rather than, as is more typical, on the noun). These processes will be covered in Chapters 5 and 11, respectively. In this section we will simply illustrate some of the more common types of inflectional morphology that cluster around the verb.

3.6.2.1. Tense-aspect-modality

These are probably the most common verb affixes. They may appear as suffixes on the verb, as in Ute (Uto Aztecan):[28]

(23) a. wýyka-y '(he) is working' ("immediate")
      b. wýyka-x̂a '(he) has/had worked' ("perfect")
      c. wýyka-pygá '(he) worked' ("remote")
      d. wýyka-vaani '(he) will work' ("future")
      e. wýyka-mi '(he) always works' ("habitual")

They may also appear as verb prefixes, as in Swahili (Bantu):[29]

(24) a. ni-na-soma 'I am reading' ("present-progressive")
      b. ni-me-soma 'I have read' ("perfect")
      c. ni-li-soma 'I read' ("past")
      d. ni-ta-soma 'I will read' ("future")
      e. n-a-soma 'I read' ("habitual")

Less commonly, tense-aspect morphology involves internal changes within the verb-stem itself, as in the irregular (but historically older and previously regular) verbs of English. Thus consider:

(25) sit/sat
      ride/rode/ridden
      sing/sang/sung
      come/came/come
      see/saw/seen
      etc.

It is also common for tense-aspect-modality morphemes to *merge* with other verb inflections — particularly grammatical agreement — into *portmanteau* ('joint') morphemes. Thus consider the following from Spanish:

(26) trabajar-é 'I will work'   trabajar-emos 'we will work'
      trabajar-ás 'you will work' trabajar-án   'y'all/they will work'
      trabajar-á 'he/she will work'

      trabaj-é 'I worked'   trabaj-amos 'we worked'
      trabaj-aste 'you worked' trabaj-aron 'y'all/they worked'
      trabaj-ó 'he/she worked'

---

28) For futher detail see Givón (1980a).

29) For details see Ashton (1944).

3.6.2.2. Negation markers
   Negation markers often cliticize on the verb, most commonly in conjunction with the tense-aspect-modal morphology. They may appear as prefixes, as in Bemba (Bantu):[30]

(27) *affirmative*   *negative*
      ba-à-boombele   **ta**-ba-à-boombele
      they-PAST-work   NEG-they-PAST-work
      'they worked'   'they didn't work'

      ba-léé-boomba   **ta**-ba-léé-boomba
      they-PROG-work   NEG-they-PROG-work
      'they are working   'they aren't working'

      ba-kà-boomba   **ta**-ba-kà-boomba
      they-FUT-work   NEG-they-FUT-work
      'they will work'   'they won't work'

Negation-markers may also appear as verb suffixes, as in Japanese:[13]

(28) bin-o   kowasi-dalo
      bottle-ACC break-FUT
      '(he) will break the bottle'

      bin-o   kowasa-**nai**-dalo
      bottle-ACC break-NEG-FUT
      '(he) won't break the bottle'

Occasionally, "double negation" is found whereby both a pre-verbal and post-verbal element are used together to mark negation. As an example, consider the following from Ute (Uto-Aztecan):[32]

(29) wúųka-y
      work-IMM
      '(he) is working'

      ka-wúųka-**wa**-y
      NEG-work-NEG-IMM
      '(he) isn't working'

---

30) For details see Givón (1972, Chapter 4).

31) Yuko Yanagida (in personal communication).

32) See Givón (1980a)

The tense-marker and the negative marker may sometimes merge to form, at least in some tenses, a **portmanteau** morpheme. As an example consider the following from Ute:[33]

(30) wúy̨ka-x̂a
work-PERF
'(he) has/had worked'

ka-wúy̨ka-**na**
NEG-work-PERF/NEG
'(he) hasn't/hadn't worked'

wúy̨ka-py̨gá '(he) worked'
work-REM
'(he) worked'

ka-wúy̨ka- **py̨á**
NEG-work-REM/NEG
'(he) didn't work'

Finally, the negation marker may on occasion also merge with a personal pronoun/agreement marker on the verb to form a **portmanteau** morpheme. As an example consider the following from Swahili:[34]

(31) ni-ta-soma
I-FUT-read
'I will read'

si-ta-soma
I/NEG-FUT-read
'I will not read'

3.6.2.3. Agreement and/or pronouns
The verb may often carry affixes "agreeing with" the subject, as in the Spanish example (26) above or, more transparently, as in Swahili:[35]

(32) **ni**-li-soma 'I read'   **tu**-li-soma 'we read'
     u-li-soma 'you read'   **m̂**-li-soma 'y'all read'
     a-li-soma 'he/she read'   **wa**-li-soma 'they read'

---

33) See Givón (1980a).

34) See Ashton (1944).

35) See Ashton (1944).

Agreement affixes or pronouns may also refer to the object, as in the following example, again from Swahili:[36]

(33) ni-li-**ji**-ona
I-PAST-REFL-see
'I saw myself'

ni-li-**ku**-ona
I-PAST-you-see
'I saw you'

ni-li-**m̂**-ona
I-PAST-him-see
'I saw him'

ni-li-**tu**-ona
I-PAST-us-see
'I saw us'

ni-li-**wa**-ona
I-PAST-you-see
'I saw y'all'

ni-li-**wa**-ona
I-PAST-them-see
'I saw them'

3.6.2.4. Case-marking morphemes

Most commonly, *benefactive* case-role markers may cliticize on the verb rather than on the noun whose semantic role in the sentence they code. Thus consider the following example from Ute:[37]

(34) a. ta'wá-ci   'u   mamá-ci   'uwáy   'apáĝa-pŋgá
man-SUBJ   that-SUBJ   woman-OBJ   that-OBJ   talk-REM
'The man talked to the woman'

b. ta'wá-ci   'u   mamá-ci   'uwáy   'áapa-ci
man-SUBJ   that-SUBJ   woman-OBJ   that-OBJ   boy-OBJ
'uwáy   'apáĝa-kŋ-pŋgá
that-OBJ   talk-BEN-REM
'The man talked to the boy **for the woman**'

36) See Ashton (1944).

37) See Givón (1980a).

In (34b) above the case-marking on the noun 'woman' and the following article ('that'/'the') is identical to that on the object noun-phrase 'boy'. But the presence of the benefactive suffix -kụ- on the verb identifies 'woman' as the benefactive object in the sentence.

In some languages, the range of case-roles that can be marked on the verb in simple sentences is wider. Thus, for example, in Hindi many *locative* case-roles may be marked on the verb by a suffix ('vector verb') that functions much like an auxiliary verb and carries the main-verb inflections. Thus consider:[38]

(35) a. ...us-ne   naukar-ko   piiTaa   to   kaii   kisaanO-ne
     he-AGT   servant-OBJ   beat   then   several   peasant-AGT
     us-e   aa-**gheraa**...
     him-OBJ   come-*surround*
     '...when he beat his servant, several peasants came **around** him....'

   b. ...us-ne   ek   caaquu   phEk-kar   maara   to
      he-AGT   one   knife   throw-do   strike   then
      '...he threw a knife and

      wo raam-ke   peT-meE   jaa-**ghusaa**...
      it   Ram-GEN   stomach-in   go-*enter*
      it went **into** Ram's stomach...'

More discussion on verb-coding of nominal case-roles will be found in Chapter 5, below.

3.6.2.5. Definitizing morphemes

Object nouns are sometimes definitized via the use of clitic/agreement pronouns on the verb. As an example, consider the following from Swahili:[39]

(36) a. ni-li-soma   kitabu
     I-PAST-read   book
     'I read **a book**'

   b. ni-li-**ki**-soma
      I-PAST-it-read
      'I read **it**'

---

38) From Hook (1974, pp. 24-25). The interpretation is my own.

39) Ashton (1944).

    c. ni-li-**ki**-soma   kitabu
       I-PAST-it-read book
       'I read **the book**'

For further discussion of this, see Chapters 10 and 11, below.

3.6.2.6. Transitivizing and de-transitivizing morphemes

    As mentioned earlier, transitivity-changing morphemes often become, over time, lexical-derivational. Their inflectional-grammatical use in a number of grammatical processes associated with changes in transitivity will be discussed in several chapters of Volume II. As an example of their morphotactics vis-à-vis the verb stem, consider the following from Bemba:[40]

(37) -mona 'see'   **-i**-mona 'see oneself'
       -mon-**eshya** 'show'   -mon-**ana** 'see each other'
       -mon-**wa** 'be seen'
       -mon-**eka** 'be visible'

3.6.2.7. Speech-act indicators

    In many languages, primarily verb-final (SOV) languages, morphemes that signal the speech-act value (declarative, interrogative, imperative) cliticize as verb suffixes. As an example consider the following from Chuave:[41]

(38) a. *Declarative*:

       ...kiapu guwai-nom-i   muruwo furuwai bei
       officer things-their-this all   strew do
       de-Ø-im-**ie** ...
       leave-non f.-3p-*DECL*
       '...they were strewing all the officers' belongings about...'

    b. *Uncertain*:

       ...nimi su-wa-m-bo   si-ke-na-m-bo
       rain hit-3sOBJ-FUT-or hit-3sOBJ-NEG-or
       fi-ke-Ø-y-**e**...
       think-NEG-non f.-*UNCERT*
       '...I don't know whether it will rain or not...'

---

40) From my own field notes.
41) Chuave is a New-Guinea Highlands language. For more detail see Thurman (1978).

c. *Interrogative*:

    ...niki-de   fi-Ø-y-**o** ...
    bad-like think-non f.-I-*INTERROG*
    '...am I angry?...'

d. *Emphatic*:

    ...mora   di   mari do-Ø-pun-**ia**...
    enough say tell be-like-non f.-we-*EMPH*
    '...we have told them completely...'

e. *Imperative*:

    ...nuwi ko-ra-ro   f-**o**...
    water fill-FUT-SS go-*IMPER*
    '...go in order to fill the water-jug...'

Speech-act indicators in this language may only appear on the verb of the final clause in a thematic paragraph, so that medial verbs within the paragraph are left *unmarked* and are assumed to have the same speech-act value as the paragraph-final verb.

3.6.2.8. Conjunction and subordination markers

In many languages, primarily verb-final (SOV) languages, morphemes which signal various modes of conjoining or subordinating one sentence to another appear as suffixes on the main verb in the sentence, and are thus in a sentence-final position. Consider the following examples from Chuave:[42]

(39) a. *Subordinate, simultaneous*:

    ...ne iki-num   moi-n-**g-i**...
    you house-your be-you-*SUBORD-SIM*
    '...while you are in your house...'

b. *Subordinate, non-simultaneous*:

    ...kan-i-**k-a**-i...
    see-I-*SUBORD-NONSIM*-that
    '...when I looked...'

c. *Conjoined, same subject*:

    ...ena tekoi u-**re**,   iki   moi-i-**koro**...
    then again come-*SS* house be-I-*DS*
    '...then (I) came back and I stayed at home...'

42) See Thurman (1979).

d. *Conjoined, different subject*:

...iki   moi-i-**koro**,   tekoi   u   boi-n-**goro**...
house be-I-DS   again   call-he-*DS*
'...I stayed at home, so then he sent for me again...'

The SS/DS markers ('switch reference') in (39(c), (d)) above refer to the subject of the *following* clause ('anticipatory switch-reference'). Subordinate clauses in Chuave occupy the beginning of thematic paragraphs. Conjoined clauses are paragraph *medial*. And speech-act and tense-marked clauses, as we have seen above, are always paragraph *final*.

3.6.2.9. Incorporated objects or adverbs

In many languages, non-referential objects of the verb, as well as instrumental and manner adverbs, may become part of the verbal word or be "incorporated" into it. As an example consider the following from Ute:[43]

(40) a. *Object*: tųvų́-pų 'earth', 'ǫrá- 'dig'
          (i) *Referential*:   tųvų́-pų   'urú   'ǫrá-pųgá
                                  earth-OBJ that-OBJ dig-REM
                                  '(he) dug the earth'

          (ii) *Non-referential*: tųvų́y-'ǫrá-na-pųgá
                                   earth-dig-HAB-REM
                                   '(he) used to dig earth'

     b. *Instrument*: wií-ci 'knife', cųkų́r'ą- 'cut'
          (i) *Referential*:   wií-ci-m   'urú   tųkúa-vi
                                  knife-OBJ-with that-OBJ meat-OBJ
                                  cųkų́r'a-pųgá
                                  cut-REM
                                  '(he) used the knife to/and cut the/some
                                  meat'

          (ii) *Non-referential*: tųkúa-vi   'urú   wií-cųkų́r'a-pųgá
                                   meat-OBJ that-OBJ knife-cut-REM
                                   '(he) cut the meat with a knife'
                                   '(he) knife-cut the meat'

     c. *Manner adverb*: mamá-ci 'woman', paĝáy'wa- 'walk'
          (i) *Referential*: mamá-ci-pani   'uwáy   paĝáy'**wa**-pųgá
                             woman-OBJ-like that-OBJ walk-REM
                             '(he) walked like that woman'

---

43) See Givón (1980a).

    (ii) *Non-referential*: mamá-paĝáy'wa-pu̧gá
                      woman-walk-REM
                      '(he) walked like a woman, in a feminine
                      manner'

3.6.3. Syntactic/distributional characterization

Verbs tend to form the obligatory *nucleus* of sentences. That is, they are most commonly the *predicate* of the sentence. Further discussion of their distribution vis-à-vis the various nominal case-roles in the sentence will be found in Chapter 4, below. Their ordering within the sentence, relative to the subjects and objects, will be discussed in Chapter 6, below.

3.7. ADJECTIVES

3.7.1. Semantic characterization

The semantic position of adjectives, as coding transitory states or permanent/inherent qualities, has already been discussed in section 3.4. above. Many adjectives, perhaps the majority, in a language which has this lexical category, come in **antonymic pairs** such as:

(41)   good/bad, long/short, tall/short, fat/thin, large/small, wide/narrow, high/low, rough/smooth, loud/quiet, fast/slow, etc.

Most commonly when such pairs are found, one of them — normally the *positive* member denoting the "possession" of a quality — codes both one extreme on a scale as well as the **generic/unmarked** property/quality representing the entire scale. This may be demonstrated through the behavior of paired adjectives in questions:[44]

(42)   a. *Question (positive)*: How tall is she?
          (i) Very tall
          (ii) Very short

      b. *Question (negative)*: How short is she?
          (i) ?Very tall
          (ii) Very short

As one can see, the range of acceptable replies to (42a) is wide, covering the entire scale of short-to-tall. On the other hand, the range of acceptable replies to (42b) is restricted to the lower range of the scale, and (42bi) is decidedly an

---

44) For further detail on the semantics of adjectives, see Givón (1970).

odd reply to (42b).

In many, perhaps most languages, quantifying modifiers such as 'many', 'few', etc. and numerals such as 'one', 'two', 'three' as well as ordinals such as 'the first', 'the second', 'the third', etc. belong morphologically and syntactically to the adjective class. Thus, their semantic description forms part and parcel of the characterization of various sub-classes of adjectives. Some further details concerning quantifiers will be found in volume II, chapter 12.

3.7.2. Morphological characterization

Since adjectives fall semantically somewhere between verbs and nouns, it is not surprising that morphologically they also tend to display intermediate characteristics. Still, much of their language-specific morphology depends on the *history* of their derivation — from erstwhile nouns or verbs. This pertains both to the historical rise of the entire class, as well as to the synchronic lexical derivation of particular adjectives.

Typically, adjectives tend to display several noun-like morphological characteristics. Thus, for example, consider the following contrast from Bemba (Bantu):[45]

(43)　a. *Verbal predicate:*　umu-ana　　a-lée-boomba
　　　　　　　　　　　　　　PREF-child　he-PROG-work
　　　　　　　　　　　　　　'The child is working'

　　　b. *Adjectival predicate*:　umu-ana　　múu-suma
　　　　　　　　　　　　　　PREF-child　PREF-good
　　　　　　　　　　　　　　'The child is good'

　　　c. *Nominal predicate*:　umu-ana　　múu-buyi
　　　　　　　　　　　　　　PREF-child　PREF-thief
　　　　　　　　　　　　　　'The child is a thief'

The nominal (non-referential) prefixes of the noun (43c) and adjective (43b) predicates above are identical. In contrast, the verbal predicate in (43a) takes a pronoun/subject-agreement prefix and a tense-aspect prefix, which adjectives — even when they agree with the subject — do not take.

In Hebrew, similarly, adjectives agree in gender/class and number with nouns they modify (or are predicates of), but not with person. The latter is a characteristic agreement pattern of verbs. This closely replicates the Bantu situation in (43) above. Further, in Hebrew a modifying adjective takes the definite article like the noun. Thus consider:

45) See Givón (1972).

(44) a. ha-yéled ha-gadól
      the-boy the-big
      'the big boy' (sg., m.)

    b. ha-yald-á ha-gdol-á
      the-girl-F the-big-F
      'the big girl' (sg., f.)

    c. he-yelad-ím   ha-gdol-ím
      the-boy-PL/M the-big-PL/M
      'the big boys' (pl., m.)

    d. ha-yelad-ót   ha-gdol-ót
      the-girl-PL/F the-big-PL/F
      'the big girls' (pl.,·f.)

In many antonymically-paired adjectives, the negative member of the pair is derived from the positive one by an affix, as in English:

(45) wise/unwise, locked/unlocked, organized/disorganized, informed/misinformed, considerate/inconsiderate

In addition, English adjectives may display other derivational affixes, which thus mark them for their derivation from nouns or verbs through various patterns. Thus consider:

(46)

noun derived	verb derived
sphere/spherical	evade/evasive
child/childish	break/breakable
prince/princely	break/broken
child/childless	bleed/bleeding
synonym/synonymous	mandate/mandatory
pride/prideful	
cycle/cyclic	
rule/regular	
medium/median	

In Ute, the small class of non-derived ('original') adjectives displays the same pluralization pattern as nouns, when those adjectives modify animate nouns (inanimates do not pluralize). Thus consider:[46]

---

46) See Givón (1980a). The situation in Ute is further complicated by the fact that the nominal/adjectival suffix -mu̥, which was most likely originally an *animacy* marker, can also mark *pluralization*, at least in some instances. Such an extension is most likely due to the fact that only animates can take the plural marker in Ute.

(47)

	noun	adjective
singular:	ta'wá-ci 'man'	míipu̧-ci 'small'
plural:	taa-ta'wá-ci-u	míi-mipú̧-ci-u
	REDUP-man-SUFF-PL	REDUP-small-SUFF-PL
	'men'	'small ones'

In addition, many adjectival senses in Ute are lexically coded as verbs, but derived adjectives may be obtained from such verbs. Such derivatives retain the stem pluralization characteristic of Ute verbs, but in addition take an *animate* suffix characteristic of derived animate nouns. Thus consider:[47]

(48) a. 'aqó-y
          stout-IMM
          '(he) is stout' (immediate relevance)

      b. 'aqó-qwa-y
          stout-PL-IMM
          '(they) are stout' (immediate relevance)

      c. 'aqó-tu̧
          thick-NOM
          'the thick one' (permanent quality)

      d. 'aqó-tu̧-mu̧
          stout-NOM-ANIM
          'the stout one' (permanent quality)

      e. 'aqó-qwa-tu̧-mu̧
          stout-PL-NOM-ANIM
          'the stout ones' (permanent quality)

Such derived adjectives thus display a *hybrid* morphology, some nominal, some verbal.

Finally, in some languages adjectives, when modifying nouns in sentential contexts, also display the case-marking morphology depending on the noun's case-role within the sentence. As an example consider the following from Latin:[48]

---

47) See Givón (1980a).

48) For details see Palmer (1954).

(49) vir   bonus   puerō   bonō   librum
man-SUBJ good-SUBJ boy-DAT good-DAT book-OBJ
bonum   dedit
good-OBJ gave
'The good man gave the good boy a good book'

3.7.3. Syntactic/distributional characterization

Adjectives may appear in sentences as either *predicates* (see Chapter 4., below) or as noun *modifiers* (see Volume II, Chapter 12). As noun modifiers they may even become affixed to the noun itself. As an example consider the following from Ute:[49]

(50) a. *Predicate adjective*: kava 'u   sá-ĝa-rų-mų   'urá-'ąy
                        horse that white-ADJ-AN be-IMM
                        'The horse is white'

     b. *Separate modifier*: kavá 'u   sá-ĝa-rų-mų   yą'ąy-kya
                        horse that white-ADJ-AN die-PERF
                        'The **white** horse died' (as contrasted to others)

     c. *Bound modifier*: sá-gavá   'u   yą'ąy-kya
                        white-horse that die-PERF
                        'The white-horse died' (habitual name of that horse)

3.8. ADVERBS

Unlike the categories noun, verb and adjective, adverbs are a rather mixed lexical class, semantically, morphologically and syntactically. Many adverbs are full sentential constructions rather than one-word lexical items (see Volume II, Chapter 21). But even single adverbial words display relatively little cross-language comparability. Unlike nouns, verbs and to some extent adjectives, adverbs tend to be *derived* from other lexical words — from nouns, verbs or adjectives. This often determines both their semantic and morphological characteristics.

3.8.1. Semantic characterization

3.8.1.1. Manner adverbs

Manner adverbs tend to modify, in some way, the meaning of the verb it-

---

49) See Givón (1980a).

self. In other words, they have the verb alone under their **semantic scope**. As examples consider:

> (51)   He worked *hard*
> She ran *fast*
> He spoke *eloquently*
> She treated him *with respect*

3.8.1.2. Time adverbs

Time adverbs tend to characterize the entire event/state, and thus bring the entire sentence under their scope. As examples consider:

> (52)   He came *yesterday*
> She left *last year*
> I'll see you *tomorrow*

3.8.1.3. Place adverbs

Somewhat hard to distinguish from locative objects (see Chapter 4, below), place adverbs take under their scope the entire sentence (rather than pertain only to the verb or verb phrase). As examples consider:

> (53)   *In Chicago* he used to work for a newspaper
> I saw him *in the street* last week
> We talked at length *at his house*

As is obvious from these examples, what makes these examples adverbs is the particular construction ('locative phrase') they enter *syntactically*, rather than a particular lexical item. But the nouns at the core of such locative constructions tend to be semantically nouns of location.

3.8.1.4. Speaker's comment adverbs

These are adverbs of three different types, involving comments that speakers may make about various aspects of the **speech situation**. Their scope is thus the *widest*.

3.8.1.4.1. Comments on desirability/rightness

Adverbs in this sub-class impart the speaker's judgment about either the desirability (from his/her point of view) of the event/state/action or its rightness/wrongness. Thus consider:

> (54)   *Fortunately* he missed his shot
> We lost, *unfortunately*
> She *quite appropriately* told them to get lost

3.8.1.4.2. Comments on the character or motives of the subject

Adverbs in this sub-class may impart a variety of judgments the speaker wishes to make about the behavior, character, motives or habits of the subject/agent participating in an event. Thus consider:

(55)   He *very cleverly* decided not to show up
       She *foolishly* rejected their advice
       Inexplicably, they decided to punt
       Uncharacteristically, he quit in the middle of the race

3.8.1.4.3. Epistemic comments

Adverbs of this sub-class impart the speaker's evaluation as to the truth, falsity, possibility or probability of a state or event. Thus consider:

(56)   She'll *probably* be back tomorrow
       Maybe she was wrong
       He finished, *supposedly*
       Surprisingly, he did show up
       This is not *necessarily* true
       Most likely she was right

3.8.2. Morphological characterization

It is almost impossible to generalize on the word-form of adverbs either within one language or cross-linguistically. It depends entirely on the historical and synchronic derivation of adverb classes or individual adverbs. For example, in English many adverbs are derived with the suffix -*ly* from lexical adjectives, as in:

(57)   slow/slow-ly, reasonable/reasonab-ly, quiet/quiet-ly, rapid/rapid-ly

But many adverbs ending in -*ly* in English have no correponding adjective, at least synchronically (*likely*), and others use the adjectival form without a derivational affix (*fast*).

In most core-Bantu languages, many derived adverbs are assigned to some characteristic 'adverbial' noun-class. These are mostly adverbs derived from nouns or adjectives. As an example consider the following from Swahili:[50]

---

50) See Ashton (1944).

(58) -dogo 'small'

m-toto   m-dogo
PREF-child   PREF-small
'small child'   (modifying adjective)

a-li-fanya   kazi   ki-dogo   tu
he-PAST-do   work   PREF-small   only
'He worked only little'   (adverb in the **ki-** (7/8, sg.) class)

-baya 'bad'

m-tu   m-baya
PREF-person   PREF-bad
'a bad person'   (modifying adjective)

a-soma   vi-baya   vi-baya
he-read   PREF-bad   PREF-bad
'He reads very poorly'   (adverb in the **vi-** (7/8, pl.) class)

In many languages, adverbs of various types are made around nouns, by constructing a prepositional or post-positional phrase. These may be manner adverbs, time adverbs or location adverbs, most commonly. Thus consider:

(59) He eats *like a pig* (manner)
      He sleeps *in the barn* (location)
      She never works *on Sunday* (time)

In some languages, noun, verb or adjective stems may become **incorporated** into the verbal word when functioning as manner adverbs. Thus consider the following from Ute:[51]

(60) a. *Noun-derived adverb*: mamá-ci 'woman'

                    mamá-paĝáy'wa-y
                    woman-walk-IMM
                    '(he) is walking **like a woman**'

      b. *Adjective-derived adverb*: piá̧-ĝa-rʉ 'sweet'

                    piá̧-'apáĝa-y
                    sweet-talk-IMM
                    '(she) is talking sweetly'

51) See Givón (1980a).

c. *Verb-derived adverb*: tṵná- 'hunt'

    tṵná-vǫrǫ-í
    hunt-walk-IMM
    '(he) is hunting around, he is walking-
    hunting'[52]

In Ute, the stem used as adverb in such a fashion is stripped of all its characteristic (suffixal) noun, adjective or verb inflections, thus signaling loss of independent word status.

Finally, the derivation of adverbs from other lexical categories may often follow a rather indirect route. Thus consider the following derivation in English, via adjectives:

(61) suppose/supposed/supposedly
      know/knowing/knowingly
      deride/derisive/derisively
      understand/understandable/understandably
      oblige/obligatory/obligatorily

3.8.3. Syntactic/distributional characterization

As will be shown in Chapter 4, below, adverbs tend to appear as **optional constituents** of sentences, rather than as obligatory members that define the core propositional meaning of events/states/actions. Their syntactic position within sentences varies enormously according to their semantic type, and certain types of adverbs retain considerable word-order flexibility.

To some extent one could predict the degree of word-order flexibility — and in some cases even the syntactic position of adverbs — from their semantic scope. As suggested in section 3.8.1., above, the semantic scope of manner adverbs is the narrowest, essentially taking in only the verb itself. In most languages (English being one glaring exception, at least occasionally) these adverbs appear as members of the verb-phrase, commonly closest to the verb,

---

52) While historically the first stem in a verb-verb compound is indeed the adverbial modifier of the second, diachronic change often conspires to reverse this situation semantically. Thus, in (60c) the verb tṵná- is semantically much more specific. The verb vǫrǫ́-, on the other hand, is considerably bleached semantically, and is used as an *aspectual* suffix almost, imparting the meaning of 'doing the action around', 'on the go', 'here and there'. This is possible in Ute precisely because 'go'/'walk' is a rather typical auxiliary verb from which a variety of tense-aspect meanings can and do develop, in Ute as well as elsewhere (cf. Givón, 1973a).

and are often incorporated into the verbal word (see (60) above). On the other hand, adverbs with wider — sentential — scope, such as those of time or speaker's comment, tend to have a greater distributional freedom, appearing before, after or in some positions inside the sentence.[53] Thus consider:

(62) a. *Last year* he bought a car
      b. He *last year* bought a car
      c. He bought a car *last year*
      d. ?He bought *last year* a car
      e. *Maybe* he bought a car
      f. He *maybe* bought a car
      g. He bought a car *maybe*
      h. ?He bought *maybe* a car

Finally, the syntactic position of some adverbs in the sentence may also depend on their diachronic origin. Thus, for example, in many languages some or all epistemic adverbs are derived from *modality verbs* (see Chapter 4, section 4.2.9.1., below), which have a characteristic position within the verb phrase — either before or after the complement verb. When such verbs are re-analyzed as epistemic operators, they retain their original syntactic and morphological character for some time. Thus, consider the following from English:

(63) They *tend* to arrive late
      She *may* come tomorrow
      He *must* have already left
      They *might* do it
      She *should* be here by now
      You *have* to come immediately

3.9. MINOR WORD CLASSES

As we have seen above, members of the four major word classes tend to appear in all languages as large, independent words — or as the large stems at

---

53) This word-order flexibility of sentence-scope adverbs is presumably controlled by discourse-pragmatic considerations of *topicality* (see Chapter 6, below), as well as occasionally — when semantically feasible — by scope. Thus (62h) may be felicitous in English under the interpretation of "What he bought was *maybe a car*", whereby the fact that he bought something is no longer under the scope of the epistemic adverb, but only the exact type of the object. Broadly, the placing of adverbs in the sentence may be another example of syntactic *iconicity*, with the general tendency being to place the adverb *closest* to the constituent that is under its semantic scope.

the core of independent words. On the other hand, members of the so-called 'minor' word classes are consistently smaller, unstressed and tend to appear as bound morphemes affixed to larger lexical-word stems. Many of these have already been surveyed in the preceding sections, namely those which characteristically form the inflectional morphology of nouns, verbs, adjectives or adverbs. Further, the inflectional-grammatical morphology associated with various syntactic constructions will be discussed repeatedly in many of the following chapters. In this section we will briefly introduce a number of inflectional-grammatical morphemes that have a higher probability — at least in some languages[54] or under some circumstances[55] — of appearing as independent words.

3.9.1. Pronouns

As we shall see in Chapter 10, below, most languages have both independent, stressed, emphatic pronouns and anaphoric, unstressed pronouns. The latter tend to be cliticized on verbs (subject or object pronouns) or on nouns (possessor pronouns). But stressed, emphatic pronouns tend to appear as independent words. Thus, consider the following contrast from Ute:[56]

(64) a. *Independent subject*:   'uwás-'urá káa-x̂a
                                he-be   sing-PERF
                                'Now as for **him**, he sang'

      b. *Independent object*:   'uwáyas-'urá pųníkya-x̂a-x̂a
                                him-be   see-PL-PERF
                                'Now speaking of **him**, they saw him'

      c. *Clitic subject*:   káa-x̂a-'u
                                sing-PERF-he
                                '... (and) he sang...'

      d. *Clitic object*:   pųníkya-x̂a-x̂ay-'u
                                see-PL-PERF-him
                                '...(and) they saw him...'

---

54) The probability of these morphemes appearing as independent words is much lower in verb-final (SOV) languages.

55) Close to the time of origination of such morphemic sub-systems, they tend to appear as independent words. In the course of time, especially in the absence of a literary tradition or without the conservative effect of an educational system, these morphemes tend to cliticize.

56) See Givón (1980a).

e. *Clitic possessor*:   tuá-ci-'u
                              child-SUFF-his
                              'his child'

3.9.2. Demonstratives and articles

As suggested in section 3.5.2.3. above, demonstratives and articles tend
to cliticize as noun inflections. But close to their diachronic point of origin
they may also appear as independent words, a situation that tends to be artificially preserved in the writing system, as in English.[57] We will discuss them in
considerable detail in Chapter 11, below. Their place within the functional domain of topic identification and topic continuity will be discussed in Chapter
22, volume II.

3.9.3. Sentential conjunctions and subordinations

In many languages, most commonly verb-final languages, sentence-
connecting operators such as the English 'and', 'or', 'but', 'if', 'when',
'though', 'because', 'while', 'since', 'in spite of', etc. do not appear as independent words, but rather as inflectional morphemes most commonly attached to the verb, often in association with the tense-aspect-modality morphemes. Their interaction with the tense-aspect-modality system will be discussed in Chapter 8, below. Their use within the functional domain of inter-
clausal connectivity will be discussed in Chapter 21, Volume II.

3.9.4. Interjections

Most languages display this mixed-bag category, with expressions such as
'yes', 'no', 'hey', 'oh', 'uh', 'hi', 'wow', 'ouch', etc. or their functional equivalents. It is not a unified category functionally, morphologically or syntactically, and it is highly language specific.

---

57) Most commonly, definite articles arise from demonstrative pronouns used as modifiers, and
indefinite articles from the numeral 'one'. For further detail see Givón (1978, 1981c).

4 | SIMPLE SENTENCES: PREDICATIONS AND CASE-ROLES

4.1. INTRODUCTION

As suggested earlier (Chapter 2), it is reasonable to describe the syntactic structure of languages as a two-tier system, whereby

(a) One describes the functional domain(s) and syntactic structure of **simple clauses** — main, declarative, affirmative, active clauses,[1] and

(b) One then describes both the function and structure of various **complex clauses** with reference to those of simple clauses.

In this chapter we will deal primarily with (a) above, i.e. the **propositional-semantic** meaning of sentences. In terms of syntactic structure, the discussion will remain incomplete, since two important aspects of the syntax of simple clauses — case marking and word-order — will be dealt with in separate chapters, Chapter 5 and Chapter 6 respectively, below.

4.1.1. Function and typology of simple clauses

In functional terms, simple sentences are responsible for conveying the bulk of new propositional information in discourse. The information is about the nature of the **state/event** ('what happened') or the types of the **arguments/participants** ('who', 'to whom', 'how', 'when', 'where', 'with what', 'for whom', etc.). In our description of the types of simple clauses most commonly found in language, we will deal with both aspects at the same time. This is because the characterization of predicate types ('verb types') is made in terms of

---

1) These four main categories (contrasting with subordinate, manipulative, negative, passive, respectively) are not the only ones by which one defines the simple clauses. Other distinctions, such as emphatic/contrastive vs. non-emphatic/non-contrastive, topicalized vs. simple etc. also play an important role in defining the notion of "markedness" in syntax. They will all be surveyed in volume II, Chapter 23. More specific questions of markedness will be dealt with in individual chapters throughout the book. For some details see Givón (1979a, ch. 2).

the "frame" of case-roles that obligatorily participate in events/states coded by these predicates. And conversely, the characterization of the various semantic case-roles must be made in terms of the predicate-types with which they form propositions. We thus separate two formal aspects of the propositional-semantic meaning of sentences:

(a)   The **propositional frame** ('semantic grid') giving the type of verb and type of case-roles of the participants; and

(b)   The **actual lexical items** filling those type slots.

When the two are combined, we have the propositional meaning of a sentence.

The major verb-types characterized below are found in all languages. Further, they are the ones most likely to carry *syntactic consequences*, in terms of the structure of sentences containing these verbs. In this sense this verb classification is universal, as is the classification of the semantic case-roles serving as the arguments of these verbs. This is not to detract from the possibility that in any individual language one may find further sub-classes of the verb classes we outline below. On the contrary, further language-specific sub-classification is common, and we will refer to it occasionally at appropriate points. In some fundamental way, *every* lexical verb is potentially in a class of its own, and could presumably display unique syntactic properties. By 'syntactic properties' or 'syntactic consequences' we mean here primarily the *case-marking behavior* of the verb's arguments. Thus we meet here the normal twin-faced problem of **taxonomy** and **coding** of classes:[2]

(a)   *Major classes* are more widely attested cross-linguistically, while *minor classes* are less widely attested; and

(b)   The *coding expression* of more general classes is stronger and more widely-attested cross-linguistically, while the coding-expression of less general classes is weaker and less widely attested or less uniform across languages.

---

2) In terms of *taxonomy*, one might suggest that classes that are more general, i.e. apply to larger sub-populations, have a greater predictive power as to the behavior of larger numbers of individuals within the total population. Presumably that greater predictability has *adaptive/survival value* (in this case *communicative* value), and this is presumably why such general classes are more widely attested cross-linguistically. In terms of *coding*, the seemingly *iconic* tendency of more general classes to receive more distinct coding expression should be attributed again to the greater adaptive utility that may accrue from coding more strongly classes whose predictive power is greater. The wider cross-language attestation of such coding behavior is again to be understood, presumably, in terms of adaptive/functional utility.

4.1.2. States, events and actions

As suggested earlier, propositions may pertain to **states**, i.e. existing conditions not involving change across time. States may be either **temporary** at one extreme or **permanent** at the other, depending on their relative position along the scale of time-stability. Propositions may also pertain to **events**, which are **changes** across time, either from an initial to a final state, if the event is **bounded**, or changes in the **process** of occurring, if the event is not construed as bounded.[3] Both states and events are defined in terms of particular sub-sections of the universe, and each sub-section normally pertains to some **individuals/arguments/participants** involved in the proposition/clause as its subjects, objects or other case-roles. These **involved participants** may now be described in terms of the type of their involvement vis-à-vis the state or event. Thus, one of them ('patient') may either **exhibit** the state or **undergo** the change in state. Another ('agent') may be the one **responsible** for initiating a change. Another yet ('dative') may be a passive but **conscious** participant aware of the change or state. Others yet may be the initial or final location relative to which a change-in-location took place. And so on with the rest of the case-roles.

Actions are events for which a responsible agent is identified. Many verbs code event types for which the assignment of such responsibility is obligatory or automatic, as part of the verb's meaning. As we shall see in Chapter 5, below (as well as informally in the following sections), most languages tend to assign the discourse-pragmatic role of **subject/topic** to the agent in simple sentences. In the various sections below, we will refer to sentential subjects only informally.

4.1.3. Patients, datives and agents

The classification of the major arguments/participants in sentences, i.e. 'case-roles', involves identifying the manner of their involvement in the state/event/action. To quite an extent, the top three case-roles are *hierarchically* related, from the least marked to the most marked.

---

3) There is nothing *logically* necessary about an event being described as either bounded or unbounded (i.e. process). The decision hinges in part on the calibration of our perceptual apparatus in terms of the speed of change (or frequency of adjacent scans) it can process. Thus, for example, a 'shot' or a 'kick' event is perceived as instantaneous — i.e. bounded on both ends — since it occurs too fast for the human perception to discriminate internal stages within it via repeated scans. On the other hand, 'finishing work' is a deliberate conceptual *construction* of the terminal boundary of a process, which may be *physically* a rather protracted wind-down.

(a)   *Patient*: Also referred to as 'accusative', this is the simplest major argument in sentences, and may be divided further into two subtypes:

    (i) *Patient of state*:   The argument whose state is described by the proposition, the one who 'is at state', the one most likely to appear as the subject of state propositions;

    (ii) *Patient of change*: The argument undergoing the change-of-state; it may either be the subject of an intransitive sentence or the object of a transitive one ('action').

(b)   *Dative*: (also called 'recipient'). The dative is a conscious participant, in addition to being also "in a state" or "undergoing change". In some sense then it adds the property of "consciousness" to the existing properties of a patient, and may thus be described as a *more marked* argument than the patient. When the dative is the subject of a state, that state is most likely to be *mental*, as in 'know', 'want', 'be afraid', 'be angry' etc. Similarly, when the dative is the subject of a change, the change is most likely to be one of mental state, such as 'learn', 'reflect upon', 'listen to', 'get angry', 'become frightened' etc. Dative participants may also be the objects of verbs, and thus most commonly register a change of mental state, as in the dative objcts of 'tell', 'teach', 'inform', etc. They may also be the dative objects of sentences coding a physical change not directly impacting the dative object, as in the recipient/dative objects of 'give', 'bring' or 'send'. In sentences containing such verbs, the change (in location) is registered upon another argument, and the dative is also the **location** with reference to which the change occurs. But most commonly the dative is also a **conscious goal** of the transaction.[4]

(c)   *Agent*: The agent is always a **conscious** participant in an event, since he is a **volitional** initiator of the change — which is thus refer-

---

4) There is one area in the verbal-cognitive map where 'patient' and 'dative' sometimes blur — at least so far as their grammatical coding is concerned. It involves the objects of verbs which induce changes in mental state, such as 'frighten', 'hurt', 'anger', 'motivate to do', etc. Many languages code the conscious participants/objects of such verbs as *patients* rather than as datives, presumably generalizing on "change of state" rather than on "consciousness".

red to as **action**.[5] In addition to being conscious — and thus perforce sharing the major property of datives — the agent is also the **responsible initiator** of the event. The agent is thus *further marked* than the dative. The assumption of responsibility for initiating actions also implies having **control** and being subject to **blame**.[6]

The implicational (or 'markedness') hierarchy of the three major case-roles may thus be given as:

(1)   a. AGENT > DATIVE > PATIENT

or

      b. BE DELIBERATE INITIATOR > BE CONSCIOUS > BE

In a curious way, this hierarchy closely parallels the top of the noun-classification hierarchy (see Chapter 3, above):

(2)   HUMAN > ANIMATE > CONCRETE

The other semantic case-roles will be defined in various sections below, when verb-types pertaining to them are described.

4.2. VERB CLASSES

4.2.1. Subjectless verbs

Verbs in this class most commonly denote natural or atmospheric phenomena, conditions of the world or the weather, whereby the event or state cannot be separated from an argument ('subject') about which the event/state is predicated. In other words, the subject and verb/predicate are here one and the same. In many languages, a "dummy" pronoun may appear in sentences with these verbs and function syntactically, at least up to a certain point, as 'subject'. However, that pronoun has no discourse reference in the normal sense in which pronouns do. As an example of such verbs consider the

---

5) Volition is obviously a conscious mental state.

6) An interesting ontology is involved here. Since people have no control over their volitions, which are mental *states*, the responsibility or blame-worthiness associated with the agent could not spring from its consciousness, a property shared with datives. Rather, it must spring from the *act of initiating* the event. The concept of act/action is thus an indispensible ingredient in the semantic definition of agents. Further, the particular ingredient of "act" to which responsibility and culpability are attributed is that of *decision* to act. Unlike volition, decision is a *deliberate* mental act (rather than a 'state'). But decision to act, by itself, does not make the agent responsible for anything except the decision. It is the actual *initiation* of the act — motivated by volition and prompted by decision — which makes the agent an agent.

following from Ute (Uto-Aztecan):[7]

(3)   a.   'uwá-y-ax̂
           rain-IMM-it
           'It is raining'

      b.   núa-y-ax̂
           wind-IMM-it
           'It is windy'

      c.   nuvuá-y-ax̂
           snow-IMM-it
           'It is snowing'

      d.   turú'ni-i-ax̂
           tornado-IMM-it
           'It is whirl-winding'

      e.   kutúruuci-i-ax̂
           hot-IMM-it
           'It is hot'

      f.   sutí'i-i-ax̂
           cold-IMM-it
           'It is cold'

All the lexical stems used in the examples above are verb stems. But they can also be made into nouns ('nominalized') with a suffix, as in:

(4)   'uwá-ru 'rain', núa-ru 'wind', nuvwá-vú 'snow'

In some languages, 'world' is used as the subject of some of these verbs. Thus consider the following from Palestinian Arabic:

(5)   id-dúnya tí-shti
      the-world she-raining
      'It is raining' (lit.: 'The world is raining')

Another way of coding such states/events is by using the nominalized verb as the subject of a verb characteristic of the event, as in:

(6)   The rain is pouring
      The wind is blowing

_____

7) See Givón (1980a).

Snow is falling
The temperature is high
etc.

But the verbs in (6) are not subjectless verbs, but rather intransitive[8] objectless verbs (section 4.2.3., below).

4.2.2. Copular sentences

These are sentences with a subject and predicate. The subject is a patient-
of-state, even when it is animate or human.[9] The predicate may be either a
noun (nominal predicate) or adjective (adjectival predicate). Further, in
some languages this sentence type obligatorily requires the semantically-de-
pleted copular verb 'be' as the surface/syntactic main verb of the construction,
as in English:

(7)   *Nominal predicate*:   He is *a teacher*
       Adjectival predicate: She is *tall*

The nominal predicate may, in turn, be either **referential** or **non-referential**
('attributive'; see Chapter 11, below), as in:

(8)   *Referential*: He is *that teacher I told you about*
       Attributive: He is *a teacher*

In many languages the verb 'be' is not necessary in less-marked tense-aspects, such as the "present" or "habitual". Thus, consider the following example from Swahili:[10]

(9)   a. *Present/habitual*: *Noun predicate*:   baba   yangu mwalimu
                                                     father my   teacher
                                                     'My father is a teacher'

---

8) Without defining "transitivity" at this point (further discussion can be found in Chapter 5,
below), we would informally assume that verbs with an agent subject and a patient direct-object are
transitive, regardless of whatever other arguments/case-roles are involved. While there are grounds
for believing that perhaps the more determinant criterion here is the presence of *patient direct-object*, some languages allow only agents (or phenomena closely resembling them) to be the subjects
of verbs which take such objects.

9) The animacy, humanness or agentiveness of the subject is irrelevant in defining this *type* of
predication, although specific noun or adjective predicates may be restricted to animates or humans (cf. 'He is *a teacher*', 'She is *wise*').

10) See Ashton (1944).

        Adjective predicate: baba yangu mkubwa
                          father my   big
                          'My father is big'

b. *Past*: *Noun predicate*:   baba yangu a-li-kuwa   mwalimu
                          father my   he-PAST-be teacher
                          'My father was a teacher'
        Adjective predicate: baba yangu a-li-kuwa   mkubwa
                          father my   he-PAST-be big
                          'My father was big'

c. *Future*: *Noun predicate*:   mtoto wangu a-ta-kuwa   mwalimu
                          child my   he-FUT-be teacher
                          'My child will be a teacher'
        Adjective predicate: mtoto wangu a-ta-kuwa mkubwa
                          child my   he-FUT-be big
                          'My child will be big'

One may consider the function of the semantically-empty copula in such cases as primarily a tense-aspect carrier. Obviously, in languages where the class 'adjective' does not exist, copular sentences display only noun predicates.

    In some languages, the copula 'be' may serve to make the semantic distinction between 'be temporarily' and 'be permanently' with the same lexical adjective serving as predicate. Thus consider the following from Spanish:

(10) a. Mi amigo **está** enfermo   (temporary; **estar**)
         'My friend is ill'

      b. Mi amigo **es** enfermo   (permanent; **ser**)
         'My friend is an invalid'

      c. Mi amigo **está** loco   (temporary; **estar**)
         'My friend is right now behaving in a crazy manner'

      d. Mi amigo **es** loco   (permanent; **ser**)
         'My friend is a lunatic'

Since nouns represent more stable, inherent properties, nominal predicates in Spanish take only the copula *ser*, as does a place-of-origin predicate which presumably cannot be changed retroactively. Thus consider:

(11) a. Mi amigo **es** pintor   (inherent; **ser**)
         'My friend is a painter'

b. Mi amigo es de España   (inherent; **ser**)
   'My friend is from Spain'

4.2.3. Objectless verbs

These are verbs with only a single argument, which then perforce becomes the subject/topic in simple sentences. The verb may denote a permanent or temporary **state**, in which case the subject may be either a patient-of-state, as in the following examples from Bemba:[11]

(12) a. a-à-shipa
     he-PERF-brave
     'He is brave'

    b. a-à-buta
      he-PERF-white
      'He is white'

    c. a-à-fina
     he-PERF-heavy
     'He is heavy'

    d. a-à-shyuuka
      he-PERF-lucky
      'He is lucky'

or a dative-of-state, as in Ute:[12]

(13) a. tuá-ci-n   nagǎmi-i
     child-SUFF-my   sick-IMM
     'My child is sick'

    b. mamá-ci 'u   nasǫtaay-'ay
      woman   the sad-IMM
      'The woman is sad'

    c. ta'wá-ci 'u   suwáay-kya
      man   the happy-PERF
      'The man was happy'

    d. múa-n   naáy-'ay
      father-my angry-IMM
      'My father is angry'

11) See Givón (1972). These adjectival senses in English lexicalize as stative verbs in Bemba.

12) See Givón (1980a). These adjectival senses in English lexicalize as stative verbs in Ute.

Verbs in this class may also denote changes/events/processes. Some of those events may involve patient-of-change subjects, as in:

(14)   a.   Soon the water *warmed up*
       b.   The leaves *rustled* gently
       c.   The rock *sank* fast
       d.   George accidentally *fell*

Others may predicate datives-of-state, as in:

(15)   a.   John *meditated* in his garden
       b.   Mary was *seething* (in anger)
       c.   She *suffered* in silence

These are admittedly less common verbal expressions in English. Most common is for event/process verbs in this class to take an agent subject, as in:

(16)   a.   He *worked*
       b.   She *sang*
       c.   He *ran*
       d.   She *danced*

But sometimes the process is not under voluntary control, as in:

(17)   a.   He *grew* up
       b.   The baby *was born* early
       c.   John *died* unexpectedly

Most commonly, an agent-subject of these verbs is both the initiator and the patient of the event. And on occasion some verbs in this class appear with a *cognate object*, as in:

(18)   a.   They danced *the rumba*
       b.   She spoke *a few words*
       c.   He sang *a song*

What one sees in (18) is a change of **perspective**, whereby the "product" of the action is presented as object, by **analogy** with prototypical patient-objects.

4.2.4   Verbs requiring a sentential subject

Most languages have a small group of verbs which, at least logically, predicate a proposition/sentence. Semantically, one may divide these into the following sub-types:

(a)   *Epistemic verbs*: 'be true', 'be false', 'be likely', 'be probable', 'be unlikely', 'be possible' etc.

(b) *Evaluative verbs:* 'be good', 'be bad', 'be nice', 'be sad', 'be regrett-
able', 'be unfortunate/fortunate' etc.

(c) *Ease-of-performance*: 'difficult', 'easy', 'possible', 'impossible'.

The first two groups involve the speaker's comment on the truth or desirability of a proposition, as in:

(19) a. That John is a crook is simply not true   (epistemic)
b. That Mary did it is sad   (evaluative)

Most languages prefer to have nominal — rather than sentential — surface-
syntactic subjects, so that sentences (19a,b) are more commonly rendered in
English via an *extraposed* structure, with an 'it' surface subject, as in:

(20) a. It is simply not true that John is a crook
b. It is sad that Mary did it

Another variant of evaluative verbal use here, with the propositional subject
denoting a future ('not yet realized') event, codes primarily expressions of obligation, command or suggestion, as in:

(21) It is *necessary/advisable/imperative* that he do it right away

The fact that in English these verbal expressions are **adjectival** has to do with
their being stative. As we shall see below (section 4.2.9.1.), they may also appear as modality verbs, in English as well as in other languages.

Ease-of-performance verbs deal with the subject/agent's ability to perform certain acts. In many languages the logical sentential subject of such
predicates cannot appear as a surface-syntactic sentence, but a number of variants — all designed to make it a noun (or pronoun) — are used. Thus consider:

(22) a. *It* was easy/difficult for John to cross the channel
b. *Crossing the channel* was easy (for John)
c. *For John to cross the channel* was easy
but not
d. **That John crossed the channel* was easy
e. **It* was easy *that John crossed the channel*

In some languages, verbs in this class may be primarily *derived*, via some
lexical derivation process, from corresponding verbs which initially belong to
a class which takes sentential *objects*. Thus, consider the following example
from Swahili, where the verbs 'know', 'can' and 'say' become verbs in the sen-

tential-subject class:[13]

(23) a. y-a-jul-**ikana**   kuwa Juma ni m̂tu m̂kuu
      it-HAB-know-STAT that   Juma be man big
      'It **is known** that Juma is an important man'

    b. y-a-wez-**ekana**   ku-fanya hivyo
      it-HAB-can-STAT to-do   thusly
      'It **is possible** to do it this way'

    c. y-a-sem-**ekana**   kuwa Juma ha-yuko
      it-HAB-say-STAT that   Juma NEG-be
      'It **is said/they say** that Juma is not here'

In Swahili, unlike in English, the sentential subject cannot appear in the surface-syntactic subject position:

(24) *kuwa Juma ni m̂tu m̂kuu y-a-jul-**ikana**
      that   Juma be man big   it-HAB-know-STAT

4.2.5. Verbs with a direct object: Semantic transitivity

4.2.5.1. Prototypical transitive verbs

There are two properties that single out the prototypical transitive verb, the major sub-groups in this class:

(a)   An *agent* subject
(b)   A *patient-of-change* object

Thus, verbs in the other, more marginal sub-groups of this class in one way or another deviate from either one or both prototypical properties. The prototype sub-group may be further sub-classified according to the type of change registered by the patient/object.

(25) *Created objects:*
    a. He built a house
    b. He painted a picture
    c. She made a dress
    d. She drew a diagram
    e. He constructed a bridge

(26) *Totally destroyed objects:*
    a. They demolished the house

---

13) For details, though not necessarily the same analysis, see Ashton (1944).

b. She smashed the glass
c. They evaporated the water

(27) *Physical change in the objects*:
   a. She cracked the pot
   b. He enlarged the bed
   c. They cut the corn
   d. She sliced the salami
   e. They bleached his hair

(28) *Change in object's location*:
   a. They moved the barn
   b. He rolled the wheelbarrow

(29) *Change with an implied instrument*:
   a. He hammered the nail   (hammer)
   b. She kicked the wall   (foot)
   c. He slapped the puppy   (palm)
   d. They knifed him   (knife)
   e. She trapped coyotes   (trap)

(30) *Surface change*:
   a. She washed his shirt
   b. They painted the barn
   c. He bathed the baby

(31) *Internal change*:
   a. They heated the solution
   b. He chilled the gazpacho

(32) *Change with implied manner*:
   a. They murdered her   ('kill' with intent)
   b. She smashed the cup   ('break' completely)
   c. They clobbered him   ('hit' hard & repeatedly)
   d. She shredded the book   ('tear' completely, into little pieces)

The prototype of a transitive verb in this group thus involves a *physical, discernible* change in the state of its patient object. One may measure the "degree of prototypicality" or "degree of deviation from prototype" of other verbs which belong syntactically to this group, partially in terms of the degree to which the change in the object is physical, obvious, concrete, accessible to observation etc. In many cases, as we shall see below, there may also be deviations from the other prototypical property of transitive verbs, i.e. that of agent-subject.

4.2.5.2. Less prototypical transitive verbs

Deviation from the transitive-verb prototype may come in a number of forms. The interesting question one could raise is why these semantically-deviant verbs appear, in many languages, in the same *syntactic* class as the transitive prototype (rather than in a semantically more compatible class or in a class of their own). The answer may be sought in two directions:

(a)   Transitivity is a matter of *degree*, partly because "obviousness of change in the object" is a matter of degree, and partly because it depends on *more than one* property.[14]

(b)   When a less-prototypical verb is coded syntactically as a member of the class of the transitive prototype, in some sense the user of the language *construes* its properties as being *similar, analogical, reminiscent* of the prototype. In other words, we have here the most common linguistic phenomenon of **metaphoric extension**.

The verbs in the sub-groups of this section may be thus considered as "*somewhat* defective but nevertheless *construed* as legitimate members of the class".

4.2.5.2.1. Verbs with a locative direct object

In many languages, it is possible to find examples such as the following in English:

(33)   a. She entered the house   (= 'go *into* the house')
       b. He approached the intersection   (= 'move *toward* the intersection')
       c. They penetrated the enemy's perimeter (= 'move *into* the perimeter')
       d. She swam the Channel   (= 'swim *across* the Channel')
       e. He rode the horse   (= 'ride *on* the horse')

In each one, in some "logical" sense, the seeming direct-object is in fact the locative **point-of-reference** (see section 4.2.6.1., below) for the subject's **spatial movement** (to, from, across, into, on) or **spatial location** (at, on, in). The most typical way languages code such verbs is by marking the locational relation of the subject vis-à-vis the object on the object, via a preposition or

---

14) See extensive discussion of transitivity as a graded, cluster phenomenon in Hopper and Thompson (1980). While their discussion is not limited to the lexical semantics of verbs, it is obviously relevant here.

post-position. But by construing these events as involving a *direct* object, the speaker introduces a different *perspective*, one of viewing some change in the object as being more *salient*. One may thus suggest that in each case in (33), the object is more important to the event than if it were merely a point-of-reference for the subject's location or movement. Thus, 'entering a house' is not merely 'moving into a house', but dramatically altering the condition of the house from "empty" to "occupied". 'Approaching the intersection' is not a mere 'movement toward the intersection', but rather a "confrontation" with it. 'Penetrating the perimeter' is not mere movement into some space, but dramatically altering the condition of that space. 'Swimming the Channel' is not mere movement across, but rather a "conquest" of the Channel. And 'riding a horse' is not merely sitting on top of it, but "controlling", "mastering" it etc. These are not necessarily the only possible interpretations of the change in saliency and perspective here, but they are the kind of metaphorical extensions commonly used in construing a **locative** as a **patient** object.

4.2.5.2.2. Verbs with a recipient or locative direct object and an implied patient

Consider the following verbal expressions from English:

(34) a. He fed the cows ('gave them food'; DO = recipient/goal)
   b. She painted the wall ('put paint on the wall'; DO = goal)
   c. They dusted the floor ('took dust off the floor'; DO = source)
   d. They dusted the crops ('put dust on the crops'; DO = goal)
   e. They robbed her ('took something from her'; DO = loser/source)

These verbs are semantically related to two-object verbs discussed in section 4.2.7., below. However, the semantically more plausible *patient* object is suppressed, most commonly because it is predictable/stereotypical — or even forms the base for a noun-derived verb ('food'/'feed', 'paint'/'paint', 'dust'/'dust', above). With the 'real' direct object thus semantically (or morphemically) incorporated into the verb, the semantic locative/recipient object is then *construed as* direct object. That is, the following changes in that object are highlighted by the expressions in (34), respectively:

(35) a. The cows were hungry, then satiated their hunger
   b. The wall was unpainted, then got painted
   c. The floor was dusty, then became clean
   d. The crops were pest-ridden, then were rid of pests
   e. She had some property, then lost it

Such systematic changes in the point of view from which the event is construed, coupled with the stereotypicality/predictability of the direct object and thus its diminished importance vis-à-vis the recipient/locative object, make it plausible to code these verbs syntactically as patient/object-taking verbs.

4.2.5.2.3. Verbs with a moving part of the subject

As seen above, the verbs of group 4.2.5.2.1. involve the movement of the subject (or the designation of its location) vis-à-vis the object. Now consider the English verbs 'hit', 'kick', 'slap' or 'punch'. In each one, a fairly stereotypical part of the subject's body moves through space to make contact with an object. Most commonly, however, that object is not construed as being a mere locative goal, but rather as an **affected** object, one which absorbs the **impact** of the event. This, again coupled with the stereotypicality and diminished importance of the 'real' object, makes it quite reasonable to construe the logically 'locative' object here as a patient, and thus to code it likewise syntactically.

4.2.5.2.4. Verbs with a dative-experiencer subject

So far, we have considered deviations from prototypical transitivity involving less-than-typical objects, ones violating the patient-object prototype. However, in many languages verbs may appear in this general syntactic class despite violation of the agent-subject prototype. These are most commonly verbs of **cognition**, **sensation** or **volition**, whose object registers — logically — no discernible impact or change. In fact, it is the experiencer-subject which registers some internal/cognitive change. Common verbs in this class are 'see', 'hear', 'know', 'understand', 'think of', 'want', 'feel', and most commonly they are semantically *states* rather than actions. But some verbs in this class may also involve volition, and are thus considered active, such as 'listen (to)', 'look (at)', 'learn'. These last-mentioned are derived, in a number of languages, from semantically-related stative verbs. Thus one finds in Swahili the following derivational relation:

(36) -sikia 'hear' (state)   ---→ -sikiliza 'listen (to)' (act)

Similarly, in Ute the following are derivationally related:

(37) nuká- 'hear'   ---→   nuká-'ni- 'listen (to)'
      puní- 'see'   ---→   puní-'ni- 'look (at)'
      sumáy- 'remember/think of' ---→ sumáy-'ni- 'think hard (about)'

The metaphoric extension of these verbs into the prototype transitive class
may be explained in terms of the subject being either an agent or at least a dative — and thus a human-animate whose importance in the construed event is
in principle high, and whose perceptual field is being *extended to* the object,
which is then metaphorically construed as affected. One must note, however,
that many languages mark such dative/experiencer subjects in a special way
which clearly codes them as non-agents. Thus, for example, in earlier stages of
English, many of these verbs were marked with the dative/experiencer as *object* and the verb displaying a neutralized third-person agreement, as in:

(38) a. me fear-th   ('I fear that...')
      b. me think-s   ('I think that...')

Further, many expressions survive in English to this day which systematically
reverse the subject-object relations of perception/cognition/volition verbs.
Thus consider:

(39) a. It seems to me that...   ('I see/think that...')
      b. It appears to me that...   ('I find it apparent that...')
      c. It grieves me that...   ('I am distressed that...')
      d. It sounds (to me) as if...   ('I consider it...')
      e. It is necessary that...   ('I want that...')
      f. It is imperative that...   ('I insist that...')
      g. It smells funny   ('I smell it and it is funny in my judg-
                                      ment')
      h. It sounds preposterous   ('I hear it & it is preposterous in my
                                      judgment')

The marking of dative subjects as dative objects is also found in Sherpa (Sino-
Tibetan), as in:[15]

(40) a. *Agent subject*: ti   mi-ti-**gi**   cenyi caaq-sung
                            the   man-DEF-ERG   cup   break-PERF
                            'The man broke the cup'

      b. *Dative subject*: ti   mi-ti-**la**   cenyi go-sung
                            the   man-DEF-DAT   cup   want-PERF
                            'The man wanted the cup'

15) The Sherpa data are from my own field notes, originally due to Koncchok Lama (in personal
communication).

In Philippine languages, dative/experiencer subjects often precipitate an obligatory "passive" structure, i.e. a reversal of the subject-object roles. Thus, consider the following from Bikol:[16]

(41) a. *Agent-subject*: nag-pákul 'ang-laláke   sa-kandíng   (active)
                          AGT-hit   TOP-man   DEF-goat
                          'The man hit the goat'

                          na-pákul   kang-laláke   'ang-kandíng (passive)
                          PAT-hit   AGT-man   TOP-goat
                          'The goat was hit by the man'

     b. *Dative-'subject'*: *nag-'ilíng 'ang-laláke sa-kandíng (*active)
                          AGT-see   TOP-man   DEF-goat

                          na-'ilíng   kang-laláke   'ang-kandíng (passive)
                          PAT-see   AGT-man   TOP-goat
    { 'The man saw the goat'   }
    { 'The goat was seen by the man' }

To sum up, then, the tendency to metaphorically extend to verbs with dative subjects the syntactic trappings of transitivity is by no means a universal solution.

4.2.5.2.5. Verbs with a reciprocal/associative object

The deviation from prototypical transitivity in this group involves the fact that the object — as well as the subject — is *equally* the agent and the construed patient of inherently reciprocal verbs. Most commonly, these are verbs such as 'kiss', 'marry', 'meet', 'join', 'fight', 'quarrel', 'make love', 'converse', etc. In many languages they take an **indirect** object marked for the **associative** case (see section 4.2.6.4., below). But in English one often finds the objects of such verbs patterning themselves syntactically — at least as an option — within the transitive class, with one of the **co-agents** thus construed as subject/agent, the other as object/patient. Thus consider:

16) The Bikol data are from my own field notes, originally due to Manuel Factora (in personal communication). There are grounds for believing that the Philippine "passive" is perhaps already an *ergative* construction (see Chapter 5, below). For some discussion of this, see Givón (1981b). The prefix *'ang-* on a Bikol noun (phrase) marks it as subject/topic (TOP). The prefix *kang-* on a noun marks it as a non-topic agent (AGT). The prefix *nag-* on a verb marks it as an active verb, i.e. with an agent topic/subject (AGT). Finally, the prefix *na-* on the verb marks it as a "passive" verb, i.e. with the patient being the topic/subject (PAT).

(42) a. He met Sylvia   (cf. 'He met *with* Sylvia')
      b. She fought him   (cf. 'She fought *with* him')
      c. They joined the group (cf. 'They joined *with* the group')

What is involved here is obviously a judgment or construction of an event from a certain perspective, whereby one of the reciprocal co-agents is viewed as more important, and coded as subject. In addition, the parenthetic semi-paraphrases on the right in (42) distinctly impart a *higher status*, one closer to agentivity, to the object, as compared with the "less controlling" or "less involved" direct object on the left in (42), when construed as a patient.

The conflict engendered by the presence of two agents and the lack of a clearcut patient is resolved above by *downgrading* one of the agents to a patient syntactic status, and thus conforming to some "canonical" transitivity. But the very same verbs are also amenable, in English and elsewhere, to a **detransitivizing** solution of this conflict, by construing both agents as conjoined subjects, as in:

(43)   John and Mary met/kissed/made love/fought/quarreled/argued

While both agents are now construed as more or less on a par in terms of importance/control/saliency,[17] many languages would code such reciprocal expressions syntactically as **intransitive**, and quite often their marking gives rise eventually to the syntactic marking of passives.[18]

4.2.5.2.6. The verb 'have'

Many languages have a stative verb 'have' whose subject is the possessor, most prototypically a human, and whose object is the possessed. The exact meaning of such a verb may vary from one language to the next, most commonly coding physical possession of objects, whole-over-part relations (with the *whole* coded as possessor and *parts* as possessed), body-part relations, the possession of mental faculties and often an *active* sense of coming into possession ('get', 'take', 'obtain'). Most commonly, a 'have' verb arises out of the semantic bleaching of active possession verbs such as 'get', 'grab', 'seize', 'take', 'obtain' etc., whereby the sense of "acting to take possession" has been bleached, leaving behind only its *implied result* of "having possession". This

---

17) It is never the case in language (unlike in logic) that two entities expressed in a certain temporal ('linear') order are really on a par. Most commonly, the one expressed first is construed to be more important than its conjunct. True, symmetrical conjunction/coordination is possible only in abstract, mathematical systems.

18) See Givón (1981b).

historical process explains why the syntactic coding of such a verb conforms to the transitive pattern of its source.

At least two other syntactic configurations can, however, code possession in language. The first is a stative expression using 'be with', and is characteristic of Bantu languages, as in Bemba:[19]

(44) n-di no-omuana
     I-be with-child
     'I have a child' (lit. 'I am with child')

In (44) the possessor is subject, thus conforming in some sense to the transitive pattern,[20] but the expression is stative rather than active. In other languages, such as Semitic or Slavic, possession is expressed by a complete reversal of the subject-object relations, with the possessed acting as the *patient-of-state* subject of 'be' and the possessor expressed as a *dative* object. Thus, consider the following from Israeli Hebrew:

(45) le-yóav hayú harbé xaverím
     to-Yoav were many friends
     'Yoav had many friends'

Languages with this type of possession expression often re-analyze it over a period of time toward bringing the more agentive/larger/possessor participant back into the subject/topic syntactic position. Thus, for example, in spoken Israeli Hebrew one already finds such an expression with the 'logical subject' of 'be' marked as *patient* object, as in:[21]

(46) ló hayá l-o **et**-ha-séfer ha-ze
     NEG was to-him DO-DEF-book DEF-this
     'He didn't have that book'

In a language such as Sherpa, which tends to mark semantically-dative 'subjects' as *dative* objects, possession is coded the same way as in Hebrew. Thus consider:[22]

---

19) See Givón (1972).

20) Again, one assumes here that agentivity is more characteristic of humans, bigger entities and 'wholes', as against non-humans, smaller entities and 'parts'.

21) For more discussion of this change and its motivation, see Givón (1976b).

22) From my own field notes, with the data originally due to Koncchok J. Lama (in personal communication).

(47) ti   mi-ti-**la**   kitab-cik   wąy
      the man-DEF-DAT   book-one   be/have
      'The man has a book'

Sherpa is a strict SOV language, and in terms of word-order 'man' is the subject of (47). But it is marked by the dative suffix -*la* and the verb is still the verb
'be'. Further, in the limited area where the verb shows agreement with the
subject, dative subjects do not control verb agreement.[23]

4.2.5.2.7. Verbs with cognate objects

As seen in section 4.2.3. above, events coded by essentially ('semantically') objectless verbs denoting certain activities may be construed as taking
an object that is in fact a noun-form of the verb, or of a semantically-related
verb (see example (18), above). The whole clause then assumes the appearance of a transitive clause, i.e. it conforms to the agent-subject and patient-
object syntactic marking pattern discussed above. In English the "created"
object may sometimes be a nominalized form of the verb, as in:

(48) a. She sang a gypsy *song*
      b. He danced an original *dance*

More commonly, however, a semantically more empty ('bleached') verb is
used with such cognate objects, as in:

(49) a. He *gave* an interesting *talk* ('He talked')
      b. She *delivered* a superb *lecture* ('She lectured')
      c. They *performed* a *song* by Schubert ('They sang')
      d. He *unleashed* a devastating *fart* ('He farted')
      e. She *took* a deep *breath* ('She breathed')
      f. They *took* the wrong *turn* ('They turned')
      g. We *had* a *meeting* ('We met')
      h. We *had* a *discussion* ('We discussed')
      (i. I *took* a quick *look* at it ('I looked at it'))
      (j. She *took* good *care* of him ('She cared for him'))

The syntactically-transitive expressions on the left in (49) clearly have different *perspectives* than their respective intransitive paraphrases on the right,
even though they are semantically (or historically-semantically) related in a
clear fashion. Presumably, a sense of "affected patient" is somehow imparted
here to the objectivized "product" of the act, which is then coded syntactically

---

23) See some discussion in Givón (1980c)

by analogy with real created objects (see (25) above).

4.2.5.3. Some residual problems of semantic transitivity

4.2.5.3.1. Humanity, animacy and agentiveness

Many languages allow a reasonable leeway in assigning non-agent subjects to prototypically-transitive verbs by analogy to real agents. Thus, in English a number of prototypically-transitive verbs can also take less-than-agen-
tive subjects, as in:

(50) a. *Liquor* killed him ('He drank liquor, and that killed him')
      b. *Hard work* killed him ('He worked hard and that killed him')
      c. *Concentration* quickened her pulse ('She concentrated, and as a
                                            result her pulse quickened')
      d. *The house* sleeps six people ('Six people can sleep in the house')
      e. *This loaf* will feed a thousand ('A thousand could be fed on this
                                            loaf')
      f. *The hammer* broke the window ('Someone broke the window
                                            with a hammer')

Presumably, the metaphoric extension here is of "being a cause", so that an
entity that cannot initiate an event willfully — but is in some way within the
causation-chain of the agent-initiated event — is re-construed as "cause", and
thus marked syntactically as agent-subject.

In some languages severe restrictions are placed on such metaphoric extensions of agentivity. DeLancey (1982) reports that in Hare-Dene (Athabascan) most inanimates cannot be thusly re-construed as agents of prototypically-transitive verbs. Thus consider:

(51) a. John lá-ni-we
         J.   die-ASP
         'John died' (intransitive)

      b. Pierre John lá-ni-h-we
         P.   J.   die-ASP-CAUSE
         'Pierre killed John' (transitive)

      c.* eyayi   John lá-ni-h-we
          disease J.   die-ASP-CAUSE
          ('The disease killed John'; disallowed)

      d. yejai   taí-tõ
         window break-ASP
         'The window broke/got broken' (intransitive)

e. John yejai ta'é-ni-se
J. window break-ASP
'John broke the window' (transitive)

f.* gowele yejai ta'é-ni-se
heat window break-ASP
('The heat broke the window'; disallowed)

This restriction is in large part a culture-based, world-view restriction, in Hare-Dene as well as in other languages with reminiscent restrictions.[24] DeLancey (1982) points out that in Hare-Dene a number of inanimates may become the subjects/agents of prototypically-transitive verbs such as 'break', 'kill' or 'dry', provided they are *visible* entities. Thus, expressions such as 'The *sun* dried the clothes', 'The *gun* killed him' or '*Liquor* killed him' are acceptable, but 'The *heat/wind* dried the clothes', '*Disease* killed him' or 'The *heat/wind* broke the window' are disallowed (cf. (51c,f), above). Agentivity is scaled very much the same in all languages, as a *cluster* of properties (rather than a discrete feature). Each property is itself scalar. Typically such scales are:[25]

(52) a. *Humanity*: human > animate > inanimate > abstract
b. *Causation*: direct cause > indirect cause > non-cause
c. *Volition*: strong intent > weak intent > non-voluntary
d. *Control*: clear control > weak control > no control
e. *Saliency*: very obvious/salient > less obvious/salient >
unobvious/nonsalient

It is rather transparent that ontologically (and probably ontogenetically) we are dealing here with one core property: **Obviousness/saliency of cause**.[26] A prototypical agent is thus human, direct cause, deliberate causer, controlling

24) A related restriction may be seen in Navajo (see Witherspoon, 1977 and Creamer, 1974).

25) For a compatible view, see DeLancey (1981).

26) To wit, a human is closer to the ego, thus more familiar and obvious. Direct causes tend to be perceptually more obvious, occupying a clear *boundary position* within the chain (as also does the *effect*, which is categorially coded as *patient*). Intermediate points in the chain are less salient. Strong intent creates a higher *probability of success*, i.e. visible effect. Ditto for strong control. Some of these scales have highly specific implications in particular languages. For example, in Navajo (Witherspoon, 1977) larger-size entities — even non-human ones — outrank smaller-size entities on the scale. This may be considered an instance of our (52e) scale of *saliency*. But it could equally be considered an instance of our (52d) scale of *control* (i.e. *power*). Similarly, older humans outrank younger humans, and males outrank females, which may be considered either an instance of our *saliency* scale ((52e), size) or of our *control* scale ((52d), power).

causer and obvious cause. Cross-cultural diversity arises when different cultures slice the dividing line at slightly different points on these scales. But the
directionality of the scales vis-à-vis the construction of agentivity is
doubtlessly universal.

4.2.5.3.2. Object suppression

Most languages have some type of mechanism via which the importance/
saliency of direct objects that are semantically prototypical patients is toned
down or 'suppressed'. In Chapter 5, below, we will consider one such process,
the so-called **anti-passive**, which is characteristic of Ergative languages.[27] But
a process in some ways akin to the anti-passive is that of **object incorporation**
into the verb. Most typically, a non-referential object, i.e. one whose individual identity does not matter for the purpose of the communication,[28] is
trimmed of most of its characteristic inflectional morphology and then incorporated into the verb stem to yield a combined single verbal word. As an
example consider the following from Ute:[29]

(53)　a.　*Referential object*:　sarí-ci　　'u　　　　sivą́ątu-ci 'uwáy
　　　　　　　　　　　　dog-SUBJ　the-SUBJ　goat-OBJ　the-OBJ

　　　　　　　　　　　　pax̂á-ux-kwa
　　　　　　　　　　　　kill-ASP-PERF
　　　　　　　　　　　　'The dog killed the goat'

　　　　b.　*Non-ref. object*:　sarí-ci　　'u　　　　sivą́ątu-pax̂á-rụ
　　　　　　　　　　　　dog-SUBJ　the-SUBJ　goat-kill-ADJ/HAB
　　　　　　　　　　　　{ 'The dog kills goats'　　　}
　　　　　　　　　　　　{ 'The dog is a goat-killer' }

The verb in (53b) above is syntactically objectless.

---

27) In Ergative languages, one consistent side-effect of the antipassive treatment of the patient
is that the marking of the agent is also *scaled down*, so that the entire clause loses syntactically both
the typical marking of a patient-object and of an agent-subject. Syntactically it is just marked as an
intransitive clause.

28) As we shall see in Chapter 11, below, the marking of referentiality in language is not always a
matter of "objective" mapping from language to some individual in the "real world" or even in the
"discourse universe", but often a matter of *saliency/importance* in the particular discourse. For an
extensive discussion see Givón (1978, 1981c, 1982c).

29) See Givón (1980c). Hopper and Thompson (1980) point out that the stereotypical direct object is not only semantically an affected patient, but also a *referential* object, and thus in discourse
terms important/salient in the *communication* (not only cognitively/perceptually salient). These
two types of saliency tend to go hand in hand.

A similar phenomenon exists in English with nominalized verb phrases, as in:

(54)   a.   He killed the deer
       b.   He is a deer-killer
       c.   He enjoys deer-killing

Sentence (54a) refers to a specific deer. Sentences (54b,c) do not refer to any particular deer, but rather to deer in general. Their word-stress strongly suggests *single word* compounds, i.e. objectless constructions.

A reminiscent situation occurs in many languages with verbs whose objects are highly stereotypical/predictable/habitual. The referential identity of such objects is thus seldom an issue in the discourse, and they are thus often suppressed, leaving the verb a surface-*intransitive*. Thus consider:

(55)   a.   We then went and *ate*   (OBJ = 'food')
       b.   He *drinks* too much   (OBJ = 'liquor')
       c.   He *hunts* for a living   (OBJ = 'game')
       d.   They *trapped* along the canyon wall   (OBJ = 'animals')
       e.   He *teaches* at Stanford   (OBJ = 'students')

4.2.5.3.3. Object creation

We have already seen above a number of instances where a non-patient object gets 'upgraded' to direct object via construing it as affected/patient. We have also seen instances where the *activity* itself, coded in a semantically-objectless verb, may be construed as object-product and thus be marked syntactically as surface direct-object. Another rule which creates direct objects is that of **dative shifting**, see Chapter 5, below.

4.2.6. Verbs with an indirect object

We will define 'indirect' object informally as one that is *not* an affected patient. We have already seen above various semantic types of non-patient objects which nevertheless get coded syntactically as direct objects, i.e. assume the form of the prototypical patient-object. Morphologically, non-patient objects have a higher probability of being marked with a prefix or suffix, often referred to then as **preposition** or **postposition**, respectively. But this is not to say that direct-objects cannot be similarly case-marked.

Semantically, the most common indirect objects are **locative, dative, associative, benefactive** or **instrumental** objects. This is obviously a rough classification that may be further elaborated, in finer and finer semantic detail, in individual languages. But in terms of overt morphology, most languages do not elaborate much further.[30] In this section we will deal only with indirect objects whose presence is *obligatory* for expressing the meaning of the verb.

4.2.6.1. Verbs with a locative object

Typically, verbs in this group code the *being at*, *moving to* or *moving from* a location. The object is then the locational *point of reference* with respect to which the subject is located or moves. Typical verbs of being in/at/on a location are:

(56) 'be', 'remain', 'exist', 'stay', 'sit', 'stand', 'lie', 'kneel', 'crouch', 'sleep', 'live' etc.

The locational object may then be further classified, semantically and commonly morphologically, according to more specific features of the spatial relation between the subject and the object, such as:

(57) 'in', 'out', 'on', 'under', 'near', 'at', 'away from', 'far from', 'in front', 'behind', 'in the middle', 'among', 'between', 'around' etc.

Quite often the preposition or postposition marking the object may be rather unspecific ('location in general'), with the rest of the semantic information carried by the verb itself. Thus, consider the following example from Bemba:[31]

(58) a. a-à-**ya**   ku-mushi
        he-PAST-go LOC-village
        'He **went to** the village'

   b. a-à-**shya** ku-mushi
      'He **went from** the village' ('left the village')

   c. a-à-**isa** ku-mushi
      'He **came to** the village'

   d. a-à-**fuma** ku-mushi
      'He **came from** the village'

Typical verbs of moving *toward a goal* are:

---

30) As suggested earlier, in principle there are as many case-role types as there are verbs in the lexicon. Some languages have a seeming passion for smaller and finer case-marking classes (cf. Finnish and Hungarian). Most languages assume that these finer details are inferred from the verb and thus need no further noun-bound coding.

31) See   Givón (1972).

(59) 'go to', 'come to', 'enter', 'ascend to', 'appear at', 'move toward', 'approach', 'arrive at', etc.

And the marking on the noun may again give the verb further specification, such as:

(60) 'to', 'into', 'on top of', 'at', 'under', etc.

Typical verbs of moving *from a source* are:

(61) 'leave', 'go from', 'come from', 'move from', 'exit', 'descend from', 'emerge out of', etc.

In (58) above the further semantic specification was *inherent* in the meaning of the verb. This is also true for verbs which take a *direct*—though semantically-locative—object, such as (see Section 4.2.5.2.1., above):

(62) 'exit', 'enter', 'approach', 'leave', 'ride', 'circle', 'scale', etc.

In some languages, however, these semantic-locational features are systematically marked on the verb by regular morphology. Thus, consider the following example from Atzugewi (Hokan), a language which practices verb-coding of this type to a seeming extreme:[32]

(63) '-w-ca-swal-mič
     it-AUX-INSTR/WIND-limp material move-down to surface
     'The limp-material (clothes) blew down (to the ground) because of the wind'

Out of the five elements in the verbal word in (63), /'-/ is the subject agreement/pronoun, /-w-/ is an auxiliary (tense-aspect), /-ca-/ is 'wind' or 'blowing wind', incorporated at the pre-verb-stem position as instrument, /-swal-/ is presumably the verb stem meaning roughly 'a limp material moving/being located', and /-mič/ is the locative specifier, meaning roughly 'down onto the surface/ground'.

The subject of verbs in this group may be either a *patient*—either of state or change — or an *agent*. The location or movement of the subject is thus denoted by the verbal expression, whereby the locative object is the point of spatial reference. As examples consider:

---

32) From Talmy (1972, p. 432). The simplified interpretation is to some extent my own. For further discussion see also Talmy (1980).

(64) *Patient-of-state subject*:   (a) John is lying on the couch
                                     (b) The book is under the couch
      Patient-of-change subject: (c) The book fell off the couch
                                     (d) John floated down the river
      Agent subject: (e) John ran to the door
                                     (f) Mary swam down the river

4.2.6.2. Verbs with a directional object

The subject of verbs in this small group is most commonly an agent. The object is most commonly dative-goal but could also be agent-source, patient-source or patient-goal. Thus consider:

(65) a. George talked to Mary (dative-goal object)
      b. George listened to Mary (agent-source object)
      c. George listened to the wind (patient-source object)
      d. George looked at the hill (patient-goal object)
      e. Mary shouted at George (dative or patient-goal object)

As one can see, these verbs involve metaphoric extension of the more concrete sense of spatial goal or source. As we shall see below, such an extension can be carried further, toward an increasingly more 'abstract sense of 'spatial direction'.

4.2.6.3. Verbs with an abstract directional object

These are verbs with either a dative or agent subject, i.e. one displaying some *mental activity*, and an object that is in some metaphoric sense the *directional goal* of that mental activity of the subject. The object may often be abstract or a nominalized proposition. As typical examples consider:

(66) a. He talked/thought/knew *about* Mary/the meeting
      b. She objected *to* John being there
      c. He was angry *at* her

In many instances, the object is clearly the *cause* of the subject's *mental state*. Thus consider:

(67) a. She mourned his death[33]
      b. He was sad *about* her leaving
      c. She was happy *because of* her absence

---

33) Here the expression lexicalizes as a transitive one, i.e. with a *direct* object. See discussion in section 4.2.5.2., above.

When the verb is stative, it tends to be lexicalized in English as an adjective.

4.2.6.4. Verbs with an associative object

Most commonly, verbs in this group code *reciprocal action*, see section 4.2.5.2.5., above. Both subject and object are agents, but only one surfaces as the syntactic subject, while the other most commonly appears as object with the pre- or post-position 'with'. As we have suggested earlier, the object of such verbs may sometimes be construed as either direct ('affected') or indirect ('associate'), as in the contrasts:

(68) a. She fought her mother (= 'against her mother')
      b. She fought *with* her mother $\left\{ \begin{array}{l} (\ = \text{'against her mother'}) \\ (\ = \text{'together with her mother'}) \end{array} \right\}$
      c. He met the committee (= 'the point of impact', 'he came to them')
      d. He met *with* the committee (= 'protracted'; 'more on a par')

In general, the use of 'with' construes the object as more on a par with the subject than if it were marked as direct object. But it can be further upgraded when marked as a *conjoined* subject, as in:

(69) a. She and her mother fought
      b. He and the committee met

4.2.7. Verbs with two nominal objects ('bi-transitive verbs')

Verbs in this group most commonly take one direct and one indirect object. Their subject is most commonly an *agent*. The direct object is most commonly a *patient of change*. We divide it further according to the type of indirect object as well as some finer properties of the direct object itself.

4.2.7.1. Verbs with a locative indirect object

These are verbs whose indirect object is either the directional-source or directional-goal of the change. The change in the direct object is one of *location* vis-à-vis the indirect object. The further sub-specification of the locative relation is marked most commonly via pre- or post-positions (see section 4.2.6.1., above, with which this group is semantically linked).[34] Typical verbs in this group are:

(70) 'put...on', 'take...off', 'remove...from', 'move...to', 'send...to', 'carry...to', 'bring...to'

---

34) That relation is a *causative* one, whereby the agent is viewed as causing the change-in-location of the patient/direct object.

Typical sentential examples are:

(71) a. She put the book *on* the table
      b. He moved the couch *to* the basement
      c. She took the cover *off* the furniture
      d. They removed him *from* the premises

4.2.7.2. Verbs with a dative-benefactive indirect object

The subject of these verbs is most commonly an *agent*. The direct object typically changes location to or from the indirect object. However, the transaction may be metaphorically extended from the most prototypical concrete locational sense as seen in section 4.2.7.1. above. Most commonly, the goal/source indirect object is a *dative/human*, and by inference it is often construed as the one *benefiting from* the transaction — i.e. the *benefactive* object (see further discussion below). The more concrete transactions involve verbs such as:

(72) a. He gave the book *to* her
      b. She brought it *to* him
      c. She received a letter *from* him

More metaphorically extended — and thus more abstract — are transactions such as:

(73) a. He told the story *to* her
      b. She showed it *to* John
      c. He received a firm promise *from* her
      d. He gave his lecture *to* a packed hall
      e. She brought bad luck *to* whoever she came into contact with

In examples (72c) and (73c), above, it is the *subject* who is the dative/benefactive/recipient, while in some sense the indirect-object is the agent-initiator. The transaction, however, is still construed from the point of view of the subject/recipient.

Some verbs that may appear in this class syntactically are semantically more complex, and in some sense condense another proposition into a seemingly simple single clause. Thus consider:

(74) a. Mary promised the ring *to* John
          (= 'She promised John *to give him the ring*')
      b. He asked a favor *from* her
          (= 'He asked her *to do him a favor*')

Finally, the dative-benefactive objects of verbs in this class quite often are switched to occupy the *direct object* position, a process termed 'dative shifting' (see extensive discussion in Chapter 5, below). Thus consider:

(75) a. He gave *her* a present
      b. She told *him* the story
      c. They brought *her* the good news
      d. She asked *him* a favor
      e. He showed *her* the house

4.2.7.3. Verbs with an instrumental-locative alternation

Verbs in this group have two nominal objects. One of these is construed semantically as a *locative* object (cf. section 4.2.7.1., above). The other is construed as an *instrumental* object (see discussion of the most common optional case-roles in section 4.4., below).[35] What makes this group distinct is that in many languages they allow a syntactic variation whereby either one of the two objects appears as the *indirect* object, marked with the appropriate morpheme (pre- or post-position) indicating its semantic case-role, while the other appears as the *direct* object, and thus in some sense is construed as the affected *patient-of-change*. In English, such a variation requires almost always changing the lexical verb altogether. Thus consider the following paired expressions:

	locative IO	instrumental IO
(76) a.	'put x *into* y'	'fill y *with* x'
b.	'take x *out of* y'	'empty y *of* x'
c.	'spread x *on* y'	'cover y *with* x'
d.	'take x *from* y'	'deprive/rob y *of* x'
e.	'supply/give x *to* y'	'supply y *with* x'
f.	'wrap/tie x *around* y'	'wrap/tie y *with* x'
g.	'place x *around* y'	'surround y *with* x'
h.	'stick x *into* y'	'stab/pierce y *with* x'
i.	'spray x *on* y'	'spray/paint y *with* x'

---

35) The notion 'instrument' is not a purely objective one, but depends on certain culture-based constructions, and is further subject to much metaphoric extension. Thus, in 'They supplied him *with food*' the dative-recipient is construed as affected patient-of-change, and 'food' as instrument, in contrast with the complement expression 'They gave food *to him*'. On the other hand, in 'They tied him *with a rope*', 'rope' is more intuitively an instrument, but may also be construed as affected patient, as in 'They tied the rope *around him*'.

In many languages no change in the lexical verb is required to bring about this variation in point-of-view. Thus consider the following example from Bemba:[36]

(77) a. a-à-cimine   indofu   **ne**-efumo (IO = instrument)
        he-PAST-stab   elephant   *with*-spear
        'He stabbed the elephant with a spear'

      b. a-à-cimine   ifumo   **mu**-ndofu (IO = location)
        he-PAST-thrust   spear   *into*-elephant
        'He thrust the spear into the elephant'

Further discussion about this variation will be found in Chapter 5, below.

4.2.7.4. Verbs with two direct objects

As we have seen above (section 4.2.7.2.), some verbs with one direct and one indirect object can appear, under some circumstances, as having two direct objects (cf. examples (75)). We shall consider these as examples of an optional variation whereby the indirect object is 'upgraded' to the surface syntactic status of direct object — without at the same time downgrading the semantically patient direct object. In some languages there are verbs which appear to take two direct objects without the same kind of variation. Semantically, such constructions are 'condensed' versions of more complex propositional structures. As examples consider:

(78) a. They elected John president (= 'elected him *to be president*')

      b. They appointed her district judge (= 'appointed her *to be district judge*')

4.2.8. Verbs with three nominal objects: Upper limits on complexity

Some verbs, in particular those coding the exchange of items between two parties, have at least in theory a three-object semantic structure. As examples consider:

---

36) See Givón (1972). There are grounds for believing that in English the verbs in the right column in (76), i.e. with the locational detail left unspecified, are semantically much richer ('more specific') than those in the left column (when different). Thus, 'fill' is 'put into', 'empty' is 'take out of', 'cover' is 'spread on', 'deprive/rob' is 'take from', 'surround' is 'place around', etc. On the other hand, the prepositions on the left are much more specified, as compared to only 'with' or its negative counterpart 'off' on the right. What I think we see here is a shift in the relative distribution of semantic material between verbs and prepositions. As suggested earlier above (sections 4.2.5.2., 4.2.6.1.), verbs may incorporate such features into their semantic structure.

(79)   a. John exchanged a bed for a sofa with Mary
       b. Mary sold a book to John for two dollars
       c. He bought a book from Mary for ten dollars

In usage, most commonly, only two of the objects — presumably the two most
salient for the particular focus of the communication — are mentioned. Thus
compare, respectively:

(80)   a. John traded beds with Mary (*Recipient* more salient than *price*)
       b. Mary sold her book for two dollars (*Price* more salient than
           recipient)
       c. John bought a book from Mary (*Donor* more salient than *price*)

One may as well note that many of the two-object verbs described in section 4.2.7.1., above, have, in some sense, an *implicit* other object as part of
their *inferential* structure. Thus, consider for example:

(81)   a. He *carried* the bag from the car to the store-room
       b. They *gave* John two dollars for his car
       c. She *brought* the boys home from school
       d. He *sent* a letter [from his location] to his uncle
       e. She *moved* the book from the shelf to the desk

The two objects we described for these verbs in section 4.2.7.1. merely reflect
the most stereotypical likely *situations* that tend to be construed in the use of
these verbs.[37]

4.2.9. Verbs with verbal/sentential complements

In Volume II, Chapter 13, we will deal in greater detail with the subject of
sentential/verbal complementation of the verbs of the various sub-groups
below. Their treatment here will involve primarily the more gross aspects of
their semantic sub-classification.

4.2.9.1. Modality verbs

Verbs in this class take a verbal complement whose subject is identical to
the subject of the main verb itself. Since that identical subject most commonly
is not repeated, the complement tends to appear syntactically as a verb or verb
phrase. In transformational terms the **equi-subject** of the complement is thus
said to be "deleted". Thus, consider:

---

37) One would do well to remember that all the event types coded by various verbs are not "objective" in any logically-fixed sense. Rather, they represent the more stable, prototypical, likely
construction culled from the potentially infinite facets of so-called "events".

(82)   John wants to work

Sentence (82) may be analyzed in terms of its meaning as containing a **main clause** with the modality verb 'want' and a **subordinate ('complement') clause** with the verb 'work'. Or:

(83)   a.   *Main clause*: John wants... [to do something]
       b.   *Complement clause*: ...John (will) work [is what John wants to do]

Modality verbs have been further sub-divided semantically according to the property of **implicativity**, either **positive** or **negative**. Briefly, an **implicative** verb when it is itself true (i.e. the clause including it is true) also implies the truth of its complement clause/verb. Thus:[38]

(84)   John *managed* to escape ⊃ John *escaped*

When a verb is **NEG-implicative**, then its truth implies the falsity of its complement, as in:

(85)   John *failed* to escape ⊃ John *didn't escape*

Finally, **non-implicative** verbs do not imply the truth of their complement one way or another. Most commonly, they code either positive or negative **intent, ability** or **disposition** toward performing the action — or being the subject of the state — in the complement. Thus consider:[39]

(86)   a.   *Positive intent*: John *wanted* to escape   (⊅ 'John *escaped*')
                                                          (⊅ 'John *didn't escape*')

       b.   *Negative intent*: John *refused* to escape (⊅ 'John *didn't escape*')
                                                          (⊅ 'John *escaped*')

The verbs most commonly found in the various sub-groups of modality verbs are:

---

38) For some traditional elaborations on this semantic classification, see Karttunen (1971) or Givón (1973a). For further elaboration beyond the logic-based tradition, see Volume II, Chapter 13, as well as Givón (1980b).

39) While in strict logical terms no inference can be drawn from 'want' and 'refuse' either positively or negatively, in terms of *pragmatic probabilities* ('conventional implication') speakers most commonly draw some inference as to which result is more *likely*. For example, 'refusing to act' coupled with sufficient power/status/resolution often leads to not acting.

(87)   implicative   non-implicative

positive	negative	positive	negative
'manage'	'fail'	'want'	'refuse'
'succeed'	'stop'	'intend'	'be reluctant to'
'start'	'decline'	'plan'	'frown upon'
'finish'[40]	'forget'	'try'	
'continue'		'decide'	
'remember'		'expect'	
		'agree'	
		'be able'	
		'contemplate'	

Verbs in this group may be further sub-divided according to other semantic criteria. Thus, for example, most of them are *stative* verbs, taking a *dative*
subject ('want', 'intend', 'be able', 'be reluctant to', 'fail', 'remember',
'forget' and others). But a few are *active* verbs, taking an *agent* subject ('try',
'stop', 'continue').

4.2.9.2. Cognition and utterance verbs

In most languages, cognition-utterance verbs take a surface sentence as
their complement, with its subject not necessarily co-referential to the subject
of the main verb. Such non-equi-subjects thus tend to appear overtly within
the complement sentence. In terms of meaning, verbs in this group most often
code mental attitude such as *knowledge, belief* or *hope* pertaining to the proposition in the complement sentence. In a few instances they may also be verbs
of *utterance* of the complement sentence.

One tradition in semantic analysis divides the verbs in this class by the
property of **presupposition** or 'factivity' (see Chapter 7, below). A verb is said
to be **factive** if its complement sentence is true either when the main clause/
verb is true or false. Thus consider:[41]

(88)   a.   John *regretted* that Mary left ⊃ Mary left
       b.   John *didn't regret* that Mary left ⊃ Mary left

---

40) The verb 'finish' exemplifies some of the complexity involved in 'implicativity'. 'He finished
working' implies that 'He worked' (i.e. positive) *prior* to the time-axis of 'finish', but that 'He
wasn't working' (i.e. negative) *after* that time-axis. For details see Givón (1973a).

41) For further discussion of 'factivity' and related issues, see Kiparski and Kiparski (1968),
Karttunen (1971) and Givón (1973a).

A verb may be considered **NEG-factive** if either its affirmative or negative implies the falsity of the complement, as in:

(89) a. John *lied* that Mary left $\supset$ Mary didn't leave

  b. John *didn't* lie that Mary left $\supset$ Mary didn't leave[42]

Finally, a verb is said to be **non-factive** when either its affirmation or denial implies nothing definite about the truth or falsity of its complement, one way or another. Thus consider:

(90) a. *Affirmative non-factive*:
 John *thought/didn't think* that Mary left $\not\supset$ $\left\{ \begin{array}{l} \text{Mary left} \\ \text{Mary didn't leave} \end{array} \right\}$

  b. *Negative non-factive*:
 John *doubted/didn't doubt* that Mary left $\not\supset$ $\left\{ \begin{array}{l} \text{Mary didn't leave} \\ \text{Mary left} \end{array} \right\}$

The semantics of these verbs is much more complicated than the dimensions outlined above, and it will be pursued further in Chapter 13, Volume II. The most common verbs falling, more or less, into the sub-classes outlined above are:

(91)

factive		non-factive	
positive	negative	positive	negative
'know'	'pretend'	'think'	'be afraid'
'understand'	'lie'	'believe'	'doubt'
'learn'		'suspect'	'be uncertain'
'perceive'		'guess'	'deny'
'remember'		'suppose'	
'forget'		'assume'	
'see'		'be sure'	
'find out'		'hope'	
'be aware'		'decide'	
'regret'		'wish'	

42) 'Lie' as well as other sometimes NEG-factive verbs such as 'pretend' are problematic. While their affirmation indeed implies the falsity of their complement sentence, their negation does so only under some intonation patterns which exclude certain *scopes* of negation (cf. Givón, 1979, Ch. 3 as well as Chapter 9, below). Thus when the scope is: 'It is not true that [John lied that Mary left him]', i.e. an *external* negation denying both assertion and presupposition associated with the bracketed expression, 'lie' appears non-factive.

	factive		non-factive
positive	negative	positive	negative
'be glad'		'say'	
'be happy'		'claim'	
'be sad'		'disclose'	
		'propose'	

The syntax of the complements of verbs in this group will be discussed in further detail in Chapter 13, Volume II. At this point we shall divide the complements further into three main types.

4.2.9.2.1. Indirect quote complements

These complements appear most commonly with *cognition* (rather than *utterance*) verbs. They do not involve literal quotation of what the subject thought/knew/said, but a certain constructed paraphrase for which the *speaker* takes editorial responsibility. That responsibility is also reflected in the control of co-reference of pronouns. The **deixis** ('pointing') of those hinges upon the speaker rather than the subject of the verb. Thus consider:

(92)   Joe said (that) *I* was a crook (I ≠ Joe)

Other deictic expressions also hinge on the position of the speaker rather than the subject. Thus consider:

(93)   a.   Joe called me from Chicago and said (that) *this* house was for sale
            (Joe couldn't have said 'this' because he was 2,000 miles away)

       b.   Joe told me last night (that) *today* would be the time to buy
            (Joe couldn't have said 'today' but rather 'tomorrow')

       c.   Joe called from Phoenix to say (that) he'd be *here* in the afternoon
            (Joe couldn't have said 'here' while in Phoenix)

4.2.9.2.2. Direct quote complements

Most languages allow direct-quote complements only with utterance verbs such as 'say'. The speaker takes a much more limited responsibility for the direct-quoted complement sentence, he merely passes it on as a more-or-less verbatim quotation, exerting less editorial tampering. Correspondingly, the control of pronominal co-reference and other deictic expressions remains vested in the *subject* of the utterance verb. Thus, compare (94) below to (92), (93) above:

(94) a. Joe said: "*I* was a crook"   (I = 'Joe')

b. Joe called from Chicago and said: "*This* house is for sale"
(He was referring to a house *in Chicago*)

c. Joe said last night: "*Today* is the time to buy"
(He was referring to *yesterday*)

d. Joe called from Phoenix and said: "I'll (still) be *here* this after-
noon"
(He was referring to *Phoenix*)

4.2.9.2.3. Embedded question complements

A limited group of cognition-utterance verbs can take **if-clauses** as their
sentential complements, with those if-clauses semantically resembling **yes/no
questions** (see Chapter 20, Volume II). Such verbs are most commonly verbs
of **negative certainty** (or negatives of verbs of certainty). As examples consider:

(95) a. He doubted *whether* she came
b. He didn't know *if* she came
c. He wasn't sure *whether* she came

Occasionally one may be able to get such a complement with a verb of high
certainty, if added explicatory material is presented:

(96) He *knew* whether she came or didn't, but he wouldn't tell us

But verbs of relatively low (though still positive) certainty do not seem compatible with such complements. Thus consider:

(97) a.* He thought whether she came or not (but wouldn't tell us)
b.* He believed whether she came or not (but wouldn't tell us)
c.* He suspected whether she came or not (but wouldn't tell us)
d.* He said whether she came or not (but wouldn't tell us)

The question embedded in the complement may also be a **WH-question**
(see Chapter 20, Volume II). In that case, the group of verbs which can take
such a complement is much wider. Thus compare:

(98) a. He knew who did it
b. He guessed who did it
c. He discovered/learned/found out who did it
d. He realized who did it
e. He said who came
f. He forgot/remembered who came

Still, some verbs — some that may take if-clause complements — reject WH-question complements. Thus consider:

(99) a.*She doubted who did it
b.?She suspected who did it
c.*She claimed who did it
d.?She was sure who did it

A major division here seems to be that of *speaker's* certainty vs. *subject's* certainty. The verbs in (98) — at least in their usage there — are *presuppositional* ('factive'), i.e. used under conditions when the speaker already knows the answer. On the other hand, the verbs in (99) — at least in their use there — are not presuppositional and simply code the degree of the subject's certainty.[43]

4.2.9.3. Manipulative verbs

Verbs in this group take one nominal object that is most commonly human/animate and thus a *conscious participant*. Further, this participant plays a double role in the event described by the manipulative-verb construction. First, it is the **manipulee** object of the main clause (whose subject is in turn the **manipulating agent**). In that role it may be termed a *dative* object. In addition, it is also the *subject-agent* of the complement sentence. This co-referential identity condition most commonly leads to the surface coding of this participant only as *object*, thus to the "transformational deletion" of its 'second' occurrence as subject/agent.[44] Finally, the complement sentence itself codes the desired state/event which the main-clause agent tries to bring about.

The more detailed semantic sub-classification of the verbs in this group will be deferred to Chapter 13, Volume II. The traditional logic-based classification closely mirrors that of modality verbs (section 4.2.9.1., above). Some manipulative verbs are thus *implicative*, so that if they (or their main clauses) are true, the complement is also true. Thus consider:

(100) She *forced* him to leave $\supset$ he *left*

These verbs thus code *successful* manipulation. Others are *NEG-implicative*, whereby if the main verb (or its main clause) is true, the complement is false.

---

43) I am indebted to Ferenc Kiefer (in personal communication) for a stimulating discussion which suggested this tentative division. The subject is far from closed, though.

44) The degree of expressing the manipulee as either purely a direct object (i.e. conforming to the *patient* prototype) or increasingly as *dative* or even *subject* is one of the major coding correlates to the scale of *binding* of the manipulation. For a detailed discussion see Chapter 13, Volume II, as well as Givón (1980b).

Thus consider:

(101) She *prevented* him from leaving ⊃ he *didn't* leave

These are thus verbs of successful *preventive* manipulation. Finally, other verbs are *non-implicative*, so that neither success nor failure of the manipulation is strictly implied by the truth of the main verb/clause. Thus consider:

(102) She *told* him to leave ≠ $\left\{ \begin{array}{l} \text{He } left \\ \text{He didn't } leave \end{array} \right\}$

These are thus verbs of *attempted manipulation*, either positive, as in (102), or negative, as in:

(103) She *forbade* him to leave ≠ $\left\{ \begin{array}{l} \text{He } didn't\ leave \\ \text{He } left \end{array} \right\}$

Verbs commonly belonging to these sub-groups are:

(104)

implicative		non-implicative	
positive	negative	positive	negative
'cause'	'prevent'	'permit'	'forbid'
'make'	'stop'	'tell'	
'have'	'talk out of'	'ask'	
'force'	'dissuade'	'order'	
'trick'	'scare away from'	'suggest'	
'help'		'tempt'	
('let'?)[45]		'allow'	
('persuade'?)		'encourage'	
'enable'			

Further semantic sub-classification of these verbs, as well as the systematic correlations between the semantics of manipulative verbs and the syntax of their complement clauses, will be discussed in Chapter 13, Volume II.

4.2.9.4. Information verbs

These are verbs whose subject is most likely an *agent*, and whose nominal object is a *dative*. In addition, they have a sentential complement whose subject is *not* restricted for co-reference. The subject/agent of the main verb *com-*

---

45) While 'let' seems to the superficial eye to be as non-implicative as 'allow', there is evidence that in common usage it is implicative. For details, see Givón (1980b) as well as Chapter 13, Volume II.

municates the propositional knowledge of the complement to the dative-object. Most commonly verbs in this class are 'tell', 'say to', 'inform', 'announce to', 'ask... if'. Their complement types may be sub-grouped along the same line as the complements of cognition-utterance verbs (section 4.2.9.2., above), i.e. into direct-quote, indirect-quote, if-clause and WH-question complements. Thus consider:

(105) a. *Direct quote*:   She told *him*: "I was a crook"
      b. *Indirect quote*:   She told *him* (that) I was a crook
      c. *If-clause*:   She asked *him* if John was a crook
      d. *WH-question*:   She told/asked *him* who the crook was

The dative object of these verbs appears in many languages as *direct* object, as in English, above. But it may also be marked with a pre- or post-position more characteristic of semantically dative participants. Thus consider the following from Israeli Hebrew, where 'tell' takes a dative and 'ask' a direct object:

(106) a. hi   amrá   **l-o**   she-Yoáv kvar   aláx
         she told   *to-him*   that Yoav already left
         'She told him that Yoav had already left'

      b. hi   shaalá **ot-o**   im Yoáv kvar   aláx
         she asked   *OBJ-him*   if Yoav already left
         'She asked him if Yoav had already left'

4.3. DOUBLE MEMBERSHIP IN VERB CLASSES

While we assigned verbs to particular classes above, one must note that many lexical verbs may belong to more than one class. This is simply another way of saying that they may have more than one distinct sense, since our verb classes are not only syntactic but also semantic. Many double — or even triple — memberships of verbs are predictable cross-linguistically, so that the same verbs have the same multiple-sense pattern in many languages. Let us illustrate this phenomenon with a number of examples. Consider first the verb 'tell':

(107) a. *With a direct and indirect-dative object (4.2.7.2.)*:
         John told the story to Mary

      b. *As an information verb (4.2.9.4.)*:
         John told Mary that he was leaving

      c. *As a manipulative verb (4.2.9.3.)*:
         John told Mary to leave

And in some languages (cf. Ute) the verb 'tell' is also the same as the verb 'say', so that it also appears as a member of the cognition-utterance class (4.2.9.2.). Consider next the verb 'forget':

(108) a. *With a direct object (4.2.5.):*
              Mary forgot the incident

    b. *As a modality verb (4.2.9.1.):*
              Mary forgot to come home

    c. *As a cognition-utterance verb (4.2.9.2.):*
              Mary forgot that it was Tuesday

Similarly with the verb 'want':

(109) a. *With a direct object (4.2.5.):*
              John wanted an apple

    b. *As a modality verb (4.2.9.1.):*
              John wanted to leave

    c. *As a manipulative verb (4.2.9.3.):*
              John wanted Mary to leave

Thus, when we say that a verb 'belongs to a particular class', it should be taken to mean that *a particular sense* of that verb belongs to that class.

4.4. OPTIONAL CASE-ROLES

4.4.0. Summary of the major case-roles

In outlining the verb classification above, we dealt with the major semantic case-roles which are *obligatory* in particular sentence types. That is, their presence — syntactically or semantically — is essential for explicating the core-meaning of the verb. In some sense they are the most important case-roles in the grammar of sentences (or, ontologically, in the propositional coding of experience). These case-roles may be now summarized informally as:

(110) a. *Agent*: Deliberate initiator of events
    b. *Dative*: Conscious participant or recipient in events or states
    c. *Patient*: Registering a non-mental state or change-of-state
    d. *Benefactive*: Conscious benefiter from an agent-initiated event;
            most commonly sub-category of dative-recipient
    e. *Instrumental*: Unconscious instrument used by the agent in
            bringing about the event

f. *Associative*: Co-agent or co-dative that is outside the focus of importance

g. *Locative*: Concrete point of spatial reference with respect to which the position or change-in-location of another participant is construed (in some further-specified manner)

h. *Manner*: The manner of a state or of an agent-initiated event

One must remember that these definitions correspond roughly to the *prototype* of these case-roles, so that metaphoric extension from these prototypes is both possible and common. One must further remember that *in principle* there are as many case-roles as there are verbs, so that these most common ones are merely the most likely, most general *classes* of case-roles.

In terms of their propositional-semantic scope, all these case-roles have a rather **narrow predication scope**.[46] This may be best explicated by contrasting "predicate scope" with a wider "sentence scope", as in the following examples:

(111) a. He went *to Chicago* (predicate scope)
b. He worked *in Chicago* (wider scope)
c. He manipulated them *very cleverly* (predicate scope)
d. *Cleverly*, he manipulated them (wider scope)
e. He spent *yesterday* there (predicate scope)
f. He worked *yesterday* (wider scope)

The optional case-roles to be discussed briefly below are all of the *narrow scope* type. Wider, sentential scope adverbial expressions will be discussed in Chapter 21, Volume II.

4.4.1. Benefactive

As mentioned in section 4.2.7.2., above, the dative-recipients of several verbs ('give', 'bring', 'send', 'tell', 'show' are the most common ones) are often construed as the **beneficiary** of the action initiated by the agent of the verb. These are obligatory dative-benefactive objects. In addition, most *active* verbs, i.e. ones with an *agent-subject*, may take an *optional* benefactive

---

46) The obvious exceptions here are the *agent* as well as *dative* and *patient* when they occupy the *subject* position. Some discussion of scope as it pertains to adverbs may be found in Chapter 3, section 3.8., above.

participant, one which is not crucial in a direct way for the semantic definition of the verb. Thus consider:

(112) a. He worked *for his father*
       b. He killed the deer *for his father*
       c. He made a table *for his father*
but not:
       d.*He understood the question *for his father* (*dative* subject)
       e.* He was tall *for his father* (*patient* subject)
       f.* The storm killed him *for his father* (non-volitional cause)

4.4.2. Instrumental

In section 4.2.7.3., above, we noted instrumental objects which are obligatory participants in predications, i.e. they are deeply involved in the semantic specification of the verb. But *active* verbs with *agent* subjects may also take appropriate optional instrumental objects. Thus consider:

(113) a. John broke the window *with a hammer*
       b. They farmed *with a big tractor*
       c. He cut the fish *with a knife*
but not:
       d.*The wind broke the window *with a hammer* (non-volitional cause)
       e.* The window broke *with a hammer* (*patient* subject)
       f.* He understood the book *with binoculars* (*dative* subject)

As we have already seen earlier (section 4.2.5.1.), when instruments are predictable or *stereotypical*, they are often incorporated into the meaning of the verb rather than expressed overtly (and thus redundantly). Thus consider:

(114) a. He tied up the captives (with rope, strap, twine, kerchief, belt)
       b. She shot him (with gun, bow, cannon)
       c. He hit the horse (with hand, stick)
       d. She kicked the table (with foot)
       e. They cut the fish open (with sharp-edged instrument)

Instrumentality (as well as patient, manner and location/direction) is indeed one of the more common semantic features that can be incorporated into the verb — either semantically, as above, or morphologically. There is in fact a continuum of instrumentality, which may express the correlation between degree of predictability/stereotypicality of an instrument, its referentiality and the probability of the instrument being 'incorporated' into the verb. The scale is roughly:

(115)

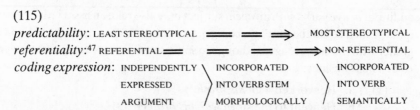

predictability: LEAST STEREOTYPICAL ══ ══ ⟹ MOST STEREOTYPICAL
referentiality:[47] REFERENTIAL══ ══ ══ ⟹ NON-REFERENTIAL
coding expression: INDEPENDENTLY \ INCORPORATED   \ INCORPORATED
                     EXPRESSED   ⟩ INTO VERB STEM   ⟩ INTO VERB
                     ARGUMENT   / MORPHOLOGICALLY / SEMANTICALLY

This correlation may be viewed as another instance of **iconicity** in grammar, where the least predictable, least stereotypical and thus most referential argument is also more distinctly coded as a separate entity.[48] To illustrate the incorporation of stereotypical instruments into the verb stem consider the following from Ute:[49]

(116) ma-cúgwa   'press to', (cugwá- 'join', 'meet')
      ma-cóĝwa-   'knead', 'press with hand'
      ma-cóy-   'squeeze', 'knead'
      ma-cá'wa-   'extend the hand'
      ma-yáakwi-   'cause to sink into' (yáakwi- 'disappear')
      ma-víciku̱-   'slap'
      ma-gú'na-   'rub', 'massage', 'touch-heal'
      ma-ĝóy'a̱   'choke' (qoy'a̱- 'slaughter')
      ma-róĝoma-   'create'
      ma-rú'na-   'rub on', 'spread', 'anoint'
      ma-rṵ́vi-   'knead', 'press together'

The old Ute root for 'hand', now extinct, is *ma-, as still appearing in ma-sṵ́ṵ-vi 'finger' (vs. ta-sṵ́ṵ-vi 'toe', from *ta- 'foot'). The common denominator in all the verbs above is the incorporated 'hand' denoting the stereotypical instrumentality of the various activities.

4.4.3. Associative

Obligatory associative case-roles, i.e. those inherently involved in the semantic definition of verbs, have been discussed in section 4.2.5.2.5., above. In

---

47) As we shall see in Chapter 11, below, referentiality in language is not a purely logical property of mapping from language to entities in some universe, but rather a pragmatically-determined property dependent upon focus, importance, topicality, saliency etc.

48) For further discussion of the sense in which *iconicity* is used here, see Haiman (in press) and Givón (1983, forthcoming).

49) See Givón (1980c).

addition, *active* verbs with an *agent* subject may also take an associative participant, which could then mean a *co-agent*, i.e. one who performs the action together with the subject agent, though in some sense in a less-focal, subservient
role. Thus consider:

(117) a.   He worked *with his brother*
        b.   He went to the store *with his brother*
        c.   He built the house *with his brother*
     but not:
        d.*He was tall *with his brother* (*patient* subject)
        e.*He knew the answer *with his brother* (*dative* subject)

The situation is somewhat blurred by the fact that the associative NP could
also be interpreted as a *co-object* rather than co-agent, as in:

(118) a.   She saw him *with his brother*
        b.   They fired *him with his brother*
        c.   They found him *with his brother*

Obviously, different restrictions are placed on the co-object associative than
on the co-agent associative. Finally, even the restriction of active verb and
agentive subject is sometimes dissolved for *co-subject* associatives, whereby
the associative 'with' begins to resemble a straight-forward **conjunction**
('and'). Thus consider:

(119) The logs floated down the river *with the other scum*
      (*patient* subject)

The presence of such examples in English strongly suggests that the asymmetrical preposition 'with' is slowly developing a more symmetrical, **coordinate**
usage akin to *and*, which of course has fewer restrictions on its distribution. In
many other languages, 'and' is simply a later sub-sense of an originally asymmetrical 'with'. Thus, consider the following from Bemba:[50]

(120) a.   ba-à-boombele   no-omunaabo   (co-agent)
        'they-PAST-work   with-friend-their
        'They worked **with** their friend'

---

50) See Givón (1972). There are grounds for believing that all so-called 'coordinate' conjunctions are diachronic offshoots of the subordinating, asymmetrical 'with'. For some more examples of the ambiguity of 'and' and 'with' in Bantu and some of its consequences in the grammar,
see also Givón (1970b). Even when two NP's are conjoined with 'and' in English, they are in
one serial order rather than the other, and that by itself is a form of *ranking*. 'Pure' conjunction
is in language — unlike in logic — illusory (Givón, 1982c).

b. ba-à-mweene   umuana   no-omunaankwe   (co-object)/(con-
   they-PAST-see child   with-friend-his joined objects)
   'They saw the boy **with/and** his friend'

c. umuana a-à-ishile   no-omunaankwe   (co-agent)
   child he-PAST-come with-friend-his
   'The boy came **with** his friend'

d. umuana no-omunaankwe ba-à-ishile   (conjoined agent
   child and-friend-his   they-PAST-come   subjects)
   'The boy **and** his friend came'

e. umukashi no-omuana ba-à-nweene   mu-meenshi
   woman   and-child they-PAST-drown in-water
   'The woman **and** the child drowned in the water'
                                   (conjoined patient subjects)

4.4.4. Manner

Manner adverbs have been discussed extensively in Chapter 3, above. As we shall see in Chapter 5, below, they are the *least referential* of all arguments of the verb, the most likely to undergo incorporation into the verb-stem (cf. (115), above) and are thus at the extreme bottom of the case-role hierarchy.

4.4.5. Time

We have discussed time adverbs briefly in Chapter 3, above. As adverbial clauses they will be further discussed in Chapter 21, vol. II. Somewhat related to them are adverbs of **duration**, **repetition**, and **frequency**, all connected semantically to tense-aspect (see Chapter 8, below). Thus, duration adverbs are compatible with events/states with a certain *protracted span*, but incompatible with *instantaneous* events. Thus consider:

(121) a. He stayed there *for a day*
      b. They feasted *for nine hours*
      c. They worked *the whole week*
      but not:
      d.? He killed her *for an hour*
      e.? The glass fell to the floor *for a second*
      f.? He found out the answer *for an hour*

However, instantaneous events are compatible with repetition and frequency adverbs, as in:

(122) a. The cup fell to the floor *again and again*
    b. He found out the right answer *every day*
    c. She kicks him *frequently*

4.4.5. Purpose

While purpose adverbs are essentially sentential/clausal constructions, they nonetheless exhibit a narrow, predicate scope. They thus share some syntactic characteristics with adverbial clauses (Chapter 21, Volume II). They exhibit most commonly an **equi-subject** restriction of the type seen in the complements of modality verbs (section 4.2.9.1., above), and in fact they often resemble the syntax of such complements rather closely. However, they are an optional argument of sentences. Their appearance is limited to active verbs with agentive subjects, for obvious semantic reasons. As examples consider:

(123) a. He ran *to catch the flight to Chicago* (= 'so that *he* may catch the flight to Chicago')
    b. She came *in order to talk to you* (= 'so that *she* may talk to you')
    c. They killed it *for the bounty* (= 'so that *they* may *collect* the bounty')
    d. He runs *for exercise* (= 'so that *he exercise*')

As one can see from examples (123c,d), purpose clauses can disguise themselves in the syntactic form of *benefactive objects* in English. However, this is done only under conditions when the verb involved in the complement clause is highly predictable/stereotypical, cf. the implausibility of the interpretation (124b) and (125b) below:

(124) He ran *for his friend* (benefactive)
    a. To *benefit* his friend
    b.*To *kill* his friend
(125) He played *for money* (purpose)
    a. He played to *gain* money
    b.*He played to *lose* money

While both benefactive and purpose share a certain semantic feature of **goal orientation**, their syntactic conflation in languages is not very common.

4.4.6. Intent

One is justified in considering intent adverbs as a sub-category of manner adverbs (see Chapter 3, above). They are just as likely as other manner adverbs to incorporate semantically into the meaning of verbs. Thus consider:

(126) a. She killed him *deliberately/accidentally*
    b.*She murdered him *accidentally* (contradictory)
    c.? She murdered him *deliberately* (redundant)

Some verbs may perhaps also incorporate accidentality, although one suspects this is a combination of pragmatically-based inference together with the semantics of an *instantaneous* event. Thus consider:

(127) a. She *accidentally* slipped and fell
    b.? She *deliberately* slipped and fell

That (127a) seems felicitous suggests that the incorporation — or the inference — is not as well entrenched for 'slip' as it is for 'murder'.[51]

4.5. SEMANTIC COMPLEXITY AND CASE-ROLES

One may, in broad terms, suggest that the *degree of complexity* of construed states/events/actions is correlated closely with the *number of distinct aspects* attributed to them. Such aspects manifest themselves at the coding level as the various *arguments* or *case-roles* obligatorily (or optionally) associated with the proposition. With this in mind, states ought to be considered the *least-complex* predications, since they (a) tend to involve most commonly only a single argument, and (b) tend to involve no change over time. Events ought to be considered *more complex* because (a) they involve both an initial and final state (change over time), and (b) they tend to involve more arguments. And finally, actions should be considered *most complex*, introducing the ontology of volition, motivation, will-to-act, as well as most commonly differentiating further between the various — separately construed — aspects of experience, such an agent-initiator, patient-changer and others.

When one goes through the verb classes described above, the following broad correlations suggest themselves, all concerning the probability of the surface expression of more elaborate, differentiated case-roles:

(128) *Probability of a separate patient/object role*:

    AGT-SUBJ > DAT-SUBJ > PAT-SUBJ

(129) *Probability of a separate propositional-object role*:

    DAT/AGT-SUBJ > PAT-SUBJ

51) Diachronically, there is a complete continuum between pragmatically-based context-dependent inference of meaning and well-coded, criterial 'lexical' meaning. For some discussion see Givón (1982c), as well as many convincing examples in García (1975).

(130) *Probability of having two distinct object roles*:

AGT-SUBJ > NON-AGT-SUBJ

(131) *Probability of having a larger number of distinct roles*:

STATE > EVENT > ACTION

Correlation (128) expresses the probability of an experience being coded as a *transitive* sentence. Correlation (129) expresses the probability of an event being coded as a *mental* event. Correlation (130) expresses the probability of an event being coded as a *bi-transitive* sentence. And correlation (131) expresses the probability of an experience being coded more *elaborately*. These are observations concerning the likely *semantic* complexity of propositions taken in isolation. As we shall see in Chapter 5, below, the case hierarchy emerging here, that of

(132) AGENT > DATIVE > PATIENT

will re-emerge to play a prominent role in determining the likelihood of what becomes the **discourse topic**. Higher semantic saliency and higher thematic saliency will thus be shown to be necessarily correlated, since it is rather unlikely that facets of experience which are cognitively *more salient* and thus linguistically *more elaborately coded* should not also turn out to be *thematically more highlighted* in human communication.

5 | CASE-MARKING TYPOLOGY: Subject, Object and Transitivity

5.1. INTRODUCTION

5.1.1. Functional levels

In the preceding chapter, in the course of dealing with the propositional-semantic structure of simple clauses, we discussed various types of **participants** in states, events and actions. We defined them as the most common **semantic case-roles** found in human language. While these case-roles are considered universal, it is not the case that all languages code them syntactically in the same way. This chapter thus concerns itself with the typologically divergent ways in which languages code their semantic case-roles as a case-marking system. We will be concerned here primarily with *morphological* coding, and in Chapter 6, below, the other major device for case-marking is discussed, namely that of *word-order*.

We have so far avoided, rather deliberately, the exact, rigorous definition of two case-roles, **subject** and **direct object**. It has been rather transparent throughout the discussion in Chapter 4, above, that these two case-roles are of a different kind from all other — semantic — case-roles. To begin with, they **co-exist** with semantic case-roles, a fact which surfaced in our references to agent-subject, patient-subject, dative-subject etc. Similarly, we also referred above to patient, dative, benefactive, instrumental, locative or associative direct objects. Clearly then, both "subject" and "direct object" are grammatical/syntactic categories coding *another* functional level in language, that of **discourse-pragmatics**, and more specifically the complex system which codes the clausal **topic**.

A more detailed discussion of the grammar of topicality, topic continuity and topic identification will be found in Chapter 22, Vol. II. Deferring the comprehensive treatment of "topic" till then is a necessary choice and is not of immediate concern. The discussion of "topic" in this chapter will remain, to quite an extent then, informal and incomplete.

5.1.2. Grammatical coding

The great bulk of cross-language typological diversity in case-marking systems is not found in the coding of semantic case-roles *per se*. Rather, it is found in the *interplay* between the coding of semantic case-roles and the coding of the pragmatic case-roles "subject" and "direct object". It is the way in which different languages approach the necessity to **jointly code** the semantic and pragmatic function of "case" — i.e. mark the roles of the various participants in propositions — which produces the typological diversity of case-marking systems. In studying this diversity, a major theme will be the **functional bind** arising from the need to code simultaneously, jointly, the semantic and pragmatic roles of nominal participants in clauses. Different case-marking types may then be viewed as different **typological solutions** to the same functional bind. In the course of the discussion, we will begin to elaborate upon one of the *leitmotifs* of this book, namely the way in which typological solutions adopted in one part of the grammar are necessarily constrained by the typological solutions adopted in other — functionally related — parts of the grammar. In this respect, the case-marking typology of a language is surely its most central typological parameter,[1] since almost all other parts of the grammar must interact with it. This is only to be expected, since the coding of propositional-semantic information remains a constant requirement in communication, regardless of what other communicative functions are to be satisfied.

5.1.3. Transitivity

We have already raised, in Chapter 4 above, the **meta-theme** of semantic transitivity. In dealing with case-marking systems, that theme gets further amplified and elaborated. The fact that so much of the syntactic/structural coding of case-roles revolves around the complex meta-phenomenon of transitivity, is itself *prima facie* evidence for the centrality of transitivity in human language. What we will observe, throughout this chapter, is the effect of discourse-pragmatics and "topicality" on the interpretation of the notion "transitive event". As a result, a psycho-linguistically unified account of transitivity will emerge, one in which the artificial dichotomy between "semantic" and "pragmatic" transitivity is resolved through the gestalt-psychological notion of **saliency**.

---

1) Case-marking devices obviously include word-order.

5.2. PRAGMATIC CASE-ROLES, CLAUSAL TOPICS AND MULTI-PROPOSITIONAL DISCOURSE

As seen in Chapter 4, above, propositional semantics involves the study of propositions ('sentences', 'clauses') and their meanings in a certain degree of isolation or abstraction from their discourse context and communicative function. This is purely a methodological *heuristic*, albeit a useful one, which allows us up to a certain point to elucidate and analyze two of the three major functional realms of language, namely **lexical meaning** and **propositional information**. But in human communication, atomic propositions are only the building blocks of a larger message unit, which we will refer to as **discourse**. And discourse, at this stage of the cognitive and cultural evolution of *homo sapiens*, is inherently **multi-propositional**.[2]

Multi-propositional discourse is not merely a concatenation ('chain') of atomic propositions. Rather, it tends to display a more elaborate, commonly **hierarchic** structure. Typically, with the **narrative** serving for the moment as the prototype for discourse,[3] the overall story is divided into chapters, chapters into episodes, episodes into macro-paragraphs and these last into smaller **thematic paragraphs**. The last-mentioned are made up of complex sentences and/or, finally, propositions ('clauses'). This hierarchic array is part of the **thematic structure** of discourse.

There is, however, another system of **coherence** that interweaves throughout thematic structure but is rather distinct functionally and syntactically. This is the system of tracking and identifying the **participants** in the story, the ones most likely to surface out as subjects and objects of clauses. We shall call it the system of **topic maintenance** or **topic continuity**. While human discourse may have loftier, more abstract **themes**, we would consider it as being prototypically about the fate, affairs, doings, trials and tribulations of individual — most commonly nominal — **topics**. Potentially, all nominal arguments in propositions are topics in this sense. However, they rank on a scale according to their importance. The various devices used to tell of the importance of topics, and the functional and cognitive space underlying this central

---

2) In the communication of canines, apes, or babies at the age of 6-10 months, discourse tends to be largely mono-propositional. See discussion in Givón (1979a, Chapters 5, 7)

3) Other discourse types are the *conversation* and *expository text*, among others. For the moment no attempt will be made to justify using the narrative as a prototype. For the internal organization of narrative text, see Longacre (1976, 1979) or Hinds (1979), *inter alia*.

grammatical complex in language, will be discussed in greater detail in Chapter 22, Volume II. At this point, it will suffice to say that the main behavioral manifestation of important topics in discourse is **continuity**, as expressed by **frequency** of occurrence. An important topic is like a *leitmotif* in thematic paragraphs, it "runs through them", it tends to occur in chains of **equi-topic** clauses. Of the many grammatical devices collaborating in the overall grammar of topic continuity, two pertain specifically to the case-marking system:

(a)   The Subject
(b)   The Direct Object

These are our two so-called pragmatic case-roles. Of the two, the subject case tends to code the most important, recurrent, continuous topic. We may call it the **primary clausal topic**. The direct-object case codes the topic next in importance, recurrence or continuity. We may call it the **secondary clausal topic**.

So far as can be ascertained, there is no human language that does not use some syntactic coding-devices, be these morphology, word-order or intonation, to code the primary clausal topic. In this sense, then, all languages have the pragmatic case-role of "subject", though they may vary in the exact type of device — or combination of devices — for coding the subject/topic.[4] On the other hand, perhaps fewer languages display the pragmatic case-role of direct-object, as a syntactically-coded device distinct from the semantic case-role of **patient**. As we have seen in Chapter 4, above, in some sense the patient is indeed the **prototype** direct-object. But the notion direct-object is only relevant if it turns out that semantic case-roles other than the patient have regular "access" to that role. As we shall see below, the various semantic case-roles may be hierarchized on a cross-linguistically valid scale according to the probability that they may accede to the two **grammaticalized** (i.e. 'syntactically coded') pragmatic case-roles of subject and direct-object.

---

4) A largely terminological argument used to rage as to whether one is talking about "subject" or "topic". The gist of it, it seems, was whether the main clausal topic was strongly or weakly coded. That is, whether the topic was coded by a maximal array of word-order, morphology and intonation devices, or whether it was coded by relatively few devices. In retrospect, the argument seems to many of us who participated at the time (cf. Li, ed., 1976 and Keenan, 1975, interalia) a bit misplaced. Other function-oriented traditions of talking about some notion of clausal-topic, under whatever terminological guise, may be found in Fibras (1966a, 1966b), Bolinger (1952, 1954), Halliday (1967), Van Dijk (1972) or Dik (1978).

5.3. THE SUBJECT CASE-ROLE

In this section we will establish — and illustrate some of the consequences of — the **topic accession hierarchy**. This hierarchy is a ranking order of the various semantic case-roles according to the likelihood of their becoming the more continuous topic *in discourse*; more specifically, however, according to the likelihood of their occupying the pragmatic case-roles of subject or direct object in simple clauses.[5] We will deal first with access to the subject case-role. As we shall see below, the same hierarchy, with one conspicuous adjustment,[6] also predicts the access to the direct-object role, provided the language has a grammaticalized direct-object case.

Tentatively one may define access-to-subject or **subjectization** as follows:

(1) "Subjectization is the assignment, by whatever coding means available in the language, of the pragmatic case-role of subject (or 'primary clausal topic') to one of the arguments ('semantic case-roles') in the clause".

The hierarchy of access to subject/topic, or **topic hierarchy** of the major semantic case-roles, may now be given as:[7]

(2)   AGT > DAT/BEN[8] > PAT > LOC > INSTR/ASSOC[9] > MANN

---

5) By simple clauses we still mean main, declarative, affirmative active clauses. From the point of view of predicting subjectization, obviously the most critical of the four properties is *active* (as against *passive*).

6) The agent, occupying the top of the hierarchy, will presumably always exercise its primacy by pre-empting the subject slot, thus removing itself from competition for the direct-object slot, when relevant.

7) We shall meet the topic hierarchy or reflections of it repeatedly in various domains of the grammar, where it has immense predictive power. Its antecedents may be found in Hawkinson and Hyman (1974), Givón (1976b) or Dik (1978), *inter alia*. Most languages draw the dividing line as to access to subjecthood in active clauses either with the *patient* or — much more rarely — *locative* case roles. To my knowledge, no clear cases exist of the *instrument* or *manner* ever becoming subjects of simple/active clauses. And the *associative*, while being semantically co-agent, may be indeed *conjoined* subject. But then it ceases to be the associative case.

8) At this point it is not clear whether a sufficient body of data exists to support a relative ranking of the dative and benefactive vis-à-vis each other. Many languages treat them in a similar fashion so far as access to the *direct-object* role is concerned. For most verbs which take a DAT/BEN subject in a simple clause, the subject is in fact a dative *rather than* a benefactive. One common exception is the verb 'receive', whose subject is clearly a benefactive, though in many languages not necessarily an agent. One may tentatively suggest that *benefactive* is "further marking" of *dative*. Since neither the instrumental nor the associative accede to subjecthood in simple clauses, no data exists to dif-

The predictive power of our topic hierarchy (2) is rather straightforward, and may be given in the following expression of descending strength of claim:

(3) a. If the simple clause has an **agent** argument, it will be the subject.

b. If the simple clause has no agent but has a **dative/benefactive** argument, it will be the subject.

c. If the simple clause has no agent, nor dative/benefactive but has a **patient** argument, it will be the subject.

d. Etc.

In the remainder of this section we will discuss evidence supporting the topic hierarchy (2), culled from lexicalization patterns in simple clauses. Evidence from access to subjecthood in **passive** clauses will be discussed in detail in Chapter 15, Volume II, where it will be shown to be fully compatible with our hierarchy. Evidence pertaining to access to **direct-objecthood** will be discussed later in this chapter.

5.3.1. The primacy of agent

There is one subjectization type, that of **ergative** languages, where at least some people have made the claim that the clause with the agent *not* being the subject is the simple clause-type of the language.[9] For the purpose of the discussion here we shall for the moment ignore these claims, which will be dealt with later.[10] Examples illustrating the predictive power of the hierarchy will for the moment be taken from non-ergative languages.

The placing of the agent at the top of the topicality hierarchy is supported by the fact that sentences such as (4a, b, c) are likely to be simple clauses, but the corresponding passives in (5, a, b, c), respectively, are not.

---

ferentiate their position on the hierarchy. Further, the number of languages which allow these arguments to be "promoted" to direct-objecthood is relatively small (see below), so that it is not clear if sufficient grounds exist to differentiate their position on the hierarchy even there. Further evidence concerning direct-objectization in simple clauses will be discussed further below.

9) Most conspicuously, Dixon (1972b) claims that in Dyrbal's transitive clauses the *ergative*-marked agent is not the topic, but rather the *absolutive*-marked non-agent is. In a more general vein, Verhaar (1982a/1982b) claims that ergative languages may be defined as those which tend to make the non-agent a clausal main topic. The argument obviously hinges on how one defines the "simple, unmarked clause" (see further discussion below).

10) As we shall see later on, the determination of what is a "simple clause" must be, inherently, a discourse-functional determination. The fact that syntactic simplicity/complexity (unmarkedness/markedness) usually goes hand in hand with functional simplicity/complexity is of course a fundamental facet of *iconicity* in language. The subject of markedness in syntax will be discussed in some detail in Chapter 23, Volume II.

(4)   a. The man talked to the woman   (AGT > DAT)
       b. The woman broke the cup   (AGT > PAT)
       c. The man went to the store   (AGT > LOC)
(5)   a. ? The woman was talked to by the man
       b. The cup was broken by the woman
       c. * The store was gone to by the man

5.3.2. The position of dative

The placing of the *dative* (and *benefactive*, see fn. 8) above all other semantic case-roles except the agent is supported by the fact that sentences such
as (6a, b, c, d, e) below are likely simple clauses, while their corresponding
passives in (7a, b, c, d, e), respectively, are not — and many of them cannot
even be passive sentences.

(6)   a. The woman saw the house   (DAT > PAT)
       b. The woman meditated in the yard   (DAT > LOC)
       c. The woman meditated with the boy   (DAT > ASSOC)
       d. The woman heard it with a hearing aid   (DAT > INSTR)[11]
       e. The woman thought hard   (DAT > MANN)
(7)   a. The house was seen by the woman
       b. * The yard was meditated in by the woman
       c. * The boy was meditated with by the woman
       d. * The hearing aid was heard it with by the woman
       e. * Hard was thought by the woman

5.3.3. The position of patient

The placement of *patient* on the hierarchy above all other case-roles but
below agent and dative/benefactive is supported by the fact that the sentences
in (8) are all likely simple clauses, but the corresponding passives in (9) clearly
are not. The range of combinations here is more restricted, due to the agent-
subject constraint on the appearance of some object arguments.

(8)   a. The book fell on the floor   (PAT > LOC)
       b. The second floor collapsed with the roof   (PAT > ASSOC)
       c. The glass broke noisily   (PAT > MANN)

---

11) Since instrumental objects prototypically appear only when there is an agent/subject in the
clause, it is likely that the meaning of 'hear' in (6d) is really an *active* meaning, something closer to
'listen', and thus the subject is really an agent rather than dative. To some extent the same may be
true for sentence (6c), where the meaning of 'meditate' may be closer to 'activity' than to 'state'.
But as we have seen in Chapter 4, above, the agent-subject restriction for associative objects is not
as stringent as the one for instrumentals.

(9)   a. *The floor was fallen on by the book
      b. *The roof was collapsed with by the second floor
      c. * Noisily was broken by the glass

5.3.4. The position of locative

In most languages locatives cannot be the subjects of simple (active) clauses. In *all* languages the associative, instrumental and manner arguments are either rare or unacceptable as subjects of simple clauses. Thus, the existence of at least some languages which admit locative subjects places them above the rest of the **oblique** arguments on our hierarchy.

Locative subjects of seemingly simple clauses may appear in Bantu languages, but only under restricted conditions and in the absence of case-roles which outrank them on our hierarchy. A major restriction placed on their subjectization is that of predicate type: only a very limited group of highly **stative** predicates may take locative subjects. As examples consider the following from Bemba:[12]

(10) a. iŋ-gaanda   ii-suma   (non-locative subject of adjective)
         PREF-house   it-good
         'The house is good'
      b. mu-ŋ-gaanda   muu-suma   (locative subject)
         in-PREF-house in/there-good
         $\left\{\begin{array}{l}\text{'In the house it is good'}\\\text{'It is good in the house'}\end{array}\right\}$
      c. im-fumu i-li na-abaana   (non-locative subject of be with/have)
         PREF-chief he-be with-children
         'The chief has children'
      d. mu-ŋ-gaanda mu-li na-abaana   (locative subject; existential)
         in-PREF-house in/there-be with-children
         $\left\{\begin{array}{l}\text{'The house has children in it'}\\\text{'In the house there are children'}\\\text{'There are children in the house'}\end{array}\right\}$

In Bemba as well as in all core-Bantu languages, the obligatory subject pronominal agreement on the verb identifies the grammaticalized subject rather clearly. Sentences (10b, d) show the locative "class" (*mu-* 'in') as the unmistakable controller of verb agreement, hence the grammatical subject.[13]

---

12) See Givón (1972).

13) For further discussion of grammatical agreement, see Chapter 10, below.

5.3.5. The position of instrumental

As we have suggested above, instrumentals, associatives and manner adverbs — i.e. the three bottom rungs of our hierarchy — do not become subjects of simple sentences. With respect to instrumentals, one may argue that sentences (11b, d f) below in fact have an instrumental subject, referring to their *physical* role in the event, as compared to — respectively — (11a, c, e):

(11)   a.   He filled the pond *with water*
       b.   *The water* filled the pond
       c.   He tied the gate *with a rope*
       d.   *The rope* tied the gate
       e.   He broke the window *with a hammer*
       f.   *The hammer* broke the window

The answer to this observation is as follows: In (11a, c, e) the instruments fulfill their role *as instruments*. That is, they are used *by an agent* as *intermediate* in the chain of causation. But that is not the case necessarily in sentences (11b, d, f), which more typically code events where no clear agent is construed or communicated. The subjects of these sentences are thus not instrumentals, but *patient* subjects. It is thus not the *physical role* of the instrument which makes it instrument, but rather its *use* by the agent.

Having said this, one may not wish to deny that some of the physical properties of instruments are in fact crucial to their *use* as instruments. In this sense, (11a, b), (11c, d) and (11e, f) are obviously semantically-related pairs. But 'water', 'rope' and 'hammer' are not *construed* as instrument in (11b, d, f). Finally, one may as well note that while (11a, c, e) are legitimate simple sentences, the corresponding (passives) (12a, b, c) are not:

(12)   a. *The water was filled the pond with by him
       b. *The rope was tied the gate with by him
       c. * The hammer was broken the window with by him

And in languages where passives with an instrumental subject are possible, similar sentences are clearly passive, thus complex.

5.3.6. The problem of dative subjects

In some languages, dative subjects are marked with a special morpheme that is similar to the morpheme marking dative *objects*, thus setting dative subjects apart from agentive or patient subjects. As an example consider the following sentences from Kannada, a Dravidian (South Indian) language. It has the rigid word-order SUBJECT-OBJECT-VERB (SOV), and the subject is normally unmarked, regardless of whether it is agent or patient. That unmarked subject normally controls the **grammatical agreement** on the verb. In this language, the phenomenon of dative subject is extremely pervasive, so that subjects playing the semantic role of "experiencer" or "recipient" receive the special dative suffix. Thus consider:[14]

(13) a. maguvi-ge   bāyārike   āgide
       child-DAT   thirst   happened
       'The child is thirsty' (lit.: 'To the child thirst happened')

     b. nana-ge nagu   baratte
        I-DAT   laughter comes
        'I feel cheerful' (lit.: 'To me laughter comes')

     c. avaḷi-ge ibbaru makkaḷu   iddaru
        she-DAT two   children are
        'She has two children' (lit.: 'To her there are two children')

     d. nina-ge ī   vicāra gottā ?
        you-DAT this   matter know-Q
        'Do you know this?' (lit.: 'Does this matter come/is it known to you?')

     e. avani-ge tāyiya   jnāpaka bantu
        he-DAT   mother-GEN memory   came
        'He remembered his mother' (lit.: 'The memory of his mother came to him')

On the surface, it seems that examples (13) from Kannada violate our hierarchy, with the *patient* out-ranking the dative, at least given one subject-identifying criterion in Kannada — the control of grammatical agreement. However, as Sridhar (1976) points out, with respect to word-order, as well as a wealth of other grammatical criteria, it is the dative NP in examples like (13) that behaves like the subject in Kannada. Sridhar goes further and points out that in some cases one could have a contrast between a dative and an 'unmarked' (nominative) subject. In each case, the nominative subject codes a **volitional act**, while the dative subject codes an **experienced state**. Thus consider:[15]

14) From Sridhar (1976).
15) From Sridhar (1976).

(14) a. avanu   jvara   barisikonḍa   (NOM subject)
          he   fever   cause-come-PAST
          'He got the fever' (intentionally, by doing something)

      b. avani-ge   jvara   bantu   (DAT subject)
          he-DAT   fever   came
          'He got a fever' (unintentionally, got hit by it)

      c. avanu   ī   suddi   tiḷidukonḍanu   (NOM subject)
          he-NOM this news learned
          'He learned this news'   (actively, intentionally)

      d. avani-ge   ī   suddi   tiḷiyitu   (DAT subject)
          he-DAT   this news   became-known
          'He came to know this news' (unintentionally, it came to him)

Thus, languages of this type mark dative-experiencer participants more consistently in their case-marking morphology, even when these occupy the subject pragmatic case-role. But the dative still outranks all non-conscious case-roles in access to subjecthood.

5.4. THE CROSS-LINGUISTIC TYPOLOGY OF SUBJECTIZATION

5.4.1. Preliminaries

While focusing in this section on the typology of **subject marking**, one must concede that in fact it is impossible to describe that typology without at the same time describing at least a healthy portion of the typology of **object marking**. This is so because what is important in the syntax/grammar of case marking is not only the *absolute* marking of assigned case-roles (be these semantic or pragmatic), but above all the *differentiation* in marking between them. One may thus view the grammar of subjectization as, in large part, the grammar of differentiating the subject from the direct-object case-role.[16]

As suggested earlier, it is possible to view the various types of coding of the same functional domain as alternative *solutions* to the same communicative task. In the case of subjectization, one may define the task as a "functional dilemma":

(15) *Functional dilemma in subjectization*:
      "How to express simultaneously the *semantic* case-role of an argument and its *pragmatic* case-role as subject"

---

16) For a cogent discussion of this relative function of case-marking systems, see Wierzbicka (1981).

One may argue that posing this as a dilemma is unwarranted, since human languages are equipped with sufficient structural devices for **double marking** the
subject, most obviously by two affixes, one tagging it as subject, the other indicating its semantic case-role. The facts are, however, that languages seem to
shy away, quite consistently, from double marking an NP in such a fashion.
When they use a reminiscent strategy, they place one mark on the NP, the
other *on the verb* (see further below). For whatever reasons then,[17] it seems
that this obvious solution is little attested in natural language, leastwise not in
a massive or widespread way.[18]

The three major coding devices used elsewhere in syntax are also used —
separately or in various combinations — to code the subject case-role:

(a)   Word-order
(b)   Morphology
(c)   Intonation

Of the three, the role of intonation (or at least of 'tone') seems to be the most
minor. In several Nilotic languages (Luo, Nandi, Maasai, Toposa, etc.)[19] a

---

17) There are two speculative lines of explanation one can offer at this point. First, one may
suggest that double marking on the NP may create a processing confusion for speakers, having to
process two functional markers on the same NP. Second, one may eventually unearth a diachronic
explanation as to why double marking is unlikely to arise via the normal channels through which
case-marking morphology arises (cf. Givón, 1975a, 1979b). These two lines of inquiry may be ultimately one and the same.

18) In Kuno's (1981) description of the Japanese case-marking system, one finds one sentence in
a footnote with double case-marking on the noun:

John-ni-wa   nihongo-ga   nigate   da
J.-DAT-TOP   Japanese-SUBJ   bad-at   be
'John is bad at Japanese'   [p. 76, fn. 9]

It is not clear from the discussion there whether this sentence is an optional variant of *John-wa
nihongo-ga nigate da* or a "stage in its derivation".
A clearer case appears in Jingpaw (Tibeto-Burman; DeLancey, in personal communication).
Thus: MaGam-gaw   MaNaw-hpe   gayat-ai
            MaGam-TOP   MaNaw-OBJ   hit-INDIC
            'MaGam hit MaNaw'

The topicalized/L-dislocated version would be:

            MaNaw-hpe-gaw,   MaGam   gayat-w-u'-ai
            MaNaw-OBJ-TOP   MaGam   hit-PAST-3s-INDIC
            'As for MaNaw, MaGam hit him'

19) For many details see Bennett (1975).

noun has a different tonal pattern depending on whether it is subject or object. All are VERB-SUBJECT-OBJECT (VSO) languages where, one may argue, the subject and object NP's are adjacent, with the verb not serving as a word- order device to separate them (see Chapter 6, below); and neither subject nor object are morphologically marked. Tone, however, is not the *only* means of differentiating between subject and object in these languages, since they do have a rigid VSO word-order that accomplishes some such distinction, up to a point. Further, there is some evidence[20] that the present tonal distinction is a leftover from an earlier morphological distinction, a very common phenomenon in African tonal languages. More broadly, intonation is used in many languages to differentiate *new/suprising/unpredictable* information from *old/predictable* information. And since the subject grammaticalized case-role is more likely to be the topic/leitmotif and thus continuous/predictable information, there is bound to be a high coincidence of "topic intonation" and "subject intonation".[21] However, this intonational phenomenon is not confined to the *grammaticalized* subject, but rather to the *topic* regardless of its grammaticalized case-role. Intonation thus tends to intersect with the case-marking devices which we will deal with here, rather than to systematically coincide with one or another.

The role of word-order in differentiating the subject and object case-roles will be discussed in Chapter 6, below. Another device commonly used as part of the morphology that codes subject and object case-roles is *grammatical agreement* on the verb. While we may refer to it on occasion in this chapter, a comprehensive treatment is deferred to Chapter 10, below.

5.4.2. The nominative-accusative case-marking type

The nominative-accusative case-marking type solves the marking dilemma of subjectization (15) by opting to display the *pragmatic* unity of the category "subject", regardless of whether the verbal clause is transitive or intransitive, and regardless of the *semantic* role of the subject. Contrastively, therefore, the (direct) object of transitive clauses will receive a different coding, be it in terms of morphology or word-order or their combination. Schematically, one may then characterize a nominative-accusative language as follows:[22]

---

20) See Maddieson et al (1973).

21) For a wealth of detail and much enlightening discussion, see Bolinger (1948, 1958, 1964, 1978, 1982).

22) For earlier schematizations in the same vein, though with slightly different terminologies, see Comrie (1978) and Dixon (1979).

(16)	the nominative coding	the accusative coding
intransitive clause	SUBJECT	/
transitive clause	SUBJECT	OBJECT

A nominative-accusative (henceforth 'nominative') language may have both the subject and the object morphologically *unmarked*, as in English. Most commonly in such languages, rigid word-order is used to differentiate the two case-roles. Thus consider the following:

(17) a. *Intransitives*: The book is good (patient-of-state subject)
The book fell (patient-of-change subject)
The man was sad (dative subject)
The man worked (agent subject)
b. *Transitive*: The man kicked the mule (agent subject)

A nominative language may also have *both* object and subject *marked*, as is the case in Korean:[23]

(18) a. *Intransitive*: Park-i   koyusu-ga   toe-iss-da
Park-NOM professor-NOM become-PAST-DECL
'Park became a professor'
b. *Transitive*: Park-i   sonyin-il ci-ss-da
Park-NOM boy-ACC hit-PAST-DECL
'Park hit the boy'

A nominative language may also have an *unmarked* subject and *marked* object, as is the case in Israeli Hebrew, at least with *definite* objects. Thus consider:[24]

(19) a. *Intransitive*:   ha-ísh   avád
the-man worked
'The man worked'

---

23) From Hwang (1982).

24) For some discussion concerning the naturalness of having a morphologically marked definite and/or animate accusative, particularly in languages with unmarked nominatives in some word-order types, see Comrie (1975, 1979).

    b. *Transitive*:   ha-ísh   kará   et-ha-séfer
                  the-man read ACC-the-book
                  'The man read the book'

Finally, at least some nominative languages have a *marked* subject and an *unmarked* object. Thus, consider the following from Mojave (Yuman):[25]

(20) a. *Intransitive*:   '-intay-č   masde:-k
                    my-mother-SUBJ fear-TNS
                    'My mother is afraid'
      b. *Transitive*:   '-intay-č   ahvay ičo:-k
                    my-mother-SUBJ dress make-TNS
                    'My mother made a dress'

5.4.3. The active vs. non-active case-marking type

    In contrast with the nominative type, which uniformly codes — in terms of morphology — the *pragmatic* case-role subject, the active/non-active type uniformly codes the *semantic* case-role of the subject. In this case-marking type, the agent-subject of an active verb is marked one way morphologically regardless of whether the verb is intransitive (i.e. "has no direct object") or is transitive ("has a direct object"). In contrast, a non-agent subject is marked differently, again regardless of the transitivity of the clause. Quite often, in addition, the direct-object is marked morphologically the same way as the non-agent subject, a system that is reminiscent of — and may be historically derived from — the ergative case-marking type (see below). As an example consider the following from Laz (Caucasian):[26]

(21) a. *Active transitive*:
        ǩoči-k   doqvilu γ·ji
        man-ACT he-kill-it pig(NOM)
        'The man killed the pig'
      b. *Active intransitive*:
        joγo-epe-k-ti   lales
        dog-PL-ACT-too they-bark
        'The dogs barked too'

---

  25) From Munro (1974). It is entirely possible that a marked nominative with unmarked accusative arises diachronically from reanalysis of an erstwhile ergative system (see below). This suggestion is discussed in Givón (1980c). Some discussions of ergativity vs. nominativity tend to assume that while ergative subjects are prototypically *morphologically* marked, nominative subjects are prototypically morphologically *unmarked* (see DeLancey, 1981). We shall return to this later.

  26) From Harris (1982, ms). The paradigm is not full here, missing a non-active transitive verb (i.e. 'see', 'be afraid of', 'know', 'want' etc.). Another off-ergative active/non-active language is Modern Tibetan (Chang and Chang, 1980).

    c. *Non-active intransitive*:
    ḳoči   doɣuru
    man(NOM) he-died
    'The man died'

In this language, the suffix *-k* marks the active subject, while the Ø nominative codes non-active subjects as well as objects.

In a number of Amerindian language families (Lakota, Muskogean and others) the active vs. non-active case-marking system does not express itself on the subject or object noun itself but rather in the **pronominal reflexes** ('agreement') on the verb. In Chickasaw (Western Muskogean), pronominal reflexes on the verb are of three kinds, roughly corresponding to *agent, patient* and *dative*. As an example consider the following:[27]

(22) a. *Active-transitive*:
       Ø-kisili-**li**
       3PAT-bit-1AGT
       'I bite him'
    b. *Active-intransitive*:
       chokma-**li**
       good-1AGT
       'I act good'
    c. *Non-active transitive*:
       paska'   **Ø**-**in**-champoli
       bread   3PAT-3DAT-like
       'She likes bread'
    d. *Non-active intransitive*:
       sa-chokma
       1PAT-good
       'I am good'

In terms of solving the functional dilemma of subjectization (15), the active/non-active type chooses to go with the semantics and disregard the pragmatics of the subject case-role.

---

27) From Munro and Gordon (1982). The division into agent/patient/dative is only rough, and several complications exist in this respect, particularly in the relative distribution of patient (series II) vs. dative (series III) pronominal forms. For a similar interpretation of a closely-related dialect, albeit with much less detail and precision, see Heath (1977).

5.4.4. The ergative-absolutive case-marking type and syntactic transitivity

5.4.4.1. Preliminaries

The ergative-absolutive (henceforth 'ergative') case-marking type displays a hybrid or intermediate solution to the functional dilemma (15), one which abides neither by the pragmatics of "subject" nor by the semantics of agent/non-agent. Rather, it abides roughly — and with many intricate variations — by the **transitivity** of the clause. In this system — as first approximation — the subject of the transitive clause (i.e. the one which has a "direct object") is marked by one marker — called the **ergative**, while the subject of the intransitive clause (i.e. the one that has no "direct object") — even when it is semantically an agent — is marked differently, by the so-called **absolutive**. Most commonly, the ergative is a marked morpheme and the absolutive is unmarked or *zero*. And further, the direct object of the transitive clause is also marked by the **absolutive** form. Schematically, the ergative-absolutive marking system may be summarized as follows:

(23)	the ergative coding	the absolutive coding
intransitive clause	/	SUBJECT
transitive clause	SUBJECT	OBJECT

Briefly, then, in ergative languages the subject of the intransitive and the object of the transitive receive the same coding, the *absolutive* case, while the subject of the transitive receives its own *ergative* case-marking.

Most commonly in ergative languages, the *ergative* case is morphologically marked, while the *absolutive* is a morphologically unmarked (or zero) case. As an example consider the following from Inuktitut (Eskimo):[28]

(24) a. *Intransitive*: innuk-Ø   takuvuq-Ø
               person-ABS   saw
               'The person saw (something)'
    b. *Transitive*: pallu-up   qimiq   takuvaa
              Paluk-ERG   dog(ABS)   saw
              'Paluk saw the dog'

28) From Kalmár (1979).

As one can see from (24b) above, semantic *agent* and semantically *active* verb are not necessary ingredients in determining the marking of clauses as "transitive" (and the subject as ergative). Rather, in most ergative languages the presence of a *direct object* is itself enough to qualify the clause as a transitive one. In many ergative languages, however, some finer discriminations as to the semantic role of the subject are made — and influence the morphology of subject marking. Thus, for example, in Sherpa (and several other Tibetan languages) many dative subjects do not receive the ergative but rather the *dative* suffix, in spite of their having a direct object. Thus consider:[29]

(25) a. *Intransitive*:
> ti   mi-ti   cam-sung
> the man-DEF(ABS) dance-PERF
> 'The man danced'

b. *Transitive, dative-subject*:
> ti   mi-ti-la   cenyi go-kyaa-sung
> the man-DEF-DAT   cup   want-AUX-PERF
> 'The man wanted the cup'

c. *Transitive, agent-subject*:
> ti   mi-ti-gi   cenyi caaq-sung
> the man-DEF-ERG   cup   break-PERF
> 'The man broke the cup'

The phenomenon of dative subjects is of course not confined to ergative languages. See the Kannada examples in section 5.3.6., above.

The choice of ergative marking of clausal subjects in ergative languages is thus sensitive, in one manner or another, not simply to "absolute" semantic elements such as "prototypical patient object" and "prototypical agent subject", but rather to a composite *degree of transitivity* of the clause. However, individual languages are not sensitive to exactly the same sub-components of transitivity, nor do they divide transitive from intransitive at exactly the same point on the various *scales* of properties which, as a cluster, determine transitivity. Perhaps the best way of dealing with this issue is through a general discussion of the phenomenon known as **split ergativity**.

---

29) From my own field notes, with the Sherpa data originally due to Koncchok J. Lama (in personal communication).

5.4.4.2. Split ergativity

Even in the most conspicuous ergative languages where the ergative-absolutive pattern is most widely spread throughout the various grammatical paradigms, it is possible to observe some *split* patterns, whereby a **non-ergative** pattern is found in some grammatical contexts. Such a pattern may be a nominative-accusative one, or an **anti-passive** one (see further below). But there is an interesting way in which all the splits seem to be determined by the cluster of scalar properties that comprise transitivity.[30] Broadly speaking, there are two distinct types of interaction between split ergativity and these scales, and we will deal with them separately.

5.4.4.2.1. Split ergativity and transitivity

The scales of transitivity-related properties along which one finds split ergativity in language may be summarized as follows:

(26) a. *Degree of agent's control or intent*:[31]
          controlled causation > uncontrolled causation
          intended causation > unintended causation
      b. *Degree of obviousness/affectedness of the patient*:
          more obvious patient > less obvious patient
          more affected patient > less affected patient
      c. *Degree of perfectivity/completeness of the event*:
          perfective > imperfective
          past > future > present
      d. *Degree of referentiality/topicality of both agent and patient*:
          anaphoric pronoun > definite NP > indefinite NP >
          non-referential NP

In the first type of split ergativity, to be discussed in this sub-section, if a clause is higher on any of the scales in (26), then it is more likely to receive ergative-absolutive case-marking. On the other hand, if it is lower on the scale, it is more likely to receive another marking pattern, be it *nominative-accusative*, *anti-passive* or *passive*. We will deal with these scales in order.

---

30) For transitivity in general and the cluster of scalar properties that comprise it, see Hopper and Thompson (1980).

31) See Chapter 4, section 4.2.5.3.1. for some introductory discussion.

5.4.4.2.1.1. The agentivity scale

We have already discussed and illustrated the effect of this scale in section 5.4.4.1., above. In all ergative languages, it is only the subjects of *transitive* clauses — i.e. ones which in some way conform to the prototype of "agent controller/deliberate initiator" — that receive the ergative marking. This property of the subject obviously goes to the heart of the definition of "transitive clause" or "transitive event". And clauses with a less agentive subject are less likely to have an ergative subject. In many ergative languages this scale may manifest itself even in *intransitive* (i.e. objectless) clauses. Thus, consider the following contrast from Modern Spoken Tibetan:[32]

(27) a. ...[the wind blew me this way, so] ŋa těe̊ lěe̊pą-reè...

                I(ABS) here come-NON-VOL

                '...so I came here...'

    b. ...[I intend to come, and] ŋɛɛ lěe̊-yōō...

                I-ERG   come-VOL

                '...and I will come...'

In a similar vein, Newari, a related language from Nepal, exhibits the following contrast between the ergative and non-ergative coding pattern under some tense-aspect conditions (see discussion further below):[33]

(28) a. *Context*: "Who is breaking the window?" (focus on AGENT)

                    (ERGATIVE pattern)

    Reply: wō mąnu-ną jhya tąjya-ną co-ną

          the man-ERG window break-AUX be-AUX

          '**The man** is breaking the window'

    b. *Context*: "What is the man doing?" (focus AWAY from AGENT)

                    (NON-ERGATIVE pattern)

    Reply: wō mąnu jhya tąjya-ną co-ną

          the man(ABS) window break-AUX be-AUX

          'The man **is breaking the window**'

The distinction in (28) is not so much between the *semantic* facts of volition and non-volition (cf. Tibetan, (27) above), but is concerned with whether the agent — and thus his/her role as deliberate initiator of the event — is *communicatively* (i.e. pragmatically) **salient**.

32) From Chang and Chang (1980). In this case, the ERG vs. ABS marking on the subject is paralleled by the VOLITIONAL vs. NON-VOLITIONAL marking on the verb. But the two systems do not parallel each other this way in all environments.

33) From my own field notes, originally due to Harsha Dhaubhadel (in personal communication).

5.4.4.2.1.2. The patienthood scale

We have already discussed and illustrated the effect of this scale in section 5.4.4.1., above. In ergative languages in general, the presence of an affected patient/object is just as important an ingredient in making clauses transitive as the presence of an agent. Thus, clauses that have a more prototypical patient/object are the obvious candidates for receiving an ergative-absolutive marking pattern. And one is thus justified in considering this as another major "split pattern" in ergative languages. The degree of affectedness (and, correlatedly, of **referentiality**) of the patient may create subtle variations in the spread of the ergative patterns within the verbal paradigm. As an example consider the behavior of three syntactically transitive (i.e. object-taking) active verbs, 'sing', 'drink' and 'break' in Newari, a Tibetan language from Nepal. The main split-ergative pattern in this language (aside from transitive vs. intransitive, of course) is between the perfective/past and the imperfective (progressive/present, future). The verb 'sing' — with a cognate object 'song' — takes an obligatory *ergative* subject in the perfect, an obligatory *nominative* subject in the progressive, and an optional ERG/NOM variation in the future. Thus consider:[34]

(29) a. wõ mạnu-nạ   mē   ha-lạ
          the man-ERG   song   sing-PERF
          'The man sang' (lit. '...sang a song')

      b. wõ mạnu   mē   ha-yi   cõ-gu   du
          the man(ABS) song   sing-IMPERF   be-NOM   be
          'The man is singing'

      c. wõ mạnu(nạ̃)   mē   ha-yi
          the man-ERG/(ABS)   song   sing-IMPERF
          'The man will sing'

With the verb 'drink' when an object is present, the ergative pattern is obligatory in the perfective/past (for both definite and indefinite/non-referential objects) and optional in both the progressive and future. Thus:[35]

(30) a. wõ mạnu-nạ   (wõ)   lạ   tó-nạ
          the man-ERG   (the)   water   drink-PERF
          'The man drank (the) water'

---

34) See fn. 33, above.

35) See fn. 33, above.

b. wō mạnu(nạ̄)   wō lạ   tó-ni   cō-gu   du
the man-ERG/(ABS) the water drink-IMPERF be-NOM be
'The man is drinking the water'

c. wō mạnu(nạ̄)   wō lạ   tó-ni
the man-ERG/(ABS) the water drink-IMPERF
'The man will drink the water'

Finally, with the verb 'break' the ergative is obligatory in *all* three major-tense-aspects:[36]

(31) a. wō mạnu-nạ̄   (wō)   jhya   tạ́jya-tạ
the man-ERG   (the)   window break-PERF
'The man broke a/the window'

b. wō mạnu-nạ̄ (wō) jhya   tạ́jya-yi   cō-gu   du
the man-ERG (the) window break-IMPERF be-NOM be
'The man is breaking the/a window'

c. wō mạnu-nā (wō) jhya   tạ́jya-yi
the man-ERG (the) window break-IMPERF
'The man will break the/a window'

As noted in Chapter 4, above, 'sing' is a verb without a real physical object, and 'sing a song', as in (29), involves the mental construction of the activity as 'object'. 'Drink' has a physical but non-solid, non-colorful object that disappears during the event, and thus its change of state is much less visible — and much less germain — than the change in the state of the *subject* from thirst to satiation. Finally, 'break' has a solid physical object whose visible change is dramatic and clear. Split ergativity in Newari thus follows a predictable gradient in terms of the transitivity parameter of prototypical object patients.

5.4.4.2.1.3. The perfectivity scale

The intimate relation between perfectivity and transitivity of events has been discussed in detail elsewhere.[37] To recapitulate briefly, a perfective/completive event is one whose boundaries — in terms of beginning and termination at precise, well-articulated points in time — are clearly specified. Most commonly this is particularly relevant to the time of *termination* of the event, i.e. the stipulation that the event has in fact occurred and has been successfully

---

36) See fn. 33, above. In another progressive form (Newari has several), the ergative pattern is optional. See section 5.4.3.2.1.1., above.

37) See Hopper and Thompson (1980).

completed.[38] The connection with transitivity lies in two obvious pragmatic inferences, which may be given as follows:

(32)   a. *Affectedness of patient*: "The more completed an event is, the more likely it is that the patient in fact *registers* to the full the effects of the action".

       b. *Effectiveness of agent*: "The more successfully completed the event is, the more likely it is that the agent *was* in fact a deliberate, direct, effective cause of that successful completion".[39]

As an example of split ergativity along the perfectivity parameter, consider the following from Sherpa:[40]

(33)   a. *PERFECT, intransitive*: ti   mi-ti   cam-sung
                                     the man-DEF(ABS) dance-PERF
                                     'The man danced'

       b. *PERFECT, transitive*: ti   mi-ti-gi   cenyi caaq-sung
                                   the man-DEF-ERG   cup   break-PERF
                                   'The man broke the cup'

       c. *IMPERF, intransitive*: ti   mi-ti   cam-ki-wi
                                    the man-DEF(ABS) dance-AUX-PERF
                                    'The man is dancing'

       d. *IMPERF, transitive*: ti   mi-ti   cenyi
                                   the man-DEF(ABS)   cup
                                   caaq-ki-wi
                                   break-AUX-IMPERF
                                   'The man is breaking the cup'

In Newari, a Nepali language distantly related to Sherpa, one finds the imperfective category, including future and progressive, further scaling itself with respect to split ergativity, so that clauses in the *future* are more likely to display an ergative pattern than clauses in the *progressive* ('present'). So that for prototypically-transitive verbs such as 'break' (see (31) above as well as (28)), the ergative pattern is obligatory in both the *past/perfective* and *future*

---

38) See more extensive discussion in Chapter 8, below.

39) Inference (32b) is, in terms of cause-and-effect, of the opposite directionality, as compared to (32a). That is, the stronger, more deliberate/willful and more direct in causation an agent is, the higher is the probability of successful completion of the task. For further discussion of this, see Givón (1980b).

40) From my own field notes, with data originally due to Koncchok J. Lama (in personal communication).

but optional under some communicative circumstances (cf. (28)) in at least
one type of *present/progressive*.

5.4.4.2.1.4. The referentiality/topicality scale

The data pertaining to this scale, as well as to some closely-related scales
to be discussed in section 5.4.4.2.2., below, is on the face of it contradictory.
One set of data, to be discussed here, follows the same directionality vis-à-vis
the scales as what we have seen above. That is, the items *higher* on the scale —
more to the left in (26) — are more likely to display ergative marking, while
the items *lower* on the scale — more to the right — are more likely to display
non-ergative (nominative, anti-passive or passive) marking. In this section we
will discuss only one segment of the relevant hierarchy, the pronoun vs. full-
DEF-NP contrast. The use of the **ergative-antipassive-passive** contrast in ergative languages and its direct interaction with scale (26d) will be discussed in
section 5.4.4.2.3., below. And the contradictory nature of the data, with other
conflicting scales, will be discussed in section 5.4.4.2.2.

The split we will illustrate below appears in ergative Mayan languages, as
well as in some ergative Austronesian languages. What one finds is that full-
NP subjects and objects, either definite or indefinite, are morphologically unmarked, so that they conform to the nominative-accusative pattern as in English (see section 5.4.2., above). But verb agreement, i.e. pronouns cliticized
(at some historical time[41]) on the verb and functioning as **anaphoric pronouns**
(see Chapter 10, below), displays an ergative-absolutive pattern. As an example consider the following from Jacaltec (Mayan):[42]

    (34) a. *Intransitive*:   x-Ø-to-pax   naj   winaj
                               ASP-A3-go-back cl-the   man
                               'The man returned'
         b. *Transitive*:   x-Ø-y-acañ   naj   winaj te'   ñah
                               ASP-A3-E3-build cl-the   man   cl-the house
                               'The man built the house'

The subject and object nouns in (34) have the same grammatical form, in all
cases preceded — since they are definite — by the classifier which functions as

---

41) See extensive discussion of the rise of grammatical agreement in Givón (1976b), as well as
further detail in Chapter 10, below.

42) From Craig (1977), but see also Craig (1976). Among Austronesian ergative languages,
Chamorro displays a reminiscent split (Chung, 1981, Cooreman, 1982).

article (and independent pronoun, when appropriate). The absolutive (A) morphology refers to the subject of the intransitive in (34a) or the object of the transitive in (34b). The ergative (E) morphology refers to the subject of the transitive in (34b). And Mayan languages of this type, once the scope of the ergative-absolutive marking is specified, are fairly typical ergative languages in terms of the functional distribution of the ergative-absolutive construction vis-à-vis other possible markings of clauses (antipassive, passive).

5.4.4.2.2. Split ergativity and the topic hierarchies

The type of split ergativity to be discussed here has been described in most detail for Australian languages, where it pertains both to the synchronic distribution of ergative-absolutive vs. nominative-accusative marking, as well as to the diachronic spread of such marking systems.[43] The scales along which this split may occur are as follows:

(35) a. *Degree of referentiality/topicality*:
             pronoun > definite-NP > indefinite-NP
       b. *Degree of individuation*:
             singular > plural
       c. *Degree of egocentricity*:
             1st person > 2nd person > 3rd person

The seemingly contradictory nature of the evidence lies in the following set of facts and/or assumptions:

(a)   In Australian languages, the higher a subject is on the scales in (35), the more likely it is to display a *nominative* (i.e. unmarked) rather than an ergative (morphologically marked) form.

(b)   But according to Hopper and Thompson's (1980) well-reasoned description of transitivity-related properties, being *higher* on any of these scales (i.e. being more to the *left*) means being *higher* on the overall transitivity scale.

(c)   And finally, as we have seen in section 5.4.4.2.1.4. above (and will further investigate in section 5.4.4.2.3., below), some split-ergative behavior goes in the *opposite* direction, i.e. in conformity with Hopper and Thompson's (1980) predictions.

---

43) For the synchronic description, see Silverstein (1976). For the diachronic discussion, see Dixon (1977).

In a recent attempt to resolve this seeming contradiction, DeLancey (1981) suggested that the split-ergative behavior of the Australian languages abides by a general principle relevant to the coding of our **point of view**:

(36) "When along a scalar dimension some elements code a more likely/ predictable *point of view*, languages would tend to leave them mor- phologically *unmarked* (or 'less marked'). On the other hand, elements which are less predictable and thus the **focus of attention** tend to be morphologically *more marked*".

In essence, DeLancey claims that the semantic principles of *transitivity* and the pragmatic principle of *topicality* are in conflict in all these cases, and that the Australian-type split-ergativity is an instance where the pragmatic princi- ple wins over the purely-semantic ones.

In part, the seeming conflict stems from one potential misunderstanding that can arise from a literal reading of Hopper and Thompson's (1980) paper. In that paper, correlations were noted between transitivity and topicality in connected discourse, and the impression was left that somehow the high-refe- rentiality categories on all the scales (35 a, b, c,) are part and parcel of the complex of "more transitive features". Such a conclusion, I believe, is both unwarranted and unwise. One can, in point of fact, explain this latter type of split ergativity in a way that will both vitiate DeLancey's original intent and give it a more solid, natural foundation. But the explanation is in large mea- sure *diachronic*.

Precisely the same split found in the Australian-ergative languages is also found in the *passive* construction of many languages. Thus, for example, Chung (1976b) reports that one of the "passives" of Indonesian — the one reinterpreted as *ergative* in subsequent works, cf. Rafferty (1978), Verhaar (1982a, 1982b) — cannot apply if the agent is *1st or 2nd person*. The restriction makes an enormous amount of *synchronic* sense in the passive construction, since promotion to subjecthood is also promotion to *higher topicality*, and 1st and 2nd persons universally outrank 3rd persons on the topicality scale (cf. Givón, 1976b, Timberlake, 1975, *inter alia*). The same restriction is reported for the *-in*-passive of Chamorro (Cooreman, in personal communication). In the same vein, Kimenyi (1976) reports that in KinyaRwanda (Bantu), the *pa- tient* object cannot become the subject of the passive if the *dative* object is an anaphoric pronoun, but only if the dative is a full NP. Again, anaphoric pro- nouns universally outrank full NP's on the topicality scale. Through dia- chronic re-analysis of the passive into the new ergative, restrictions that originally were topicality-related and made sense for the passive are transferred wholesale to the new ergative construction.

The argument may then be summarized as follows:

(a) The split ergativity that correlates with *transitivity* properties, such as "agentivity", "patienthood" and "perfectivity", is indeed a general and predictable feature of ergative languages, arising directly from the fact that their case-marking typology is sensitive above all to transitivity.

(b) The Australian-type split ergativity, which correlates to *topicality* properties of the subject/agent, will appear only in ergative constructions which arise from the reanalysis of erstwhile *passives*.

5.4.4.2.3. The ergative-antipassive variation

In many, though not all, ergative languages, there is an alternative construction type which is used, under distinct conditions, to code transitive sentences. For reasons that turn out to be fully justified, it is called the **anti-passive (AP)** construction. There are several facets of the antipassive which suggest a resemblance to the structural properties of an *intransitive* clause. First, the object in the AP construction is not coded by the normal (unmarked) *absolutive* case-marker characteristic of the ergative construction, but rather by an *oblique/indirect-object* marker, most commonly a marked pre- or post-position.[44] In that sense, to begin with, the AP-clause "does not have a direct object", and thus displays one major characteristic of an intransitive clause. Second, most commonly as a result, the agent/subject loses its ergative case-marking, and reverts to the *absolutive* (unmarked) case. To illustrate this, consider the following from Inuktitut (Eskimo):[45]

(37) a. *Ergative*: inu-up   qimmiq-Ø takuvaa
             person-ERG   dog-ABS   saw
             'A/the person saw **the** dog'

---

44) In Nez Perce (Penutial; see Rude, 1982), a language with many ergative characteristics, the direct object — thus *absolutive* case — is morphologically marked with the post-position *-nel-na*. In the anti-passive, it *loses* rather than gains marking. This is of course understandable in terms of the need to maintain a *contrast* between the DO/absolutive and the IO/unmarked. But such a situation is relatively rare in ergative languages, and there are other grounds for considering Nez-Perce a less-than-typical ergative language.

45) From Kalmár (1980).

   b. *Anti-passive*: innuk-Ø   qimmir-mik takuvuq-Ø
                   person-ABS dog-OBLQ   saw
                   'A/the person saw **a** dog'
   c. *Normal intransitive*: innuk-Ø   takuvuq-Ø
                   person-ABS saw
                   'The person saw (something)'

The verb-form in (37a) is marked as a two-argument verb. In both the intransitive (37c) and the anti-passive (37b) it is marked as a one-argument verb, i.e. intransitive. And in both the subject reverts to the absolutive case.

The conditions under which the anti-passive clause-type occurs in ergative languages are predictable rather substantially from the degree of *referentiality/topicality/discourse importance* of the direct object in the clause. This may in turn be captured by scale (26d), reproduced below in a slightly modified version:

(38) a. *Referentiality*:
          DEF-NP > INDEF-NP > NON-REF-NP
     b. *Topicality*:
          more important/continuous topic > less important/
          continuous topic

Scales (38a), (38b) are two aspects of the very same topicality scale. The traditionally more "semantic" aspect is captured in (38a) — and will be discussed in detail in Chapter 11, below. The more discourse-pragmatic reflection of the same scale, given in (38b), will be discussed extensively in Chapter 22, Volume II.[46] The "split" in ergative languages, between conditions under which the ergative clause-type is used and those under which the anti-passive clause-type is used, may thus be considered another supportive instance for our postulate concerning the relation between split ergativity and transitivity. The evidence may be now summarized as follows.

5.4.4.2.3.1. The Eskimo evidence

Kalmár (1979, 1980) shows rather conclusively that in Inuktitut-Eskimo the anti-passive is used when the object is either *indefinite, less-topical, less-referential*, provides more *new information* or, in the sense defined in Givón (1983a,

---

46) For early versions currently available in print, see Givón (ed. 1983a) and Givón (1983b, 1983c).

1983b, 1983c) is a *less continuous/important topic*. In terms of so-called formal "subject properties"[47], the ERG-marked subject of the ergative clause and the ABS-marked subject of the anti-passive clause remain, equally, the surface subjects of the two clause-types.

5.4.4.2.3.2. The Dyrbal evidence

Dixon (1972b) suggests that in Dyrbal, an Australian ergative language, the *absolutive* case — regardless of whether it is marking the subject of an intransitive clause, the object in the ergative-transitive clause or the agent in the anti-passive two-argument clause — indeed always marks the *subject/topic* of the clause. Thus, the anti-passive device, which removes the object from topicality/subjecthood and downgrades it to an oblique case (and correlatedly installs the *agent* in the subject/topic slot), operates in the discourse-pragmatic context of a *less referential* or *less topical* object.

5.4.4.2.3.3. The Nez-Perce evidence

Rude (1982) shows that in Nez Perce, a Sahaptan-Penutial language with many ergative properties, the object in the anti-passive construction is more typically *indefinite, non-referential* or *plural*. In other words, it is lower on the referentiality/topicality hierarchy than the typical definite, referential and singular object of the ergative construction.

5.4.4.2.3.4. The Chamorro evidence

Cooreman (1982, 1983, in preparation) shows that in Chamorro, an Austronesian ergative language, the object in the anti-passive construction is consistently *less topical/continuous/important* in discourse than the object in the ergative construction. Cooreman's findings are particularly important in this respect because they are based on careful, quantitative text studies, where "degree of topicality" was defined by two exact measures, one assessing the degree of *continuity/recurrence/predictability* of the topic vis-à-vis its *preceding* discourse environment, the other assessing the degree of the topic's *importance/persistence* vis-à-vis its *succeeding* discourse environment.[48]

---

47) "Coding properties" of the subject (cf. Keenan, 1975, 1976a) include word-order, case-marking and control of verb agreement. "Behavioral" or "deep-grammatical" properties of the subject include the control of various grammatical processes, such as reflexivization, reciprocalization, equi-NP deletion in verb complement, identical-subject deletion in continuous discourse and others (cf. Anderson, 1976, Dixon, 1972, Sridhar, 1976 or Kalmár, 1980). Kalmár's (1980) reanalysis of Eskimo clearly challenges claims made earlier by Anderson (1976) and Woodbury (1975) concerning the "deep-ergative" nature of Eskimo. For this topic, see further discussion in section 5.4.3.3., below.

48) For the general approach, quantitative methodology and its application to a typological cross-section of languages, see Givón (ed., 1983a).

5.4.4.2.4. The coding of transitivity in Ergative languages: Ergative, passive and anti-passive

We are now in a position to address a central theme running through this investigation into the ergative case-marking system, namely the way "transitivity" is coded in ergative languages. In particular, we are in the position of being able to contrast the three major construction-types that occur in ergative languages,

(a) Ergative
(b) Passive
(c) Anti-passive

as to their specific use in the coding of transitivity. As was suggested in Chapter 4, above, the two major components of construing an event as transitive are:

(i) The presence of a *deliberate initiator agent*
(ii) The presence of a *clearly affected patient*

As we shall see in Chapter 15, Volume II, one of the major functional parameters of passivization is to code semantically-transitive events that have lost transitivity because of severe downgrading of the topicality/referentiality of the *agent* (accompanied by a predictable *up*grading of the topicality/referentiality of the patient).[49] The antipassive represents the opposite parameter of loss of transitivity, i.e. the one due to downgrading the referentiality/topicality of the *patient/object*. The thing that is unique to ergative languages in this respect is that once a clause is rendered intransitive by downgrading (or altogether eliminating) its underlying semantic patient/object, the marking on the agent is also readjusted, from *ergative* (characteristic of transitive subjects) to *absolutive* (characteristic of intransitive subjects). The relation between the topicality/referentiality of the agent and patient in the three constructions in ergative languages can be best summarized following Cooreman's (1982, 1983) text-study of Chamorro:

(39)

clause type	relative topicality of AGT and PAT
ergative	AGT > PAT
antipassive	AGT ≫ PAT
passive	AGT ≪ PAT

---

49) For discussion already available in print, see Givón (1979, Chapter 2 and 1981b).

What one must also note is that similar relationships between the three major ways of coding semantically-transitive events in syntax also exist in *nominative* languages. Passivization there achieves the same results as in ergative languages, above. And a number of processes exist by which a language may downgrade the status of highly predictable, stereotypical, non-referential or topically unimportant objects. These are rules such as *object incorporation, deletion of non-specified object* or *demotion from direct object* (see further below). Thus consider:

(40) a. *Transitive*: John taught the class brilliantly
      b. *Passive*: The class was taught brilliantly [agent suppression]
      c. *Unspecified object*: John taught brilliantly [object suppression]
      d. *Transitive*: John lent the money to an industrialist
      e. *Passive*: The money was lent to an industrialist [agent suppression]
      f. *Unspecified object*: John lends to industrialists [object suppression]
      g. *Non-referential object*: John is a money-lender [object incorporation]
      h. *Dative-shifting*: John lent the industrialist lots of money [object demotion]

The major difference between the anti-passive of ergative languages and its various functional equivalents in nominative-accusative languages is that in the latter no adjustment in the case-marking of the subject is made when the object is downgraded, suppressed, demoted or deleted due to low referentiality/topicality — because the subject of both transitive and intransitive clauses is marked by the *same* nominative case.

5.4.4.3. Deep and surface ergativity

Anderson (1976) suggested that while most ergative languages display the difference between the ergative-marked subject of transitive and the absolutive-marked (or rather 'unmarked') subject of the intransitive in their *morphology*, the grammatical behavior of the ergative subject of transitives and the absolute subject of intransitives is identical, so far as various rules governing "subject properties" are concerned.[50] Anderson called such erga-

---

50) See fn. 47, above. At this point in the presentation we are not in a position to discuss these rules comprehensively, since they involve by and large the syntax of complex clauses, most of which are to be treated in Volume II.

tive languages **surface-ergative**. He then contrasted these with two other ergative languages, Dyrbal (Australian, cf. Dixon, 1972) and Eskimo (cf. Woodbury, 1975) in which — so it was claimed — subject/topic properties were vested in the absolutive NP, regardless of whether it was the subject of the intransitive or the patient-object of the transitive clause. Such languages were
then called **deep-ergative**.

The great bulk of so-called subject properties used to define the behavior
of "deep" ergative languages turn out to be pragmatic **topic** properties, associated with deletion under identity in various grammatical environments
(see Dixon, 1972 as well as Heath, 1979). The existence of "deep" ergative
languages thus poses a grave challenge to what has been said above concerning the hierarchy of access to subjecthood. This is so because in such languages presumably the patient ('absolutive') is more topical/subject-like than
the agent ('ergative') in the ergative-transitive clause. As mentioned earlier,
our notion of hierarchy of access to subjecthood also assumes that the *passive*
clause-type is the *marked*, less-frequent one in discourse, and that the *active* is
the *unmarked*, neutral and more common in discourse, in the coding of transitive events. If the descriptions of Dyrbal and Eskimo were to be taken at face
value, then they indeed combine the following properties which normally do
not go together:

(41) a. The *ergative* clause-type is the unmarked, neutral, more fre-
          quent means of coding transitive events in discourse; but
      b. In such ergative-transitive clauses, the *absolutive-patient* — rather
          than the *ergative-agent* — is vested with subject/topic properties.

Turning first to Eskimo, Kalmár (1979, 1980) has shown that the language is *not* "deep" ergative, but rather "surface" ergative. In other words,
the notion of "subject" applies regardless of whether it is the absolutive-sub-
ject of the intransitive or the ergative-subject of the transitive. This analysis
also makes it clear that the ergative clause-type is the unmarked, most frequent means of coding transitive events in Eskimo discourse.

The status of Dyrbal remains a bit murky. Heath (1979) has challenged
Dixon's (1972) "deep" ergative analysis, showing many instances in text
where the ergative-agent NP — rather than the absolutive-patient — controls
subject/topic properties. However, a quantified text-study of Dyrbal has yet
to be done, one which would resolve the two issues in terms of discourse-fre-
quency:

(a)   Which of the two NP types in transitive clauses is *more frequently*
        the topic in discourse; and

(b)   Which clause type — ergative or antipassive — is the *unmarked*,
        more-frequent one in the coding of transitive events in discourse.

More recently, Verhaar (1982a, 1982b) has claimed that colloquial Indonesian is "deep-ergative" in the same sense claimed for Dyrbal. But a text-
frequency study (Verhaar, 1983) has shown that in discourse the ergative-
agent is more topical than the absolutive-patient of transitive clauses. In the
same vein, Mallinson and Blake (1981) have claimed that Tagalog (Philippine) is a "deep" ergative language. But again, a quantified text study (Cooreman, Fox and Givón, 1983) has demonstrated conclusively that the ergative-
agent of the transitive clause is more topical than the absolutive-patient.
Clearly then, the concept of "deep" ergativity remains, for the moment, in a
state of limbo, and more text-based studies must be done in order to determine whether Dyrbal is indeed a unique human language.[51]

5.4.5. The Philippine verb-coding case-marking type

As suggested earlier, case-marking systems of various types may be viewed as different solutions to the same functional dilemma — the need to code
simultaneously the semantic and pragmatic functions of nominal participants
in clauses. With respect to subjectization, the Philippine solution is in a way
rather elegant. Nouns that are *not* in the pragmatic case-role of subject/topic
are marked for their *semantic* roles, by prefixes. The subject/topic noun is
marked by prefix for its *pragmatic* role. And the verb is marked (by various
prefixes/infixes/suffixes) for the *semantic* role of the subject/topic. As an illustration consider the following from Bikol:[52]

---

51) A dissenting comment may be seen in Dixon (1979b), and a dissent from that dissent in
Heath (1980). Another likely conclusion to this argument may be, eventually, that Dyrbal is a
mixed ergative language, whereby some "subject properties" ('topic-related processes') are controlled only by the absolutive, regardless of semantic case-role, while others are controlled by
either the ergative subject of transitives or by the absolutive subject of intransitives.

52) From my own field notes, with the data originally due to Manuel Factora (in personal communication). The presentation here is slightly simplified. Sentences (42b), (42c) are thus, potentially, passive sentences (i.e. with a non-agent subject/topic), and will be discussed in greater detail
in Chapter 15, Volume II. For further detail see also Givón (1981b).

(42) a. *Agent topic*:
nag-ta'ó   'ang-laláke   ning-líbro   sa-babáye
AGT-give   TOP-man   PAT-book   DAT-woman
'The man gave a book to the woman'

b. *Patient topic*:
na-ta'ó   kang-laláke   'ang-líbro   sa-babáye
PAT-give   AGT-man   TOP-book   DAT-woman

$\left\{\begin{array}{l}\text{'The book was given to the woman by the man'}\\\text{'The man gave the book to the woman'}\\\text{'As for the book, the man gave it to the woman'}\end{array}\right\}$

c. *Dative topic*:
na-ta'o-hán   kang-laláke   ning-líbro   'ang-babáye
DAT-give-DAT   AGT-man   PAT-book   TOP-woman

$\left\{\begin{array}{l}\text{'The woman was given a book by the man'}\\\text{'As for the woman, the man gave her a book'}\end{array}\right\}$

5.5. THE DIRECT-OBJECT CASE-ROLE

5.5.1. Preliminaries

As suggested earlier, while the subject pragmatic case codes the *primary* clausal topic, the direct-object (DO) codes the *secondary* topic in the clause. It is observed cross-linguistically, as we shall see later, so that the morphological coding of the direct-object is considerably *weaker* than that of the subject. There are several reasons why such differential coding-strength is natural:

(a)   Both transitive and intransitive verbs have subjects, but only transitive verbs have direct objects. Thus, if a clause has only one argument/participant, the probability is higher that it would be its subject.

(b)   When a clause has only two arguments, and one of them is already well-marked as subject, the other one may be semantically either patient, dative, locative, associative, benefactive etc., so that it is crucial to provide for some *semantic* case-role marking. However, pragmatically it is already tagged as secondary topic by contrast with the well-coded subject. There is thus no compelling reason to further mark it for its *pragmatic* role.

(c)   Finally, the most important, recurrent, continuous topic in the thematic paragraph becomes the well-coded subject. The direct object is thus bound to be a less important/recurrent/continuous topic. The fact that it is also bound to be *less distinctly coded* thus follows from general considerations of iconicity.

In many languages, given the considerations outlined above, there are no *morphological* provisions for marking the direct-object as distinct from the semantic case-role of patient. Rather, word-order or intonation may be used to indicate which of the participants — apart from the subject — is more topical.

When the direct-object is a morphologically distinct case-role, the language is faced with the same *functional dilemma* already seen for the subject.

(43) *Functional dilemma in objectization*:
"How to express simultaneously the *semantic* case-role of an argument and its *pragmatic* case-role as secondary topic (i.e. DO)"

The way various languages solve this dilemma, by combining the common syntactic coding devices of word-order, morphology and intonation, forms the basis for our typology of objectization.

5.5.2. The topic hierarchy of accession to direct-objecthood

The access to direct objecthood is governed, not surprisingly, by the very same topic hierarchy of the semantic case-roles which governs the access to subjecthood (see (2), section 5.3., above). The only difference is, of course, that the *agent* is irrelevant to this hierarchy, given its automatic access to the primary topic slot, i.e. subject. The hierarchy of access to objecthood is then:

(44) DAT/BEN > PAT > LOC > INSTR/ASSOC > MANN

The support for this hierarchy in terms of grammatical behavior will be outlined in the typological sub-sections below. A text-frequency study in support of the hierarchy — in particular of the relative positions of *patient, dative/benefactive* and *locative*, may be found in Givón (1981a).

5.5.3. The direct object as a pragmatic case

While the treatment of the subject as 'topic' is a well-established tradition in Linguistics,[53] the direct object has most commonly been considered a

---

53) See for example Li (ed., 1976) for a general survey from a largely grammatical point of view. For text-oriented quantitative studies, see Givón (ed., 1983a).

"grammatical" case-role, i.e. a purely structural phenomenon.[54] It would perhaps be worth the time to illustrate the kind of considerations that point toward treating this structural phenomenon as having firm *functional* correlates.

While the ultimate proof of the DO's pragmatic function as secondary topic must come from text studies, where "topicality" is defined in measurable, quantifiable terms,[55] there are clear indications from sentence-level data of DO/IO alternation that this is indeed the case. Thus, consider for example:

(45) a. *Context*: Who did Mary give the book to? (PAT-topic, DAT-focus)

     b. *Reply*: She gave the book to Bill (PAT is DO)

     c.   ?She gave Bill the book (?DAT is DO)

     d. *Context*: What did Mary give to Bill? (DAT-topic, PAT-focus)

     e. *Reply*: She gave him a book (DAT is DO)

     f.   ?She gave a book to him (?PAT is DO)

While emphatic contrastive stress may, in English, salvage the inappropriate responses (45c, f), it is clear that (45b, e), respectively, where the more topical ('out of focus') object surfaces as the DO, are much more natural replies to the respective questions (45a, d).[56] The question context thus establishes one of the two objects as the focus of new information (see Chapter 7, below), leaving the other to be the *secondary topic* — given that the subject already is the primary topic.

---

54) Relational Grammarians (cf. Perlmutter and Postal, 1974, Johnson, 1974, Kimenyi, 1976, *inter alia*) have discussed the DO as a purely formal, structural category. In the long grammatical tradition preceding them, there was no attempt to separate clearly the semantic category *patient/ accusative* from the structural category object or direct-object. To my knowledge, the first explicit claim that this structural category has a systematic functional correlate, the secondary clausal *topic*, is due to Givón (1979a). Relational Grammarians nevertheless deserve much of the credit for separating the semantic from the "grammatical" strands of "object", an endeavor that directly led to my own suggestion that the "grammatical" — much like their "grammatical subject" — coded a systematic *discourse function*.

55) For that methodology see Givón (ed., 1983a). For a specific text study in a language — Nez Perce — with optional promotion of many non-patient objects to DO, see Rude (1983).

56) When the DO is stressed contrastively, the IO becomes "more topical" by default. However, the stress-focus answer is a more *marked* one than (45b, e), and is thus appropriate to a more marked discourse environment, rather than to the neutral (non contrastive) questions (45a, d).

Another indication that the DO is more topical than the IO — when an option such as the variation in (45) is available — is the high frequency of pronouns — as against full NP's — found in the DO position. Thus, in Givón (1982a) the number of pronouns in that position, for DAT/BEN arguments that display this option (i.e. capable of 'dative shifting', see below) was counted. Out of a total of 38 DO's, 34 were pronouns. Out of the total of 7 DAT/BEN objects in the IO position in the same text, all were full NP's. In general, pronouns are much more continuous/important/persistent topics than definite nouns.[57]

The following alternation of DO and IO (cf. Chapter 4, section 4.2.7.3.) also displays the same topic-focus relation, with the DO being more topical:

(46) a. *Context*: What did she do with the paint? (INSTR-topic)
      b. *Reply*: She sprayed *it* on the wall   (INSTR is DO)
                   (*implied*: All the paint was sprayed, though not necessarily the whole wall)
      c. *Context*: What did she do to the wall? (LOC-topic)
      d. *Reply*: She sprayed *it* with paint (LOC is DO)
                   (*implied*: The entire wall was sprayed, though not necessarily all the paint)

The implicit *semantic* effect associated with the pragmatics of direct objecthood is hardly surprising:[58] As we have seen in Chapter 4, above, the prototypical object is a highly affected *patient*. The alternations in (45) and (46) above — especially the latter — are thus both pragmatic and semantic in nature. But this merely reflects a certain unity in the fundamental notion of *saliency*, which may be more semantic (i.e. focus upon the object's being "visibly affected") or more pragmatic (i.e. focus upon the object's being an "important topic in the communication"). That the two go hand in hand is, in some fundamental way, to be expected.

5.5.4. The cross-linguistic typology of objectization

5.5.4.1. Promotion to direct object: Preliminaries

The typology given below pertains to a process that we will refer to as "promotion to DO". The term is borrowed from Relational Grammar (see for example Chung, 1975, 1976a) and will be used to mean:

---

57) For the higher topicality of pronouns over definite nouns, see Givón (ed., 1983a).

58) The original semantic observation is due to Anderson (1970).

(47) *Promotion to DO*: "The placing, by whatever grammatical means,
of a *non-patient* object into the position of direct
object, whose grammatical coding (most commonly by morphology) is otherwise characteristic of patient objects".

This process has also been called "dative shifting".[59] Our hierarchy (44) of accession to the DO slot receives its strongest support from the restrictions on
objectization.

5.5.4.2. The word-order type: Israeli Hebrew and Sherpa

Languages of this type display no *morphological* means of separating the
DO pragmatic role from the patient semantic role. That is, the morphology
unambiguously codes only the *semantic* case-roles. However, the more topical of the various objects — when more than one is present — is coded by
word-order, that is by placing it *before* all other objects. As an example consider the following from Israeli Hebrew:

(48) a. *Context*: To whom did he give the book?   (PAT-topic,
                                                      DAT-focus)

   b. *Reply*:   hu   natán   et-ha-séfer   la-ishá   (PAT-DAT)
                 he   gave   ACC-the-book   to-the-woman
                 'He gave the book to the woman'

   c. *Context*: What did he give to the woman?   (DAT-topic,
                                                        PAT-focus)

   d. *Reply*:   hu   natán   la   et-ha-séfer   (DAT-PAT)
                 he   gave   to-her ACC-the-book
                 'He gave her the book'

As can be seen above, the relative order relation, i.e. the word-order device
coding this alternation, is the same in Hebrew as in English (cf. (45) above).
But there is no change in the case-marking morphology, which continues to
code the underlying semantic case-roles.

   The same type of word-order alternation without change in the semanti-
cally-based case morphology can be seen in Sherpa, as in:[60]

---

59) As for example in Givón (1981a).

60) From my own field notes, with the data originally due to Koncchok J. Lama (in personal
communication).

(49) a. *Context*: Where did he put the book?   (PAT-topic)
   b. *Reply*:   (PAT-LOC word order)
ti-gi	kitab-yi	coxts-i-kha-la	žax-sung
he-ERG	book-ACC	table-GEN-on-DAT	put-PERF
      'He put the book on the table'
   c. *Context*: What did he put on the table?   (LOC-topic)
   d. *Reply*:   (LOC-PAT word-order)
ti-gi	coxts-i-kha-la	kitab-yi	žax-sung
he-ERG	table-GEN-on-DAT	book-ACC	put-PERF
      'He put on the table a book'

Languages such as Hebrew and Sherpa may be viewed as ones in which our functional dilemma in objectization (cf. (43) above) does not arise, since the morphology and the word-order carry separate functions:

(a) The morphology remains the major coding device of semantic case-role; and

(b) The word-order alternation codes the pragmatic relations of secondary topic vs. less important topics.

This separation is consistent with what is known elsewhere concerning the coding of pragmatic case-roles. Thus, for example, Keenan (1975) notes that the most "easily transferable" subject-coding property in passivization is the characteristic word-order ('position'). Li and Thompson (1976) labeled languages where only word-order (but not case-marking morphology or subject-controlled grammatical agreement) codes subjects/topics "topic prominent languages". Finally, in Givón (1983c) it was shown that in language registers where grammatical morphology is almost entirely absent, such as plantation Pidgins and Early Second Language acquisition, similar word-order principles for coding the pragmatics of topicality already operate in very much the same way (see also Chapter 22, Volume II for further elaboration).

5.5.4.3. Limited optional promotion: English

As can be seen from example (45) above, English allows a limited range of promotion of non-patient objects to DO, whereby they lose their semantically relevant case-markers ('propositions') and become morphologically unmarked, like the prototypical patient. This operation in English is restricted to DAT/BEN objects, i.e. to the top of our hierarchy (44) of access to objecthood. Further, this operation in English is characteristic of a relatively small group of verbs whose non-patient object ('indirect object') is dative-benefactive, i.e. verbs such as:

(50) 'give', 'bring', 'send', 'tell', 'show', 'teach', 'do favor'

Typical examples are:

(51) Do *me* a favor
      Show *him* the door
      Tell *her* a story
      Teach *them* a lesson
      Bring *us* some tea
      Send *him* a note
      Give *her* a book

In a text-study of two-object clauses containing such verbs (Givón, 1982a), their dative-benefactive objects were "promoted" to DO *84 percent* of the time, while only *16 percent* appeared as IO, with either 'to' or 'for' marking their semantic case-role. The study also included verbs with patient objects and an *optional* benefactive argument (cf. Chapter 4, section 4.4.1.) These are examples such as:

(52) Cut *me* some meat
      Write *me* a song
      Schedule *us* an appointment
      etc.

In contrast with dative and/or benefactive objects, semantically *locative* objects appeared *100 percent* in the text as *indirect* objects. The data thus serves to validate the first segment of our hierarchy (44), showing the DAT/BEN object in English to have a much stronger claim on the DO slot than the locative object.

   Limiting "promotion" to DO to mostly DAT/BEN objects serves an important function of making the semantic role of the non-patient "promoted" DO reasonably transparent. By promotion to DO, objects in English lose their semantic case-role marking. The DAT and/or BEN participants are semantically — inherently — maximally differentiated from the prototypical patient. They are typically *human, conscious, involved*; while the patient is typically *inanimate, unconscious, uninvolved*. Thus, sentences such as those in (51) and (52) above, in spite of lack of *morphological* distinction between the two objects (both unmarked and thus seemingly 'direct'), allow consistent role-disambiguation of the object by two pocesses:

(a) Maximal semantic differentiation; and

(b) Fairly rigid word-order, which dictates that a "promoted" DAT/ BEN object should always precede the semantic patient.

On the other hand, the LOC or INSTR objects, both semantically inanimate, do not get promoted to DO in English, but retain their semantic case markers.

That such an explanation is useful may be supported by the fact that when the patient argument is itself human, the acceptability of promoting an optional benefactive to DO decreases dramatically, presumably because of an increase in potential ambiguity of semantic roles. Thus consider:

(53) a. *Tell *me* someone a story   (vs. Tell someone a story *for me*)
      b. *See *me* Mary   (vs. See Mary *for me*)
      c. *Write *me* Joe   (vs. Write Joe *for me*)
      d. *Write *me* Joe a letter   (vs. Write Joe a letter *for me*)
      e. *Send *me* Mary a letter   (vs. Send Mary a letter *for me*)
      f. *Show *me* Joe the house   (vs. Show Joe the house *for me*)
      g. *Give *me* Mary a kiss   (vs. Give Mary a kiss *for me*)
      h. *Kiss *me* Mary   (vs. Kiss Mary *for me*)

In each case in (53), a human-dative object is present in addition to the "promoted" benefactive. In each case potential role confusion blocks the "promotion" of the BEN-object to DO. The English system of promoting DAT/BEN objects to DO without added morphological provisions for disambiguating semantic case-roles is thus of necessity a rather restricted instrument.

5.5.4.4. Obligatory promotion of DAT/BEN objects: Ute, Bantu, Tsotsil

In languages displaying this type of promotion to DO, only DAT/BEN objects can undergo this process, as in English. Such languages thus once again validate our hierarchy of access to objecthood (44). In this group, however, DAT/BEN must obligatorily appear as DO's. In Relational Grammar terms they are thus "obligatorily promoted".[61] As we have seen above, in English this state of affairs is clearly manifested at the *text frequency* level, where 84 percent of all DAT/BEN objects appear as DO's.

While English makes no provision for clear coding of the semantic role of the DAT/BEN object when it occupies the DO position, languages in this group do. They achieve such coding by a combination of means:

---

61) The reference to "obligatory promotion" is somewhat nonsensical, since there is no evidence for the "underlying" indirect/prepositional object status of the DAT/BEN object prior to that "obligatory promotion".

(a)   The use of *word-order*, as seen in all types above, via which the pro-
      moted DO appears before all other objects, including the semantic
      patient;

(b)   But in addition the verb itself carries a morpheme indicating that
      the direct object is semantically dative-benefactive.

As an example of this type, consider the following sentences from Ute. In
this language, the word-order device by itself (cf. Hebrew, Sherpa) is used for
topical indirect objects further down the hierarchy. Thus consider:[62]

(54) a. 'áapa-ci   'u   tṵkúa-vi   'urú   wií-ci-m
        boy-SUBJ   the-SUBJ   meat-OBJ   the-OBJ   knife-with
        cikávi'na-pṵgá
        cut-REMOTE
        'The boy cut the meat with a knife'   (meat = topic)

     b. 'áapa-ci   'u   wií-ci-m   'urú   tṵkúa-vi
        boy-SUBJ   the-SUBJ   knife-with   the-OBJ   meat-OBJ
        cikávi'na-pṵgá
        cut-REMOTE
        'The boy used the knife to cut meat'   (knife = topic)

A small group of verbs take an obligatory dative object, such as 'give', 'tell' or
'show', and such dative objects are morphologically unmarked, appearing as
direct objects *without* further marking on the verb. However, they may exhibit
the same word-order variation as in (54) above. Thus consider:

(55) a. mamá-ci   'u   'áapa-ci   'uwáy   pṵsáriniya-pṵ
        woman-SUBJ   the-SUBJ   boy-OBJ   the-OBJ story-OBJ
        máy-pṵgá
        tell-REMOTE
        'The woman told the boy a story'   (topic = boy)

     b. mamá-ci   'u   pṵsáriniya-pṵ 'urú   'áapa-ci
        woman-SUBJ   the-SUBJ   story-OBJ   the-OBJ boy-OBJ
        máy-pṵgá
        tell-REMOTE
        'The woman told the story to the boy'   (topic = story)

---

62) From Givón (1980a). The subject in Ute is marked by a *silenced* (devoiced) final vowel, most
commonly the last noun-suffix vowel. The direct object is thus marked *in contrast* by a fully voiced
final vowel.

Finally, optional benefactive objects, those which are not involved in defining
the meaning of the verb, must obligatorily appear as DO's, with the verb taking the BEN suffix -ku̧-, as in:

(56) a. 'áapací   'u   sivá̧a̧tu-ci 'uwáy   pax̂á-pu̧gá
        boy-SUBJ the-SUBJ goat-OBJ   the-OBJ kill-REMOTE
        'The boy killed the goat'

b. 'áapací   'u   mamá-ci   'uwáy   sivá̧a̧tu-ci
   boy-SUBJ the-SUBJ woman-OBJ the-OBJ goat-OBJ
   'uwáy   pax̂á-ku̧-pu̧gá
   the-OBJ kill-BEN-REMOTE
   'The boy killed the goat for the woman'

In cases such as (56), the benefactive DO must appear as the *first* object, and
does not allow word-order flexibility.

The Ute system described above is shared by Bemba (Core-Bantu, SVO)
and Tsotsil (Mayan, VSO).[63] It is in essence a three-tier system in terms of
coping with the functional dilemma of objectization (cf. (43) above):

(a)   The word-order strategy, as in Hebrew or Sherpa, is used for in-
      direct objects lower on the hierarchy (44) than DAT/BEN;

(b)   The limited promotion strategy, as in English, is confined to verbs
      whose obligatory DAT/BEN objects can be assigned their seman-
      tic role via the meaning of the verb; and

(c)   The obligatory promotion of optional BEN objects is used, to-
      gether with the verb-coding of the promoted optional benefactive
      object, for all other verbs.

5.5.4.5. Extended promotion via verb-coding: KinyaRwanda

KinyaRwanda, a Lake-Bantu language, represents probably the most
extensive use of the above verb-coding strategy to widen the range of object
types that may be made into direct object. As in Ute, Bemba or Tsotsil, the
objectization of benefactive objects is obligatory. But inanimate indirect objects much lower on the topic hierarchy may also be "promoted" to DO, each
with its specific verb suffix. Thus consider:[64]

---

63) See further details on Bemba (core-Bantu) and Tsotsil (Mayan) in Givón (1981a). The Tsotsil data there are originally from Aissen (1978, 1979). Within core-Bantu, a few languages (see
KinyaRwanda, below) show a more expanded promotional system.

64) The data is originally from Kimenyi (1976).

(57) a. *PAT-topic*: umugore y-ooher-eje   umubooyi **ku**-isoko
                        woman   she-sent-ASP cook   *to*-market
                        'The woman sent the cook to the market'
      b. *LOC-topic*: umugore y-ooher-eje-**ho**   isoko   umubooyi
                        woman   she-sent-ASP-LOC market cook
                        'The woman sent to the market the cook'
      c. *PAT-topic*: umualimu a-ra-andika   ibaruwa **n**-karamu
                        teacher   he-ASP-write letter   *with*-pen
                        'The teacher wrote the letter with a pen'
      d. *INSTR-topic*: umualimu a-ra-andik-**iishya** ikaramu ibaruwa
                        teacher he-ASP-write-INSTR pen   letter
                        'The teacher used the pen to write a letter'
      e. *PAT-topic*: Mariya y-a-tets-e   inkoko **n**-agahiinda
                        Mary   she-PAST-cook-ASP chicken *with*-sorrow
                        'Mary cooked the chicken with regret'
      f. *MANN-topic*: Mariya y-a-tek-**an**-ye   agahiinda
                        Mary   she-PAST-cook-MANN-ASP sorrow
                        inkoko
                        chicken
                        'Mary regretfully cooked the chicken'
      g. *PAT-topic*: Mariya y-a-tets-e   inkoko **ni**-Yohani
                        Mary   she-PAST-cook-ASP chicken *with*-John
                        'Mary cooked the chicken with John'
      h. *ASSOC-topic*: Mariya y-a-tek-**an**-ye   Yohani
                        Mary   she-PAST-cook-ASSOC-ASP John
                        inkoko
                        chicken
                        'Mary cooked with John a chicken'
      i. *PAT-topic*: Karooli y-a-fash-ije   abaantu **ku**-busa
                        Charles he-PAST-help-ASP people *for*-nothing
                        'Charles helped the people for nothing'
      j. *PURP-topic*: Karooli y-a-fash-**ir**-ije   ubusa abaantu
                        Charles he-PAST-help-BEN-ASP nothing people
                        'Charles for nothing helped people'

While KinyaRwanda is, to my knowledge, the most extreme in extending the
use of the verb-coding strategy and thus allowing a wider range of promotion
to DO, beyond the DAT/BEN object, other languages have gone a smaller
distance in the same direction. Thus, for example, in Indonesian the verb suf-

fix -*i*- is similarly used in the promotion (optional) of dative-recipient and locative-goal objects to DO, while the suffix -*kan*- is used in the promotion (optional) of benefactives, instrumentals and object genitives.[65]

5.5.4.6. The serial-verb sources of object case-marking

In the preceding sections we have surveyed various approaches languages may take in solving the functional dilemma of objectization (43). Another possible case-marking type involves the use of serial verbs as semantic case-markers for objects. This case-marking system is based on a fact already discussed in Chapter 4, above, namely that verb-object combinations are often highly *specific* semantically, so that one may read the case-role of a noun off the meaning of its governing verb. In such a system, with the agent/subject excluded, each verb in the series serves implicitly as the semantic case-role marker of an adjacent noun. As an example consider the following from various Niger-Congo languages:[66]

(58) a. *Patient*: ìywi **awá** utsì ikù   (Yatye)
          boy *took* door shut
          'The boy shut the door'

      b. *Instrumental*: mo **fi** àdé   gé nākằ   (Yoruba)
          I   *took* machete cut wood
          'I cut wood **with** the machete'

      c. *Dative*: mo sọ   **fún** ọ   (Yoruba)
          I   said *give* you
          'I said **to** you'

      d. *Benefactive*: nám útom ẹ́mì **nì** mì   (Efik)
          do   work this *give* me
          'Do this work **for** me'

---

65) See Chung (1975, 1976a) as well as P. Hopper and J. Verhaar (in personal communication).

66) From Givón (1975a), where an extensive survey of the literature may be found. This case-marking type is endemic in Benue-Congo and other Niger-Congo branches. It is also found in the South-East-Asia basin (Mandarin, cf. Li and Thompson, 1973, 1975; Mon-Khmer, Thai and others, see Goral, forthcoming). Diachronically, serial-verbs of this type tend to cliticize, over time, on the nouns whose case-role they indicate, thus becoming bound case morphology (Givón, 1975a, 1979b). In many languages this system of generating case-markers is confined to the locative cases, as in Ute (Givón, 1980a, 1979b) or Bikol (Austronesian, from my own field notes). Occasionally, due to certain word-orders, case-marking verbs cliticize on the main verb rather than on the noun whose semantic function they code. This is presumably one diachronic source of verb-coding case morphology. Such a process is fairly extensive in Hindi (Hook, 1974; the interpretation is my own).

e. *Locative*: Ọ́ gbàrà ọ́sọ́ **gáa** áhyà   (Igbo)
        he ran   *go* market
        'He ran **to** the market'

f. *Comparative*: abakashi ba-boomba **uku-cila** abaana (Bemba)
        women   they-work *to-exceed* children
        'Women work **more than** children'

g. *Manner*: mo **fi** ọgbọ̀n   gé igi   (Yoruba)
        I   *took* cleverness cut tree
        'I clever-**ly** cut the tree'

5.5.4.7. The nominal-genitive source of object case-marking

Another common source for object case-marking, most prevalent in the diachronic rise of *locative* case morphology, is complex genitive-nominal expressions. When genitive modifiers follow the head noun, as is common in VO languages (see Chapter 6, below), one tends to obtain *prepositional* markers via this type of reanalysis, whereby the erstwhile head noun becomes the case-marker. As an example consider the following from Bemba (Bantu):[67]

(59)   independent noun source   complex locative construction

      i-saamba 'bottom'   pa-**i-saamba** lya-ngaanda
                         at-*bottom*   of-house
                         '**under** the house'

      umu-ulu   'sky'   pa-**mu-ulu** wa-ngaanda
                         at-*sky*   of-house
                         '**on top of** the house'

      aka-ti   'center'   pa-**ka-ti** ka-ngaanda
                         at-*center* of-house
                         '**in the middle of** the house'

      in-taanshi 'face'   ku-**n-taanshi** ya-ngaanda
                         at-*face*   of-house
                         '**in front of** the house'

      in-numa   'back'   ku-**n-numa** ya-ngaanda
                         at-*back*   of-house
                         '**behind** the house'

      in-shi   'ground'   ku-**n-shi** ya-ngaanda
                         at-*ground* of-house
                         '**under** the house'

---

67) See Givón (1972, 1979b). The same process has been going on in English.

in-se   'outside'   pa-**n-se**   ya-ngaanda
                                  at-*outside* of-house
                                  '**out of** the house'
    im-bali   'shade'   ku-**m-bali** ya-ngaanda
                                  at-*shade*   of-house
                                  '**on the other side of** the house'

In OV languages, where genitive modifiers most commonly precede the head noun (see Chapter 6, below), similar constructions give rise to *postpositional* locative case-markers. Thus consider the following from Kru (Niger-Congo):[68]

(60) a. sra   **kpō**   'on top of the house'
          house *top*
      b. tu-na **sonti**   'under the tree'
          tree-the *base*
      c. sra   **ju**   'in front of the house'
          house *front*
      d. sra   **wakaey**   'near the house'
          house *side*
      e. sra   **bweti**   'under the house'
          house *bottom*
      f. blokūn **kli**   'inside the box'
          box   *cavity*
      g. sra   **de**   'behind the house'
          house *back*

5.5.5. Further typological issues in objectization

5.5.5.1. Marked vs. unmarked accusatives (patients)

As we have seen above, in some languages (Hebrew, Sherpa) the direct-object pragmatic case is coded only by word-order, without morphology (which thus remains a semantically-oriented coding device). When one surveys the languages in which there is a morphologically distinct DO case, into which various non-patient objects may then be promoted and in the process lose their semantic case-role markers, the following correlation seems to emerge:

---

68) See Givón (1975a, 1979b). A similar process may be found in Tibetan languages.

(61) *Correlation between unmarked accusative and DO case*:
"The great majority[69] of languages with a morphologically distinct DO case are those in which the accusative (patient) case — which becomes the DO case — is *morphologically unmarked*".

This correlation would thus group English, Bemba, Indonesian, Kinya-Rwanda and Tsotsil as those that (a) promote IO to DO and (b) have an unmarked accusative. Ute is technically an exception to this rule, since the accusative/DO is marked, albeit only by the voicing of a devoiced but extant vowel.[70] And Nez Perce (see fn. 69), is a glaring exception. On the other hand, languages such as Sherpa, Hebrew or Japanese, with a morphologically-marked accusative, do not engage in the same type of promotion to DO.

If correlation (61) indeed proves to be sound, one may offer the following explanation for its existence:

(a) The functional dilemma in promoting non-patient objects to the DO position (cf. (43)) was how to preserve some *structural/coding* indication of their semantic case-role.

(b) By losing their original semantic case-role markers to become DO, non-patient objects increase their probability of being semantically misinterpreted.

(c) If on top of that they would also acquire a *marked* case morphology that is initially characteristic of the semantic *patient*, the probability of processing confusion is increased.

(d) Finally, even when the DO takes the form of the *unmarked* accusative case, stringent provisions are made, via (i) limiting the promotion to DAT/BEN objects (as in English, Bemba, Tsotsil, Ute) and/or (ii) by providing an auxiliary system of *verb-coding* the semantic function of non-patient DO's (Bemba, Ute, Tsotsil, Indonesian, KinyaRwanda, Nez Perce), in order to preserve their semantic case-role.

---

69) The only exception I am aware of thus far is Nez Perce (Rude, 1982, 1983), in which the accusative/DO case is marked by suffix but an extensive promotion-to-DO system, with verb suffixes coding the semantic case-roles of the various non-patient objects, does exist.

70) There are reasons to believe that silenced vowels in Ute are still considered "present", at least by older speakers (see Givón, 1980a, Ch. 1).

5.5.5.2. Why the accusative is the least-marked object case

The fact that the patient/accusative is the object case *most likely* to appear morphologically unmarked still demands explanation. Why is it that in all languages it — rather than the pragmatically higher on the topic hierarchy DAT/BEN object — consistently displays a higher potential for becoming the pragmatic DO case (just as the *agent* consistently displays a higher probability of becoming the *subject* case)? A number of factors seem to combine in making this status of the accusative in some sense natural.

(a)   *Semantic predictability from the verb*

The patient is the argument/participant "most affected by the event" or "displaying the most salient change". It is thus semantically most intimately bound up with the meaning of the verb, and its role in the event is thus easiest to predict from the semantics of the verb. Obligatory dative, benefactive or locative objects have a progressively more *abstract*, less predictable relation to the verb. And optional participants such as instrumental, associative, manner or purpose are more abstract yet and less predictable. In terms of the need for *explicit semantic-role* marking, object arguments are thus ranked:

(62)   INSTR/ASSOC/PURP/MANN > DAT/BEN/LOC > PAT

(b)   *Text frequency of patient objects*

The accusative/patient object is the most frequent non-subject argument in text. In text counts of English fiction, *64 percent* of all non-subject arguments are patient-objects.[71] Thus, in actual speech production the *secondary topic* — after the subject, which is primary — is most likely to be the *patient*. Re-interpretation of the semantic case-marking "accusative" as a pragmatic case-marking "direct-object" is the *least costly* inferential extension from semantic to pragmatic case that speakers are likely to make. (In the same vein, reinterpreting the morphological *agent* case-marker as a *subject* case-marker, at least for transitive clauses, is of a similarly high probability).

5.6. CASE MARKING VS. CASE DIFFERENTIATION

As noted in Chapter 4, section 4.2.9.3. above, nominal objects of manipulative verbs ('tell', 'order', 'force', 'make', 'ask', 'prevent' etc.) have a double role. Vis-à-vis the complement verb they are *agents*. Vis-à-vis the manipulative main verb they are *datives*. In terms of morphological marking, they

---

71) For the text counts and further discussion, see Givón (1981a).

often appear as *direct objects*, i.e. they show the case-marking most often characteristic of the semantic *patient*. Case marking systems, however, are not made to explicitly mark *every* argument, but rather — ideally — to maximally *differentiate* between arguments in actual sentential contexts. By leaving one of two opposites in a contrast *unmarked*, the system achieves just as much — and possibly even greater — differentiation, at a greater *economy*.[72] Thus, consider the two senses of 'tell' below:

(63) a. Mary told *John* a story   (Mary told the story *to John*)
      b. Mary told *John* to do the dishes (*Mary told *to John* to do the dishes)

In (63a) there are two nominal objects, and the option of marking the dative explicitly (with *to*) is open. In (63b), there is only one nominal object, the dative. It is structurally quite dissimilar to the sentential complement, and thus receives DO coding.

Consider next the contrast between human and inanimate accusatives in the following examples:

(64) a. They gave *John* a book
      b. They gave the book *to John*
      c. ? They gave *John* Mary
      d. They gave Mary *to John*

While (64a), where the dative differs from the patient in animacy and referentiality is acceptable, (64c) where no such differentiation exists is odd, and (64d) thus preferred.

A more general illustration of this principle is the tendency, in many languages, for both subjects and DO's to go morphologically unmarked. Since their position vis-à-vis the verb — i.e. word-order — is by itself a powerful case-marking device (see Chapter 6, below), it is more likely that only more oblique arguments — appearing less frequently in text — will require more explicit markings (see also section 5.5.5.2., above).[73]

---

72) The gestalt of marked/unmarked and figure/ground is probably the single most powerful explanatory principle in interpreting the facts of language as both a cognitive map and a communicative coding system.

73) For an earlier, and perhaps a bit simplistic discussion of these possibilities, in the context of trying to explain word-order change, see Vennemann (1973a).

Next, we have noted earlier that in Ergative languages the absolutive case is most commonly morphologically *unmarked*, while the subject-of-transitive role is most commonly marked. This may be viewed as one more instance of *case differentiation*, whereby clauses with a single argument display that argument as unmarked ('absolutive'), while when a second argument — the agent — is added, it must receive explicit marking.

Finally, we have noted in Chapter 4, above (section 4.2.5.2.) that certain verbs whose objects are *semantically* locative, recipient or associative — all three being object types that most commonly appear *marked* — may take those objects as surface DO's. Thus recall:

(65) a. He approached the house   (*to* the house)
      b. He left the house   (*from* the house)
      c. He fed the cows   (*to* the cows)
      d. He robbed the beggar   (*from* the beggar)
      e. She fought him   (*with* him)

There are two reasons why such direct objects are a likely phenomenon:

(a)   There are no other objects requiring differentiation in such expressions; and

(b)   The semantic role of the object is substantially predictable from the meaning of the verb.

Such considerations underscore the fact that overt, morphological case-marking is not an automatic feature of case-coding systems. Rather, it is used economically and with discrimination, when role differentiation is required and when the semantics of the verb is not enough to predict the semantic role of nominal participants.[74]

---

74) For further discussion of case-marking from the perspective of *relative* differentiation (as against *absolute* marking), see Wierzbicka (1981).

6 | WORD-ORDER TYPOLOGY

6.1. INTRODUCTION

In the preceding chapter we discussed the grammatical coding of case-roles, both semantic and pragmatic, primarily in reference to the use of bound morphology. In this chapter we will deal with the use of the other major coding device, word-order, in fulfilling the same general function. The discussion will center, at least initially, on the use of word-order in coding case-roles in simple clauses (main, declarative, affirmative, active). Still, there are several points where we must proceed beyond the syntax of simple clauses — and discuss various facets of the grammar not yet sketched out in detail here — in order to present a more comprehensive view of word-order. Such areas will involve the syntax of **noun phrases** (see Chapter 12, Volume II), the syntax of **subordinate clauses** (see Chapters 13, 16 and 21, Volume II) and the typology of bound morphemes.

There are several ways in which languages use word-order in syntax, and we will concentrate here, at least initially, on what has been traditionally called the **semantic** or **grammatical** use of word-order, to distinguish by relative position between the three most common elements in verbal clauses:

(a) The verb
(b) The subject
(c) The direct object

Calling this use "semantic" is probably misleading, since the categories "subject" and "direct object", as we have seen in Chapter 5, above, are in large measure pragmatic. This is true more for "subject" than for "direct object", which tends to correspond more closely to the semantic category "patient". The term **grammatical** word-order, though more neutral, carries little indication of the actual function performed. However, it suggests **grammaticalization**, which is broadly what happens to the notion "topic" when it becomes a structural category such as "subject" or "direct object".[1]

Two other uses of word-order in syntax are pragmatically based, and display some potential for grammaticalization:

(a)   Its use in the grammar of topic continuity
(b)   Its use in the grammar of contrast and emphasis

The two are in fact related, and will be dealt with in some detail in chapers 17, 18 and 22, Volume II. However, some mention of them must be made in later sections of this chapter, particularly with respect to word-order flexibility.

The reason why word-order tends to be a device for signaling the case-role of only *two* participants — subject and object — is because it is a limited instrument, employing the relative position of nominals *before* or *after* the verb as the critical perceptual clue.[2] As we have observed in Chapters 4 and 5 above, arguments beyond the direct object (or patient) tend to be morphologically marked, and this persistent fact is by itself an indirect corroboration of the limits of coding by relative position vis-à-vis the verb.

6.2. DEGREE OF RIGIDITY OF WORD-ORDER

As we shall see later, word-order flexibility ('variation') is used in most languages, at least to some extent, to code pragmatic distinctions such as topic-comment, definite-indefinite, emphatic-neutral, etc. But individual languages vary enormously as to the *degree* to which they employ such flexibility. Languages that use it more extensively are usually called **flexible-order languages**. Those that use it sparingly are called, by contrast, **rigid-order languages**. But the distinction is obviously artificial, since we are dealing with a fine *gradient*. The underlying factors controlling this gradient will be discussed in Chapter 22, Volume II.

6.3. CONSISTENCY AND "PURITY" OF RIGID WORD-ORDER TYPES

There is a certain legitimate tradition in making predictions from the rigid word-order type in simple clauses (i.e. the relative ordering of verb, subject, object) as to a number of *dependent* ('derived') parameters in word-order. These dependent parameters are presumably:

---

1) For a discussion of subjects as grammaticalized topics see Givón (1976b and 1979a, Ch. 5).

2) For some psycholinguistic evidence concerning the limitation of using word-order to code the case-roles of nouns, see Fodor and Garrett (1967).

(a)   Basic word-order in **complex clauses**
(b)   The order of nouns vs. modifiers in **noun phrases**
(c)   The morphotactics of prefixes or suffixes in **bound morphology**

If a language has not undergone word-order change within the last two to three thousand years of its history[3], it is expected to be "topologically consistent" in the way these dependent variables agree with the independent variable of basic word-order of **simple clauses**. The major typological predictions that may be made with respect to these three dependencies are summarized below, following Greenberg's pioneering work:[4]

(1)   a. Word-order in complex clauses should be the same as in simple clauses.
       b. If a language has the order OBJECT-VERB (OV) in its simple clauses, it should have the order MODIFIER-NOUN (M-N) in its noun phrases. While if it has the order VERB-OBJECT (VO) in simple clauses, it should have the order NOUN-MODIFIER (N-M) in noun phrases.
       c. If a language has the order OBJECT-VERB (OV) in its simple clauses, it should have a predominantly **suffixal** morphology. While if it has the order VERB-OBJECT (VO) in its simple clauses, it should have a predominantly **prefixal** morphology.

There are two issues that must be mentioned concerning the predictions in (1) above. First, we must note that typological consistency of languages is governed primarily by *diachronic change* (see fn. 3). So the common intervention of syntactic change, particularly of word-order change, creates many "inconsistent" languages. And second, that the "typological consistency" of the idealized sort expressed in (1) above is rarely perfect even without the intervention of major word-order change. It is only a probabilistic approximation. Thus, within a language that has not changed its basic word-order type in any

---

3) Contrary to Lehmann (1973) and Hawkins (1980), I will assume here that languages don't change their dependent variables to "fit" the word-order of simple clauses via a simple process of analogy. Rather, complex diachronic processes controlled by many independent factors are involved in imposing — over a long time span — a modicum of "typological consistency" within a language. The figure of two to three thousand years is a conservative guess, although we know frozen dependent features of an older typological state to persist longer (cf. Li and Thompson's (1973) discussion of word-order change in Mandarin Chinese). For further discussion see Givón (1971a, 1975a, 1979b).

4) Greenberg (1966).

way, specific instances of the rise of syntactic constructions and bound morphologies may occur in a perfectly natural way that would nevertheless be inconsistent with the predictions made in (1). We will deal with some of these
issues further below.

6.4.   RIGID WORD-ORDER TYPES

6.4.1. The basic word-order in simple clauses

6.4.1.1. The subject-verb-object (SVO) word-order: English

English is one of the most consistent and rigid SVO languages, so far as
word-order in its simple clauses is concerned. It does have a number of variant
orders, such as in L-dislocation, R-dislocation or Y-movement (see Chapter
18, Volume II), questions (Chapter 20, volume II) or focus constructions
(Chapter 17, Volume II). But these are marked, complex clauses. Thus consider:

(2)   a. The man hit *the ball*   (direct object)
      b. The man went *to the store*   (indirect object)
      c. The woman knew *that her house was on fire*   (sentential com-
          plement)
      d. The woman wanted *to leave*   (sentential complement)
      e. The woman told the man *to leave*   (sentential complement)
      f. The man was *tall*   (adjectival predicate)
      g. The man was *a teacher*   (nominal predicate)

We have already discussed the flexibility shown in **dative shifting** (see
Chapter 5, above) in the relative positions of direct and indirect object, as in:

(3)   a. Mary gave the book to John
      b. Mary gave John a book

An *existential-presentative* fronting of locatives, precipitating a VS word-
order, is also possible in English (see further discussion in Chapter 19, Volume II):[5]

(4)   a. And *there* came Bronson (OVS)
      b. *Under the bridge* stood a dilapidated shack (OVS)
      c. Once upon a time, *in a distant land, there* lived a king... (OVS)

A verb-subject "inverse" (VS) word-order is also found in yes/no questions

---

5) See also Hetzron (1971), Gary (1974) and Givón (1976b, 1976c) for further discussion.

(Chapter 20, Volume II), as in:

(5)   a. *Did* he do it?
      b. *Can* she leave?
      c. *Was* he there?

Object fronting — thus OSV order — is possible in English in a number of complex clauses:

(6)   a. *Whom* did you see? (WH-question; cf. Chapter 20, Volume II)
      b. It was *Bill* that I saw (cleft-focus; cf. Chapter 17, Volume II)
      c. Potatoes I like (Y-movement; Cf. Chapter 18, Volume II)
      d. *Bill*, I saw him yesterday (L-dislocation; cf. Chapter 18, Volume II)

Finally, moving the subject to the end of the clause — thus VOS order — is also a possible complex pattern:

(7)   He saw me, Bill   (R-dislocation; cf. Chapter 18, Volume II)

The use of these various *marked* word-orders in complex clauses of roughly similar functions and structures is fairly typical in rigid SVO languages.

6.4.1.2. The subject-object-verb (SOV) word-order: Sherpa

Sherpa, a Tibetan language (Sino-Tibetan) from Nepal is a rigid SOV language. As examples of word-order in simple clauses consider:[6]

(8)   a. ti 'ang-di   tu'pe no   (adjectival predicate)
         the baby-DEF small be
         'The baby is small'

      b. ti mi-ti   dyeken yin   (nominal predicate)
         the man-DEF teacher be
         'The man is a teacher'

      c. ti mi-ti-gi   laĝa kyaa-sung   (direct object)
         the man-DEF-ERG work do-PERF
         'The man did work'

      d. ti mi-ti-gi   cenyi caaq-sung   (direct object)
         the man-DEF-ERG cup   break-PERF
         'The man broke the cup'

6) All the Sherpa examples are from my own field notes and originally due to Koncchok J. Lama (in personal communication).

    e. ŋaa   yambur-la   gal-yin   (indirect object)
       I(ABS) Katmandu-LOC go-PERF
       'I went to Katmandu'

    f. sentential complement:
       ti   mi-ti   laĝa ki-tup no-(u)p kyaa-sung
       the man-DEF workdo-INF want-INF do-PERF
       'The man wanted to work'

More complex sentential complements in Sherpa, as well as in many other (though not all[7]) rigid SOV languages, may either precede or follow the main verb. Thus consider:

  (9)   a. SO-COMP-V:
         ti-gi   pumpetsa-la derma tu   si-kyaa-sung
         he-ERG woman-DAT dishes wash-IMP tell-AUX-PERF
         'He told the woman to wash the dishes'

      b. SOV-COMP:
         ti-gi   pumpetsa-la si-kyaa-sung   derma tu
         he-ERG woman-DAT tell-AUX-PERF dishes wash-IMP
         'He told the woman to wash the dishes'

      c. SO-COMP-V:
         ti-gi   pumpetsa-la ŋyee-acu shi-sung   si-kyaa-sung
         he-ERG woman-DAT my-brother die-PERF tell-AUX-PERF
         'He told the woman that his/my brother died'

      d. SOV-COMP:
         ti-gi   pumpetsa-la si-kyaa-sung   ŋyee-acu shi-sung
         he-ERG woman-DAT tell-AUX-PERF my-brother die-PERF
         'He told the woman that his/my brother died'

As we have seen in Chapter 5, above, order-variation of the dative-shifting type is possible in Sherpa, as in:

  (10) a. DAT-ACC word order:
         ti mi-ti-gi   pumpetsa-la kitab-yi   biin-sung
         the man-DEF-ERG woman-DAT book-ACC give-PERF
         'The man gave the woman a book'

---

7) At least some New Guinea Highland SOV languages, such as Chuave (Thurman, 1978), do not allow these 'large' V-complements to follow the main verb. But otherwise, the post-verbal position — at least optional — of such complements is very common in rigid SOV languages, presumably for reasons of processing simplification.

b. ACC-DAT word-order:

ti mi-ti-gi kitab-yi pumpetsa-la biin-sung
the man-DEF-ERG book-ACC woman-DAT give-PERF
'The man gave a book to the woman'

Preposing objects is a rather limited process in Sherpa, probably limited to the functional equivalent of L-dislocation ('topic switching'), as in:

(11) a. khyoro ŋye-khamba łaa-sung (SOV; simple clause)
you-ERG my-house visit-PERF
'You visited my house'

b. ŋye-khamba khyoro łaa-sung (OSV; L-dislocation)
my-house you-ERG visit-PERF
'As for my house, you visited it'

Less rigid SOV languages, such as Japanese, presumably allow preposing an object even for Y-movement ('contrastive topicalization').[8]
Finally, Sherpa displays a movement rule in WH-questions by which the WH-pronoun, regardless of its grammatical role, is placed *directly before* the verb. Thus consider:

(12) a. ŋaa yambur-la gaal-sung (SOV; simple clause)
I(ABS) Katmandu-LOC go-PERF
'I went to Katmandu'

b. yambur-la **su** gaal-sung? (OSV; subject-WH-
Katmandu-LOC *who* go-PERF question)
'**Who** went to Katmandu?'

There are reasons for believing that such placement of WH-pronouns is typical only of SOV languages, though certainly not of all SOV languages.[9]

6.4.1.3. The verb-subject-object (VSO) word-order: Jacaltec
Jacaltec (Mayan) is a fairly rigid VSO language in its simple clauses. Thus consider:[10]

(13) a. xa' ix te' hum wet an (direct and
gave CL-she CL-the book to-me pl indirect objects)
'She gave the book to me'

8) See Kuno (1981).

9) The same was described for Kartvelian (Caucasian) languages in Harris (1983), but see also discussion in Comrie (1983).

10) All the Jacaltec examples here are from Craig (1977).

b. xahtoj naj   yibañ no'   cheh   (indirect object)
   go-up   CL-he on   CL-the horse
   'He climbed on the horse'

c. smak naj   ix   (direct object)
   hit   CL-he CL-her
   'He hit her'

d. sonlom   naj   (nominal predicate)
   marimba-player CL-he
   'He is a marimba player'

e. caw ay ka'   (equivalent of
   very be heat   adjectival predicate)
   'It is very hot'

f. ay no' hin txitam   (existential-possessive)
   be CL my pig
   'I have a pig' (*lit.*: 'My pig exists')

g. c'ul   ye ix   (adjectival predicate)
   good be CL-she
   'She is fine'

Sentences (13e) and (13g), with the predicate *preceding* the copula 'be', are less typical of VSO languages. The copula *ay* is most commonly in the initial position and is thus more typical, as in (13f) above or in:

(14) ay mac xa-x'apani   (existential)
      be who already-arrived
      'There's someone who's already arrived'

And in other VSO languages the verb 'be', at least in its locative sense, is sentence initial, as in the following from Nandi (Nilotic):[11]

(15) mî:téy kípe:t kerîcho
      he-be Kipes Kericho
      'Kibet is in Kericho'

The basic VSO order is maintained when the objects/complements are sentential, as in the following (again from Jacaltec):

---

11) From Creider (1975, 1976).

(16) a. s-kan   hin-c'ul   Ø-w-il-a'   naj
        E3-want   my-stomach   A3-E1-see-FUT   CL-him
        'I would like to see him' (*lit*.: 'My stomach wants to see him')

     b. x-Ø-y-iptze   ix   xo'   Ø-s-tx'ah-a'   xil
        ASP-A3-E3-force   CL-she   CL-her   A3-E3-wash-FUT   Cl-the
        kape
        clothes
        'She forced her to wash the clothes'

     c. xal   hin-mam   an   **chubil**   xcam   no'   cheh
        said   my-father   pl   *that*   died   CL-the   horse
        'My father said that the horse died'

The use of word-order variants in complex clauses of various kinds is widespread in Jacaltec. Thus consider the fronting of constituents in cleft-focus constructions:

(17) a. smak naj   ix   (neutral)
        hit   CL-he   CL-her
        'He hit her'

     b. ha'   naj   xmak-ni   ix   (subject cleft)
        FOC   CL-he   hit-SUF   CL-her
        'It was **he** who hit her'

     c. ha'   ix   smak   naj   (object cleft)
        FOC   CL-her   hit   CL-he
        'It was **her** that he hit'

Fronting for topic-switching (L-dislocation) is also possible, as in:

(18) a. smak naj   Pel   ix   (neutral)
        hit   CL   Peter   CL-her
        'Peter hit her'

     b. naj Pel   smak naj   ix   (subject L-dislocation)
        CL Peter   hit   CL-he   CL-her
        'Peter, he hit her'

     c. ix   Malin   smak naj   ix   (object L-dislocation)
        CL   Mary   hit   CL-he   CL-her
        'Mary, Peter hit her'

Finally, fronting also occurs in forming WH-questions, as in:

(19) a. mac xwat'e-n   te' meẍa tu'   (subject WH)
        who made-SUFF CL table that
        'Who made that table?'

    b. mac chacolo'   (DO WH)
        who you-will-help
        'Whom will you help?'

    c. mac yiñ chach   to munil   (IO WH)
        who for you   go work
        'For whom are you going to work?'

6.4.1.4. The verb-object-subject (VOS) word-order: Malagasy
Malagasy (Austronesian) is a rigid VOS ('subject last') language, in terms of word-order in its simple clauses. Thus consider:[12]

(20) a. lasa ny mpianatra   (intransitive subject)
        gone the students
        'The students left'

    b. manasa lamba   Rasoa   (transitive, direct object)
        wash   clothes Rasoa
        'Rasoa is washing clothes'

    c. nanome vola   an-Rabe   aho   (transitive, two objects)
        gave   money OBJ-Rabe I
        'I gave money to Rabe'

    d. manaiky manasa ny zaza Rasoa   (V-complement)
        agree   wash   the baby Rasoa
        'Rasoa agrees to wash the baby'

    e. mampa-manasa lamba   an-Rasoa   aho   (V-complement)
        CAUSE-wash   clothes OBJ-Rasoa I
        'I made Rasoa wash clothes'

Only the loosest, sentential complement of cognition/utterance verbs may appear *following* the subject (i.e. VSO), as in:

(21) mihevitra Rabe **fa** handeha ho any Antsirabe rehampitso
     think   Rabe *that* go   FUT there Antsirabe tomorrow
     'Rabe thinks that he'll go to Antsirabe tomorrow'

12) All the Malagasy examples below are from Keenan (1976b).

Preposing subjects or objects in front of the verb is permissible in several types of complex clauses, as in L-dislocation:

(22) a. SUBJ L-dislocation:
Rasoa **dia** manasa lamba
Rasoa TOP wash clothes
'Rasoa, she's washing clothes'

b. OBJ L-dislocation:
raha io lamba io **dia** mbola manasa azy Rasoa
if that clothes that TOP still wash it Rasoa
'As for the clothes, Rasoa is still washing them'

Similarly, in cleft-focusing the focused constituent is moved before the verb, as in:

(23) a. Rasoa **no** manasa ny lamba   (subject focus)
Rasoa FOC wash the clothes
'It is **Rasoa** who is washing the clothes'

b. ny lamba **no** manasa Rasoa   (object focus)
the clothes FOC wash Rasoa
'It is **the clothes** that Rasoa is washing'

In forming WH-questions, the movement in front of the verb is optional:

(24) a. VOS neutral order:
manasa lamba **amin'inona** Rasoa?
wash clothes with-what Rasoa?
'With what is Rasoa wahing clothes?'

b. Fronted WH-focus order:
amin'ona **no** manasa lamba Rasoa
with-what FOC wash clothes Rasoa
'With **what** is Rasoa washing clothes?'

Finally, in indefinite-subject/existential constructions (see Chapter 19, Volume II), fronting of the subject vis-à-vis the main lexical verb[13] is the normal pattern:

(25) a. mitomany ny zaza   (definite SUBJ; V-S)
cry the child
'The child is crying'

---

13) One may argue that the sequence 'be-SUBJ' represents a VS word-order. However, vis-à-vis the main verb 'cry' in (25b), 'child' is in a pre-verbal position, and 'be' may be viewed as the *inflectional morphology* of such a construction.

b. misy zaza mitomany   (indefinite SUBJ; BE-S-V)
   be   child cry

$\left\{ \begin{array}{l} \text{'A child is crying'} \\ \text{'There's a child crying'} \end{array} \right\}$

6.4.1.5. The object-verb-subject (OVS) word-order

While Greenberg (1966) suggests that this is one of the theoretically possible but factually unattested *grammaticalized* word-orders, some recent reports suggest that it may be found as the 'neutral' word-order in Carib languages. Thus, consider the following from Hixkaryana:[14]

(26) a. kana yanɨmno   bɨryekomo
         fish he-caught-it boy
         'The boy caught a fish'

      b. ɨtohra   exko Waraka yakoro kelnano   rohetxe rowya
         not-going be   Waraka with   she-said-it my-wife to-me
         '"Don't go with Warake", my wife said to me'

The available reports make it reasonably clear, however, that the OVS word-order is not rigid. And a quantified *discourse* study justifying the treatment of OVS
as the *neutral* word-order in Hixkaryana has not yet been undertaken. The OVS
word-order as one of several variants was also identified for Tlingit and Haida
(Athabascan)[15], where the data strongly suggested that it was not a rigid,
grammaticalized word-order. In Ute (Uto-Aztecan)[16] the OVS word-order is
the second most frequent in discourse, after SOV. But the language has complete, pragmatically-controlled word-order freedom (see further below), so
that to call *any* word-order under such circumstances 'neutral' is less than
meaningful.

6.4.1.6. The verb-agent-patient-dative word-order variant of VSO

One may argue that in Philippine languages, which are most commonly
described as VSO, promoting a non-agent to a subject/topic position does not
change the word-order, but only the *morphology*. So that the neutral word-
order remains verb-agent-patient-dative/oblique. As an example of this

14) From Derbyshire and Pullum (1981), but see also Derbyshire (1977, 1979a, 1979b, 1981).

15) See Dryer (1982) and Eastman and Edwards (1981), respectively, for further discussion. In
both cases the authors conclude that these are flexible word-order languages with pragmatic control over the variation.

16) See Givón (1983d) for a detailed, quantified discourse study of word-order pragmatics in
Ute.

theoretical possibility consider the following from Bikol:[17]

(27) a. *agent-topic*: nag-ta'o   'ang-lakáke ning-líbro sa-babáye
                        AGT-give TOP-man   PAT-book DAT-woman
                        'The man gave a book to the woman'

      b. *patient-topic*: na-ta'ó   kang-laláke 'ang-líbro sa-babáye
                        PAT-give AGT-man   TOP-book DAT-woman
                        'The book was given to the woman by the man'

      c. *dative-topic*: na-ta'o-hán   kang-laláke ning-líbro
                        DAT-give-DAT AGT-man   PAT-book
                        'ang-babáye
                        TOP-woman
                        'The woman was given a book by the man'

There are two facts that mitigate such a description of Philippine languages. First, the relative order of the nominal arguments following the verb is relatively free, and while agent-patient-oblique is a preferred order, wide latitude is allowed. And second, it has been suggested[18] that these languages have already undergone a re-analysis toward *ergative* typology, whereby the NP marked with the erstwhile topic prefix *'ang-* is not necessarily always the main topic/subject of the clause. And finally, it can be shown that the agent even in the ergative Philippine languages is most frequently the most topical (i.e. 'main clausal topic') element in the clause.[19] Thus, the difference between VSO and V-AGT-PAT is to some extent illusory.

6.4.2. The relative order of nouns vs. modifiers in noun phrases

As suggested in section 6.3. above, a rough though by no means perfect correlation exists between the order of verb and object (VO, OV) in the simple clause and the order of noun and modifier (NM, MN, respectively) in the noun phrase. This and other typological correlations pertaining to the basic word-order have on occasion been interpreted to mean that certain "principles of harmony" prevail in language, by which a language somehow strives to be

---

17) From my own field notes, with the data originally due to Manuel Factora (in personal communication).

18) Cf. for example Egerod (1975), Payne (1982), Givón (1981b), Cooreman, Fox and Givón (1983), Fox (forthcoming), *inter alia*.

19) See Fox (forthcoming) and Cooreman, Fox and Givón (1983).

"typologically consistent".[20] A more likely explanation must hinge on the *diachronic* processes via which various noun-modifying constructions arise, and the various pathways of *analogy* through which certain features are spread from one area of the grammar into others.[21] The issues — and facts — involved in such an interpretation of word-order correlations and typological consistency are far from resolved, and referring to them at this stage of the investigation should not imply a closure.

6.4.2.1. Pre-nominal modifiers: Japanese

Japanese is a relatively rigid SOV language, displaying largely pre-nominal modifiers in its NP. It thus abides by Greenberg's (1966) prediction (1b), above. As illustrations consider:[22]

(28) a. ooki hito-wa   (adjective-noun)
        big   man-TOP
        'the big man'

     b. sono   hito-wa   (demonstrative-noun)
        that(vis.) man-TOP
        'that man'

     c. san-satsu-no   hon-o   (numeral-noun)
        three-CL-GEN   book-OBJ
        'three books'

     d. watashi-no   hon-o   (genitive/possessive-noun)
        I-GEN   book-OBJ
        'my book'

     e. kaisha-no   sacho-wa   (genitive/nominal-noun)
        company-GEN   president-TOP
        'company president'

     f. Fukuda Takeo   (surname-name)
        F.   T.
        'Takeo Fukuda'

20) See for example Vennemann (1973a), Lehmann (1973) or Hawkins (1980), *inter alia*, or along similar lines Lightfoot (1976a, 1976b).

21) See for example discussion in Givón (1971, 1975a, 1979b).

22) The Japanese examples in this section are due to Ira Plotkin (in personal communication).

g. onna-no-hito-o   mitta   hito-ga (REL clause-noun)
   female-GEN-person-OBJ   saw   person-SUBJ
   'the person who saw the woman'

6.4.2.2. Post-nominal modifiers: Hebrew

Modern Israeli Hebrew and Semitic languages in general[23] are predominantly VO languages, and have been so for at least four millenia. Hebrew is thus typologically consistent in displaying overwhelmingly post-nominal modifiers in its NP. Thus consider:[24]

(29) a. ha-ísh   ha-gadól   (noun-adjective)
      the-man the-big
      'the big man'

    b. ha-ishá   ha-zot   (noun-demonstrative)
      the-woman the-this
      'this woman'

    c. ísh exád   (noun-one)
      man one
      'one man'

    d. ha-séfer shel-í   (noun-genitive/possessive)
      the-book of-me
      'my book'

    e. ha-séfer shel-Yoséf   (noun-genitive/nominal)
      the book of-Joseph
      'Joseph's book'

---

23) Ethiopian-Semitic languages such as Amharic, Harare, Gurage, Tigrinya etc. have adopted a rigid SOV word-order due, presumably, to contact with a vast Cushitic substratum. Pre-proto Semitic may have been at some time an SOV language (Givón, 1977a), but the time lag had bleached out most word-order correlates (though not all *bound-morphology* correlates) by the time of the classical period (again excluding Akkadia, which reverted back to SOV via contact with a Sumerian substratum).

24) Most numeral modifiers as well as many quantifiers, which are diachronically head nouns of a genitival compound, synchronically precede the head noun in Hebrew, as in:
   shnéy   anasím ; ktsát   avóda
  *two-of men *edge-of work
  'two men'   'a little work'
This of course illustrates how a perfectly natural diachronic reanalysis creates, ultimately, typological inconsistencies in the synchronic grammar.

    f. bét   ha-séfer   (nominal compound)
       house-of the-book
       'school' (*lit.*: 'house of the book')

    g. Natán Yalín-Mór   (name-surname)
       N.   Y.-M.
       'Nathan Yalin-Mor'

    h. ha-séfer she-natáti le-Yoséf   (noun-RELclause)
       the-book that-gave-I to-Joseph
       'the book that I gave to Joseph'

    i. ha-dód   mi-Yrushaláyim   (noun-prepositional phrase)
       the-uncle from-Jerusalem
       'the uncle from Jerusalem'

6.4.2.3. Typological inconsistency in NP syntax

As suggested earlier, a language may be rigidly consistent in its basic word-order in simple clauses without necessarily conforming to Greenberg's (1966) prediction (1b). Overall, different modifier types tend to display different probabilities of being "inconsistent" with the basic, clausal word-order. While the data is not one hundred per cent conclusive, one may suggest the following implicational hierarchy of conformity to basic/clausal word-order:

(30)   *most likely to conform to prediction (1b)*

             nominal (compounding) modifiers
             genitive/possessive modifiers
             noun-complements
             adjectives
             relative clauses
             numerals/quantifiers
             determiners

    least likely to conform to prediction (1b)

One must keep in mind, however, that these overall probabilities do not necessarily take into account specific diachronic sources via which modifying constructions arise, and that in many cases there exists a diachronic source *both* for a pre-nominal and post-nominal position of the same modifier type. And such double sources are often independent of the OV/VO basic word-order typology. This is true, for example, for numerals (see fn. 24), for genitive/possessive modifiers (cf. Givón, 1979b) and for relative clauses (cf. Givón, 1979b). Further, a certain type of modifier often arises by analogy with another type, and several possible analogical pathways may exist for the very same modifier type. Thus, for example, adjectival modifiers in English and German have most likely arisen by analogy with the **genitival**, pre-nominal pattern. But more complex adjectival modifiers in English are almost certain to have been patterned on the post-nominal **relative-clause** mold, as in:

(31) a. a country *rich in natural resources*
      b. a pattern *consistent with past performance*

In the nominal syntax of modern English, which is a rigid SVO language in terms of basic clausal syntax, one finds a mixture of pre- and post-nominal modifiers, each with its peculiar history. Thus consider:

(32) a. the man *I saw yesterday*   (noun-RELclause)
      b. the *big* man   (adjective-noun)
      c. the man *from U.N.C.L.E.*   (noun-PREPphrase)
      d. *one* minute   (numeral-noun)
      e. a passion *for climbing mountains*   (noun-noun complement)
      f. *many* mistakes   (quantifier-noun)
      g. the house *of the rising sun*   (noun-genitive/possessive)
      h. *my uncle's* house   (genitive/possessive-noun)
      i. *bird*-house   (modifier noun-noun)
      j. *the* horse   (article-noun)
      k. *a* cow   (article-noun)
      l. *this* house   (demonstrative-noun)

Synchronically, one may observe that the *large-size* modifiers in (32) are all post-nominal, while the small-size ones are pre-nominal. Coupled to this observation is also the fact that most of the pre-nominal patterns are diachronically *older*, harkening back to the period of OV syntax in the history of English. In contrast, most of the larger-size modifiers are historically younger, presumably arising during a period of VO syntax. But as suggested earlier, this may be a mere coincidence.[25]

Finally, it is observed that SOV languages tend to be most consistent in terms of prediction (1b), SVO languages least consistent, and VSO/VOS fairly consistent (cf. Greenberg, 1966, Hawkins, 1980). But this may again reflect complexities arising from the directionality of diachronic change in word-order, as well as various historical accidents.[26]

---

25) There is no historical evidence for an earlier pre-nominal relative clause in Old English, for example.

26) See discussion in Givón (1979a, Chapters 6,7).

6.5. WORD-ORDER FLEXIBILITY

As we have seen in section 6.4.1., above, even languages which adhere most rigidly to a "basic" word-order type retain some flexibility in using variant word-orders in *complex* clauses ('highly marked contexts'). But other languages display much greater flexibility, one that is most commonly controlled by discourse-pragmatic considerations pertaining to new vs. old, topical vs. non-topical, continuous vs. disruptive information, etc. We have already observed one such 'minor' variation in Chapter 5, above, in conjunction with the promotion of non-patient objects to the pragmatic case of direct-object. In this section we will survey similar variations pertaining to the relative positions — in simple clauses/contexts — of the three major constituents, verb, subject and (direct) object.

6.5.1. The pragmatics of word-order variation in Ute

Ute (Numic, Uto-Aztecan) is currently in an early stage of drifting away from an erstwhile SOV word-order. This early stage of the drift is characterized by great word-order flexibility, whereby the variants (VS vs. SV, VO vs. OV) are controlled by the pragmatics of **topic continuity**.[27] When a sentence is produced in isolation, thus maximally *out of context* and the topic thus highly *discontinuous/surprising*, the SV, OV or SOV orders are predominant, recapitulating the historically older SOV type. In connected discourse, however, the degree of predictability/continuity of an NP-topic determines its position vis-à-vis the verb: Pre-verbal when new, discontinuous and unpredictable; post-verbal when old, continuous and predictable. Thus, consider the following examples concerning the subject's relative position:[28]

(33) a. *Most predictable*: .... páĝa-kwa-pугá...   (Ø-pronoun)
         walk-go-REMOTE
         '....and then (he) left...'

     b. *Intermediate*:   .... páĝa-kwa-pугá   ta'wáci 'u... (VS)
         walk-go-REMOTE man   the
         '....and the man left...'

---

27) For an exhaustive, quantified discourse study of word-order pragmatics in Ute, see Givón (1983d). For similar albeit unquantified and more limited studies in other SOV dialect areas, see Eastman and Edwards (1981) and Dryer (1982) for Athabascan, and Derbyshire (1981) for Carib. Classical Latin presumably displayed a similar degree of flexibility.

28) Following Givón (1980a, Ch. 17) and (1983d).

c. *Most discontinuous*:

   (i) *Definite*: ...; ta'wáci-'urá 'u páĝa-kwa-pųgá... (SV)
                      man-be   the walk-go-REMOTE
                      '...now as for the man, he left...'

   (ii) *Indefinite*: ...; ta'wáci páĝa-kwa-pųgá...   (SV)
                       man   walk-go-REMOTE
                       '...so then a man left...'

The use of zero-pronouns (33a) is found typically when the referential distance to the last participation in a preceding clause is *one* clause. The order VS with full NP's, which cannot be indefinite, is found typically when the referential distance is *one to three* clauses back. And the order SV is found either with first introduction of participants into the discourse, including indefinites, or with definites being re-introduced into the discourse over a referential distance ('gap of absence') of *ten to fifteen* clauses.

The same principle, though with different absolute numerical values, controls the OV/VO variation. Thus consider:

(34) a. *Most predictable*: ....(x'urá) pųníkyay-kay-pųgá-amų.... (Ø)
                            (then)   see-PL-REMOTE-they
                            '...then they saw (him)...'

     b. *Intermediate*:   ....x'urá pųníkyay-kya-pųgá-amų   (VO)
                            then   see-PL-REMOTE-they
                            mamá-ci   'uwáy...
                            woman-OBJ the-OBJ
                            '...then they saw the woman...'

     c. *Most discontinuous*:

        (i) *Definite*:   ....x'urá mamá-ci   'uwáy   (OV)
                            then   woman-OBJ the-OBJ
                            pųníkyay-kya-amų...
                            see-PL-REMOTE-they
                            '...then they saw the woman...'

        (ii) *Indefinite*: ....x'urá mamá-ci   (OV)
                            then   woman-OBJ
                            pųníkyay-kya-pųgá-amų...
                            see-PL-REMOTE-they
                            '...then they saw a woman...'

Since the subject, being the primary topic, is likely to be a more impor-
tant/continuous discourse topic, one expects a language such as Ute to display
a higher preponderance of post-verbal subjects than objects, and this is indeed the case. The overall distribution of the various word-orders in Ute, with
full NP's and independent pronouns counted together, is as follows:[29]

(35)   PERCENT DISTRIBUTION OF WORD-ORDERS IN UTE

word order	with DO	with LOC-object	total objects
SVO	13	7	9.2
VSO	9	9	7.4
OSV	13	4	7.4
VOS	/	/	/
SOV	32	64	52
OVS	27	18	20

If one focuses on the percentages with *direct objects* only, post-verbal subjects
appear in *36 percent* of the sample (OVS, VSO, VOS), while post-verbal direct objects appear in only *22 percent* of the sample (SVO, VSO, VOS). Finally, the OVS word-order, with the subject *highly topical* and the object of
low topicality, is the most frequent word-order after the historically older
SOV.

The pragmatic principle which controls word-order variation in Ute, one
which has been shown to apply similarly elsewhere,[30] may be summarized as:

(36)   "More surprising/disruptive/new information *precedes*
       more continuous/predictable/old information"

As we shall see below, other languages make use of the same principle, although more commonly applying it only to the subject, while keeping the object's position rigid, most commonly post-verbally (VO).

6.5.2. Definiteness, indefiniteness and word-order variation in Mandarin

While the Mandarin data below pertain only to the definite/indefinite
contrast, and are not derived from text studies (but rather are based on isolated sentences), they seem to abide by exactly the opposite pragmatic principle governing word-order variation from that in Ute (cf. (36) above). That is:

29) See Givón (1983d).

30) A comprehensive treatment of topic continuity and the role of word-order within the system
coding this functional domain may be found in Chapter 22, Volume II, as well as in Givón (1983a,
1983b, 1983c). Earlier versions may be found in Givón (1978) and (1979, Ch. 2).

(37) "More indefinite/discontinuous/new information *follows*
more definite/continuous/old information"

Thus, consider the following:[31]

(38) a. *INDEF-subject*: lái   kèrén le   (VS)
come guest ASP
'A guest arrived'

b. *DEF-subject*: kèrén lái   le   (SV)
guest come ASP
'The guest arrived'

c. *INDEF*-object: wǒ dǎ-pò   le   zh'uāngzi   (VO)
I   hit-break ASP window
'I broke a window'

d. *DEF-object*: wǒ bǎ   zh'uāngzi dǎ-pò   le   (OV)
I   ACC   window   hit-break ASP
'I broke the window'

There are several reasons why the counter-principle (37) may be of less validity cross-linguistically. First, it is based on selected isolated sentences rather
than on a quantified discourse study. Second, Chinese also has a morphological way of signaling the DEF/INDEF contrast, maintaining therein a fixed SVO
order (see fn. 31). Third, all the examples cited for the indefinite VS order are
from *presentative* verbs such as 'be', 'exist', 'arrive', 'enter' etc. For such
verbs, one may reasonably argue that the presentative verb itself is *semantically depleted*, and normally another predicate — semantically less stereotypical and more complex — participates in presentative constructions, so that it
follows the indefinite subject. Thus consider the following presentative devices in English:

(39) a. A man came yesterday *into my office* and *demanded* to....
b. There's a girl *in my soup*....
c. There's a man who *wants* to see you....
d. There was once a king who *loved* cream cheese....

31) The Mandarin data here are from Charles Li (in personal communication), but see also Li
and Thompson (1975) as well as discussion in Givón (1978). Chinese also has another — purely
morphological — device for signaling the DEF/INDEF contrast, with the basic order SVO maintained throughout and demonstratives used to definitize, the numeral 'one' to indefinitize. The
word-order device reported here may be thus not necessarily the most common device in current
Mandarin, though it may characterize older stages of the language.

It is thus entirely possible, although quantified discourse studies must demonstrate this, that the so-called presentative VSO order is really not a syntactic phenomenon in word-order so much as a morphological phenomenon in marking indefinite subjects.[32]

6.5.3. The pragmatics of the subject position in Biblical Hebrew

In Early Biblical Hebrew, the same word-order principle (36) as in Ute applies, but only with respect to the pre- or post-verbal position of the *subject*. Thus consider:[33]

(40) a. ...va-yavo'u shney ha-mal'axim Sdom-a   b-a-ʕerev,   (VS)
             and-came two   the-angels   Sodom-LOC in-the-evening
        '...So the two angels came to Sodom in the evening,

    b. vi-Loṭ yoshev bi-sha ar Sdom;   (SV)
       and-Lot sitting at-gate-of Sodom
       and Lot was sitting at the city's gate;

    c. va-yar' Loṭ   (VS)
       and-saw Lot
       and Lot saw (them)

    d. va-yaqom   (pronominal agreement)
       and-rose-he
       and (he) got up

    e. vayishtaḥw....   (Ø NP/pronominal agreement)
       and-bowed
       and prostrated himself...'   [Genesis, 19:1]

In clause (40a) above the subject — two angels sent by God — is definite and was mentioned in the preceding paragraph. So the VS order is used. In (40b) Lot is introduced for the first time, with the SV word-order. Following a slight thematic discontinuity[34], Lot is still mentioned as full NP in (40c) — but with the more continuous VS word-order. Finally, the tight thematic continuity in (40d, e) involves mentioning the subject only as Ø, i.e. via the obligatory sub-

---

32) For an extensive discussion of existential-presentative constructions, see Chapter 19, Volume II. For an earlier discussion, see Hetzron (1971) or Givón (1976c), *inter alia*.

33) For more details see Givón (1977b) and A. Fox (1983).

34) The more discontinuous/disruptive word-order, SV, in Early Biblical Hebrew is used to code either *topic* discontinuity or *action/theme* discontinuity — or, since they most commonly coincide, both. See further discussion in Givón (1977b). The same is true of the use of similar devices elsewhere (cf. Hopper, 1979, Givón, 1983a). For further detail see also Chapter 22, Volume II.

ject pronoun on the verb.

Unlike Israeli Hebrew, where the VS word-order is used as an existential-presentative device to introduce indefinite subjects, and the basic word-order has gravitated closer to rigid SVO,[35] in Biblical Hebrew the few indefinite subjects found in the text are introduced via the discontinuous SV word-order. As an example consider:

(41) a. SV, returning DEF-subject:
          ....va-yaqom   David
          and-rose   David
          '....and David got up

      b. Ø, continuous DEF-subject:
          va-yered   'el midbar   Pa'ran;
          and-descended to desert-of Paran
          and went down to the Paran desert;

      c. SV, INDEF-subject:
          vi-'ish   bi-Maˁon u-maˁase-hu   bi-Karmel...
          and-man in-Maon   and-business-his in-Carmel
          and **there was a man** in Maon who had **his business** in Carmel...'
                                                    [Samuel I, 25:1-2]

The pragmatic principle controlling the VS/SV word-order variation in Biblical Hebrew is thus the same as seen in Ute, above. However, it does not apply to the object quite as freely. Definite objects which are re-introduced (rather than recurring in a co-referential series) indeed appear *pre*-verbally, as in:

(42) a. VO, continuing DEF-object:
          ...va-yiqaḥ   'alohim 'et-ha'adam
          and-took   God   ACC-the-man
          '...and God took Adam

      b. PRO, continuing DEF-object:
          va-yaniḥe-hu bi-gan   ˁeden
          and-put-him in-garden-of Eden
          and put him in the Garden of Eden

      c. SUBORD clause:
          li-ˁovd-o u-li-shomr-o;
          to-work-it and-to-guard-it
          to work and guard it;

35) For the pragmatics of the VS word-order in Israeli Hebrew, see Givón (1976c).

d. VO, continuing DEF-object:

va-yiṣav   YHWH 'elohim ʕal   ha-'adam le-'mor:
and-ordered YHWH God   unto the-man to-say
and God ordered Adam:

e. OV, new object in contrast:

"mi-kol ʕeṣ   ha-gan   'axol to'xel,
from-all tree-of the-garden eating you-shall-eat
"You may eat **from all the trees** in the garden,

f. OV, new object in contrast:

u-me-ʕeṣ   ha-daʕat   ṭov ve-raʕ   lo'
and-from-tree-of the-knowledge-of good and-bad NEG
to'xel…"…'
you-shall-eat
but **from the tree of knowledge** you may not eat…"…'

[Genesis, 2:15-17]

However, indefinite objects usually appear *post*-verbally, as in:

(43) VO; INDEF-object:
…va-yiqaḥ   ben   baqar raḥ   va-ṭov …..
and-he-took son-of cattle tender and-good
'…and he took **a tender, good calf**…'   [Genesis, 18:7]

6.5.4. Subject position in Spanish: A conflict of pragmatic principles

Spanish exhibits, on cursory inspection, the same wɔɹd-order behavior
with respect to the SV/VS variation as Early Biblical Hebrew, above. It is a
VO language in much the same way , with contrastive objects preposed to
OV, as a *marked* order. The principle of a new or re-introduced subject appearing *pre-verbally* has been established in a number of recent studies.[36] To illustrate this, consider the following passage:

(44) a. PRO/agreement; continuing DEF-subject:

…pués, comió su cena,
then ate-he his meal
'…well then he ate his dinner,

b. SV; switch subject:

pero su amiga   no   comió la suya,
but his girlfriend NEG ate-she the hers
but his girlfriend didn't eat hers,

36) See details in Silva-Corvalán (1977) and Bentivoglio (1983), as well as further discussion in
Givón (ed., 1983a, Introduction).

c. PRO/agreement; continuing DEF-subject:
así   se-sentába   hallá   llorando.
thus REFL-sitting there   crying
she just sat there crying.

d. SV; intermediately-continuous DEF-subject:
Poco mas   tarde se-levantó   la   amiga   y...
little more late   REFL-rose the   girlfriend and subject)
A little later the girlfriend finally got up and...'

However, Spanish already employs the VS word-order in existential-presentative devices, one which at least superficially follows the opposite principle, (37), as in Mandarin (but see discussion in section 6.5.2., above). Thus consider:[37]

(45) ... luego vino   un amigo suyo y...
then   came a   friend his   and
'...so then a friend of his came and...'

That Spanish follows principle (37) universally was indeed suggested by Bolinger (1954), based on isolated sentential examples such as:

(46) a. *Context*:   'What does John do?' (TOP-subject, FOC-predicate)
b. *Utterance*: Juán canta
'John sings'   ('What John does is *sing*')
c. *Context*:   'Who sings?'   (TOP-predicate, FOC-subject)
d. *Utterance*: Canta Juán
'Sings John'   ('The one who sings is *John*')

There are a number of problems with Bolinger's suggestion. To begin with, the examples are not based on text studies, but are isolates. Further, if the questions in (46a, c) were indeed the discourse context for (46b, d), respectively, the more natural answers would omit the first elements in (46b, d) and preserve only the focal element. Finally, (46b, d) are indeed more *marked*, contrastive utterances, uncharacteristic of the most continuous/topical subject as illustrated in either (44c) or (44d), above.[38]

---

37) See further discussion in Bentivoglio (1983).

38) Relying on isolated sentences as examples, rather than on continuous discourse, has led Bolinger (1954) to the same — I think hard to substantiate — conclusions as the Prague School, in viewing TOPIC-COMMENT as the natural pragmatic principle controlling word-order (cf. Fibras, 1966a, 1966b). For further discussion, see Givón (1983a, Introduction, and 1983c).

6.5.5. "Free word-order" languages

Hale (1980) has recently suggested that Walbiri, an Australian language, has totally free word-order that is not governed by any pragmatic principle. Since the suggestion is not based on the study of discourse, texts or actual communication, but rather on the existence of isolated sentences with various word-orders, it is at the moment premature to evaluate this possibility.[39]

6.6. MIXED WORD-ORDER TYPES AT THE CLAUSE LEVEL

6.6.1. Preliminaries

As suggested earlier, typological consistency in "basic" word-order is mediated by diachronic change, and only languages which have never changed typologically, or those whose earlier typological change has been followed by millenia of typological stability, display complete typological consistency. The mixed word-order types surveyed in this section are thus, quite often, the product of typological change in word-order, which left one 'basic' word-order in some contexts, and another 'basic' word-order in others. Quite often one may in fact predict the contexts in which word-order changes may occur first, and those in which *conservative* word-order is more likely to be found. While diachronic change is not the focus of the discussion below, it is hard to avoid making repeated reference to it, if one is to make sense out of synchronic typological facts.

6.6.2. Different word-order in main vs. subordinate clauses

In general, subordinate (complex) clauses tend to preserve earlier word-orders which have become "frozen", although the opposite (i.e. conservatism of main clauses) has also been reported.[40] As an example consider Kru, a Niger-Congo language where the diachronically older OV order still occurs in a number of subordinate/complex clause types, as in:[41]

(47) a. nyeyu-na bla nyino-na   (SVO, main clause)
      man-the hit woman-the
      'The man hit the woman'

---

39) The situation becomes a bit more confusing when Hale (1980) goes on to suggest that Navajo, a rigid SOV language, is also a free-word-order (i.e. *W-star*, in his parlance) language.

40) See further detail in Givón (1975a) and Hyman (1975). German may be an example where the OV word-order in subordinate clauses is *innovative*, while the VO of main clauses is conservative. For further discussion see Givón (1979a, Chapters 2, 6).

41) From Givón (1975a).

b. nyeyu-na jila **boe** nyino-na   bla   (OV,V-complement)
   man-the want SUB woman-the hit
   'The man wants to hit the woman'

c. n-pni   nyeyu-na **bẹ́ẹ́** nyino-na   bla   (OV, V-comple-
   I-squeeze man-the SUB woman-the hit   ment)
   'I forced the man to hit the woman'

d. nyeyu-na **mũ** nyino-na   bla   (OV, future-modal
   man-the FUT woman-the hit   scope; historically
   'The man will hit the woman'   V-complement)

e. nyeyu-na **si**   nyino-na   bla   (OV, negative; histo-
   man-the NEG woman-the hit   rically V-complement)
   'The man didn't hit the woman'

A similar situation may be found in German, although here it may be that the OV word-order in subordinate clauses is actually innovative. Thus consider:[42]

(48) a. Der Mann isst   den Apfel   (VO, main clause)
         the man   eats the apple
         'The man eats the apple'

      b. Der Mann **der**   den Apfel isst   (OV, REl-clause)
         the man   SUB the apple eats
         'The man who eats the apple'

      c. Ich weiss **dass** der Mann den Apfel isst   (OV, verb-
         I   know SUB the Man   the apple eats   complement)
         'I know that the man eats the apple'

      d. **Wenn** der Mann den Apfel isst...   (OV, adverbial
         when the man   the apple eats   SUBORD-clause)
         'When the man eats the apple...'

      e. Der Mann **wird** den Apfel essen   (OV, future-modal
         the man   FUT the apple eat-INF   scope; historically
         'The man will eat the apple'   V-complement)

---

42) From Austrian, with the data due to Anna Meyer (in personal communication).

    f. OV, perfect-auxiliary; historically V-complement:
        Der Mann **hat**   den Apfel gegessen
        the man   AUX the apple PARTICIP-eat-INF
        'The man ate/has eaten the apple'

    g. OV, progressive auxiliary; historically V-complement:
        Der Mann **ist**   den Apfel am Essen
        the man   AUX the apple at   eat-INF
        'The man is eating the apple'

    h. OV, passive auxiliary; historically V-complement:
        Der Apfel **wurde** von dem Mann gegessen
        the apple AUX by   the man   PARTICIP-eat-INF
        'The apple was eaten by the man'

6.6.3. Different word-order of direct vs. indirect objects

Often in ex-SOV languages, direct objects display the more conservative OV word-order, while indirect objects display the innovative VO order. In several Mende and Voltaic (Niger-Congo) languages this variation has become rigid or 'grammaticalized'. Thus consider the following from Kpelle (Mende):[43]

(49) a. è   kâli kaa   (OV, PAT-object)
             he hoe saw
             'He saw the hoe'

        b. è   lì   naa   (VO, LOC-object)
             he went there
             'He went there'

        c. é   sɛŋ-kâu tèe kâloŋ-pí   (OV PAT-object, VO
             he money sent chief-to   DAT-object)
             'He sent the money to the chief'

        d. è   wúru tèe à   bóa   (OV PAT-object, VO
             he stick cut with knife   INSTR-object)
             'He cut the stick with a knife'

6.6.4. Different word-order in referential vs. non-referential objects

Non-referential (generic) direct objects are quite often **incorporated** into the verb, and thus become morphologically frozen (see Chapter 3, section

---

43) From W. Welmers (in personal communication), but see also Givón (1975a) and Hyman (1975).

3.6.2.9, as well as further discussion in Chapter 11, below). When subsequently a language changes the position of the object vis-à-vis the verb, a variation may ensue whereby one word-order applies to non-referential objects and another to referential ones. As an illustration of this possibility, consider Ute, where referential objects appear in both the OV and VO word-order, depending on topicality/continuity (see section 6.5.1., above) but non-referential objects are incorporated pre-verbally, in the more conservative OV word-order:[44]

(50) a. ta'wá-ci sivą́ą̀tu-ci paxá-ux-pųgá   (OV, INDEF-object)
        man   goat-OBJ kill-ASP-REM
        'The man killed a goat'

     b. ta'wá-ci paxá-ux-pųgá   sivą́ą̀tu-ci 'uwáy (VO, DEF-con-
        man   kill-ASP-REM   goat-OBJ the-OBJ tinuous object)
        'The man killed the goat'

     c. ta'wá-ci sivą́ą̀tu-paxá-na-pųgá-vaci   (OV, NON-REF-ob-
        man   goat-kill-HAB-REM-DIGRESS ject, incorporated)
        'The man used to kill goats'

     d. ta'wá-ci sivą́ą̀tu-paxá-mi-tų   'urá-'ąy (OV, NON-REF-ob-
        man   goat-kill-HAB-NOM be-IMM   ject, nominalized)
        'The man is a goat-killer'

If Ute eventually completes its drift to VO, only incorporated non-referential objects (as well as other incorporated non-referential elements such as manner adverbs and instrumentals) would remain in the conservative OV order. Example (50d) above also suggests that the frozen VP-nominalization compounds of English (see further below) may be interpreted in a similar light.

6.6.5. Different word-order in nominal vs. sentential objects

In many strict SOV languages, sentential complements may *follow* the verb, while nominal objects rigidly precede it. Thus consider the following from Sherpa:[45]

---

44) From Givón (1980a).

45) From my own field notes, with the data originally due to Koncchok J. Lama (in personal communication).

(51) a. ŋyee   cenyi caaq-yin   (OV, nominal object)
        I-ERG cup   break-PERF
        'I broke the cup'

      b. ŋyee   si-kyaa-yin   laĝa kyaa-yin   (VO, sentential
        I-ERG say-AUX-PERF work do-PERF   object)
        'I said (that) I worked'

The same may be also seen in Wara (Voltaic, Niger-Congo), a language where
the direct object displays the conservative OV order but sentential (as well as
indirect) objects appear post-verbally, as in:[46]

(52) a. i   laabo liee-ni   (OV, nominal object)
        he cow   kill-PERF
        'He killed a cow'

      b. i   waa-ni   a   mi-fi   tamã   (VO, sentential
        he say-PERF SUB you-buy dolo   complement)
        'He said that you bought dolo'

      c. i   laa tumu-se-ni   (VO, sentential complement)
        he go cultivate-INF-PERF
        'He went to cultivate'

6.6.6. Different word-order in definite vs. indefinite NP's

Recall the Mandarin example discussed in section 6.5.2., above where
for both objects and subjects the pre-verbal position (SV, OV) coded definites and the post-verbal (VS, VO), indefinites.

6.6.7. Different word-order in continuous vs. discontinuous topics

Recall the discussion of pragmatic control of flexible word-order (cf.
Ute, section 6.5.1., above), where more discontinuous topics — including indefinites — appeared pre-verbally (SV, OV) and more continuous ones post-
verbally (VS, VO).

6.6.8. Different word-order in free vs. nominalized clauses

In English the current basic word-order is rigidly VO, but VP nominaliza-
tions exhibit the OV word-order, as in:

(53)   'house painter', 'garbage collector', 'street cleaning', 'deer hunting'

Such examples also illustrate a differential order for non-referential, incorpo-

---

46) See Givón (1975a).

rated objects (see section 6.6.4., above).

A similar situation is seen in Nupe (Niger-Congo), again a largely SVO dialect with frozen OV nominalized VP-compounds, as in:[47]

(54) *free word order (VO)*   *nominalized word-order (OV)*

gbè	elo		elo-gbè
hunt	deer		deer-hunt
'to hunt a deer'			'deer-hunting'
pá	eya		eya-pá
drive	car		car-drive
'to drive a car'			'car-driving'

A complement case may be shown in Akkadian (Semitic), where the language changed to OV following contact with OV substratum (Sumerian) but old nominalized VP-compounds remained VO, as in:[48]

(55) *free word-order (OV)*   *nominalized word-order (VO)*

a. ina idi umma-nīya illakū   ālikūt did amma-nīya
at side-of troops-my they-go   goer(s) side troops-my
'they go alongside my troops'   'goer(s) at the side of my troops'

b. ana šarr-im ikrub   ikrib šarr-i
for king-GEN he-prayed   prayer-of king-GEN
'he prayed for the king'   'prayer for the king'

c. abull-am inaṣṣar   maṣṣar abul-im
gate-ACC he-guards   watcher-of gate-GEN
'he guards the gate'   'gate-keeper'

d. dull-am ippeš   āpiš dull-im
work-ACC he-does   doer-of work-GEN
'he does work'   'worker'

6.6.9. Different order for pronominal vs. nominal NP's

In many languages, one finds that pronominal and full-NP objects are positioned differentially vis-à-vis the verb. This is characteristic of many ex-SOV languages (or families), where the clitic pronouns *froze* at a pre-verbal position, while full NPs go by the more innovative VO word-order. As an

47) From Madugo (1978), but see also discussion in Givón (1979b).

48) From Bucellati (1970), see also discussion in Givón (1977a, 1979b).

example consider the following from Swahili (Bantu):[49]

(56) a. ni-li-soma   kitabu   (VO, full NP object)
        I-PAST-read book
        'I read a book'

    b. ni-li-ki-soma   (OV, clitic object pronoun)
        I-PAST-it-read
        'I read it'

A discrepancy between nominal and pronominal order may involve both subject and object, as in Amharic (Ethiopian-Semitic, SOV):

(57) a. set-wa   wämbär säbbär-ač   (SOV, nominal)
        woman-the chair   broke-she
        'The woman broke a chair'

    b. säbbär-ač-ɨw   (VSO, pronominal)
        broke-she-it
        'She broke it'

Pronominal elements themselves may display different morphotactic positions vis-à-vis the verb in different tense-aspects of the verb. Thus, in Hebrew the perfect pronominal order is VSO, the imperfect SVO:

(58) a. riʕi-tí-hu   (VSO, perfect/past)
        saw-I-him
        'I saw him'

    b. 'e-rʕé-hu   (SVO, imperfect/future)
        I-will-see-him
        'I will see him'

In many SOV languages post-verbal subject agreement appears and is not a frozen relic of an older VS nominal word-order, but rather arises via other diachronic channels. Thus, consider the following from Hittite (Indo-European):[50]

---

49) See Ashton (1944). For a diachronically-oriented discussion, see Givón (1971, 1975a, 1977a, 1979b). A similar dichotomy between OV pronominal order and VO nominal order may be seen in Romance, Iroquois and others.

50) From Justus (1976, 1978). For some discussion of one diachronic channel via which SOV languages may acquire post-verbal pronominal agreement see Givón (1977a).

(59) ...ta lugal-i   sallugal-ga tarue-ni...
     to king-DAT queen-and reported-we
     '...we reported (it) to the king and queen...'

In some SOV languages such post-verbal agreement is fused with the tense-aspect auxiliaries, as in Sherpa:[51]

(60) a. cenyi caaq-yin   (1st person subject)
        cup   break-PERF/1st
        '(I/we) broke the cup'

     b. cenyi caaq-sung   (non-1st-person subject)
        cup   break-PERF/non-1st
        '(he/she/you/they) broke the cup'

One last type of discrepancy between nominal and pronominal syntax involves the so-called **second position clitic pronouns** (see Steele, 1977), common in many language families. This involves placing anaphoric/clitic/agreement pronouns (see Chapter 10, below) not on the verb but as suffixes on the first lexical word in the clause. Since the most frequent first word in connected narrative discourse is likely to be the verb, this type of pronominal placement may result eventually in a post-verbal pronominal position. As an example consider the following from Ute, where these pronouns may refer either to subject or object:[52]

(61) a. 'áavu̧-n tu̧ká-y
        now-I   eat-IMM
        'Now I am eating'

     b. kací-n tu̧ká-wa
        NEG-I eat-NEG
        'I am not eating'

     c. tu̧kúa-vi-n tu̧ká-y
        meat-OBJ-I eat-IMM
        'I am eating meat'

     d. tu̧ká-yi-n tu̧kúa-vi 'uwáy
        eat-IMM-I meat-OBJ the-OBJ
        'I am eating the meat'

---

51) From my own field notes, originally due to Koncchok J. Lama (in personal communication).

52) See Givón (1980a).

e. kac-áx̂ tu̜ká-wa
   NEG-it eat-NEG
   '(I) am not eating it'

f. tu̜ká-y-ax̂
   eat-IMM-it
   '(I) am eating it'

6.7. BASIC WORD-ORDER AND WORD-ORDER WITHIN NOUN PHRASES

6.7.1. Preliminaries

As suggested earlier, Greenberg's (1966) typological prediction (1b) is not absolute, first because there is not always a direct causal correlation between the VO/OV parameter and the MN/NM parameter of word-order, and second because of typological change. Most commonly, word-order change tends to start at the simple, main-clause level, and only later on to spread — if at all — into more complex, marked environments, including also the relative order of modifiers vis-à-vis the head noun in the noun phrase.[53] Thus, for example, both English and Mandarin are currently SVO, but the NP syntax of both reveals many *pre*-nominal modifiers, more so in Mandarin than in English, which presumably harken back to an earlier stage of SOV syntax.[54] As an illustration of this, consider the following from Akkadian (Semitic), a VO language which changed to OV presumably via substratum contact:[55]

(62) a. SOV, main clause:
        awil-um   alp-am   ana di'āš-im   īgur
        man-SUBJ   ox-OBJ   for threshing-GEN   hired
        'The man hired the ox for threshing'

     b. SOV in REL-clause, N-REL in the NP:
        awil-um   ša   eli-šu   kišp-ī   iddu
        man-SUBJ   *that*   upon-him magic-OBJ/PL cast
        'the man who cast magic upon him'

     c. N-ADJ in the NP:
        rē'ū   damaguti
        shepherd   good
        'the good shepherd'

---

53) See discussion in Givón (1971, 1979a, Chapter 2).

54) For Mandarin word-order change, see Li and Thompson (1973).

55) From Bucelatti (1970); see discussion in Givón (1977a).

   d. N-DEM in the NP:
      awil-um   šū
      man-SUBJ this
      'this man'

Typological consistency between VP and NP syntax is thus to some extent a
fiction, though perhaps a useful one. In the following sub-sections some of the
more problematic correlations will be discussed.

6.7.2. Possessive/genitive modifiers

   The position of genitive/possessive modifiers vis-à-vis the head noun is
the most consistent correlation between VP and NP word-order as expressed
in (1b) above. Nevertheless, even this correlation is not absolute, since natural diachronic processes exist via which pre- or post-nominal genitives may
arise in either VO or OV languages. The process involves the **grammaticalization** (syntacticization) or either left-dislocated or right-dislocated constructions with these modifiers (for L- and R-dislocation, see Chapter 18, Volume
II). Thus, consider the following:[56]

   (63) a. *Pre-N, VO language (Krio):*   Jóhn in-ǫ́s
                                            John his-house
                                            'John's house'

         b. *Post-N, VO language (Hebrew):* bet-ó   shel-Yoséf
                                            house-his of-Joseph
                                            'Joseph's house'

         c. *Pre-N, OV language (Chuave):*   na-non nam-i
                                            my-pig my-this
                                            'my pig'

---

56) See further detail in Givón (1979b). The Krio (Creole, Sierra Leone) data are from my own
field notes and originally due to Sori Yilla (in personal communication). The Chuave (New Guinea
Highlands) data are from Thurman (1987). Ute is in the process of drifting away from SOV, but the
pre-nominal genitive *independent* pronoun (unlike the post-nominal clitic pronoun) predates the
change, as do examples such as (63d), which comes from my own field notes. Normally, non-dislo-
cated genitive modifiers are *pre*-nominal, thus conforming to the OV pattern, as in:
núumaróĝomapųgá-tų mǫ'ǫ́-vi
god-GEN   hand
'God's hand'
But R-dislocated examples such as (63d) appear sporadically in informal language. For evidence
suggesting that the English pre-nominal genitive also came from an L-dislocated pattern, see Janda
(1978).

d. *Post-N, OV language (Ute)*:   máayas mǫ'ǫ́-naaĝa-tux
                                       his   hand-in-to
                                       núumaróĝomapȣgá-tȣ
                                       God-GEN
                                       'into God's hand'

6.7.3. REL-clause modifiers

The position of relative clauses vis-à-vis the head noun quite often represents the history of syntacticization of pre-posed or post-posed **paratactic** topic sentences, and either pre-posed or post-posed REL-sentences may arise in either VO or OV languages. Thus, for example, Justus (1976, 1978) shows that in Indo-European languages a pre-posed topic sentence gave rise to the current REL-modifier. As an illustration of the potential for such reanalysis, consider the following from Bambara (Mende, Niger-Congo):[57]

(64) cę **min** ye   mùru sàn, n ye   o   ye
      man *REL* PAST knife buy I PAST *him* see
      'The man who bought the knife, I saw him'

Direct/patient objects conform to the OV pattern in Bambara. When the topic-sentence 'The man (who) bought the knife' is embedded in Bambara, which is an *optional* process, one obtains (65) below where the syntacticized REL-clause is *post*-nominal:

(65) n ye   cę **min** ye   mùru sàn ye
      I PAST man REL PAST knife buy see
      'I saw the man who bought the knife'

In languages showing the Bambara pattern of relativization, the *entire* topic-sentence occupies the position within the main clause of the *head* noun, and this gives rise to post-nominal REL-clauses in an OV language, following grammaticalization of subject-REL sentences as in (65) above.

Preposed REL/topic-sentences are quite common in informal, conversational Englsih, as well as in the speech of early childhood in English. Thus, the following is a plausible example:

(66) *y'know, that man came yesterday, right? Well,* he left
      this morning

---

57) Relativization will be discussed in Chapter 16, Volume II. For earlier discussion see Givón (1979a, Chapter 4), where the source of the Bambara data is also acknowledged. For an extensive discussion of the rise of syntactic constructions via the grammaticalization of paratactic ones, see Givón (1979a, Chapters 5,6).

The function of the italicized portion in (66) is the same as that of REL-clauses, identifying the referent ('man') by using a proposition known to the hearer in which that referent was a participant.

Finally, it has been shown[58] that in otherwise rigid SOV languages, post-nominal REL-clauses may arise from **non-restrictive**, paratactic construc-tions that *follow* the head noun. Schematically, such a possibility may be illus-trated in English as:

(67)   a.   The man, *I saw him yesterday*, he came again today   (parataxis)
         b.   The man *I saw yesterday* came again today   (syntacticized)

Relatively little simplification — especially if anaphora is handled by subject agreement (see Chapter 10, below) — is needed to reanalyze (67a) into (67b), even less so if a *non-restrictive* REL-clause is used, as in:

(68)   a.   The man, *whom I saw yesterday*, left today   (parataxis)
         b.   The man *whom I saw yesterday* left today   (syntacticized)

6.7.4. Quantifiers or numeral modifiers

As in the case of other modifiers, above, the diachronic processes via which numeral/quantifying modifiers arise may determine their pre- or post-nominal position in a way not directly predictable from Greenberg's (1966) correlation (1b). Consider first quantifying expressions where a **classifier** is in-volved (see Chapter 12, Volume II),[59] so that within the entire construction the numeral occurs as a modifier on the classifier, the classifier is the *head* noun, and what eventually emerges as the head noun is a *genitive* modifier. The following example from English illustrates this:

(69)   two *head* of cattle

The pre-nominal position of a modifying numeral such as 'two' above, in a lan-guage which developed a grammaticalized numeral classifier system, is thus predictable not directly from the OV/VO syntax of simple clauses, but rather from the conflation of

(a)   A genitival construction of numeral classifiers; and
(b)   The pre-or post-nominal (the latter as in (69) above) position of genitive modifiers.

---

58) See Langdon (1977). Theo Vennemann (in personal communication) has suggested that the same happened in the history of German relative clauses. For futher discussion see Givón (1979a, Chapters 5,6).

59) For an extensive background on numeral classifiers see Greenberg (1978).

Thus, if the *of* genitive were pre-nominal in English, (69) would re-translate into (70), with a post-nominal numeral modifier:

(70) *of cattle* two head

A similar case, without the presence of numeral classifiers, may be seen in Hebrew and other Semitic languages. In general, these are VO languages with mostly post-nominal modifiers (cf. section 6.4.2.2., above). However, all numerals except for 'one' are *pre*-nominal, as in:

(71) séfer 'exád
book one
'one book'

shnéy sfarím
two-of book-PL
'two books'

shloshá sfarím
three-of book-PL
'three books'

etc.

Historically, the numeral 'one' is a post-nominal adjective meaning 'lone', 'unique'. The rest of the numerals, however, are historically *head* nouns modified by a genitive noun — which then became re-analyzed as the head noun syntactically. The form of these numerals was originally the **construct state** form of head nouns in a compound. This "inconsistent" pre-nominal position of numeral modifiers in an otherwise consistent VO language thus arises naturally from the re-analysis of a "consistent" *post*-nominal modifying construction.

6.7.5. Adjectival modifiers

In many languages, word-order flexibility allows adjective modifers to appear both pre- and post-nominally. The difference between the two is initially pragmatic, but often becomes "semanticized". This phenomenon has been described for Romance languages, where pre-nominal adjectives initially took the value of **non-restrictive** modifiers (non-contrastive; see discussion in Chapter 12, Volume II), while post-nominal modifiers are **restrictive** and thus used in the grammar of establishing unique reference, much like restrictive relative clauses. Eventually the non-restrictive adjectives developed highly specific semantic variations. Thus consider the following from

Spanish:[60]

(72) a. hombre pobre 'poor man', 'man who is poor' (restrictive; N-A)
      b. pobre hombre 'pitiable man'   (non-restrictive; A-N)

The pre-nominal adjective in Romance has a high potential for co-lexicalizing with the head noun in a compound. This potential is already reflected in the meaning shift in (72b) in Spanish, but is perhaps further along in French, where the post-nominal position remains reserved for restrictive modifying adjectives, with full lexical stress, while the pre-nominal, non-restrictive position is less stressed and thus bears some trimmings of a co-lexicalized compound. This phonological reduction may also be seen in some Spanish pre-nominal adjectives. Thus consider:[61]

(73) a. una mujer grande   'a big woman'
          one woman big

      b. ?una grande mujer
          one big   woman

      c. un   gran mujer   'a swell woman', 'a terrific woman',
          one big   woman   'a great woman'

      d. ?un mujer grande
          one woman big

In other languages, of essentially OV topology, the same variation may result in actual co-lexicalization. Thus, for example, in Ute, post-nominal adjectives are complete words with adjectival suffixal morphology and a restrictive usage. While pre-nominal ones, including numerals on occasion, may drop the morphology and fuse as *prefixes* to the noun stem, as in:[62]

---

60) Following Bolinger (1952). The underlying pragmatic principle controlling this order variation is actually of more universal applicability, and may be given as:
    (a) "More *specific*, narrowing, restrictive information tends to come *later*, while more *general*, non-restrictive, non-narrowing information tends to come *earlier*".
Essentially, this is an information processing principle of "going from the generic to the specific", or "increasing the load of processing gradually". For further discussion see Wilkins and Kimenyi (1975).

61) These data are characteristic of colloquial – rather than official – Spanish.

62) See Givón (1980a).

(74) a. kavá sá-ĝa-rų-mų   (N-ADJ; restrictive)
         horse white-ADJ-ANIM
         'a white horse'

     b. sá-gavà   (ADJ-N; non-restrictive, co-lexicalized)
         white-horse
         'a white-horse'

All this is simply to illustrate how the OV/VO typological dimension does not necessarily determine the relative position of adjectival modifiers.

6.7.6. Definite articles and demonstratives

The position of definitizers and demonstratives before or after the head noun is notoriously independent of the OV/VO typological dimension. What is of interest here is that a language may have the option of using *both* positions, thus creating a pragmatic contrast not unlike the one described above for adjectives — and eventually affecting a separation between demonstratives and definite articles, even as the first category was clearly the precursor of the second.[63] As an example for the potential of this variation, consider the following from Bemba (Bantu), an SVO language:[64]

(75) | deictic grade | pre-nominal | post-nominal |
| --- | --- | --- |
| *near speaker* | u-no muuntu | umuntu u-no |
| *near hearer* | u-yo muuntu | umuntu u-yo |
| *near both* | u-yu muuntu | umuntu u-yu |
| *remote* | u-lya muuntu | umuntu u-lya |

The *pre*-nominal demonstrative in (75), modifying the head noun *umuntu* 'person', is non-restricitve, non-contrastive or 'neutral', and its tonal pattern is different from that of the *post*-nominal demonstrative, which is restrictive and contrastive. The sense conveyed is that if the deictic position of the noun is critical for affecting unique reference ('definite description'), post-nominal demonstratives are used. While if it is incidental for establishing unique reference, the pre-nominal deictic is used. Eventually, in Bemba and elsewhere in Bantu, such a situation leads to reinterpreting one demonstrative in the pre-nominal position — most commonly the more *remote* one — as the *definite article*. This involves the "bleaching" of the concrete *spatial* deixis, while retain-

---

63) For the intimate relation between demonstratives ('deictics') and the definite article, see Chapter 11, below as well as Givón (1978).

64) See Givón (1972, Chapter 1).

ing the more abstract, temporal *discourse* deixis. This tendency is already evident in Bemba, where the frequency of only two of the demonstratives —
most remote and most proximate to the speaker—is very high pre-nominally.
The situation is virtually grammaticalized in Swahili, where the less-stressed
pre-nominal position is reserved for the remote demonstrative, which functions as a definite article; while the normal, contrastive demonstrative with
spatial deictic values tends to follow the head noun. Thus consider:[65]

(76) a. yùle m̂tóto   'the child'
      b. m̂tòto yúle   'that child over there'

One may interpret the rise of the pre-nominal articles in current Romance languages in very much the same fashion, with the optional position of
demonstratives in Latin — before or after the head noun — broadly echoing
the Bemba situation. But at the time when Latin allowed such word-order variation, it was an ex-SOV language drifting away toward VO. And in other languages at a comparable position on the drift continuum from OV to VO,
exactly the opposite controlling word-order principle may emerge. Thus in
Ute (Uto-Aztecan), it is the *pre*-nominal position of demonstratives that (a) is
contrastive and (b) allows the use of all three deictic grades (near, remote-visible, remote-invisible); while the post-nominal position is (a) non-contrastive,
and (b) restricted mostly to the *remote* demonstrative, which has thus become
a definite article. As examples consider:[66]

(77) a. 'ú   'áapaci   'that boy (invisible)'
      b. 'áapaci 'ù   'the boy'

Finally, a post-nominal ex-demonstrative definite article may also develop in
a rigid VO language, such as Indonesian.[67] In sum, thus, any correlation between the VO/OV typological dimension and the position of definite articles
is mediated by pragmatic principles controlling word-order, by highly specific
processes of grammaticalization and word-order change, and perhaps by
other factors as well, so much so that a firm correlation seldom, if ever, exists.

---

65) See Ashton (1944). For further discussion see Chapter 11, below as well as Givón (1978).

66) See Givón (1980a). For further discussion of the drift-continuum from OV to VO see Givón
(1975a, 1977a, 1979a, Ch. 7). For discussion of the pragmatic control of word-order variation at
early stages of that drift, see Givón (1983d).

67) The article *itu* 'the', in post-nominal position, is also – when stressed – the demonstrative
'that'. See Soemarmo (1970).

6.8. BASIC WORD-ORDER AND BOUND MORPHOLOGY

6.8.1. Preliminaries

In this section we will discuss briefly Greenberg's (1966) prediction (1c) that OV languages would tend to have suffixal morphology and VO languages prefixal morphology. This generalization seems stronger in OV languages with no evidence of a different earlier word-order and subsequent word-order change. And in general, the longer a language has maintained a rigid OV or VO word-order, the more it is likely to bear out Greenberg's predictions. Which strongly suggests that the correlation between basic word-order and morphotactics is mediated by the specific diachronic processes via which various morphemic categories arise. It is the syntactic word-order prevailing within specific constructions that give rise to specific morphologies — by the reanalysis of one word within the constructions as a function-word and thus a "morpheme" — which most commonly determines the resulting morphotactics.[68] So-called inconsistencies between morphotactics and basic word-order quite often turn out to be nothing of the kind. In the following sub-sections we will survey some of the more common, both strong and weak, correlations.

6.8.2. Case-marking morphology

Within nominal morphology, case-marking morphemes offer perhaps the best correlation between basic word-order and morphotactics. There are two universal primal sources[69] of case-markers. The first is the reanalysis of **serial verbs** (see Chapter 5, section 5.5.4.6., above) as case-marking morphemes on objects. Reconsider first the Niger-Congo examples:[70]

(78) a. iywi **awá**-utsì ikù   ('take' reanalyzed as
         boy *took*-door shut   *accusative*; Yatye)
         'The boy shut **the door**'

---

68) See Givón (1971a, 1975a, 1979b) for further discussion.

69) Some case-markers may arise from re-analysis of others. Thus, for example, it is common for the *locative-directional* ('to') to become a *dative-directional* ('to'), as in English, Hebrew, Bantu etc. and eventually a *definite/human accusative* (as in Spanish). Dative may be reanalyzed as *dative-subjects* (cf. Kannada, Sherpa, Newari etc.) and eventually as *nominatives*. Accusatives may be reanalyzed as *absolutives* – thus at least for a while perhaps *topic* – in the change from nominative to ergative typology (cf. Dyrbal, Eskimo, Samoan etc.). And *genitives* or *instrumentals/associatives* may become *ergative* case markers and thus eventually be reanalyzed into *nominative* markers (cf. Sherpa, Japanese, Newari, Samoan, Dyrbal etc.; for this latter possibility, see Givón (1980c)).

70) For the original data see Givón (1975a).

b. mo **fi**-àdé   gé nākā̀   ('take' reanalyzed as *instru-*
   I   *took*-machete cut wood   *mental*; Yoruba)
   'I cut wood **with the machete**'

c. mo sǫ **fún**-ǫ   ('give' reanalyzed as *dative*;
   I   said *give*-you   Yoruba)
   'I said **to you**'

d. ǫ́ gbàrà ǫ̀sǫ́ **gáa**-áhyà   ('go' reanalyzed as *locative-*
   he ran   *go*-market   *directional*; Yoruba)
   'He ran **to the market**'

Both Yoruba and Yatye in the examples above are rigid SVO languages, and were rigid SVO at the time the serial-verb typology arose. The reanalysis of the verb as case-marker merely translates "verb precedes object" to "preposition precedes noun". But a related language, Ijo, gave rise to virtually the same case-marking system under a strict SOV word-order, i.e. to *suffixal* case markers. Thus compare:[71]

(79) a. yé-**akị̀**-nị̣   ụ-bę́   (*accusative* from
     thing-*take*-ASP him-tell   'take')
     'tell him **a thing**'

   b. erí ogidi-**akị̣**-nị̣   indi pęị-mị́   (*instrumental* from
     he machete-*take*-ASP fish cut-ASP   'take')
     'He cut fish **with the machete**'

   c. dúma tun-ni   a-**pị́rị̣**   (*dative/benefactive*
     song sing-ASP her-*give*   from 'go')
     'sing a song **for her**'

   d. erí ụwǫ́ụ-**dùo** węnị̣-mị̣   (*locative-directional*
     he road-*go* walk-ASP   from 'go')
     'He walked **along the road**'

Here the reanalysis proceeds just as directly from "verb follows object" to "post-position follows noun".

The second primal source of case-marking morphemes is *de-nominal*, from re-analyzing genitival compounds (see Chapter 5, section 5.5.4.7., above). Tnere (cf. examples (59) and (60), chapter 5 for the data), the erstwhile locative *head noun* of the construction becomes reanalyzed as a

---

71) See Givón (1975a). The Ijo data is originally from Williamson (1965).

locative case-marker, while the erstwhile *genitive* modifier becomes the new head noun, as in the English complex locative expression:

(80)   on top **of the house**   ⇒   **on top of** the house
        GENITIVE   LOCATIVE
        MODIFIER   PREPOSITION

In a language with post-nominal genitives, this diachronic reanalysis gives rise to locative *prepositions*. While in a language with pre-nominal genitives, the same reanalysis gives rise to locative *post-positions*. Now, as suggested earlier, the position of genitive modifiers is one of the most reliable correlations between basic word-order (OV/VO) and NP syntax (MOD-N/N-MOD, respectively). Therefore, to the extent that OV languages display pre-nominal genitives and VO languages post-nominal ones, reanalyses as in (80) will indeed yield the predictable correlation (1c) between OV/VO and suffix/prefix, respectively. But as we have seen above (section 6.7.2.), the correlation between basic word-order and genitive word-order is not absolute. In terms of universal predictability, one must add, possible discrepancies arising from this source are not large, given that this diachronic source of case-markers is normally confined to a narrow area of *locational* cases, most commonly *non-directional* (static) ones.

6.8.3. Tense-aspect-modal morphology

Here, over a wide cross-language sample, the correlation between basic word-order and morphotactics (1c) is perhaps the strongest. Tense-aspect-modal markers arise almost always from *main verbs*. Their complements then get reanalyzed as main verbs, while the erstwhile main verb becomes a tense-aspect-modal affix. This may be illustrated schematically as:[72]

(81)   He **wants** to leave   ⇒   He **wants-to**-leave
        MAIN   FUTURE
        VERB   TENSE

When such reanalysis occurs in a VO language, where the main verb *precedes* complement verbs, it gives rise to *prefixal* tense-aspect-modal morphology. Thus, consider the following from Swahili:[73]

---

72)   See discussion in Givón (1973a, 1982a). The reanalyzed main verbs most commonly become *aspect* or *modal* markers, and tense arises later on from the reanalysis of these two.

73)   See Ashton (1944) and discussion in Givón (1973a, 1975a).

(82) a. a-**li**-soma   kitabu   ('be' [-**li**] reanalyzed as PAST)
        he-PAST-read   book
        'He **read** a book'

     b. a-**ta**-soma   kitabu   ('want' [-**táka**] reanalyzed as
        a-FUT-read   book   FUTURE)
        'He **will read** a book'

     c. a-**me**-soma   kitabu   ('finish' [*-**mála**] reanalyzed
        he-PERF-read   book   as PERFECT)
        'He **has read** a book'

     d. a-**na**-soma   kitabu   ('have' [-**na**] reanalyzed as
        he-PROG-read   book   PROGRESSIVE)[74]
        'He is reading a book'

On the other hand, when such reanalysis takes place in an OV language,
where the main verb *follows* the complement, it gives rise to *suffixal* tense-aspect-modal morphology. Thus, consider the following from Ute:[75]

(83) a. wúu̧ka-**xa**   ('have/be' reanalyzed as
        work-PERF   PERFECT)
        '(he) worked'

     b. wúu̧ka-**pu̧gá**   ('have' [-**ga**]   reanalyzed, following a
        work-REM   nominalized complement,
        '(he) worked (long ago)'   as REMOTE PAST)

     c. wúu̧ka-**xwa**-pu̧gá   ('go' [-**kwa**] reanalyzed
        work-ITER-REM   as ITERATIVE)
        '(he) kept on working'

     d. wúu̧ka-**uca**   ('start' [*-**kucá**] reanalyzed
        work-INCEP   as INCEPTIVE)
        (he) was about to work'

     e. wúu̧ka-**vaa**(ni)   ('go/pass [*-**páa**] reanalyzed
        work-FUT   as FUTURE/MODAL)
        (he) will work'

---

74) The analysis here was indirect, with -*na* first leading to a *perfect* aspect and the perfect then
reanalyzed as *present progressive*. For details see Wald (1973).

75) See Givón (1980a).

6.8.4. Negation markers

Negative markers on the verb conform to Greenberg's (1966) prediction ((1c) above) only when they arise from main verbs in a fashion similar to that of tense-aspect-modals (see above). Consider the following examples from Bemba (Bantu), a VO language:[76]

(84) a. uku-bula   'to fail', 'to avoid' (infinitive)

     b. a-à-boomba
        he-PAST-work
        'he worked'

     c. uku-**buláa**-boomba   'not to work' (NEG-infinitive)
        INF-*fail*-work

     d. a-à-**buláa**-boomba
        he-PAST-*fail*-work
        { 'He failed to work' }
        { 'He didn't work' }

Verbs which give rise to NEG-markers in such a fashion are most commonly negative modality verbs, either NEG-implicative such as 'fail', 'stop', 'avoid', 'lack' or NEG-non-implicative such as 'refuse', 'decline'. Presumably then, if the modality verb (for that group see Chapter 4, section 4.2.9.1., above) *follows* the complement verb, as is the case in OV languages, the resulting NEG-marker would be a a verb *suffix*.

While such a correlation is widespread, it is not absolute. This is due to the fact that negative markers may also arise from the reanalysis of *negative intensifiers*. The latter co-exist with the bona-fide, diachronically older NEG-markers, to render more specific, emphatic senses. As a general example consider the following from Modern French:

(85) a. je **ne**   sais   **pas**   (**pas** 'step')
        I   NEG   know   *step*
        'I don't know'

     b. je **ne**   connais **personne**   (**personne** 'person')
        I   NEG   know   *person*
        'I don't know **anybody**'

---

76) See Givón (1972, Chapter 3), with further discussion in Givón (1973a).

c. je **ne** sais **rien** (**rien/ren** 'thing')
I NEG know *thing*
'I don't know **anything**'

The post-verbal position of these intensifiers conforms to their **object** origin in a VO language. Of the three, *pas* may be unstressed, or stressed for emphatic negation, while *personne* and *rien* are stressed and normally emphatic. On the other hand, *ne*, the old pre-verbal negative is unstressed. And in the colloquial dialect *ne* drops out altogether, leaving most commonly *pas* as the neutral, non-emphatic generalized negative *suffix* in a VO language, as in:[77]

(86) je-sais-**pas**
I-know-NEG
'I don't know'

In constrast, the same diachronic source in an OV language, where NEG-intensifying objects would *precede* the verb, will give rise to a negative *prefix*. In illustration of this consider the following from Ute:[78]

(87) a. **kac-ín** wýyka-**wa**
NEG-I work-NEG
'I am **not** working' (emphatic)

b. **ká**-wýyka-**wa**
NEG-work-NEG
'(I) am not working' (less emphatic)

The pre-verbal NEG-prefix may appear as an independent word as in (87a) or in the negative exclamation *kác* 'no'. If the clause contains no clitics (pronominal or others), the pre-verbal NEG-marker shrinks and becomes a less stressed NEG-prefix on the verb. In contrast, the NEG-suffix *-wa* is older, unremovable, never stressed and has a wealth of morphonemic variants (*-'wa, -'a, -na*), all attesting to its older diachronic status, as well as identifying it as a sure bet for dropping out altogether within a few generations, leaving an OV language with a perfectly natural prefixal NEG-marker.

---

77) A similar but earlier change made the intensifier *ne-ought* 'no-thing' in English as the *post-verbal* NEG-marker, as in *didn't, can't, shouldn't, isn't, haven't* etc., while the older, unstressed, pre-verbal *ne* disappeared. Similarly, in colloquial Arabic dialects, **ma-biddi** 'iśśi 'I don't want *anything*' NEG-want thing
has given rise to the contraction **ma-biddi-š** 'I don't want' and later to **biddi-š** 'I don't want' (all from colloquial Palestinian).

78) See Givón (1980a).

6.8.5. Verb derivational morphemes

The most common derivational morphemes on verbs are those affecting transitivization ('causativization', see Chapter 14, Volume II) and detransitivization ('passivization', 'reciprocation', 'stativization', 'reflexivization', see Chapter 15, Volume II). When such morphemes arise diachronically from main verbs, as is most common with **causative** affixes, they cliticize as prefixes in a VO language and as suffixes in an OV language. As an example consider the following from Spanish (VO) and Sherpa (OV):[79]

(88) a. Yo le **hize** comer a   Juán   (Spanish; VO)
     I   him *made* eat   DAT John
     'I made John eat'

   b. nyee   mi-ti-la   laĝá ki **ci**-yin   (Sherpa; OV)
      I-ERG   man-DEF-DAT   work do CAUS-PERF
      'I made the man work'

The causative construction (88a) in Spanish is relatively recent, with the causative morpheme still functioning morphologically as main verb. On the other hand, the Sherpa causative suffix *-ci* in (88b) has already diverged from its cognate *-ki* 'do', 'make' phonologically, and it is not clear which of the two is the main verb in (88b).[80]

What complicates typological neatness is that causative affixes may also arise from an object nominal source, and when that is the case, OV languages would yield causative *prefixes* and VO languages, *suffixes*.[81]

The prefixal or suffixal position of detransitivizing affixes vis-à-vis the verb again depends on their diachronic source. When they arise from main ('auxiliary') verbs, they would cliticize in conformance with Greenberg's

---

79) The Sherpa data is from my own field notes, originally due to Koncchok J. Lama (in personal communication).

80) The fact that *-ki-* in (88b) does not take an infinitival complement form (*ki-tup*) may suggest that it is the main verb, and *-ci-* already a grammatical suffix.

81) Langdon (1977) points out that in Yuman languages, which are rather strict OV languages, causative derivational markers may arise from pre-verbal *instrumental objects*, thus giving rise to causative *prefixes* rather naturally in an OV typology. An etymological connection between the *causative* derivational suffix (reconstructible in cor-Bantu as *-li-į-*, with the *-li-* part being cognate to the benefactive verb-suffix) and the *instrumental* promotion-to-DO suffix has also been observed in KinyaRwanda (Bantu, see Chapter 5, section 5.5.4.5., above). It is possible, however, that in KinyaRwanda the direction of the diachronic extension is the reverse, i.e. *from* causative *to* instrumental.

(1966) prediction (1c), as prefixes in VO languages and as suffixes in OV languages. In illustration consider the following contrast of English (VO) with Ute (OV):[82]

(89) a. He *was*-killed by a bear
      b. 'uwáy   pax̂á-ta-pугá
          he-OBJ kill-PASS-REM
          'He was killed' (agent obligatorily unspecified)

In both languages the passive marker is reconstructible to 'be', but in English it is a pre-verbal auxiliary that would have cliticized had the writing system allowed it to, while in Ute it is a verb suffix.

When de-transitivizers arise from other sources, typological predictions may require more detailed etymological/diachronic information. Thus, a very common source of **reflexive** detransitivizers is a reflexive object pronoun, which may then cliticize on the verb in the position where object pronouns normally do. Now, in a language such as Spanish or Bemba (Bantu), where nominal syntax is VO but pronominal syntax is OV (see section 6.6.9, above), the detransitivizing morphology arising from such a source would conform to prediction (1c) rather trivially. Thus, consider the following from Spanish:

(90) a. Juán **se**-vió   en el   espejo   (reflexive)
          John REF-saw in the mirror
          'John saw himself in the mirror'

      b. **se**-vió   a   Juán en la calle   (impersonal passive)
          REF-saw DAT John in the street
          ⎰ 'John was seen in the street'   ⎱
          ⎨ 'Someone saw John in the street' ⎬
          ⎱ 'They saw John in the street'   ⎰

---

82) See Givón (1980a) and further discussion in Givón (1981b). The suffix -*ta*- marking the impersonal passive in Ute is cognate to -*ra*-, which is the stem of 'be', as in '*u-rá*, '*a-rá*, *ma-rá* etc. The perfect tense-aspect -**ka*- in Ute is also an older passive suffix, and may be still found in nominalized objects, as in *kwiy'á*- 'to fence around', **kwiy'á-ka-tу**   'a fence', 'a thing that has a fence-PASS-NOM
been fenced'; or **pọ'ọ́**- 'write', **pọ'ọ́-kwa-tу**   'book', 'letter', 'a thing that has been written'
write-PASS-NOM
Since the suffix -*tу* is a *subject* nominalizing/relativizing suffix, the only way to obtain it in object nominalization is by assuming an older function of -*ka*- as a passive suffix. On the other hand, when objects are nominalized by a more characteristic object suffix, such as -*pу*, the nominalization is formed without the -ka- suffix. Thus consider *kwicá*- 'defecate', *kwicá-pу* 'feces', etc.

Since the reflexive has developed in Spanish (and many other languages) into an impersonal passive,[83] passive-marking morphology thus arises conforming to the position of object pronouns vis-à-vis the verb rather than to the position of the main verb vis-à-vis its complement.

6.8.6. Noun derivational morphemes

Noun derivational morphemes often arise from the reanalysis of **head nouns** in genitival compounds or other similar noun compounds. As an example consider the following reanalysis in English:

> (91)   mail-*man* [méyl-mn]

Nominal modifiers in English *precede* the head noun. But in (91), the erstwhile head has become a derivational suffix, in a VO language which maintains the old genitival-nominal compounding pattern of an OV language. A similar pattern may be seen in innovating the **diminutive** derivation in Ute, where the language is much closer to its original OV syntax, and where genitive and nominal compounding displays a compatible pre-head pattern. Thus consider:[84]

> (92)   a.   sarí-ci   tuá-ci
>   dog-GEN   child-NOM
>   { 'the child of the dog' }
>   { 'the dog's child' }
>
>   b   sarí-taa-ci
>   dog-DIM-NOM
>   'a puppy', 'a small dog'

In (92a) 'dog' is a genitive modifier preceding the head noun 'child'. In (92b) *-taa-* (ex *tuá-ci*) is a derivational diminutive suffix on 'dog'.

On the other hand, in a language with post-nominal genitives, and thus presumably VO syntax (see Hebrew, section 6.4.2.2., above), the same process is expected to yield derivational *prefixes*. As an example consider the following from Israeli Hebrew:

> (93)   a.   báyit   'house'

---

83) For further discussion of this diachronic development in Spanish and elsewhere, as well as of other diachronic channels giving rise to passive constructions, see Givón (1981b).

84) See Givón (1980a).

b. bet-séfer   'school-house'
   house-of-book

c. bet-kafé   'coffee-house'
   house-of-coffee

d. bet-sóhar   'jailhouse'
   house-of-detention

e. bet-holím   'hospital'
   house-of-sick-PL

In (93a) 'house' receives the normal lexical stress. In (93b-e) it is unstressed and in fact is further contracted in rapid speech to eliminate most of the morpheme altogether, yielding [pt-] or even [t-] as the derivational prefix. What is important to remember, then, is that the correlation between the OV/VO dimension and the suffix/prefix dimension here is indirect, mediated by the syntax of genitive-nominal compounds. And while that typological feature is relatively reliable as a correlation to basic word-order, the predictability is nevertheless not absolute (cf. section 6.7.2., above).

6.9 CONCLUDING REMARKS

Perhaps the most important thing to emphasize in the discussion of word-order typology and the various typological predictions one may draw from it is the central theme of how synchronic typology is forever mediated by diachronic change in word-order and by the diachronic processes through which paratactic constructions give rise to syntactic ones, and syntactic constructions in turn give rise to bound morphology. While the subject of diachronic syntax is outside the main focus of this book, it is not likely that one can develop a coherent view of typology without at the same time elaborating a coherent view of diachronic change.[85]

---

85) For an extensive discussion of this, see Givón (1979a, Chapter 6).

7 | INFORMATION-THEORETIC PRELIMINARIES TO DISCOURSE PRAGMATICS

7.1. INTRODUCTION

As we have suggested earlier above, the sentence — or **proposition** — is the basic unit of information processing in human language. Smaller units, such as words, may carry **meanings** which are represented in the lexicon. They do not, however, carry information ('message') *per se*. Although they can stand for whole propositions and thus carry information, as in (1b) below:

(1) a. *Question*: Who did it?
     b. *Answer*: The butler.

Further, information structure in human language most commonly involves units larger than the single proposition. In this sense human communication is **multi-propositional**. Another name used to refer to it is **discourse**, which whenever appropriate we can then break down into smaller hierarchic sub-units (story, chapter, section, paragraph etc.).

While this book is primarily about syntax, every chapter from now on is in one way or another involved in coding **discourse function** and/or **discourse structure**. This chapter should thus be considered as supplying a set of preliminary notions, most of which will be further amplified and elaborated in subsequent chapters, in this volume as well as in Volume II.

In the discussion throughout we will restrict ourselves, at this point, to largely one major discourse type, the **narrative**. In this type, a single speaker controls the floor for long chunks of speech time, actively producing the discourse. The role of the interlocutor(s) ('hearer(s)'), while important in terms of *feedback*, is relatively passive and non-verbal, involving primarily gestures, facial expressions, eye contact or movement, short exclamations etc. The fact that such feedback may be dispensed with altogether in the extreme — written — form of this discourse genre clearly attests to the more marginal role feedback plays in it, as compared with the other major genre, **conversation**.[1]

7.2. MULTI-PROPOSITIONAL DISCOURSE AND THE GENESIS OF FOREGROUND/BACKGROUND

7.2.1. Tautology, contradiction and informational coherence

A discourse may be likened to a *knowledge system* or *data base*. When two propositions are part of the same discourse, then they perforce stand in some relation of **informational coherence** vis-à-vis each other. If the discourse is abstracted, to be taken only as a chain ('concatenation') of propositions in sequence, then one may say that the informational coherence between two propositions must be a function of their **relative distance** within the chain. But however large that distance may be, so long as they are within the same discourse, *some* coherence relation between them must exist. In other words, the requirement for informational coherence — of whatever kind and strength — between individual propositions within a discourse is a *critical property* for a set of propositions being a discourse — rather than a disparate set.

At the most fundamental ontological level, the relation of informational coherence between two propositions in the same discourse may be stripped down to their being at some point on a continuum between two extremes:[2]

(a)   Tautology
(b)   Contradiction

Tautology is a relation of **informational redundancy**, whereby if the data-base already holds one of the propositions, adding the other would add no more new information to that data-base. Contradiction is a relation of **informational incompatibility**, whereby if the data base already holds one proposi-

---

1) Unlike narrative, conversation involves frequent exchange of the speaker-hearer roles and control of turn-taking. Information is processed in both directions. The *thematic coherence* of the entire discourse covers both speakers'/hearers' contributions. Such coherence is much more complex, involving at various extremes either *joint planning*, antagonistic *tugs of war* or various *asymmetries* in the control of the rate of flow of information and its directionality. The same is also true in terms of the topic identification ('reference') system in conversation. It is assumed, however, that ultimately information-processing frameworks relevant to narrative will reveal themselves to be equally relevant to the analysis of conversation. One such demonstration may be found in Givón (1983c).

2) The initial impetus for this formulation was Wittgenstein's *Tractatus* (1918), though it is not clear that the use I made of it (Givón, 1979a, Chapter 8) is necessarily predictable from Wittgenstein's.

tion, adding the other is impossible without severely disrupting the very informational coherence of the data base. It is clear that if information processing — or the flow of discourse — is to proceed at any pace at all or to any benefit at all,[3] the coherence relation between subsequent propositions in the chain of discourse could stand neither at the extreme of contradiction nor at the extreme of tautology. Rather, discourse is an informational *hybrid* or an informational *compromise*, whereby each proposition in the chain of discourse adds *some* information, so that it is not totally tautological and thus informationally redundant, given the pre-existing data base; nor is it totally novel, without any overlap with pre-existing knowledge — and thus unintegrable and the functional equivalent of a contradiction.[4]

Not only is the *process* of discourse an informational compromise, but each proposition ('sentence') transacted within a coherent discourse must itself be such an informational compromise, containing at least some **old information** that would insure its linkage to the coherence network of the already-transacted discourse, as well as at least some **new information** to supersede total redundancy. The dichotomy between new and old information in discourse as well as in sentences is thus a natural consequence of the coherence requirement of multi-propositional discourse. Under another guise, this is also the dichotomy between **foreground** and **background** information.

7.2.2. Being in the middle and the cumulation of background

If human discourse is indeed multi-propositional, and if the coherence units of such discourse are of sufficient length, say 10-20 propositions at the least,[5] then it is easy to see that when one produces a proposition in the chain of discourse, one has a high probability — 80 to 90 percent, respectively — of

3) An underlying assumption, derived from the theory of speech acts (see Chapter 20, Volume II) is that information is transacted by the speaker at least in part because the hearer welcomes it. For various formulations see Grice (1968/1975) as well as Cole and Morgan (eds, 1975).

4) There is nothing logically contradictory in a proposition that is totally novel to a data-base so that no relation of *informational coherence* holds between it and any other portion of the knowledge system. This is so because the relation of *coherence* within a discourse is not identical to the relation of logical *consistency* in a formal system. The parallels between the two systems are nonetheless revealing, so that one may use the tautotlogy/contradiction dichotomy in logic as a *metaphor* for the dichotomy between "totally redundant" and "totally new" information in discourse.

5) This is a very modest figure, given that books, stories, lectures etc. often have coherence spans of a thousand or more propositions. The figure of ten to twenty proposition corresponds, on an average, to roughly the thematic *paragraph* in connected narrative.

being *in the middle* of the discourse rather than at the beginning or the end. Further, one has at least a 50 percent chance, on the average, of having at least half of the total discourse already transacted — and thus being **background information** — at the time of producing any single proposition in discourse. Given that many discourses, such as stories, books or lectures are a thousand propositions long or longer, the amount of background information potentially relevant to — i.e. part of the coherence structure of — the production of any new proposition within connected discourse may be exceedingly high, even excluding from consideration *generic* background knowledge.[6] Discourse is thus **cumulative** in adding new information chunks to the pre-existing store of background information.[7] This cumulativeness applies both to the *specific* discourse as a coherence system and to the *generic* knowledge as a coherence system. It also entails two **hardware** capabilities of the brain:

(a)   Long-term memory/storage of stable *generic* information ('lexicon')

(b)   Long-term — and short-term — memory/storage of *specific* ('episodic') information

Without these two, neither coherence system, however evident to the outside observer, would have meaning or existence to the actual communicator(s). Long-term memory is thus required for processing both types of information, while short-term memory is relevant to the processing of specific ('episodic') information, most of which is presumably due to partaking in the same communicative transaction.[8]

---

6) See discussion below. In an obvious sense, *generic* background knowledge, shared by the speaker and hearer more or less permanently as a result of living in the same universe, partaking in the same culture/community, speaking the same language and commanding the same lexicon, is of extreme relevance for information processing. It thus forms a higher *coherence system* for each organism through its lifetime, and for each culture/community through its generic lifetime.

7) See Karttunen (1974), as well as further discussion , below, concerning the *communicative contract*.

8) Participating in the same communicative transaction must then be a *sub-species* of participating in the same *experience*, witnessing the same *event*, being on stage during the same *scene*. Discourse — i.e. communication — is thus a way of sharing experiences, events or scenes with others who were not actually there, so that they may add them to their own pool of knowledge, and thus come to experience them too, however vicariously. In many story-telling traditions, the bare facts of the story line are quite familiar to the hearer, whose attention is nevertheless captured due to the narrator's ability to recreate the scene vividly and make the hearer experience it as if he were there.

7.2.3. Thematic structure and shifting coherence

We suggested in section 7.2.1. above that the coherence relation between two propositions in a discourse may depend upon their relative distance within the discourse. This preliminary formulation of the *relativity* of coherence involved a deliberate simplification of the *thematic* ('coherence') structure of the discourse, abstracting it into a mere chain of sequentially-produced propositions. But discourse quite commonly has a deeper, hierarchic structure, roughly along the schema of:[9]

(2)   story

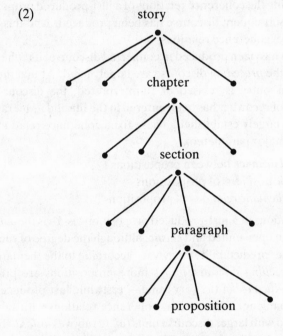

One may look at the **coherence relations** of any proposition in the discourse from two points of view:

(a)   Coherence vis-à-vis the *preceding* discourse; and
(b)   Coherence vis-à-vis the *subsequent* discourse.

These two points of view correspond, broadly, to the needs of the two participants in the discourse transaction, the **speaker** and the **hearer**. From the point

---

9) See Longacre (1976, 1979) and Hinds (1979) for the hierarchic structure of narrative discourse.

of view of the hearer, first, the dominant (though by no means exclusive) concern at any specific point in the discourse — say when a new proposition is produced by the speaker — is how to **perceive** the coherence relations of the new proposition vis-à-vis the *background* of the preceding discourse. From the point of view of the speaker, however, the dominant concern at the very same point is how to **produce** the subsequent discourse with firm coherence relations to what has preceded. Now, this is not to suggest that these two concerns do not overlap to some extent. In particular, the hearer must often reserve his final judgment concerning the coherence relations of a just-produced proposition until more of the subsequent discourse has been produced. And this is the gist of the *relativity* of coherence relations.

Once a proposition has been produced in connected discourse, its coherence relations vis-à-vis the *preceding* discourse are largely fixed. At that moment, and until the discourse is revised or re-interpreted, the discourse background is a matter of record, it has been **entered in the file** and its hierarchic structure has been largely established. These fixed coherence relations are mediated via three major parameters:

(i)   The *temporal distance* between propositions
(ii)   The *hierarchic positions* of propositions
(iii)   The *specific thematic relations* of propositions[10]

The coherence relations of a just-produced proposition vis-à-vis the *subsequent* discourse remain open ended and *elastic*, although the degree of such elasticity (or its converse, predictability) may vary according to the thematic organization of the *preceding* discourse.[11] As more propositions are produced, the thematic *significance* of the very same — erstwhile just-produced — proposition keeps changing, as its various coherence relations with subsequent propositions and with larger discourse units (cf. (2) above) *unfold*. To

10) By 'specific thematic relations' one means here the traditional rhetorical categories such as *sequentiality*, *temporality*, *causality*, *conditionality*, *contrast* etc. These are most commonly coded in English grammar via conjunctions and subordinators such as 'and', 'or', 'but', 'when', 'if', 'because', 'before', 'after', 'in spite of' etc. For more detail see Longacre (1976, 1979, forthcoming). This general subject will be discussed in detail in Chapter 21, Volume II.

11) Some previously-produced discourses are sufficiently clear and elaborate as to suggest quite strongly the next turn in the narrative. Others are by design or lack of design rather opaque. But the degree of *thematic* predictability of human discourse seldom if ever approaches the *deductive* predictability obtained between antecedents and their implications in a logical system (see discussion in Givón, 1982c).

an adjacent proposition it may stand in an 'and', 'but', 'if', 'when' or 'be-cause' relation. To a proposition further down the line it may be a background of **presupposed** knowledge. To a topic/participant in any subsequent proposition it may include an antecedent coreferent topic. From this perspective, then, the thematic relations of all propositions in connected discourse remain open, in a flux. Though one expects such openness to taper off as distance increases.[12]

7.2.4. Thematic structure and the four unities

Beyond distance, specific thematic relations, backgroundedness and the possibility of coreference, the notions **thematic structure** and **coherence relations** remain somewhat opaque. They can, nevertheless, be brought down to earth considerably by the use of the **three unities** observed in the works of the Classical Greek playwrights:

(3)   a. Unity of time
       b. Unity of place
       c. Unity of action

To these three one may now add a fourth, one so obvious that it remained implicit in the classical tradition:

       d. Unity of participants

Given these four unities, the hierarchic structure of narrative discourse may be illuminated by making the following observation:

(4)   "The four unities — or continuities — are more likely to be maintained *within* any particular discourse unit than *across* its boundary with another unit".

And more specifically, the **hierarchy** of discourse units may be captured in making the subsequent observation:

(5)   "More *major*, higher discourse nodes are those at whose boundaries one observes a *greater* number of breakages and discontinuities in the four unities".

---

12) For example, it has been noticed (Givón, ed., 1983a) that with respect to topic identification and coreference relations, the referential distance of roughly twenty clauses ('propositions') to the left is probably some upper bounds in the grammar of topic identification, ones beyond which many languages tend to treat a re-entering topic as if it had just entered into the discourse *file* for the first time. This figure should some day correlate with a putative psychological dimension of "active episodic memory-file".

While changes or continuities of the four unities are not necessarily by them-selves the ultimate thematic gist of the discourse, they are quite commonly the most tangible correlates of thematicity, the heuristics via which thematicity may be tracked.

7.3. THE FUNCTION OF SHARED BACKGROUND INFORMATION IN COMMUNICATION

7.3.1. Sharing a universe: Information vs. manipulation

Three types of **speech acts** are most commonly and distinctly coded in the syntax of human languages:

(a) *Declarative*: Transfer of information from speaker to hearer
(b) *Interrogative*: Request by speaker of information from hearer
(c) *Imperative*: Attempt by speaker to elicit action from hearer

Of the three, (a) is an act of transferring information to others, while both (b) and (c) are acts of manipulating the behavior of others. One may call these two broad types **informative** and **manipulative**, respectively.

In the discussion thus far we have adhered tacitly to the assumption that human communication, or discourse, is largely informative. While this re-quires detailed empirical justification, and while it may depend enormously on the specific **discourse type**,[13] there is a sense in which such an assumption is reasonable. For example, if one disregards academic discourse (largely infor-mative), exams (largely manipulative) or law codiciles (largely manipulative), and if one harkens to informal everyday verbal interaction among adult hu-mans,[14] one is likely to concede that over large stretches of text declarative sentences outnumber interrogatives and imperatives combined by a wide margin. But even if we can justify this tacit assumption about the *prototype* status of the informative speech act, we must ask ourselves why that is the case.

In seeking an answer to this question, perhaps the best strategy one could employ is to contrast our evolved stage of complex multi-propositional dis-course with two social situations where the opposite is true; that is:

13) Some specific genres such as the exam/interrogation or the law may be overwhelmingly man-ipulative. But there is some sense in which these are neither the prototypical discourse, nor the most common overall, nor the ontogenetically or phylogenetically prior ones.

14) There are solid grounds for suspecting that in early childhood most speech acts are primarily manipulative. For discussion see Givón (1979a, Ch. 7).

(a)   Discourse is *not* multi-propositional; and

(b)   Discourse is predominantly *manipulative*

Such social situations are those of *children* during the first few months of life and *higher mammals* throughout life. The social and communicative situation of these two systems may be jointly characterized as follows:[15]

(6)	parameter	higher mammals & early childhood	human adults
a.	*Discourse length*:	mono-propositional	multi-propositional
b.	*Speech act prototype*:	manipulative	informative
c.	*Role of immediate, deictically obvious context*:	predominant	less predominant
d.	*Richness of code*:	impoverished	elaborate
e.	*Social circle*:	closed, genetically homogeneous	open, genetically divergent
f.	*Cultural complexity*:	low	high
g.	*Cultural change*:	slow[16]	fast

It should now be obvious why communication in higher mammals and early childhood is primarily manipulative:

(a)   All discourse topics are present within the immediately accessible deictic range of the speaker and hearer.

(b)   All the information pertinent to the communicative situation is shared.

(c)   The culture is stable, the body of generic knowledge does not require frequent updating.[17]

(d)   The participants belong to a homogeneous and socially-rigid closed circle within which motivation, status, obligation, action prob-

---

15) For discussion see Givón (1979a, Chapters 5, 7).

16) Cultural change among adult higher mammals is virtually nonexistent. Here the human child obviously differs enormously, since the pace of change in its cultural universe is extremely fast — and is accompanied by the parallel development of the adult communicative system.

17) Here again the early childhood situation is different, but may be viewed at any particular time as the early stages approximating to this model.

abilities and social consequences are largely common knowledge.[18]
(e)   The participants share a high degree of empathy, not to mention
      telepathy.

Under such circumstances, there is no particular reason to indulge in informational transactions; the shared *background* for interaction is clear, and all that remains is to transact the *real purpose* of the communication — manipulating the other to do something for you.

There is nothing outrageous in extrapolating from the discussion above the reason why adult human communication is based on the informative speech act as the prototype:

(i)   Communicative topics may be outside the immediate, deictically-
       accessible range.
(ii)   Much pertinent information is *not* held in common.
(iii) Fast change requires periodic updating of the body of shared
       background knowledge.
(iv)   The participants are often strangers, whose motivation, *bona fides*,
       status, obligations and entitlements, action probabilities etc. must
       first be determined.
(v)   The participants may be lacking in empathy and most likely incapa-
       ble of telepathy.

Under such conditions, even granted that the ultimate purpose of the communicative transaction is indeed to manipulate the other toward some target action, the interlocutors must first — and in fact constantly — create, recreate and repair the body of shared knowledge which is the absolute prerequisite for the ultimate communicative transaction.

The culture and communication pattern of higher mammals and early childhood is that of the **society of intimates**. The culture and communication pattern of adult humans is that of the **society of strangers**. Within the latter, given the ascent of the informative speech act as the prototypical one in discourse, the cumulation of background information, in addition to providing the background for the ultimate — manipulative — goal, also performs the vital function of *facilitation* of the informative transaction itself.

---

18) The asymmetry in the communicative exchange between child and care-taker in this early stage is obvious. But caretakers make strong assumptions about the child's motivation from the beginning, i.e. food, heat, comfort, physical contact etc. While the child obviously does not do the same, it is not clear whether at that early age the child is at all aware of the sad fact that its mind is not totally accessible to the care-taker.

7.3.2. New vs. old information

Two fundamental cognitive prerequisites for maintaining coherence and thematic continuity in producing and processing multi-propositional discourse are **memory capacity** and **categorization schemata**. One may in fact wish to argue that the categorization schema specific to the processing of discourse is its **thematic/coherence structure**. Given these two prerequisites, one may now suggest the following property of multi-propositional discourse in terms of the ratio of new to old information:

(7)   **Ratio of new to old information in the production of multi-propositional discourse:**

"At the moment of producing a new proposition — i.e. a chunk of *new information* — in multi-propositional discourse, the ratio of new information within that proposition to *old information* in the discourse *background/context* required for the successful interpretation ('thematic integration') of the proposition, is very large".

There is nothing logically necessary about property (7). One could easily conceive of another discourse type — mono-propositional discourse — where a large bulk of *specific* background ('old') information is not as crucial for thematic integration of a new proposition into the existing body of knowledge/ information.[19] Further, one could hypothesize another mode of processing of multi-propositional discourse, whereby speakers would not rely upon such a large bulk of background information, but rather would explicitly supply it at any point before producing a propositional chunk of new information. But it is easy to see that if such a processing method is used exclusively, the time required to process a single proposition bearing new information would stretch for all practical purposes *ad infinitum*. This conundrum will be illustrated for the two major uses of old information in discourse.

(a)   *Participant deixis*: The referential identification of participants-topics

---

19) As discussed in section 7.3.1., above, such a processing system relies heavily on the existence of a (presumably) equally large body of shared *generic* background information. The difference between the two processing modes, at some crude level, lies in whether background information is *permanently shared* or *specifically assembled* for a particular occasion. Multi-propositional discourse is thus a method of assembling background on a contingency basis for particular communicative occasions.

(b)   *Propositional deixis*: The epistemic-modal, foreground/background, asserted/presupposed identification of propositions

7.3.2.1. The use of old information in participant deixis

Let us illustrate the use of old information in this process, also called **topic identification** (see Chapter 11, below as well as Chapter 22, Volume II), by considering a fairly rudimentary example, such as:

(8)   The man who came yesterday is a crook
(9)   a. There's *a man*,
       b. *he* came yesterday,
       c. *he's* a crook.
(10)   a. There's *a man*;
       b. *That man that there is* came yesterday;
       c. *That man that there is who came yesterday* is a crook.

The most efficient, streamlined, compressed version of this simple chunk of information is (8) above. It relies, in the speaker's assumption that the hearer could identify the referent, on two pieces of old information:

(a)   The participant 'man' has already been introduced previously; and
(b)   The knowledge about that participant 'coming yesterday' is available to the hearer for identifying that man uniquely.

A more expanded, less streamlined version (9) introduces the man (9a), introduces the identifying event (9b) and then processes the new information (9c). But in both (9b) and (9c) the anaphoric pronoun 'he' is used, which signifies reliance on the accessibility of (9a) to the hearer. However, our hypothetical alternative mode of processing proscribed such availability. Perhaps a more realistic approximation of such an alternative mode is then (10), with its rather cumbersome redundancies. But even (10) does not yet eliminate the use of old information in participant deixis, since in (10b) the deictic expression 'that man' is used, depending on the availability of (10a). And in (10c) 'that man' is used again, as well as 'who' which in turn can only be processed if (10b) were available as background knowledge. In sum, then, not only is background information *useful* for establishing referent identification in multi-propositional discourse, it is *indispensible* for affecting such a function. Remove it and the entire function collapses.

7.3.2.2. The use of old information in propositional deixis

Let us now illustrate the use of old information in some of the processes falling under the general label of propositional deixis. Within the grammar of any language, specific coding means are available for tagging certain clauses ('sentences', 'propositions') as being *old*, **presupposed** or *shared-background* information, while identifying others in contrast as *new*, **asserted**, *foreground* information. Consider first the example of relative clauses (cf. Chapter 16, Volume II), as in:

(11) The woman *that Joe saw yesterday* left

(12) a. Joe saw a woman yesterday,
     b. and she left

(13) a. *Speaker A*: The woman that Joe saw yesterday left
     b. *Speaker B*: No, she didn't leave.
     c. *Speaker C*: ?No, Joe didn't see her yesterday

In (11) above the information in the italicized object REL-clause is logically the same as in (12a). However, in (12) two propositions are processed on a par, both *asserted*. While in (11) only one of them — the one equivalent to (12b) — is asserted, and the other — the one equivalent to (12a) — is presupposed. The speaker takes for granted that the hearer is already *familiar* with the event coded in that proposition, that he's not likely to challenge its *truth*. This is illustrated in (13), where a challenge such as (13b) to (13a) is felicitous (see section 7.4., below) but a challenge such as (13c) is infelicitous, signaling a breakdown in the communicative contract. In a similar vein, the italicized sentences in the verb complement (14a) and adverbial clause (14b) below are presupposed/backgrounded:

(14) a. Mary regretted that *John left*
     b. Because *John left*, Mary left too

It would be easy to demonstrate that foregrounding/backgrounding differentiation as in (11), (14a) and (14b) would be impossible to affect without reliance on shared background information. The amount of cumbersome redundancy required for maintaining communication in a system that did not rely on background information would be enormous. Even if the particular grammatical devices in (11), (14a), (14b) were not available, the need to rely on background information for establishing thematic relations between propositions in connected discourse would presumably persist. In short, blocking the availability of old information would make it impossible to process the thematic structure of discourse within a finite time.

7.4. THE SPEAKER-HEARER CONTRACT AND PROPOSITIONAL MODALITIES

7.4.1. The logic-bound tradition: Truth, necessity, possibility

In the dominant tradition of logical analysis of propositions,[20] propositional modalities pertain to **truth relations** between atomic propositions and some universe, be it 'the' Real World or some Universe of Discourse. In addition to the cardinal modalities **true** and **false**, translated in language as 'affirmative' and 'negative', the logical tradition also established several **modes of truth**, three of which turn out to be of particular interest to linguists:[21]

(15) **Traditional modes of truth**
   a. Necessary truth (*analytic* in the Kantian/Peircean tradition)
   b. Factual truth   (*synthetic* in the Kantian/Peircean tradition)
   c. Possible truth (*conditional* in the Kantian/Peircean tradition)

These three modalities are rigidly defined within this tradition as properties vested in individual propositions. Such an approach is a natural consequence of the tradition being *pragmatics-free*, involving neither speaker nor hearer nor speech act nor communicative intent. Nevertheless, it is possible to show that a similar tri-partite system of modalities also exists in human language when studied from a discourse-pragmatic perspective, one which bears some clear isomorphism to the Kant/Peirce/Carnap tradition of propositional modalities in logic. This pragmatically-based system of modalities will be discussed in section 7.4.3., below.

7.4.2. Logic-bound pragmatics: Presupposition and assertion

The logic-bound tradition described in 7.4.1., above, did not directly take account of the contrast between presupposition and assertion. The closest precursor of 'presupposition' in that tradition was the Kantian **analytic truth** (Carnap's **necessary truth**). This mode of truth requires no justification via factual evidence. Rather it is taken for granted as part of the **logical structure** of reasoning, part of the **definition** of terms/rules, etc. Within a later tradition,[22] the notion of presupposition was developed as an extension of logic,

20) As in for example Russell (1905, 1919), Carnap (1947, 1959), *inter alia*.

21) The three are taken, informally, from Carnap (1947, p.175). The identification with the Kantian/Peircean tradition is meant to be only suggestive and informal, since it is not clear whether full logical equivalence holds between the two systems.

22) Strawson (1950), Herzberger (1971), Keenan (1969, 1972), Horn (1972), Oh and Dinneen (eds, 1979), *inter alia*.

roughly meaning "precondition for meaningfulness" of atomic propositions
— as contrasted with "preconditions for truth". This was best illustrated by
taking two propositions, A and B, and showing how regardless of whether B is
true or false, A must be equally true as a *necessary precondition* for B having
its *meaning*. As an example consider the following:

(16) a. Mary regretted that Joe left
      b. Mary didn't regret that Joe left
      c. Joe left

In order to use the verb 'regret' felicitously in either (16a) or (16b), (16c) must
be true. So that (16c) is "presupposed" by both (16a) and (16b). While this
tradition represents a clear advance over traditional logic in accounting for the
linguistic facts, it remains in essence anti-pragmatic. Neither the hearer nor
the speakers are mentioned in this account of "shared background", and the
objectivization of communication as "propositions" disembodied of the
speech act and communicative intent persists in this tradition.

7.4.3. Discourse-pragmatics: The communicative contract

Another way of organizing the facts which appeared previously under the
labels of "necessary truth" and "presupposed truth" is by viewing sentential
modalities as a matter of **epistemic contract** between the speaker and hearer in
communication. We can then recast the three Kantian/Carnapian propositional modalities as follows:[23]

(17) a. **Uncontested knowledge** (including *necessary* truth, *analytic*
                                          truth and *presupposed* truth)
      b. **Realis-asserted knowledge** (including *factual/synthetic* truth)
      c. **Irrealis-asserted knowledge** (including *possible/conditional* truth)

The reason that knowledge/information may be uncontested at a particular
point in discourse/communication is one of several:

(18) a. *Deictic obviousness*: The information is present in the im-
                                    mediate perceptual field of both speaker
                                    and hearer, or is derived from the speak-
                                    er's *direct experience*.
      b. *Shared presupposition*: The information is part of what the
                                    speaker assumes that the hearer already

---

23) See Givón (1982b). For further discussion of *evidentiality*, see Chapter 8, below.

knows due to previous *experience* or previously *shared information* in the discourse.

c. *Divine revelation*: Information both speaker and hearer subscribe to, as coming from unimpeachable *higher sources*.[24]

d. *A priori synthetic*: *Generic* knowledge that is held in common due to living in the same *universe/culture*, as coded in the same *lexicon*.

e. *Analytic truth*: Knowledge shared due to subscribing to the same *mode of thought, logic*, or *rules of various games*.

What such a formulation does is recognize that both the Kantian/Carnapian and the early presuppositional traditions chose to limit their horizons in treating "knowledge taken for granted", due to their reluctance to admit the pragmatics of speaker-hearer and communicative context into consideration. And that further, in human language as used in communication, a number of other categories of knowledge/information are given the same privileged status of **uncontested knowledge**, due to systematic conventions that hold for all users of human language. The three propositional modalities in (17) may now be re-described in terms of their communicative parameters.

(19) **Propositional modalities and the communicative contract**

contract clause	uncontested knowledge	realis assertion	irrealis assertion
a. *speaker's assumption about hearer's knowledge of P*	familiar with P or believes in P	unfamiliar with P	unfamiliar with P
b. *strength of speaker's belief in P*	strongest	strong	weak

contract clause	uncontested knowledge	realis assertion	irrealis assertion
c. *need for speaker to support P with evidence*	not necessary	necessary	not possible
d. *strength of speaker's evidence supporting P*	not an issue	stronger	weaker
e. *speaker's willingness to tolerate challenge to P*	least willing	more willing	most willing
f. *probability of hearer challenging P*	low	intermediate	high

As we can see, this re-formulation of the Kantian/Carnapian modalities subsumes their traditional properties as well as those noted by the later presuppositional-logical tradition. However, it construes those traditional properties not in terms of truth, but rather in terms of various *attitudes*[25] of the speaker and hearer. These include, in particular, the strength of the *speaker's beliefs* and their likely consequences, as well as the speaker's expectations about the *hearer's beliefs*, their strength and likely consequences. In the subsequent discussion, we will refer to the three modalities informally as presupposition, realis-assertion and irrealis assertion. Whenever the difference between realis and irrealis is irrelevant, we will distinguish only between presupposition and assertion.

Within this framework of pragmatically-based propositional modalities, one must remember that the epistemic status of a particular proposition vis-à-

25) For other versions of these attitudes, in particular various *sincerity conditions* associated with *speech acts* analysis, see Austin (1962), Grice (1968/1975), Searle (1970), Gordon and Lakoff (1971) and Cole and Morgan (eds, 1975), *inter alia*.

vis the discourse depends on its proximity to the speech act itself. Thus, a proposition is typically produced first as an **assertion**, and at that time is open to **challenge** by the hearer. But if the hearer chooses not to challenge it, then the speaker may proceed on the assumption that the unchallenged proposition has now been converted into shared **background information** — thus acquiring the status of **presupposition**. And in fact, there are grounds for believing that the longer an assertion goes unchallenged, the stronger would be the speaker's tendency to consider it presupposed/unchallengeable (Givón, 1982b). This is one more facet of the relativity and elasticity of coherence relations in discourse.

7.5. FOCUS OF NEW INFORMATION AND THE SCOPE OF ASSERTION

So far, in discussing the difference between presupposed and asserted information, we have allowed a certain simplification to prevail, whereby *entire* propositions are either presupposed or asserted. But this, in reality, is seldom if ever the case, for a reason already noted in section 7.2.1. above: Propositions produced in connected discourse, in order to maintain both coherence and interest, must stand somewhere between the two extremes of tautology (informational redundancy) and contradiction (informational incoherence). Propositions in real discourse context, then, are most commonly informational hybrids, so that some portions of them are *old*, *presupposed*, or *background* information, presumably serving to anchor them within the coherence structure of discourse (see discussion further below), while other portions are under the scope of asserted *new information*. Most commonly, the *subject* ('main clausal topic') tends to be part of the old information in clauses, while the rest of the clause has a higher likelihood of being new information. This normal tendency is evident in the common interpretation of negative sentences, where the subject is normally left outside the scope of negation:[26]

(20) a. The king of France **is bald**

b. The king of France **is not bald**

---

26) Philosophers tended to assume, traditionally (viz Russell, 1905 and Strawson, 1950, *inter alia*) that the negative (20b) is ambiguous, one reading being "internal" which indeed spares the presupposition ('There is a king in France, but he's *not bald*'), the other being "external" and taking both presupposition and assertion, at least potentially, under its scope ('*It is not true that* there is a king in France, *nor* that he's bald'). For arguments against this interpretation of common syntactic negation, see Chapter 9, below, as well as Givón (1979a, Chapter 3).

The most common negation pattern in language pertains only to the asserted parts, leaving presupposed portions outside its scope (see Chapter 9, below). While the subject is the most common presupposed, non-asserted part of any sentence in connected discourse, it is by no means the only one. Other nominal participants may be excluded from the scope of assertion, such as the object in (21b) below:

(21)   a. *Context*: What did she do with the cheese?
       b. *Reply*: She **ate** it

Neither 'she' (subject) nor 'it' (object) are totally new information in (21b), but only the verb 'ate'.

As we have suggested in Chapter 5, above, when both a direct and an indirect object are present in the sentence, the more common tendency is for the direct object to be old/presupposed ('topical') information, and for the indirect object to be the new, asserted information. Thus, in (22b) below, both subject and DO are 'topics', while both verb and IO are asserted new information:

(22)   a. *Context*: What did they do next?
       b. *Reply*: He **invited** her **over to his house**

While such tendencies are indeed more common, all languages have the mechanisms for reversing them and topicalizing less-likely portions of the proposition such as the verb, while making various nominals the focus of new information. Thus, in (23) below, with its cleft-focus patterns (see Chapter 17, Volume II), in each case only a single nominal participant is under the focus of asserted new information:

(23)   a. **It was Jóe** who invited Mary over to his house   (subject cleft)
       b. **It was Máry** that Joe invited over to his house   (DO cleft)
       c. **It was to his house** that Joe invited Mary   (IO cleft)

Sentences with *all* constituents under the scope of assertion are relatively rare and tend to be discourse-initial. As a classical example consider:

(24)   Once upon **a time**, in **a faraway land**, there lived **a princess**...

But more commonly, in ordinary language, even story-initial sequences involve **topic negotiations**, whereby the new topic is given a *coherence* relation to something already accepted as shared information. Typical examples are:

(25) a. *End of topic negotiation*: ...Now, if **you** are asking for **a story**,
                                                here's one **my grandfather** used to tell.
         Story opening: **He** was caught in a blizzard in the dead of winter
                            in '83...
      b. *End of topic negotiation*: ...**You** wanna hear about **Joe**? I'll tell
                                                you about **Joe**.
         Story opening: **Joe** was born in...
      c. *End of topic negotiation*: ...The topic of today's lecture is
                                                ZZYZX.
         Story opening: **ZZYZX** is a small ghost-town in the Mojave
                            desert...
      d. *End of topic negotiation*: ...Could you tell me **what time** it is?
         Story opening: **It** is 4:00 PM

Topic negotiations preceding a discourse serve to establish the *relevance* of
entering into this *particular* discourse, vis-à-vis who is present (I, you, he), who
is talking (I), who is listening (you) and their various goals and expectations,
their assumed prior knowledge etc. In other words, discourse seldom if ever
begins from ground zero in terms of specific shared background information.

7.6. THE RATE OF INCREMENTING NEW INFORMA-TION: THE "ONE CHUNK PER CLAUSE" PRINCIPLE

In the preceding section it was suggested that asserted declarative sentences in connected discourse are informational hybrids, containing some
new information and some presupposed, backgrounded or topical old information. In this section we will survey a range of evidence suggesting that in
fact most asserted clauses in connected discourse contain *only one* item —
henceforth **chunk** — of new information. In other words, in the processing of
human discourse, the following principle seems to hold:[27]

(26) **The One-Chunk-Per-Clause processing principle**
      "The majority of sentence/clauses in connected discourse will have
      only *one chunk* — be it a nominal, predicate (verb, adjective) or
      adverbial word/phrase — under the scope of asserted new informa-
      tion. All other elements in the clause will tend to be topical,
      background or presupposed old information".

---

27) For the first formulation of this principle and more supporting evidence, see Givón (1975b).

If principle (26) indeed holds, it would mean that intransitive clauses, with only subject and verb, would tend to vest new information in the verb, since the subject is most commonly the connecting topical **leitmotif** and thus old information. And that in transitive (or two-argument) clauses, either the verb or the object would tend to be old information ('topical') as well. This would predict that the majority of discourse contexts for transitive clauses would more closely resemble (27a) and (27b) below, rather than, say, (27c):

(27) a. *Context*: What did John see then?
          Reply: He saw **a dog**.   (object focus of new information)
      b. *Context*: What did John do to the dog?
          Reply: He **fed** it   (verb focus of new information)
      c. *Context*: What did John do then?
          Reply: He **fed a dog**   (both verb and object focus
                                                  of new information)

The evidence supporting principle (26) comes from diverse sources. First, consider languages where, within the tense-aspect system, a special morpheme codes the following distinction:[28]

(28) a. The verb is *included* in the scope of new information
                                    vs.
      b. The verb is *excluded* from the scope of new information

Given that the subject is normally excluded from asserted scope, variant (28a), which turns out to be the more *marked, less frequent* one in discourse, is used mostly when the clause is intransitive (one argument). While variant (28b), which turns out to be the *unmarked, more frequent* one in discourse, is used mostly — almost obligatorily — when the clause is transitive (two or more arguments). This means that when a direct or indirect object (or an adverb) is present, in connected discourse the verb would be most commonly *excluded* from the scope of new information, much like the subject, and thus only one argument — the single chunk — will fall under the scope of asserted new information.

The next piece of evidence involves the use of WH-questions. As will be seen later on (Chapter 20, Volume II), WH-questions tend to elicit new information in the context when the entire clause is familiar ('presupposed'), with the exception of a single element. What is requested then is that *one chunk* of

---

28) See Chapter 8, below, as well as the original description in Givón (1975b).

new information, be it the subject, object, indirect object or various adverbials (but much less commonly, though occasionally, the verb). Typical examples of the normal WH-pattern are:

(29) a. *Subject*: Who killed the dog?
  b. *DO*: Whom did John kill?
  c. *IO*: To whom did John send the letter?
  d. *Locative*: Where did Mary go?
  e. *Time*: When did she leave?
  f. *Manner*: How did he break the code?
  g. *Verb or predicate phrase*: What did she do?

On the other hand, double or triple WH-questions such as (30) below are clearly a rare, marked pattern:[29]

(30) Who did what to whom?

What this means is that the principal method of eliciting specific constituent responses imposes principle (26) on the solicited response.

The next piece of evidence does not pertain to the exclusion of the verb from the scope of new information, but rather to the exclusion of one object in bi-transitive (two-object) clauses in connected discourse. When both direct and indirect object are present, one of them — most commonly the DO (see Chapter 5, above) — tends to be **topical** or old information, leaving the other alone under the scope of asserted new information. The existence of this strategy of discourse processing is supported by text-counts from English.[30]

The next piece of evidence concerns optional adverbial arguments, such as manner, benefactive, purpose, time or instrumentality. In text, they most commonly *attract* the focus of new information, to exclude the verb as well as other obligatory non-subject arguments. The rationale for such behavior is presumably that if an optional argument is added to a clause, it must be communicatively most salient — i.e. the focus of new information. This would mean, among other things, that responses such as (31b, d, f, h) below are more likely to be elicited by the **narrow focus** questions (31a, c, e, g), respectively, than by the **wide focus** question (31i):

(31) a. How hard did he work? ('He worked' is presupposed)
  b. He worked **very hard**.

29) See Wachowicz (1976).

30) See Givón (1981a).

c. What did he plow with?   ('He plowed' is presupposed)
d. He plowed **with a tractor**.
e. When did he arrive?   ('He arrived' is presupposed)
f. He arrived **at five o'clock**.
g. For whom did he build the house'   ('He built the house' is pre-
                                      supposed)
h. He built the house **for his mother**.
i. What did he do?   ('He acted' is presupposed)

With some optional adverbials, this tendency is actually grammaticalized. This is the case with 'deliberately' below, so that (32a) with *narrow scope* is a much more natural elicitation of (32c) than is (32b) with the *wide scope*:

(32) a. Did he kill the goat accidentally? (narrow scope elicitation)
      b. What did he do then? (wide scope elicitation)
      c. He killed the goat **deliberately**.

Finally, one can present some text-count evidence concerning the distribution of definite vs. indefinite nominal arguments in actual discourse, in support of the contention that at least *on the average*, in running text in English, the tendency is to have *less than two chunks* of new information per proposition. To illustrate this type of evidence, 110 declarative verbal clauses were analyzed, taken from four consecutive pages of a detective novel.[31] Each clause had at least one non-verbal/non-sentential complement ('object'). Thus, one-argument clauses, with only subject and verb, were not counted (since in those, given the topicality of subjects in general, our point would hold redundantly). Adverbial clauses and REL-clauses were not included. And the assumption was made, a priori, that all subjects were definite.[32] Finally, just to be on the safe side, all verbs were counted as *new information*, disregarding presumably emphatic and negative clauses in which the verbs may not in fact be new information.[33] The 110 clauses then automatically contained *110 chunks* of verbal new information. Of the total of 110 verbal clauses, *67* had one object, *39* had two objects and *4* had 3 objects. The total

31) MacDonald (1951/1971), pp. 25-28.

32) Similar texts were counted in Givón (1979a, Ch. 2), where it was found that on the average subjects in low-brow English fiction were *95 percent* definite.

33) The verb is part of the presupposed, old information portion of focus sentences (see Chapter 17, Volume II). A similar argument can be made for negative sentences (see Chapter 9, below).

number of object chunks in the sample was then *157 chunks*. Of these only *46 object chunks* were indefinite or new information. Added to the *110 verb chunks*, the total was then *156 chunks* of new information per 110 clauses ('propositions'), or *1.41 chunks per proposition*. By eliminating from the sample most presuppositional (verb complements of cognition verbs, REL-clauses, WH-questions, syntactic CLEFT-focus constructions, adverbial clauses) and one-argument clauses, the sample was deliberatly biased toward over-representing new information, so that the average in a less-biased, more realistic sample would have been even closer to *one chunk* per proposition.[34] So, while one must keep in mind that the results represent an average, and that within the text some asserted clauses may have added *no* chunks of new information (thus presumably serving more as background information) and others may have had two or three chunks, the average *flow* of new information in narrative discourse, if the chunks are defined as verbal, nominal, adverbial or adjectival words,[35] approximates the proposed value set in principle (26) above.

The reasons why asserted clauses in connected, coherent discourse should contain some old and some new information have already been given in section 7.2.1. above, namely:

(a)   Sentences with *only* new information will be incoherent; and
(b)   Sentences with *only* old information would be redundant.

But principle (26) is not logically necessary given the twin requirements of **coherence** ('connectivity') and **informativeness** ('interest'). Further, if **efficiency** were the major concern in processing connected discourse, principle (26) is obviously an inefficient dampener on the processor. If such a principle is nonetheless a fact, then it must be motivated by either one of the following considerations:

34) It is assumed here that if the entire proposition is known to the hearer, i.e. codes a state/event familiar to him, then it must also be the case that the identity of the topics/participants in such a proposition is *not* new information to the hearer.

35) The identification of lexical words with chunks of information is reasonable, since they carry the major load of semantic information in the clause. Grammatical morphemes, on the whole, tend to code propositional *roles* and discourse-pragmatic *functions*. It is likely that a slight correction may have to be made to this way of reckoning 'chunks', to take into account modified *phrases*, in particular noun phrases with nominal, adjectival or verbal modifiers. There is some evidence, however, that within such noun phrases — especially if the modifiers are restrictive — it is the *modifier* word rather than the head noun which carries the focus of new information. In which case the correction would turn out to be somewhat trivial.

(i)   Transmission *speed* of the processing channel
(ii)   Integration *speed* of the storage space
(iii) Integration *mode* of the storage space

Of these three, (i) and (ii) are of less interest, but must be resolved empirically one way or another. They presumably represent two possible bottlenecks in the processing of **episodic information**, and it may well be that the two turn out to be one and the same, and thus one major mechanical aspect of the neurological **hardware**.[36] The possibility that principle (26) may be motivated by consideration (iii) above, i.e. by some less mechanical properties of the **software** or the manner by which new episodic information is integrated within the already existing **coherence structure** of the storage, is obviously more attractive. We will discuss it below.

7.7. THE ROLE OF OLD INFORMATION IN INTEGRATING NEW INFORMATION

We have suggested throughout (but see initially section 7.2.1., above) that propositions in connected discourse must contain *some* old information in order to integrate or "address" the new information onto the appropriate location within the storage space. If principle (26) of "one chunk per proposition" turns out to indeed hold for human language, it raises the following complex hypothesis:

(33) a. *Modality of integration of new information*: "The chunks of old, topical, background information in the proposition constitute its **addressing mechanism**, referring it to the right pre-established location, to be filed there within the coherence network of the discourse".

b. *Strength of integration of new information*: "The more chunks of old information the proposition has, the more *securely*, more *permanently* and the *less tentatively* it can then be integrated into the coherence structure of the discourse".

c. *Speed of integration of new information*: "The more chunks of old information the proposition has, the *faster* will be the pro-

---

36) Upper limits on processing speed have been observed in other areas of speech processing, some pertaining to the number of phonemes per second (cf. Miller and Taylor, 1948), others to the numbers of words per minute (cf. Orr, Friedman and Williams, 1965). See further discussion in Lieberman *et al* (1967).

cess of integrating it into the coherence structure of the discourse, because the search through the pre-existing network would proceed on the basis of a larger number of *clues*, and will thus have less **indeterminancy** in it".

Portions (33b) and (33c) of hypothesis (33) may be viewed as a psycho-linguistic research program, one that ought eventually to dovetail with an equally complex neuro-linguistic research program. If (33b), (33c) turn out to be the case, then our processing principle of "one chunk per proposition" will receive a natural, if initially less obvious, explanation.

One might as well note, further, that a counter-hypothesis may be formulated, one which could construe the effect of principle (26) in a somewhat different direction. That is:[37]

(34)   *Cost of integrating information*:
  a.   *Cost of old information*: "The more old information chunks there are in a proposition, the more complex — thus *slower* — will be the task of integrating it into the pre-existing coherence network, since a larger number of addresses will have to be checked systematically".
  b.   *Cost of new information*: "The more new information chunks there are in a proposition, the more complex — thus *slower* — will be the task of integrating it into the pre-existing coherence network, *if* a large enough number of old information chunks are supplied. Or, alternatively, the less successful the integration task will be — and the more **disorder** will arise in the system as a whole — if a sufficient number of old information chunks are *not* supplied".

If (34a) turns out to be true, then it follows that the ideal clause-type for discourse-processing is one that contains only *two chunks* of information, one new, the other old.

It may turn out, finally, that (33c) and (34a) are not totally contradictory, but rather represent the two extreme upper limits on information processing in discourse. So that up to a certain point (say 2-3-4 chunks of old information per proposition) clause (33c) holds, but above that point clause (34a) holds. This would suggest an *optimal* number of "addresses" per chunk of new infor-

---

37) For this suggestion I am indebted to Doug Moran (in personal communication).

mation, one that will be *larger than one* but obviously not infinite. Again, all three possibilities are in fact parts of a complex program for future research.

7.8. MOVING FROM SPECIFIC TO GENERIC INFORMATION

In section 7.3.1., earlier, we contrasted higher mammal (and early childhood) communication with adult human language, suggesting, among other things, that the role of the immediately available **situational context** is paramount in the phylogenetically and ontogenetically earlier communicative modes. We further suggested that those early modes also rely much more heavily on the stable pool of shared **generic information**. Between the use of shared immediate context and shared generic information, it was argued, the early communicative modes can get away with little incrementation of **specific knowledge** via propositional, informative discourse. The discussion from that point onward tracked primarily the *use* of specific, discourse-coded information in communication and the *manner* of processing such information. Such specific information tends, on the whole, to involve specific events/states, obtaining at specific times and places and involving referentially unique participants. It was further assumed that such information is processed and stored in something like **episodic memory** or **episodic storage**.

Underlying all transactions of specific information — and making them all possible — is a different, vast pool of stored knowledge, the *generic* one, pertaining to how things are *in general*, what events are *likely* to occur, *how* and *why*, how participants are *likely* to behave under diverse and generally understood circumstances, what are likely *motivations* for behavior and likely *causes* of events. Within the linguistically-coded system, much of this information turns out to be stored in the **lexicon**, as meanings of words which stand for various *types* of states, events, objects, persons, institutions, customs, behavior patterns, ideas etc.

While at the two extremes, specific and generic information seem to contrast rather drastically, one can easily see that there is a potential continuum of *degree of generality* of information. Thus, specific individuals may indulge in generic activities in generic times and places, as in:

(35)   John always smokes wherever he goes

Conversely, generic groups may together indulge in the same activity at the same specific time and place, as in:

(36)   Everybody held their breath as the news came on

In some cultural groups, knowledge of some important specific persons, events or objects is generically shared, as in:

(37) a. Louis XIV   (in France)
     b. Plato   (in Western civilization)
     c. Word War II   (in most of the human world)
     d. The Sun   (for all humans & perhaps all animates)

The process of transforming specific information available to the individual into generic information shared by all members of the culture is thus, presumably, a gradual transition.

One may view the process by which an individual ('organism') adds to its storage of new information — first specific and then generalized — and the process by which the culture ('species') adds information to its pool of culturally-shared knowledge (Science, Libraries, Computers) as fundamentally the same process but practiced at different meta-levels. New information must always penetrate the system as **specific information**. But at that level already the process involves the *contract* between speaker and hearer. Two steps of inductive/abductive **generalization** must then take place within the individual absorbing new information:

(a) Generalization about the *similarity of events/states* pertaining to the same referential token, thus creating the notion of *type of event/state*; and
(b) Generalization about the *similarity of individual tokens* which participate in similar events/states, thus creating the notion of *type of individual*.[38]

In addition, for generic information to be the generically shared background within the culture, another potentially gradual process of spreading it to more and more individual speakers must take place.

Within the storage pool of a single speaker, there must be open access from *episodic storage* to *generic/lexical storage*. This is so because the two generalization processes suggested above both require cross-comparisons

---

38) The asymmetry between 'event' and 'individual' is grounded in necessary ontological facts: An event at a different time could never be the *same* event, only a *similar* one. But an individual at a different time could either be the *very same token* individual or a similar one (i.e. member of the type). This dichotomy is due to our construction of events ('verbs', 'states') as being prototypically *less time-stable*, while individuals ('nouns') are prototypically more time-stable, and thus capable of maintaining their referential identity across large time-spans. For discussion, see Chapter 3, above, as well as Givón (1979a, Ch. 8).

within the pool of episodic memory in order to consolidate generic information — and then presumably move it on to the more stable pool of lexical storage. Therefore, while one would want to posit the existence of both cognitive/neurological capacities, one must also provide for connections between the two. Within the culture ('species'), one may view science as the systematization of this process of generalization, via which specific information gets generalized, to the point where it affects changes in the culture's *generic view* of its universe. The probabilistic, inductive/abductive nature of such a process in science must surely resemble the process of moving from specific to generic information within the individual.[39]

---

39) See further discussion in Givón (1982b).

8 | TENSE-ASPECT-MODALITY

8.1. INTRODUCTION

8.1.1. Tense-aspect-modality in the grammar

Of all grammatical sub-systems, tense-aspect-modality is probably the most complex and frustrating to the linguist. For one thing, it is an obligatory category without which simple sentences cannot be produced. Because of this, one must confront tense-aspect-modality (henceforth TAM) relatively early in studying the structure of simple clauses of a language, in some sense earlier than the complexity of TAM vis-à-vis other areas of the grammar would warrant. While being an obligatory component of simple sentences, TAM in fact constitutes one of the major devices coding the *connectedness* — or coherence — of sentences in their wider discourse context. TAM is thus intimately involved in the grammar of complex constructions and complex discourse functions, so that the label 'simple' as applied to the common TAM markers that may appear, as various options, in simple clauses, is to some extent illusory.

8.1.2. Semantics vs. pragmatics of TAM

The various categories comprising the complex system of TAM are clusters of semantic and discourse-pragmatic features. As *lexical semantic* features, they are intimately involved in the meaning-structure of verbs ('predicates'). As *propositional-semantic* features, they code various facets of the state, event or action. And as *discourse-pragmatic* features, they play a crucial role in the sequencing of propositions in discourse, in foregrounding or backgrounding them, and in indicating their time/truth/certainty/probability modalities vis-à-vis the speaker-hearer contract. This clustering of all three functional realms around one coding sub-system in the grammar is far from accidental. As we have seen earlier (cf. Chapter 3), of all lexical categories the *verb* is most intimately associated with coding states/events/actions in the proposition. There exists, thus, a *gradation* from the lexical-semantic properties of verbs, to their propositional-semantic properties in coding states/ events/actions, and onward to their contextualized properties in connected discourse. The TAM system in grammars thus reflects this gradation, whereby some features may be viewed as having a narrower, lexical-semantic scope, others as having a wider propositional scope, and others yet as having the widest, discourse-pragmatic scope. It is also common for the same coding unit, say a morpheme, to code a *cluster* of lexical, propositional and discourse functions.

8.1.3. Deictic foci in sentences

As suggested earlier (cf. Chapter 7, above), the connectedness/coherence of propositions in discourse is coded in the grammar of human languages by two — or sometimes three — complexes of grammatical devices:

(a)   The grammar of **topic identification** ('participant deixis')

(b)   The grammar of **propositional identification** ('propositional modalities', 'propositional deixis')

(c)   The grammar of **connectives** (conjunctions, subordinators)

The first complex tends to cluster as *nominal* morphology, primarily as case-markers and articles. The second complex tends to cluster as *verbal* morphology, primarily the TAM system. The third complex may either occupy a *presentential* position, as in English and most VO languages, or else be part of the *verbal* morphology cluster and thus, possibly, be associated with the TAM system, as is characteristic of OV languages. Both (b) and (c) are thus associated, in various ways, with **propositional deixis**, i.e. anchoring entire propositions (rather than their sub-components) relative to other propositions, temporal or thematic contexts, etc.[1]

8.1.4. TAM morphology

As suggested in Chapter 3, above, TAM morphology tends to cluster — and often cliticize — around the verb. This is in part due to the history of the

---

1) Prototypically and phylogenetically/ontogenetically, topic/participant deixis tends to be *spatial*, while propositional deixis tends to be *temporal*. This is probably predictable from the categorial prototypes of noun and verb (cf. Chapter 3, above), whereby nouns are *time-stable* and thus identifying them uniquely by points in time is not a useful strategy for deixis. On the other hand, verbs are *time-unstable*, existing only at particular times, so that identifying them uniquely by points in time is more likely to be a viable deictic strategy. See further discussion in Hopper and Thompson (1983) and Givón (1979a).

markers, most of which arise via re-analysis of erstwhile **main verbs**.[2] Such reanalysis is gradual and protracted. Consquently, at the initial point of this process the TAM marker-to-be is to all intents and purposes a main verb itself, semantically, syntactically and morphologically. As such, it is often referred to as an **auxiliary verb**. As the TAM marker becomes more specialized as a grammatical morpheme, it gradually loses its original verbal meaning, syntax and morphology, becoming de-stressed and phonologically compressed/shortened. This eventually leads to full **cliticization**, as prefix or suffix on the verb.[3] Depending upon the presence of other — often older — verbal morphemes around the verbal word during this process of cliticization, verbal inflectional morphology and the distribution of TAM markers within it can become quite murky and communicatively less-than-transparent. TAM markers may eventually fuse into *portmanteaux* with each other, with negation markers or with pronominal/agreement markers. Potentially neat morphotactics which, when present, often signal important semantic and pragmatic *scope* relations, may thus become offset by diachronic change, yielding bizarre synchronic states. For this reason, the morphological status of the very same semantic/pragmatic categories of TAM may exhibit vast cross-language variability, a phenomenon that will be illustrated at various junctures below.

8.1.5. Chapter organization

We will first introduce the *semantic space* and/or discourse-pragmatic *functional domain(s)* underlying TAM systems. In doing so, I would like to acknowledge a number of more recent antecedents. They will not be cited at specific points, since on the whole I have not adhered to any particular one. Nevertheless, their overall influence and my eventual indebtedness to them is hereby acknowledged.[4]

Having outlined the functional domains of TAM, we will proceed to examine a number of TAM systems from different language types, endeavoring to establish at least the beginning of a universal *typology*, i.e. the most

---

2) For further discussion of this, see Givón (1973a).

3) See Givón (1971a, 1975a).

4) They are Bull (1968), Comrie (1976), Chung and Timberlake (forthcoming) and Hopper (1979, 1982 ed.). The materials here also owe something to my own ealier work (Givón 1972, Chapter 4, 1977b, 1982a). Of special value for the development of my own thinking on TAM systems has been the work of Bickerton (1975, 1976, 1977a, 1977b, 1981), also of Bickerton and Odo (1976) and Bickerton and Givón (1976).

likely ways by which a language may code the TAM domain. We will do this by discussing first the universal **Creole** TAM system, which is in some sense a **prototype** of TAM systems, and then we will introduce and illustrate more idiosyncratic and language-specific cases.

The great morphological variety of TAM systems will be illustrated throughout. Lastly, we will deal with a number of sub-areas of TAM systems which link them to other areas of the grammar.

8.2. THE SEMANTIC/FUNCTIONAL DOMAIN OF TENSE-ASPECT-MODALITY

8.2.1. Preliminaries

In this section we will discuss the notional ('categorial') space, semantic as well as pragmatic, underlying TAM systems in human language. The categories established here will be referred to later in describing language-specific TAM systems. These are the most common, universally-attested categories. A few others will be introduced later on, during the discussion of some specific systems.

The division within the TAM notional space into **tense**, **aspect** and **modality** is far from spurious. In one way or another, these three represent three different *points of departure* in our experience of **time**. Tense involves primarily — though not exclusively — our experience/concept of time as *points in a sequence*, and thus the notions of **precedence** and **subsequence**. Aspects of various kinds involve our notion of the **boundedness** of time-spans, i.e. various configurations of *beginning*, *ending* and *middle* points. But in the semantic space of aspect, nearly always some element of tense is also involved, in terms of establishing a **point-of-reference** along sequential time. Finally, modality (see Chapter 7, above) encompasses among other things our notions of **reality**, in the sense of "having factual existence at *some* real time" ('true'), "having existence at *no* real time" ('false'), or "having *potential* existence in some *yet-to-be* time" ('possible'). In describing the three major categories and their sub-components or variants, we will initially maintain the pretense that each forms a separate, self-contained functional domain. Such pretense is convenient for the purpose of exposition, but is probably ultimately not warranted. Synchronically, diachronically and ontogenetically, TAM categories are interconnected, as well as connected to other regions of our conceptual map.[5]

8.2.2. Tense and sequential time

There are two fundamental features involved in our concept of time as reflected in tense systems:

(a) **Sequentiality**: Tense is a way of construing time as a succession of *points*, each one occupying a *fixed position* in the linear order, thus either preceding or following other discrete points in the sequence. Within such a sequence, **precedence** means "existing/occurring before", and **subsequence** "existing/occurring after".[6]

(b) **Point of reference**: Within the flow of linear time, one may establish a point of reference — the **time axis** — with respect to which the 'past' precedes and the 'future' follows. The most common universal point of reference is the **time of speech**, anchored to the speaker at the time of performing the *speech act*. This is the 'now', taken for granted as the *unmarked* time axis, unless another, more marked one is explicitly specified.[7]

The interaction between the two features of tense may be expressed diagrammatically as follows:

(1)

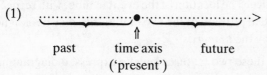

past   time axis   future
('present')

Given such representation, 'past', 'present' and 'future' may now be defined rigorously and exclusively by their positions on the ordered time dimension relative to the time-axis. 'Always' ('habitual') may be defined as either

(a) At all times; or
(b) Unspecified for time

Within past and future, moreover, one may now make further distinctions such as 'near past', 'remote past' etc. based on *relative proximity* to the time axis. The present may be further sub-divided through the *aspectual* property of *duration* (see below) into 'continuous/durative present' or 'instantaneous present'. Finally, the time-axis itself may be either **absolute** ('now', 'time of

---

6) For discussion of the ordered dimension 'time', see Givón (1979a, Chapter 8).

7) The time-axis in tense systems is *speech-act anchored*. But an embryonic, *event-anchored* time-axis exists as part of the semantic structure of all non-stative verbs. For the original discussion, see Givón (1973a).

speech') or **relative** ('then'; i.e. fixed by other means, most commonly by *time adverbial* words or by reference to *other events*).

8.2.3. Duration, continuity and punctuality

We have already noted in Chapter 3, above, that **duration**, i.e. the degree of *diffuseness* vs. *compactness* in time, is an important variable characterizing the semantics of verbs. Some verbs were seen as *instantaneous* ('hit', 'shoot', 'kick', 'expire', 'blink' etc.). Others tended to be extended **states** ('know', 'wish', 'be angry', 'be tall' etc.). And the bulk of the verbal lexicon occupies various intermediate positions between these two extremes. When the feature of duration is used within an aspectual system, it is most common to find only the binary contrast between *durative/continuous/progressive* and *punctual/compact*. The semantic space underlying this distinction is the product of interaction between two basic features, one already familiar from the discussion of tense, above:

(a) **Boundedness**: The durative aspect construes an event as having *no initial or terminal boundaries*. In contrast, the punctual aspect construes an event as *having such boundaries*.

(b) **Point of reference**: The location of the event in time, with respect to which the relative position of the two boundaries may be assigned, is again given by the *time-axis*.

The interaction between these two features may be expressed diagrammatically as follows:

(2) *Durative ('unbounded')*:

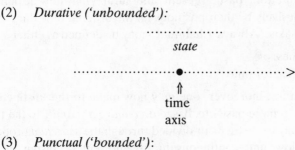

(3) *Punctual ('bounded')*:

Most commonly, predicates that are semantically *states* are already durative by definition and thus do not take the durative aspect *per se*. The durative aspect thus applies only to *punctual* verbs, and thereby converts them into states. Thus consider:

(4)   a. She knew the answer (state)
      b.*She was knowing the answer
      c. She read the book (compact event)
      d. She was reading the book (durative state)

While a compact event such as (4c) receives its time-axis ('point of reference') *implicitly* in discourse,[8] the durative (4d) often requires an *explicit* point of reference, as in:

(5)   When I came into the room, she **was reading** the book

The restriction in (4b) does not hold in languages where the marker used to code *present tense* is also extended by inference to mean *progressive*. Such an extension holds only for bounded events but not for verbs that are semantically stative. Thus consider the following from Israeli Hebrew:

(6)   a. hu koré et   ha-séfer
          he read ACC the-book
          'He **is reading** the book'
      b. hu yodéa et   ha-tshuvá
          he know ACC the-answer
          'He **knows** the answer'

The participial form of the verb is identical in (6a, b). In Israeli Hebrew this form may code either the *present* or the *habitual* tense. With the punctual verb in (6a) the present *progressive* is a natural interpretation. With the stative verb in (6b), the most likely interpretation is the *habitual*; a less likely but possible one — given the proper context — is the *present* non-progressive, as in:

(7)   axsháv hu yodéa et   ha-tshuvá
      now   he know ACC the-answer
      '**Now** he knows the answer!'

---

8) As we shall see later, bounded events tend to be the sequential backbone of narratives, while unbounded states tend to be occasional background interruptions in the sequential flow. A clause in sequence depicting an event is thus most likely to receive its time-axis from the preceding clause. This is less often the case with clauses depicting unbounded states, which often disrupt the thematic continuity and demand a re-established point of reference.

But the progressive remains an impossible interpretation of (6b) and (7).

The time-axis for the progressive may be the implicit 'now', or it may be *relativized* as in (4d), and one may view this as a *tense* phenomenon rather than an inherent feature of the durative aspect. Finally, lacking *both* boundaries also means, redundantly, lacking a *terminal* boundary, a feature that characterizes the *imperfective/incompletive* aspect, see below.

8.2.4. Perfectivity

As seen above, durativeness involves the lack of *both* boundaries. But the initial and terminal boundaries which are missing in the durative are not on a par. The missing terminal boundary is a consequence of the location of the time-axis — *in the middle* of the event/state. It is missing because it has *not yet arrived*, the state/event is *in the middle*. On the other hand, the initial boundary is missing because it *has not been construed*. In purely logical terms, thus, an *event* in the middle of occurring must have had a beginning, however remote in the past. If not, it couldn't possibly be an event, but rather a permanent state.

The contrast between **perfective** ('completive') and **imperfective** ('incompletive') involves the **terminal boundary** of events, as well as its relationship to the *time-axis*. These two features interact in the following ways:

(a)   **Termination**: An event is *perfective* if at the time axis it has been *completed, terminated, accomplished*. That is, it has a terminal boundary at the time axis. In contrast, an event is *imperfective* when no terminal boundary is present at the time axis.

(b)   **Point of reference**: The time-axis pertains to the *end point* of a perfective event, or where the end point would be construed if the event were bounded, for an imperfective event.[9]

Diagrammatically, the perfectivity contrast may be represented as:

---

9) Obviously, in a logical sense, an unterminated event has no *set* endpoint. Nevertheless, I think it would be erroneous to assume that the time-axis for the imperfective/incompletive is *in the middle* of the event, just like it is for the durative aspect. Rather, the cognitive/communicative *focus* in construing perfectivity is that of *termination*, while in construing durativeness it is of *being in the middle*. This aspectual distinction arises, diachronically and perhaps ontogenetically/phylogenetically, from the semantic structure of specific verb types. Thus, some verbs depict unbounded *activity* ('read', 'work', 'walk', 'dance', 'talk'), while others depict *achievement* or *completion*, (e.g. 'die', 'kill', 'make', 'swallow', 'arrive', 'gobble up', 'finish', 'succeed', 'grab', 'obtain' etc.).

(8) *Perfective/completive*:

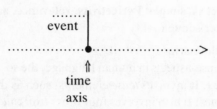

(9) *Imperfective/incompletive*:

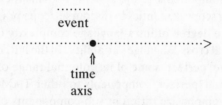

Within TAM systems, cross-linguistically, the most common imperfective aspect is the *durative/continuous*. Quite common too is the *habitual-state* and/or *repetitive/distributive* aspect. And many languages also group the *future* with the imperfective aspect. This latter grouping follows the reasonable inference:

(10) "If an event has not yet occurred, its terminal boundary is not yet specified, even if its initial boundary is already envisioned".

While English does not have a unified morphological category of 'imperfective', one may illustrate the various semantic categories that most commonly fall into the imperfective grouping as follows:

(11) a. *Durative*:   He is **working** (present)
                      He was **working** (past)
   b. *Habitual*:   He always **works**
   c. *Repetitive*:   He **works** on and off
   d. *Future*:   He **will** work

By elimination, one can see that the most common category associated with the 'perfective' is the *past*, when it is not further modified by durative, repetitive or habitual aspects. This is presumably so because once an event has occurred, its terminal boundary is more likely to be a matter of record, in retrospect.[10]

8.2.5. Perfect vs. simple: Perfectivity, relevance, anteriority, counter-sequentiality

8.2.5.1. Preliminaries

Of all tense-aspects in human language, the so-called **perfect** is by far the most complex. It involves *tense* elements, such as the *time-axis*, *sequentiality* and *precedence*. It also involves four other *aspectual* elements, each overlapping to some extent with other sub-components of the TAM system. More than other components of the system, it spans the entire functional range, from narrow scope semantics to discourse-scope pragmatics. The result of all this is a large degree of intra-language complexity of the perfect, as well as subtle but real cross-language variability. In the latter respect, a language may load onto the 'perfect' some of its potential range of features, while shifting other potential 'perfect' components to other TAM markers. Different languages thus emphasize different sub-components of the perfect. Nevertheless, the incidence of coding all four major sub-components of the perfect with one morphemic category in the TAM system is quite high. We will discuss these sub-components in order.[11]

8.2.5.2. Perfectivity and accomplishment

As noted in section 8.2.4., above, **perfectivity** involves the presence of a terminal boundary of an event/state *at* some time-axis. The way perfectivity is manifest in the perfect is through an interaction with **anteriority** (see below), whereby the terminal boundary is construed at some time *prior to* the time-axis. Consider first the following exchange:

10) This systematic asymmetry between the past ('fact', 'truth', 'certainty') and the future ('possible', 'uncertain', 'hazy') runs through the grammar at various levels, cf. Chapter 7, section 7.4., above. Thus, the IRREALIS modality overlaps to quite an extent with FUTURE. The reasons for this are most likely cognitive, having to do with differences in the strength and stability of the cognitive representation of *memorized* vs. *imagined* events/states.

11) The great complexity of the perfect is also evident from the vast amount of literature, often covering similar grounds in non-similar ways, that has been produced about this subject over the years. For a number of recent treatments and more comprehensive bibliographies, see Hopper (ed., 1982). The perfect is also intimately connected to many other categories in the grammar *outside* the TAM system, such as passive, adjectives, stativity or possession. For a useful account of these interconnections, see Anderson (1982).

(12) a. *Speaker i*:   Go do the dishes.
      b. *Speaker ii*: I**'ve** already **done** them.

In (12b), the time-axis is now ('time of speech'), and the speaker is asserting the completion ('boundedness') of the event at *some* time *prior* to that time-axis. That time-axis may be moved to either the past or future, as in:

(13) a. When she came home, he **had** already **done** the dishes.
      b. When she comes home, he **will** have already **done** the dishes.

The completion/boundary of the event may precede the time-axis by a large gap, or it may be placed *just before* the time-axis, but the normal case for actions/events (as against *states*) is for *some* gap to exist between that completion/boundary and the time axis.

When the perfect is used with *states*, the completion/boundary tends to come *at* the time-axis. Thus, compare (14a, b, c) below to (12) and (13) above:

(14) a. He **has been** here for an hour now.
      b. When she came home, he **had been** there for an hour already.
      c. When she comes home, he **will have been** there for an hour already.

One can thus diagram the perfectivity component of the perfect as follows:

(15) a. *For actions/events*:

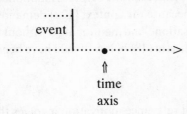

      b. *For states*:

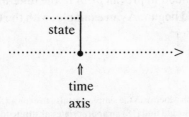

One may wish to argue that the following constitutes a counter-example to the claim that for states the boundary of a perfect-marked event is *at* the time-axis:

(16)   When she came home, he **had** already **been** there and gone.

However, the use of 'be' in (16) is subtly different than in (14b). Rather than depicting a *state*, it depicts an *event* such as 'come', as can be illustrated in the close equivalency of:

(17)   When she came home, he **had** already **come** and **gone**.

8.2.5.3. Lingering/current relevance

So far, the perfectivity sub-component of the perfect has been described mostly in *semantic* terms. The lingering/current relevance feature, in contrast, already exhibits some *discourse-pragmatic* valuation. What was said above with respect to the terminal boundary and its position relative to the time-axis still holds, and is crucial for understanding lingering/current relevance. But added to it is the notion of *communicative motivation* for mentioning an event/ state, that had already terminated some time *prior to* the time-axis, *later on* in the chain of discourse, when the time-axis has already moved to a *subsequent* event/state. This can be discussed by referring again to example (12), replicated below:

(12)   a.   *Speaker i*:   Go do the dishes.
      b.   *Speaker ii*:   I**'ve** already **done** them.

The reason why an event that ended a while before is mentioned at the *particular* point in time in (12b) is because the context (12a) demands its mention at this later point in the conversation. And mentioning it without the perfect, but rather merely as a past event, as in (18) below, would have been less appropriate in the context (12a):[12]

(18)   ?I *did* them.

As to states, the current relevance motivation involves the mention of a state which began and continued to prevail *prior to* the time-axis at a point in the discourse *long after* it had begun. As an example, with the time-axis again being time of speech, consider:

---

12)   There is a style-level in English which uses the simple *past* also to express the *perfect*. And it is conceivable that a user of that style would find (18) an appropriate substitute for (12b). Most commonly, however, (18) is an appropriate response to either '*Did* you do the dishes?' or 'You *didn't* do the dishes', both focusing on whether the event did or didn't occur in the past *without* hinging its lingering/current *relevance* to a *particular* time-axis.

(19) a. *Speaker i:*   Why are you so tired?   (time axis 'now')
      b. *Speaker ii:* I **have been** working all afternoon. (till now; rele-
                                                              vant to 'now')
      c.   ?I **was** working all afternoon.

As can be seen, (19c) is an inappropriate answer in terms of the relevance to the context established in (19a).

Typically, the time-axis 'now' is used in face-to-face communication, particularly conversation, where time-of-speech is the *unmarked* point of reference. But relevance can also be anchored relative to a *marked* point of reference, most commonly some time in the past. Thus, consider the transformation of (19) above into a past description, as in:

(20) a. ... so he asked me why I **was** tired,   (time axis 'then')
      b. so I told him I **had been** working all afternoon... (till then; re-
                                                              levant to 'then')

The reported speech in (20b) refers to a state that began *prior to* what was reported in (20a). Its relevance, however, is to the reported *question* in (20a), and that is presumably the communicative motivation for its interjection into the discourse at that particular — out-of-sequence — point. The relation between the **relevance** feature of the perfect and the **out-of-sequence** feature (see section 8.2.5.5., below), may thus be characterized by the following probabilistic inference:

(21) "If some event is mentioned within the discourse *out-of-sequence*
      (rather than at the earlier sequential time-point when it occur-
      red), the reason must be because it is somehow *relevant* at that
      later point".

8.2.5.4. Anteriority

The discussion above has already illustrated the fact that some features of the perfect, most explicitly perfectivity, involve a relation of **anteriority** or **pre-cedence** vis-à-vis some time-axis. The relation pertains to some **end point** of an action/event, or to some **mid-point** of a state (whose end-point most typically occurs *at* the time-axis).[13] Thus, while diagrams (15a, b) above focus upon the

---

13) Here again, I think what underlies this difference is some feature of *cognitive saliency*, whereby events are more salient at their *completion*, while states are more salient at their *middle*. As Hopper and Thompson (1980) have pointed out, the prototypical transitive event is *perfective/completed*.

end-point boundary relevant to perfectivity, what is relevant to anteriority is
the **gap** that prevails between some time-point in a preceding state/event and
the time-axis. This aspect of the perfect is the one which makes it possible for
us to explain the rather common diachronic shift from *perfect* to *past tense*.[14]
The anteriority aspect of the perfect may be diagrammatically given as:

(22)   *Anteriority for events*:

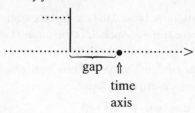

(23)   *Anteriority for states*:

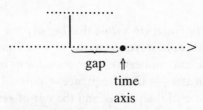

8.2.5.5. Counter-sequentiality

In order to understand this last major feature of the perfect, one must
consider the position of the perfect-marked clause within a **clause-chain** in discourse, particularly in narrative. The most *iconic*, natural way of coding, in
narrative, a sequence of events that are *thematically coherent* as sub-parts of a
single episode ('paragraph'), is by presenting the events — each coded by a
clause — in the *time-sequence* in which they originally occurred. When this is
indeed the presentation strategy pursued in discourse, the perfect aspect —
which is the *marked* case — is *not* used. However, when an event in the chain
occurs earlier in actual time, but is reported *later* in the clause-chain of discourse — later than another event that actually followed in real time, then that
out-of-sequence event is coded by the perfect ('anterior'). To illustrate this
diagrammatically, consider:

---

14) See discussion in Givón (1982a).

(24) a. ...A, B, C, D, E,..... (real time sequence of events)
      b. ...A, B, C, D, E,..... (narration in same sequence as real events)
      c. ...A, B, D, **C**, E,..... (clause **C** presented counter-sequentially)

In (24b), the sequence of events (24a) is depicted in the same sequence as they occurred in real time. All clauses will be marked by the *unmarked* (not the perfect) form. In (24c), clause **C**, which in real time *preceded* D, is reported in narrative *after* D. Clause C is the out-of-sequence one, and it will be marked by the perfect/anterior. As an example consider the following:

(25) a. *In sequence*:
          ... he came into the room, looked around, saw the exhibit on the desk, sat down and relaxed...
      b. *Counter-sequence*:
          ... he came into the room and looked around. *He had already seen the exhibit on the desk*. He sat down and relaxed...

The perfect inflection of the verb of the italicized clause in (25b) clearly tags it as having occurred, in real time, *before* the clause which directly precedes it in the narrative.

8.2.5.6. What binds the perfect complex together

While each of the sub-components of the perfect can be described independently up to a certain point, it is nonetheless most common to find the perfect in many languages — perhaps most languages — as a conflation of all these sub-components, each of which may be more *salient* in particular *contexts*. But each one of these features may also appear, by itself or in combinations with other elements, in other portions of the TAM system or in other domains of the grammar. Thus, the perfectivity feature is a necessary feature of the *perfective/imperfective* contrast. The anteriority feature is a necessary ingredient of *tense*. Perfectivity is a regular ingredient in the *lexical-semantic* structure of verbs. Perfectivity/completion/accomplishment is a necessary ingredient of many *possession* constructions. Perfectivity or terminal boundary or end result is a common ingredient of *stative* or *passive* ('detransitive') derivations of event verbs. This multiple network of semantic overlap is manifest both synchronically and diachronically. The best way to account for it at this juncture, in anticipation of eventual psycho-linguistic confirmation, is to present the various overlaps discussed above as hypotheses about *pragmatic* ('probabilistic') *inference*.[15] To wit:

---

15) Unlike deductive/logical inference, pragmatic/probabilistic inference deals with possible/ likely connections (rather than with necessary connection). For an extensive discussion, see Givón (1982c).

(26) a. *Perfectivity* > Anteriority: "If an event is *terminated* before
         some time axis, that event must have *preceded* that time-axis".
      b. *Anteriority* > Counter-sequentiality: "If an event *precedes*
         another event in real time but *follows* it in narrative report, that
         first event must then be out-of-sequence".
      c. *Counter-sequentiality* > Current relevance: (See (21) above) "If
         an event occurs *counter-sequentially* in narrative report, it must
         then be *relevant* to a later point in time — later than its original
         time-point in the natural sequence".
      d. *Perfectivity* > Current Relevance: "If an event is construed as
         having a *terminal boundary* relative to some time-axis, then that
         event must surely be *relevant* to that time-axis".

While the inferences in (26) are only suggested connections, inferences much
like them have been shown to motivate diachronic change within the TAM
system,[16] outside the TAM system,[17] and in between the TAM system and
other parts of the grammar.[18]

8.2.6. Modality: Fact vs. possibility

8.2.6.1. Preliminaries

As seen in Chapter 7, above, the four major sentential modalities most
commonly and most distinctly coded in human language are:

(a) *Presupposition*:   P is true by prior agreement
(b) *Realis-assertion*,   (i)   *Affirmative*: P is strongly-asserted as true
                            (ii) *Negative*: P is strongly-asserted as false
(c) *Irrealis-assertion*: P is weakly-asserted as possibly true

In this section we will deal, among the four epistemic modalities above,
primarily with the contrast between **realis-assertion** (b) and **irrealis-assertion**
(c). Toward the end of the chapter, in dealing with TAM categories in subor-
dinate/embedded clauses, the discussion will be widened to deal with a
number of non-epistemic modalities. The subject of modalities will be raised
again, and later, from a different perspective, in Chapters 9 and 11, below. It is
also highly relevant to the topics discussed in Chapters 13 and 20, Volume II.

---

16) See Anderson (1982), Givón (1977b, 1982a), *inter alia.*

17) See Givón (1981b, 1982c), Benveniste (1968), *inter alia.*

18) See Anderson (1982), Benveniste (1968), *inter alia.*

8.2.6.2. Realis and irrealis in simple clauses

Of the four major tenses, past, present, future and habitual, the past and present are clearly **realis** ('fact') tenses, dealing with events/states that either have occurred or are in the process of occurring. The future is a clear **irrealis** tense, dealing with hypothetical, possible, uncertain states or events that have not yet occurred. Thus consider:

(27) a. *Past*:   Joe cut a log (assertion of fact)
      b. *Present*: Joe is cutting a log (assertion of fact)
      c. *Future*:   Joe will cut a log (assertion of possibility)

The most common test for realis/irrealis involves the **referentiality** of indefinite arguments under the scope of these modalities (see Chapter 11, below). Briefly, in both (27a, b), which are *realis* modalities, belief in the truth of the whole sentence implies also belief in the *existence* of a *unique* object — 'a log' — to which the sentence pertains. On the other hand, in the *irrealis* (27c) 'a log' is ambiguous, and may be used either to mean a *unique* log or only *some*, *unspecified* log, a mere member of the *genus* 'log'. Such an interpretation is called **non-referential** or **generic**.

The status of the habitual tense is mixed. On the one hand, it represents a clear *strong assertion of facts*, in the sense defined for the realis modality in Chapter 7, above. Thus, (28) below is presumably uttered felicitously by a speaker holding a strong belief that *in the past* a number of *similar* events have occurred, with a certain regularity, to warrant making a *generic* statement by using the habitual:

(28)   Joe always cuts **logs**

On the other hand, 'logs' in (28) does not refer to any *individual* log, nor does it refer specifically to any *unique group* of logs. Rather, it is a *generic*, non-referential expression. And in this sense, the habitual resembles irrealis. The same may be demonstrated with a singular indefinite object. Thus, consider (29) below:

(29)   Every day Joe cuts **a log**, then...

'A log' in (29) again does not refer to a specific log. Rather, it is non-referential.

Another source of the *irrealis* modality in simple clauses comes from various probabilistic operators, such as *epistemic adverbs* and *modals*. Thus, compare:

(30) a. Joe caught a whale   (past; realis)
      b. **Maybe** Joe caught a whale   (past + adverb; irrealis)
      c. Joe **may have** caught a whale   (past + modal; irrealis)

While 'a whale' in (30a) must be referential, in both (30b, c) it may also be interpreted as non-referential.

Finally, another source of the *irrealis* modality in main clauses is the scope of *modal* ('world creating') *verbs*, which do not imply the existence of their objects even in the past tense. These are, briefly, verbs that depict imaginary worlds, states or events. For example compare:

(31) a. Joe **caught** a whale   (past, realis, implicative verb)
      b. Joe **looked for** a whale   (past, realis, irrealis scope
                                          of non-implicative verb)
      c. Joe **wanted** a whale   (past, realis, irrealis scope
                                          of non-implic. verb)
      d. Joe **imagined** a whale   (past, realis, irrealis scope
                                          of non-implic. verb)
      e. Joe **dreamed of** a whale   (past, realis, irrealis scope
                                          of non-implic. verb)

While in (31a) 'a whale' is referential, in (31b) through (31e) 'a whale' may also be interpreted non-referentially.

8.2.6.3. Modality in complex clauses

This subject will be discussed later in this chapter as well as in a number of chapters in volume II. The treatment here is thus expository. A number of complex clauses, both embedded/subordinate and non-embedded, are obligatorily *irrealis* in their modality. The major ones are the following:

(32) a. *Conditional adverbs*: **If** Joe catches a whale, then...
      b. *Imperatives*: **Go** catch a whale!
      c. *Yes/no questions*: **Did** Joe catch a whale?
      d. *Complements of non-implicative modality verbs*:
                              Joe **wanted** to catch a whale.
      e. *Complements of non-implicative manipulative verbs*:
                              Mary **told** Joe to catch a whale.
      f. *Complements of non-factive cognition verbs*:
                              Mary **thought** that Joe caught a whale.

In all the examples in (32), the object 'a whale' may be interpreted non-referentially.

In contrast, a number of complex clauses, at least when combined with
the *past* tense, impose the realis modality. Thus compare:

(33) a. *Because adverbial clauses*: **Because** Joe caught a whale, he...
      b. *When adverbial clauses*: **When** Joe caught a whale, he...
      c. *In-spite-of adverbial clauses*: **In spite of** the fact that Joe caught
                                 a whale, he...
      d. *Participial adverbs*: **Having caught a whale**, Joe steamed home.
                               Catching a whale at last, Joe steamed home.
      e. *Relative clauses*: The man **who caught a whale yesterday** left.
      f. *Cleft-focus clauses*: It is Joe **who caught a whale**.
      g. *Complements of implicative modality verbs*:
                              Joe **managed** to catch a whale
      h. *Complements of implicative manipulative verbs*:
                              Mary **forced** Joe to catch a whale
      i. *Complements of factive cognition verbs*:
                              Mary **regretted** that Joe caught a whale

In all the examples in (33) above, 'a whale' *cannot* be interpreted non-referentially. What unites all clause types in (33), of course, is the fact that they are
either *presupposed* or *strongly asserted* (33g, h), and that further, no grammatical element that imposes *irrealis* intervenes. As we shall see later, there
are grounds for considering *realis* the unmarked, natural, neutral case, and *irrealis* as the marked, exceptional case in human language.

8.2.7. Tense-aspect-modality in discourse: Foreground vs. background

So far we have looked at the TAM system primarily — though not exclusively — in terms of the properties of individual clauses. In this section we will
consider the use of the TAM system in multi-propositional discourse, as one
major *focus* of coding the *connectedness/coherence* relations of propositions.
There is one fundamental pragmatic notion that must be borne in mind in
order to understand the role of the TAM system in dicourse:[19]

(34) *Foreground vs. background*:
        "In connected discourse, some aspects of the description — coded
        in some sentences/clauses — are considered the *gist*, *backbone*,

---

19) For the precursors of the following discussion and much empirical support, see Givón
(1977b), Hopper (1979) and Hopper and Thompson (1980).

main line of the episode/description/communication. They are the **foreground** of the discourse. Others are considered *satellites, side-trips, supportive* portions of the description/episode/communication. Those are the **background** portions of the discourse".

While the division between *foreground* and *background* in discourse is reminiscent of the division between *asserted* vs. *presupposed* information (see Chapter 7, above), it is not identical. *Asserted* new information in connected discourse is most often divided into the *main line* of the description, imparting the most crucial *skeletal* gist of the story, and *background* lacunae or digressions. The latter supply background information *on line*, as it is *needed*, at the points when it is judged *relevant*.

There is a strong *probabilistic* correlation in connected discourse between the various TAM distinctions described earlier and the foreground/background distinction. The various correlations may be summarized as follows:[20]

(35) DISCOURSE FOREGROUND/BACKGROUND
      CORRELATIONS OF TENSE-ASPECT-MODALITY

feature	foreground	background
tense	past	present, future, habitual
sequentiality	in-sequence	out-of-sequence, anterior, perfect
durativity	compact/punctual	durative/continuous
perfectivity	perfective/completive	imperfective/incompletive
modality	realis	irrealis
(*activeness*)	(action/event)	(state)
(*syntax*)	(main clauses)	(subordinate clause)

The first thing one must emphasize with regard to these correlations, is that they are not absolute but rather probabilistic. The second is that they pertain most typically to *narrative* discourse, and are less evident in *face-to-face* conversation, and even less so in specialized *procedural* discourse. Nonetheless, they represent the basis for a function-based elucidation of *markedness* in TAM systems. There is nothing logically necessary about these correlations.

---

20) This formulation owes much to the *transitivity* correlations described in Hopper and Thompson (1980), as well as to Bickerton (1975, 1976).

Rather, they represent the cultural-cognitive-perceptual facts concerning what humans are most likely to consider *noteworthy*, *informative*, *salient*, *memorable* or *outstanding* in the coding and communication of experience. Each single correlation may spring from solid cognitive-perceptual grounds, though at the moment we can only present such putative grounds as hypotheses. To wit:[21]

(36) a. *Tense*: "An event that has already happened should be more firmly coded in memory and more easily retrieved and reported than an event that is still ongoing or merely hypothesized".

b. *Sequence*: "It should be easier to code, recall and report events in the natural, temporal or causal order in which they occurred, rather than in a counter-sequence order".[22]

c. *Durativity*: "Sharply-bounded, compact, fast changes in the normal inert state of affairs should be more salient in coding and recalling than diffusely-bounded slow-changing states".[23]

d. *Perfectivity*: "Completed events should be easier to code and recall than still-ongoing, incompleted ones (cf. (36a), above). A sharp terminal boundary should be easier to code and recall than a diffuse one" (cf. (36c), above).

e. *Modality*: "Events that have actually happened should be more salient for coding and retrieval than hypothesized events" (cf. (36a), above).

21) Bickerton (1976) has proposed very similar constraints, but has suggested that they are genetically wired into the neurological structure of the human organism. This may indeed be true, but should not necessarily impinge on their being functionally based and survival motivated. The status of the psychological-cognitive evidence in support of these hypotheses is not yet clear to me.

22) Some evidence supporting this hypothesis in episodic memory is presented by Mandler (1978). In addition, Mandler and Johnson (1977) show that some prototypical *thematic* organization of stories, which they call "story grammar", is also involved in the coding and recall of stories. Sequential and causal connections may be viewed as one type of localized thematic organization.

23) See discussion in Givón (1979a, Chapter 3) concerning the normal background of inertia vis-à-vis which events — rather than non-events — are cognitively/perceptually more salient. For some psycholinguistic evidence supporting this suggestion, see H. Clark (1971) and E. Clark (1971).

If such hypotheses as given in (36) turn out to be psychologically valid, they would then constitute the *motivation* — or at least the cognitive basis for motivation — for the clear *markedness* behavior seen in the use of tense-aspect-modality in discourse as summarized in (35) above. The investigation of syntactic structure and function does not then concern only the structural definition of markedness, but also its broader functional explanation. This topic will be discussed again in Chapter 23, Volume II.

8.3. THE CODING OF TENSE-ASPECT-MODALITY: TOWARD A TYPOLOGY

8.3.1. Preliminaries

In the preceding section we surveyed the functional domains of tense-aspect-modality, discussing each feature more or less in isolation. In this section we will deal with the same features from two other perspectives:

(a)   How the TAM features combine within a system
(b)   How TAM systems are coded morpho-syntactically

The bulk of the treatment will involve descriptions of a number of TAM systems from typologically-diverse languages. These descriptions will serve first to illustrate the interplay between *universality* and *language-specificity* in the organization and coding of TAM systems. Rather than considering this a fully motivated typology, where major types are distinguished from minor subtypes by some principled means, one may view this section as a precursor to an *eventual* typology. The ordering of the various types is not significant, except for the first one, which describes the most *prototypical* TAM system, that of Creole languages.[24]

8.3.2. The TAM system of Creoles

Creole languages are a unique source of data reflecting on language universals. Briefly, they are **contact languages** created by children of the speakers of *Pidgin* languages. Pidgins have only a *minimal syntax*, with virtually no

---

24) For discussion justifying the choice of Creole TAM as the universal prototype, see Givón (1982a). The features underlying it are the most common ones found cross-linguistically, in one way or another running like a *leitmotif* or recurrent theme through all other TAM systems.

complex/embedded constructions or morphology.[25] Further, the speech of the Pidgin community is even more variable than the norm in non-contact language communities. The Pidgin itself is a rather *restricted* communicative code, in terms of expressive power, topics of discussion, speed of communication and independence of immediate context. The parent generation thus displays imperfect learning of a second language. Given both the variability and limited expressive range of the parents' Pidgin, the children never try to acquire it. Rather, they extract the only reasonably stable feature from the Pidgin — the lexicon, and then go on to *invent the Creole grammar* from scratch, presumably relying on their human-universal faculty of language/communication.[26]

Any Creole TAM system sufficiently close to its point of origin turns out to have three TAM markers ('auxiliaries') contrasting with *zero* ('the unmarked'). These will be illustrated with data from Hawaii English Creole, following Bickerton.[27] The markers and their functions are summarized in (37) below.

(37) *TAM markers of Hawaii English Creole*

marker	semantic/pragmatic value	comments on discourse distribution
Ø	-punctual/non-durative -completed/perfective -simple/non-perfect -realis -in sequence [-past][28]	overwhelmingly past-event descriptions in discourse, or present resulting states of past events. Backbone of narrative description in discourse, relating primarily to foregrounded events in natural sequence;
'stay'	-durative/non-punctual -iterative/repetitive -habitual/timeless	background/side-trips in discourse; primarily states, out of sequence;

25) Earlier works, cf. Bickerton (1975, 1976, 1977), Bickerton and Odo (1976), Bickerton and Givón (1976) or Givón (1979a) *inter alia*, have tended to over -emphasize the non-systematic, variable nature of the Pidgin code. More recently it has been shown that Pidgins and/or natural second language acquisition display(s) many universal properties of the *pre-syntactic* mode of communication (cf. Givón, 1979a Ch. 5 and 1983c).

26) For the initial argument supporting this interpretation of the genesis of Creoles, see Bickerton (1975, 1976, 1977) and Givón (1973/1979c), *inter alia*.

27) See citations in fn. 26. The reformulation here follows Givón (1982a).

28) Bickerton (1975) initially defined the function of Ø in purely semantic terms, as "past of actions and present of states". The re-interpretation here is more discourse-pragmatic oriented.

marker	semantic/pragmatic value	comments on discourse distribution
'go(n)'[29]	-irrealis/hypothesis -future -conditional/possible -imperative	background/side-trips or subordinate clauses in discourse; breaking the main-line narrative sequence;
'bin'	-perfect/plu-perfect -anterior -lookback	background/side-trips in discourse; frequently in subordinate clauses; counter-sequence in terms of temporal order of the actions/events on the main line of narrative;

In terms of markedness, the Creole *zero* codes all the **unmarked** categories (cf. (35) and (36) above), while each one of the three makers, *go(n)*, *bin* and *stay*, codes one of the **marked** categories.

The sequential, foregrounding use of *zero* may be seen in the following passage, here contrasting with the perfect/anterior *bin*:[30]

(38) a. ...I **go** out of the way,
     b. I **fix** that dog up...
     c. [that dog **bin** come nice and fat,
     d. all the hair **bin** grow...]
     e. I **spray**-im with malathion 'n all,
     f. I **bring**-im down the beach special...

'...So I went out of my way, I fixed that dog up — the dog had become nice and fat, all his hair had grown back — I sprayed him with malathion, I brought him down to the beach specially...'

Passage (38) also illustrates the counter-sequence use of the perfect *bin*. A common feature of this usage is that, in addition to breaking the action sequence, the use of *bin* also involves breaking the continuity of the *topics/participants*, here switching from 'I' to 'dog' as subject.

The perfect *bin* appears typically in subordinate clauses, which again pre-

---

29) In Hawaii English Creole, as well as in other Creoles, there is less-than-consistent coding of the imperative vis-à-vis the marker *go/gon*. *Go* codes either imperatives (probably the original situation) or future/conditional, while *gon* codes only future/conditional (probably the original situation). For further discussion, see Givón (1982a).

30) From Bickerton's tape K-22, side 2.

sent out-of-sequence, backgrounded material, as in:[31]

(39) …main thing, I *get* some receipt, eh,
       showing that I **bin** pay-im…   (*bin* in V-complement)
       '…the main thing is, I got a receipt, eh,
       showing that I (had) paid him…'

(40) …because you know, the time I **bin** go   (*bin* in ADV-
       to borrow money…   clause)
       '…because you know, that time when I went/had gone to borrow
       money…'

The use of *go/gon* to code various irrealis categories is illustrated in the
following passages:[32]

(41) a. *Future*: …the guy say he **gon** fix me up with, da kine, vinyl floor…
                   '… the guy said that he was going to fix me up with that
                   vinyl flooring…'
       b. *Conditional*: …that's two hundred something dollar I can save
                   if he **gon** get-im for me…
                   '…that's two hundred or so dollars I could save if
                   he was going to get it for me…'
       c. *Imperative*: …but the guy tell the Mexican boy:
                   "**Go** ask the guy for downpayment…"…
                   '…but the guy told the Mexican boy:
                   "Ask the guy for downpayment…"…'

Quite consistently, the irrealis *go(n)* in the Hawaii English Creole transcripts
appears mostly in *subordinate clauses* or *quoted speech*, underscoring the
background properties of this feature.
       The use of the durative *stay* may be seen in:[33]

(42) a. *Habitual-repeated*: …I don't know, he **stay** come in…
                   'I don't know, he kept coming in…'
       b. *Habitual-copula*: …I no blame-im tho, he **stay** in business, no?…
                   '…I don't blame him though, he is in busi-
                   ness, eh?…'

31) From Bickerton's group tape B-152, p. 43 of transcript.
32) From Bickerton's group tape B-152, p. 43 of transcript.
33) From Bickerton's group tape B-152, p. 43 of transcript.

    c. *Durative-potential*:   ...so I bump into him, he tell me:
                       "Yeah, **stay** come in, **stay** come in..."...
                       '...So I bumped into him and he told me:
                       "Yeah, it's coming in, it's coming in..."...'
    d. *Habitual-durative*:   ...so the Mexican guy, he **stay** work for me...
                       '...So the Mexican guy kept/was working
        for me...'

One of the most striking features of the Creole TAM system is the complete rigidity of the linear order used in combining TAM markers. Bickerton (1975) noted this universal order as:

    (43) (ANTERIOR) (MODAL) (DURATIVE) V

For Hawaii English Creole this translates as:

    (44) (bin) (go) (stay) V

Such combinations may be seen in:

    (45) a. *go-stay-V*: ...whatever I save from the house rent, I **go stay**
                       pay...[34]
                       '...whatever I save from the house rent, I'll keep
                       paying...'
        b. *bin-stay-V*: ...you know where we **bin stay** go before...[35]
                       '...you know where we had been going before...'
        c. *bin-go-V*: ...ah...I say, I **bin go** order, see...[36]
                       '...huh, so I said, I had been meaning to order, you
                       see...'
        d. *bin-go-stay-V*: ...no, shit, I **bin go stay** figure only about
                       twenty...[37]
                       '...no, shit, I would have been figuring on only
                       twenty...'

The significance of the rigid order (43)/(44) of the Creole TAM markers may be explained in reference to their **scope** of application:

---

34) Bickerton (1975, p. 12).

35) Bickerton (1975, p. 12).

36) Bickerton's group tape B-152, p. 43 of transcript.

37) Bickerton's (1975, p. 12).

(a)   The durative/non-punctual has the narrowest, **verbal** scope;
(b)   The irrealis/modal has a wider, **propositional** scope;
(c)   The perfect/anterior has the widest, **discourse** scope;

Such scope facts may be translated into linear order via a simple principle of morpho-syntactic iconicity:[38]

(46)   "An operator that takes *only* the operand under its scope, will be placed *closer* to the operand than operators that take the operand plus other items. The *wider* the scope of an operator is and the more items it takes under its scope *in addition to* the operand, the *farther away* from the operand it will be placed".

Since Creoles have no diachronic — but only ontogenetic — history, they show the most transparent one-to-one correlation between semantic/pragmatic scope and morpho-syntactic ('coding') scope. Such transparency is seldom if ever matched in diachronically mature languages.[39]

8.3.3. English: Tense and bound morphology

The TAM system of English is remarkably close to that of Creoles, with only one feature added to the Creole semantic-pragmatic structure, that of **past tense**. The core of the system may be summarized as:

(47)   (tense) (modal/irrealis) (have/perfect) (be/durative) V

The element **tense** is not a free operator, but a bound suffix on whatever follows it. Further, for some stylistic levels **tense** is dispensed with, and the system is then even more reminiscent of the Creole one, i.e:

(48)   (modal) (have) (be) V

The semantics and pragmatics of 'modal', 'have' and 'be' in English mirror closely the 'irrealis', 'perfect' and 'durative' discussed above. In the more formal style, **past** corresponds to the Creole *zero*, while in the more informal/immediate style, English has a similar *zero* to code the same function. As examples of both styles, consider the following, where *zero* or *past* is italicized and the **perfect** is bracketed. Both (49a, b) below are taken from the same magazine article:[40]

38) For justification of principle (46) as an iconicity principle, see Givón (forthcoming).

39) For further discussion of the role of diachronic change in introducing more marked features into language, see Givón (1979a, Chapter 6).

40) *The New Yorker*, Dec. 31, 1979, "Profiles", pp. 33-39. In English the two styles differ, among other things, along the dimension of *immediacy* (see discussion in section 8.3.6., below).

(49) a. ...He *entered* the Star's marble lobby; *passed* a glass case that displayed old newspapers...; *exchanged* greetings with the security guard; and *took* an elevator to the third floor. He *unlocked* his office; he *went* in; *hung up* his coat, tie and stetson; and *gave* the morning mail a quick glance. He *cackled* with pleasure at an abusive anonymous letter. "I get at least one of these a day" he *told* his companion... Oliphant [had portrayed] a petulant Henry Kissinger in full papal atire...

      b. ...The man *enters*, and *begins* examining the pictures in sequence, reading the notes beneath each one — standing close, standing back, moving in again. Occasionally he *makes* a comment to his companion. "Pen and water-color over chalk" he *remarks*... At a picture labeled "Crayons and watercolors heightened with gouache" he *tries* to figure out where the gouache [has been applied]; it *is* hard to decide. "That's nice" he *says* about the next one... "The first smoking-bomb cartoon!" *exclaims* the man, laughing delightedly. He *looks* closer. "Except it doesn't say 'The World' on the bomb". When he [has seen] all the pictures, he *adjusts* his stetson and *departs*...

While English TAM auxiliaries closely resemble their Creole counterparts, the bound morphology of English reflects the diachronically gradual development of the system, whereby the more recent auxiliaries are slowly supplanting an older, suffixally-marked system. Morphologically ('structurally') such a mixed system is highly *marked* and seemingly confusing. The relative order of the English auxiliaries (cf. (47)/(48) above) also reflects diachronic history rather than, purely, synchronic scope.[41] Such deviation from the Creole prototype is typical in diachronically-mature languages.

8.3.4. Early Biblical Hebrew: Topic shift, thematic continuity and old inflections

In semantic and pragmatic terms, Early Biblical Hebrew (henceforth EBH) resembles the Creole prototype to quite an extent. The morphology, however, involves diachronically-old inflections, with no auxiliaries. The major contrast in that morphology is between the *simple/sequential* form with subject agreement prefixes, called traditionally 'imperfect', and the *perfect/anterior* form with subject agreement suffixes, called traditionally 'perfect'.

---

41) See discussion in Givón (1982a).

The unmarked, topic-continuity, sequential-action ('theme continuity') use of the *imperfect* can be seen in:[42]

(50) ... va-yisʕú   me-rifidím   va-yavóʼu
      and-they-travel-IMP from-Rephidim and-they-come-IMP
      midbár sináy,
      desert-of Sinai
      '...and they traveled from Rephidim and entered the Sinai desert,

      va-yahanú   sham ba-midbár,   va-yáhen
      and-they-camp-IMP there in-the-desert and-he-camp-IMP
      sham yisraʼél néged   ha-hár...
      there Israel   against the-mountain
      and they camped there in the desert, so Israel camped there near the mountain...'

[Exodus, 19:2]

The subject/topic of all clauses in (50) remains the same (the people of Israel), and the action is in natural temporal sequence. In the passage which directly follows, subject/topic shifting precipitates the use of the *perfect*:

(51) ... u-Moshé   ʕalá   ʼel ha-ʼelohím, va-yiqráʼ
      and-Moses   climb-he-PERF to the-God   and-he-call-IMP
      ʼeláv   YHWH...
      to-him   Jehovah
      '...and Moses **had gone up** toward God; so then God called him...'

[Exodus, 19:3]

The use of the perfect in (51) codes two parallel *discontinuities* in the narrative:[43]

(a) *Topic switch* from 'Israel' to 'Moses'; and
(b) *Action/theme switch* from the camping at the foot of the mountain to Moses' activities elsewhere.

As suggested earlier above (see Chapter 7, section 7.2.4.), major breaks in both continuities tend to coincide in narrative discourse.

---

42) For the designation Early Biblical Hebrew, see Givón (1977b). The transcription used here largely follows Israeli Hebrew pronunciation of the text.

43) Both discontinuities are also coded, in parallel fashion, by the SV word-order (see discussion in Chapter 6, above, as well as Givón, 1977b). This contrasts with the VS word-order which codes the more continuous topic and theme.

As elsewhere, the perfect/anterior occurs in high frequency in subordinate clauses, as in:

(52) a. *V-complement*:

...va-yár'   ve-hinéh   ḥarvú   pnéy
and-he-see-IMP   and-lo   dry-they-PERF   faces-of
ha-'adamá...
the-earth
'...and he saw that the surface of the earth **had dried up**...'
                                                    [Genesis, 8:13]

   b. *REL-clause*:

...kól néfesh   ha-ḥayá   ha-roméset   'asher sharṣú
all spirit-of the-living the-crawling that spawn-they-PERF
ha-máyim...
the-water
'...all the crawling live creatures that the water **had spawned**...'
                                                    [Genesis, 1:21]

The *durative* in EBH is marked by the participial-nominal form of the verb, a category that is in the process of being re-analyzed from nominal to verbal status.[44] In (53) below it is used to code the *habitual* as an adjectival or REL-clause modifier:

(53)   ...déshe'   ʕésev   mazríaʕ   zéraʕ...
         loan-of   grass   seed-PART-of   seed
   { '...(all) grasses **seeding** their seeds...' }
   { '...(all) grasses **that seed** their seed...' }
                                                    [Genesis, 1:11]

In (54) it is used to code the *progressive*:

(54)   ...va-yishmeʕú   'et   qól   ha-'elohím mithaléx
         and-they-hear-IMP   ACC   voice-of   the-God   walk-PART
         ba-gán...
         in-the-garden
         '...and they heard the voice of God (as he was) **walking** in the garden...'
                                                    [Genesis, 3:8]

---

44) This process is reminiscent of the reanalysis of V-*ing* in English, in conjunction with *be at* (cf. 'He is *a*-court*ing*'), to mark the durative. The nominal use of this category in later stages of Biblical Hebrew becomes lexicalized/fossilized (Givón, 1977b).

The irrealis/modal category in EBH is not coded uniformly. Special verb-forms exist for coding the imperative and the subjunctive ('jussive'). The future and conditional are often marked by the imperfect (i.e. the simple, sequential, unmarked form). The counterfact conditional is often marked by the perfect/anterior.[45]

The inflectional nature of the EBH TAM system almost completely eliminates the possibility of combinations, as in Creoles or English, among the various TAM markers — and features. This makes for a more impoverished coding system, with inflections often used in multiple functions that may be coded distinctly in the Creole, or in other languages with an auxiliary-verb TAM system. Thus, the perfect by itself (rather than the Creole combination of perfect plus irrealis) is used to code counterfact conditionals, as in:[46]

(55) ...pen yishláḥ   yad-ó   ve-laqáḥ   me-ʕéṣ
      lest he-send-IMP hand-his and-take-he-PERF from-tree-of
      ha-ḥayím ve-'axál...
      the-life   and-eat-he-PERF
      '...lest he extended his hand and **took** (fruit) from the tree of life
      and **ate**...'

[Genesis, 3:22]

In the same vein, where in the Creole the combination of durative and perfect may be used to code *past-durative*, in EBH the participle/durative is used to code this combination by itself, and 'past' is simply inferred from the context, as in:

(56) ...va-yɨhí   rív   beyn   roʕéy   miqnéh
      and-it-be-IMP quarrel between shepherds-of flock-of
      'avrahám u-veyn   roʕéy   miqnéh loṭ,
      Abraham and-between shepherds-of flock-of Lot
      '...and there **was** a quarrel between Abraham's and Lot's shepherds,

---

45) Bickerton (1975) notes that in Creoles counterfact conditionals are marked by a combination of the *modal/irrealis* and and the *perfect/anterior*. Such a combination is of course impossible in the inflectional system of EBH.

46) The imperfect is also used in the same line to code that function. It is God's concept of the event as something that *should never happen under any circumstances* which makes this passage a *counterfact* rather than a simple ('possible') conditional. For discussion, see Givón (1977b).

ve-ha-knaʕaní   ve-ha-prizí   yoshév   ba-'áreṣ...
and-the-Canaanite and-the-Perizzite *sitting*-PART in-the-land
and (at that time) the Canaanites and the Perizzites **were occupying**
the country...'

[Genesis, 13:7]

8.3.5. Bemba: Expanded tense and the focus aspect

Like other core-Bantu languages, Bemba has a largely prefixal, transparent, agglutinative TAM morphology, normally allowing the concatenation of two to three prefixes plus, on occasion, a diachronically older suffix. Such a system allows explicitly at least some of the combinatorial possibilities seen in Creoles. The most common combination is the adding of the *durative* marker to various *tense* categories, as in:[47]

(57)   a.   *Remote past*:
       (i)   *Simple*:   a-à-boomb-ele
                    he-PAST-work-SIMPLE
                    'He worked' (sometime before yesterday)
       (ii)   *Durative*:   a-à-léé-boomba
                    he-PAST-DUR-work

$$\left.\begin{array}{l}\text{'He was working'}\\ \text{'He used to work'}\\ \text{'He kept on working'}\end{array}\right\}$$

     b.   *Tomorrow-future*:
       (i)   *Simple*:   a-kà-boomba
                    he-FUT-work
                    'He will work' (sometime tomorrow)
       (ii)   *Durative*:   a-kà-láá-boomba
                    he-FUT-DUR-work

$$\left.\begin{array}{l}\text{'He will be working'}\\ \text{'He will keep working'}\end{array}\right\}$$

In semantic/pragmatic terms, the Bemba TAM system displays all the prototype Creole features discussed above. It makes, in the past tense, a major distinction between *perfect/current relevance* and the *simple/unmarked/sequential* form. The durative has distinct marking in both past and future (it is obligatory in the present). The *future/modal* has a distinct form, and, as is

---

47) For details see Givón (1972, Chapter 4).

common, other *irrealis* categories (conditional, counterfact conditional, subjunctive, imperative) have special forms of their own. Two features of the Bemba TAM system, however, are fairly uncommon:

(a) The extreme elaboration within the *tense* system; and
(b) The pragmatic feature of *focus of assertion*.

The Bemba tense system recognizes — and codes explicitly — *four* time sub-divisions in both the past and future. They are defined in terms of *distance* from the *time axis*, with the past preceding and the future following it. Thus consider:

(58) a. *Remote past*: a-**à**-boomb-ele 'He worked' (before yesterday)
     a-PAST-work-SIMPLE

 b. *Yesterday-past*: a-**á**-boomb-ele   'He worked'   (yesterday)
     he-PAST-work-SIMPLE

 c. *Today-past*: a-**àcí**-boomba   'He worked'   (earlier today)
     he-PAST-work

 d. *Immediate past*: a-**á**-boomba 'He worked'   (within 3-4 hours)
     he-PAST-work

 e. *Immediate future*: a-**áláa**-boomba 'He will work' (within 3-4 hours)
     he-FUT-work

 f. *Today-future*: a-**lé é**-boomba   'He'll work'   (later today)
     he-FUT-work

 g. *Tomorrow-future*: a-**kà**-boomba   'He'll work'   (tomorrow)
     he-FUT-work

 h. *Remote future*: a-**ká**-boomba   'He'll work' (after tomorrow)
     he-FUT-work

Within this elaborate system, the more remote categories of both past and future tend to use the *absolute* time-axis, i.e. time of speech. The less remote categories, on the other hand, are more amenable to adopting a *relative* time axis, which either precedes (past) or follows (future) the time of speech. The present progressive is in that respect the *least marked*, since it most easily adopts a relative time axis. In this respect Bemba resembles English:

(59) a. He is **walking** in the yard   (absolute time-axis)
 b. I saw him **walking** in the yard   (relative to past time-axis)
 c. **Walking** in the yard, he saw a rabbit (relative to past time-axis)
 d. The man **walking** in the yard will then approach you (relative to
     future time-axis)

The Bemba facts thus allow us to formulate a hypothesis concerning the semantic **markedness** of tenses in relation to their distance from the time-axis:[48]

(60) "The *closer* a tense division is to the universal/unmarked time-axis of *time-of-speech*, the *less marked* it is, and the wider *freedom of distribution* it will exhibit".

The second remarkable feature of the Bemba TAM system is the pragmatic *focus* aspect. Within the entire system, there are seven minimal pairs displaying this contrast, which has to do with what, within the sentence, falls under the scope of new information (see discussion in Chapter 7, above). Thus, consider the following examples from English, where (61a) can be the answer either to the **wide-scope** question (61b) — including the *verb* under the scope of new information — or to the **narrow-scope** question (61c) which excludes the verb from the scope of new information:

(61) a. He went to the village.
 b. What did he do then? (VP scope)
 c. Where did he go then? (COMP scope)

In Bemba, the two senses of (61a), i.e. in answer to either (61b) or (61c), will be coded by different aspectual markers. This may be illustrated by one of the seven minimal pairs:

(62) a. a-à-**lí**-iile ku-mushi (VP scope, verb *included*)
 he-PAST-FOC-go to-village
 'He **went to the village**' ('What he did was go to the village')
 b. a-à-iile ku-mushi (COMP scope, verb *excluded*)
 he-PAST-go to-village
 'He went **to the village**' ('Where he went was to the village')

In terms of functional/semantic distribution, the category in (62a) — the one which *includes* the verb under the scope of new information — is the *marked* one. It is excluded from more backgrounded presuppositional environments, such as REL-clauses, V-complements, ADV-clauses, WH-questions, cleft-focus constructions and negative sentences. Further, it is the COMP-scope (excluding the verb) in Bemba that is used most commonly in *foregrounded*, *sequential-action*, *main-line* clauses, thus displaying itself

---

48) For many supporting data and arguments in Bemba, see Givón (1972, Chapter 4). For discussion of the distributional correlates of functional/semantic markedness, see Givón (1979a, Chapter 2).

clearly as the *unmarked* member of the pair in multi-propositional discourse.
This unmarked status of the narrower focus of new information is obviously
related to the processing principle "one chunk per proposition" discussed in
Chapter 7, above.

8.3.6. Ute: The immediate relevance tense-aspect

At first glance, the TAM system of Ute (Uto-Aztecan) shows a certain
skewing from the general semantic-pragmatic organization outlined in section
8.2., above. It thus seems to deviate more strongly from the Creole TAM prototype. Of the major TAM features, *irrealis* is clearly marked (excluding the
imperative) by the suffix -*vaa*-/-*paa*- or its variants. Thus consider:[49]

(63) a. *Future*: wýýka-vaa-ni
                    work-MOD-MAIN
                    'I **will work**'

      b. *V-COMP of modality verb*: wýýka-vaa-ci   'ásti-'i
                    work-MOD-SUBORD want-IMM
                    'I want **to work**'

      c. *V-COMP of manipulation verb*:
                    mamá-ci   'u   ta'wá-ci   'uwáy
                    woman-SUBJ the-SUBJ man-OBJ the-OBJ
                    wýýka-vaa-ku   máy-kya
                    work-MOD-SUBORD   tell-ANT
                    'The woman told the man **to work**'

      d. *Hortative*: wýýka-vaa-rami!
                    work-MOD-we-II
                    '**Let's** work!' (you and I)

      e. *Intentional*: wýýka-vaa-ci-n
                    work-MOD-SUBORD-I
                    'I **intend to**/am **about to** work'

      f. *Counterfact* (in combination with the *anterior*):
                    'uwás-'urú   wýýka-vaa-qa-tų
                    he-TOP   work-MOD-ANT-NOM
                    'He **should/could/might** have worked' (but didn't)

      g. *Predictive*: wýýka-vaa-pų
                    work-MOD-NOM
                    '(he) **may/might/could/should** work'

49) For more details on the Ute TAM system, see Givón (1980a, Chapter 4). In the Ute orthog-
raphy used here, bold-faced vowels are *devoiced*.

h. *Uncertainty*:   wúy̨ka-va-**ci**
                    work-MOD-NOM/SUBORD
                    '**Maybe** he works/is working'

The *main-line*, *foregrounded*, *sequential* thread of Ute narrative may be rendered in either one of two *deictic* modes: Immediate and remote. Traditional stories about long-past events typically use the *remote* mode, as in:

(64)   ...wíitys   'urá-pygá,
       past   be-REM
       '...it **was** a long time ago,

       sináwa-**vi** 'urá-pygá,
       S.-SUBJ   be-REM
       there **was** S. ("copycat" character),

       my̨í-ta-s   'úmy̨   wicí-ci-u   núu-ci-u
       early-PART-CONJ the-SUBJ bird-SUBJ-PL human-SUBJ-PL
       'urá-qa-pygá...
       be-PL-REM
       and in those early days the birds were human...'

Even though (64) recites the opening lines of the story, where *states* (rather than sequential actions) constitute the main line of the narrative, that main line is the **foreground**, and it is conveyed by the **remote** aspectual suffix -*pygá*. In either the sequential action portions of traditional narratives or in the informal narrative dealing with more recent events, the speaker may choose to render the foreground of the description in the **immediate** aspect, making it more vivid, more deictically immediate and more directly relevant to the present situation and participants. Such coding of the event places the hearer *in the middle* of the scene. It is reminiscent of the English so-called 'historical present' (see discussion earlier above). As an example consider:

(65)   ...ný-'urá   kaní-naag̨a-tux   yygá-y,
       I-TOP   house-in-to   enter-IMM
       '...so I **enter** the house,

       mamá-ci-'urá   'uwáy   py̨níkya-y...
       woman-OBJ-TOP   the-OBJ   see-IMM
       and I **see** the woman...'

Rather than have a present-progressive category derived from a *durative* aspect, which *per-se* is not coded in Ute, the language uses the *immediate* tense-aspect, above, to code the present-progressive, as in:

(66) a. *Context*:   What are you doing?
      b. *Reply*:   tu̧ká-yi-n
                       eat-IMM-I
                       'I **am eating**'

However, it is clear that it is not the category *durative* that precipitates the use
of the immediate in this fashion, but rather the category of *present relevance* or
being *deictically immediate* to the scene. Thus, in narrative about the past,
using either the remote or the immediate markers, no special provisions are
made for duratives: they are simply inferred from the verb or the thematic
context.

The immediate-relevance feature of the immediate aspect in Ute also absorbs one function usually associated with the perfect, that of the *present perfect*. Thus consider:

(67) a. *Context*: Would you like to eat?
      b. *Reply*:   kací-n,   wíitu̧s   tu̧ká-y
                      NEG-I   past   eat-IMM
                      'No, I'**ve already eaten**'

The pre-emption of the lingering relevance feature by the immediate aspect in Ute leaves the anterior/perfect primarily with the *counter-sequence*
function. A variant of the anterior marker *-ka-* (or *-kya-*, *-qa-*, *-x̂a-*, *-kwa-*)
may be used to intersperse with either the immediate or the remote aspect.
Thus contrast:

(68) a. *With the immediate*:
          (i)   ...kaní-naag̑a-tux yu̧gá-y,
                 house-in-to   enter-IMM
                 '...so he **enters** the house
          (ii)   na'áy-naag̑a-tu̧ pu̧ní'ni-y;
                 REFL-in-DIR   look-IMM
                 and **looks** around him;
          (iii) mamá-ci-'urá   'uwáy   'apág̑a-qa...
                 woman-OBJ-TOP   the-OBJ   talk-ANT
                 he **has already talked** to the woman...'
      b. *With the remote*:
          (i)   ...kaní-naag̑a-tux yu̧gá-pu̧gá,
                 house-in-to   enter-REM
                 '...so he **entered** the house

   (ii)   na'áy-naaĝa-tṵ   pṵní'ni-pṵgá,
           REFL-in-DIR   look-REM
           and **looked** around him;
   (iii) mamá-ci-'urá   'uwáy   'apáĝa-qa-pṵgá...
           woman-OBJ-TOP   the-OBJ talk-ANT-REM
           he **had already talked** to the woman...'

A final note concerns the use of the perfect/anterior in Ute, in conversational style, to mark the foregrounded *past* in the very first clause of a chain, after which the foreground description is shifted to the immediate. Consider:

(69) *Context*: So what happened?
       Reply: mamá-ci-'urá   yṵgá-qa;
               woman-SUBJ-TOP   enter-ANT
               'A woman **entered**;

               pináxwa-'urá   karṵ-y,
               later-TOP   sit-IMM
               then she **sits** down,

               pináxwa 'apáĝa-y,   'aváaaant   'apáĝa-y...
               later   talk-IMM   much-INTENS talk-IMM
               and she **starts** talking, and boy she **talks**!...'

One way of interpreting the use of the anterior/perfect in such chain-initial positions is to point out that in principle the chain-initial position is *out-of-sequence*, since it establishes the beginning of a *new* sequence ('thematic paragraph'). Similar uses of the perfect/anterior may be seen in Creoles.[50]

8.3.7. Sherpa: Perfective/imperfective and evidentiality

The major morphologically-coded distinction in the Sherpa (Sino-Tibetan)[51] TAM system is between the **perfective**, which covers the past, and **imperfective**, which covers the habitual, present and future. The last three are in the process of being differentiated from each other by additional morphological means, but historically they are all derived from the imperfective. Further, Sherpa is a *split-ergative* language (see Chapter 5, above) where transitive clauses exhibit ergative-absolutive morphology only in the perfective; otherwise they exhibit nominative-accusative morphology. As an example consider:

50) For further discussion of this, see Givón (1982a).

51) The Sherpa data are from my own field notes, originally due to Koncchok J. Lama (in personal communication). Some of it has been discussed previously in Givón (1982b).

(70) a. *Past/perfective*:   ti-gi   laĝá   ky-aa-no   (ERG subject)
                                  he-ERG work do-AUX-PERF
                                  'He worked'
      b. *Present/imperfective*: ti laĝa ki-yin   way (NOM subject)
                                  he work do-AUX be
                                  'He is working'
      c. *Future/imperfective*: ti laĝá ki-wi   (NOM subject)
                                  he work do-AUX
                                  'He will work'

The other feature of interest in the Sherpa TAM system is that of **evidentiality**. Briefly, evidentiality markers in general are often associated with
TAM morphemes, and many of them arise diachronically from erstwhile
verbs, much like TAM markers. They code the speaker's evaluation of the
source of evidence of information processed in declarative sentences (see
Chapter 7, section 7.4.3., above). Evidentiality is thus, ultimately, the source
of the speaker's *certainty* and the hearer's willingness to *challenge* asserted information. Most commonly, information is classified for evidentiary purposes
along the following parameters:[52]

(a)   *Direct* vs. *indirect* experience as source of information
(b)   *Visual, auditory* and other *sensory modalities* as source of information;
(c)   *Experience* vs. *hearsay* as source of information;
(d)   *Experience* vs. *inference* as source of information.

The cross-linguistic evidence suggests that speakers hierarchize these sources
universally as to their *evidentiary strength* or reliability:

(71) a. *Personal deixis hierarchy*:
          SPEAKER > HEARER > THIRD PARTY
      b. *Directness hierarchy*:
          SENSORY EXPERIENCE > INFERENCE
      c. *Sensory modality hierarchy*:
          VISION > HEARING > OTHER SENSES > FEELING
      d. *Space deixis hierarchy*:
          NEAR > FAR
      e. *Time deixis hierarchy*:
          PRESENT > IMMEDIATE PAST > REMOTE PAST

52) For a general discussion and cross-linguistic evidence, see Chafe and Nichols (forthcoming)
and Givón (1982b).

In terms of distribution within the grammar, evidentiary markers are found in *declarative* but not in manipulative speech acts. They pertain to *realis* (past, present) but not to irrealis (future). Clauses where the *speaker* is a *conscious participant* in the reported event/state are exempted from the contrast since *automatically* direct experience by the speaker counts as having the highest evidentiary strength (cf. (71a)). Clauses where the *hearer* is a *conscious participant* in the state/event reported are likewise exempted, presumably because of the following *communicative principle*:

(72) "The *speaker* cannot claim evidentiary authority over states/events in which the *hearer* was a conscious participant (and the speaker was not), since (a) the hearer's evidentiary support is stronger, and (b) there's no reason to inform the hearer of things he knows better than the speaker".

Principle (72) is part and parcel of the communicative contract.[53] Finally, evidentiality contrasts do not appear in *presupposed* clauses, since they are presumably agreed to in advance by some speaker-hearer conventions, and thus require no evidentiary justification (see Chapter 7, section 7.4.3., above).

Let us briefly illustrate the evidentiary contrast in Sherpa. In the perfective/past, two 3rd-person auxiliaries/agreements can be used, one coding *direct evidence* by the speaker, the other *indirect* or *hearsay* evidence. Thus consider:

(73) a. ti-gi   cenyi caaq-**sung**
          he-ERG cup   break-PERF$_i$
          'He broke the cup'   (and I have *direct evidence*)

      b. ti-gi   cenyi caaq-**no**
          he-ERG cup   break-PERF$_{ii}$
          'He broke the cup' (and I have only *indirect/hearsay* evidence)

      c. ŋyee   cenyi caaq-**yin**
          I-ERG   cup   break-PERF
          'I broke the cup' (no need to defend the evidence)

A similar contrast is found in the present/imperfective:

---

53) See Chapter 7, section 7.4.3., above, as well as Grice (1968/1975) and Gordon and Lakoff (1971).

(74) a. ti laĝa ki-yin **no**
he work do-IMP AUX$_i$
'He is working' (and I have *direct evidence*)

b. ti laĝa ki-yin **way**
he work do-IMPER AUX$_{ii}$
'He is working' (and I have only *indirect/hearsay* evidence)

c. ŋa laĝa ki-yin **way**
I work do-IMP AUX
'I am working' (no need to defend the evidence)

In contrast, in the future/imperfective a form equivalent to (73a) or (74a) above is not possible. Thus consider:

(75) a. ti laĝa ki-**wi**
he work do-IMP
'He will work' (impossible to have evidentiary support)

b. ŋa laĝa ki-**din**
I work do-IMP
'I will work' (impossible to have evidentiary support)

Other aspectual distinctions, such as *durative* or *perfect/anterior*, are not explicitly coded in Sherpa TAM morphology, although presumably they can be inferred from the context.

8.3.8. Bikol: Realis vs. irrealis

In Bikol (Philippine), as in many other Austronesian languages, the major morphological distinction in the TAM system is between *realis* (prefix *n-ag-* for agent-topic) and *irrealis* (prefix *m-ag-* for agent-topic). Realis then covers the past, present and habitual, while irrealis covers the future, together with other future-projecting modal categories. In illustration consider:[54]

(76) a. **nag**-bakál 'ang-laláke ning-líbro (realis/past)
AGT-buy TOP-man ACC-book
'The man **bought** a book'

b. **nag**-ba-bakál 'ang-laláke ning-líbro (realis/progressive)
AGT-PROG-buy TOP-man ACC-book
'The man **is buying** a book'

---

54) The Bikol data are from my own field notes, originally due to Manuel Factora (in personal communication).

    c. **mag**-bakál 'ang-laláke ning-líbro   (irrealis/future)
       AGT-buy TOP-man   ACC-book
       'The man **will buy** a book'

    d. muyá na   **mag**-bakál 'ang-laláke ning-líbro (irrealis/V-COMP)
       want that AGT-buy TOP-man ACC-book
       'The man wants **to buy** a book'

    e. nag-sabí 'ang-laláke sa-babáye   (irrealis/V-COMP)
       AGT-tell TOP-man   DAT-woman
       na **mag**-bakál ning-líbro
       that AGT-buy ACC-book
       'The man told the woman **to buy** a book'

The *durative* aspect is marked (cf. (76b)) by first-syllable reduplication, and may appear either in the realis or irrealis. Finally, the perfect/anterior is not morphologically coded.

8.3.9. Chuave: Clause chaining and switch reference

    Chuave (New Guinea Highlands)[55] is a *clause-chaining* language. Such languages employ a different mode of coding discourse structure. Information is presented in long "chains" or thematic paragraphs in which *mood*, *speech act* and *tense/modality* are coded only in the *paragraph-final* clause. The assumption is thus that non-final asserted verbs must have the same values as the final one, with respect to these categories. And presumably value-changes precipitate the initiation of a new paragraph. Furher, the "chain" is divided into two main parts:

    (a)   *Background/presupposed/topical clauses*: These have no speech-act, mood or TAM value. They include clauses that fall elsewhere under the grammatical categories of ADV-clauses, REL-clauses, V-complements and conjoined TOPIC-clauses. They are marked as being either *simultaneous* (SIM) or *non-simultaneous* (NSIM) with the asserted clause(s). And they cannot appear anywhere except at the beginning of the "chain".

    (b)   *Foreground/asserted/sequential clauses*: These represent the main line of the sequential information. Among them, *medial clauses* appear first and take their speech-act, tense and mood/modality values from the *chain-final* clause.

---

55) The Chuave data cited below are from Thurman (1978). For further details on clause-chaining languages, see Longacre (1972).

Let us first illustrate the variety of chain-initial *topic clauses* in Chuave:

(77)   a. *ADV-clause*:

       ne   iki-num   moi-n-g-i   (TOPIC, SIM)
       you   house-your   be-you-TOP-SIM
       'While you are in the house,

       tei   u-na-y-e   (ASSERTED, FINAL)
       there come-IRREAL-I-DECL
       I will come there'

   b. *ADV-clause*:

       kan-i-k-a-i   (TOPIC, NSIM)
       see-I-TOP-NSIM-that
       'When I looked,

       kiapu   guwai-nom-i-   muruwo furuwai-bei
       officer   thing-their-that all   strew-do
       de-Ø-im-ie   (ASSERTED, FINAL)
       leave-REAL-they-DECL
       they were strewing all the officers' things about'

   c. *REL-clause*:

       gan   moi-n-g-u-a   (TOPIC, NSIM)
       child   be-he-TOP-him-NSIM
       'The child who is here,

       Gomia tei   awi   d-o   (IMPER, FINAL)
       Gomia there send   leave-IMPER
       send (him) to Gomia!'

   d. *V-complement*:

       kasu di-in-g-a   (TOPIC, NSIM)
       lie   say-there-TOP-NSIM
       'that they told a lie

       fai-ke-Ø-m-a   (ASSERTED, FINAL)
       right-NEG-REAL-it-EMPH
       is not right'

Topic clauses in Chuave discourse may number more than one at the beginning of a chain, and a second topic clause may be of an asserted or *foregrounded* value vis-à-vis the one preceding it, but of a presupposed or *backgrounded* value vis-à-vis the following clause(s). Thus compare (78a) and (78b) below:

(78) a. *One topic clause*:

kan-i-k-a-i   (TOPIC, NSIM)
see-I-TOP-NSIM-that
'when I looked,

kiapu guwai-nom-i   (ASSERTED, MEDIAL)
officer things-their-that
muro furuwai-bei de-in-goro
all   strew-do leave-they-DS
they were strewing about all the officers' belongings

niki-de fi-Ø-y-e   (ASSERTED, FINAL)
bad-be think-REAL-I-DECL
and I got angry'

   b. *Two topic clauses*:

kan-i-k-a-i   (TOPIC$_i$, NSIM)
see-I-TOP-NSIM-that
'When I looked,

kiapu   guwai-nom-i   muruwo furuwai-bei
officer   things-their-that   all   strew-do
de-in-g-a   (TOPIC$_{ii}$, NSIM)
leave-they-TOP-NSIM
then because they were strewing about all the officers'
belongings,

niki-de fi-Ø-y-e   (ASSERTED, FINAL)
bad-be think-REAL-I-DECL
I got angry'

The second interesting feature of the Chuave-type clause-chaining paragraph structure is the use of **anticipatory switch-reference** in the medial asserted clauses, the ones which carry the bulk of foregrounded, sequential information. The switch-reference markers — DS 'different subject' and SS
'same subject' — appear as suffixes on the medial verbs, at the position normally reserved for TAM markers in an SOV language. They are *anticipatory*
because they alert the hearer to subject continuation or change in the *subsequent* clause. As an example consider:[56]

56) Further discussion of switch reference, within the grammar of *topic continuity*, may be found
in Chapter 22, Volume II. For many cross-language details, see Munro (ed., 1980) and Haiman and
Munro (eds, 1983).

(79) a. ...meina i ne-**ro**
money get eat-SS
'...(I) took the money

b. ena tekoi u-**re**
then again come-SS
and then I came back

c. iki moi-o-**koro**
house be-I-DS
and stayed home;

d. tekoi u boi-n-**goro**
again call-out-he-DS
so then he sent for me again,

e. inako de-**ro**
return leave-SS
so (I) came back

f. fu-i-**goro**
go-I-DS
and went there;

g. tokoi numba lin-lin numba-i naro-Ø-m-e
again number one-one number-that give-me-REAL-he-DECL
and again he made me foreman of the work-line'.

The tense-modal distinction between *realis* and *irrealis* is the major TAM feature marked on finite, chain-final clauses. The aspectual feature *durative* can be marked in any clause by the auxiliary verb 'be'. *Foreground/sequentiality* in discourse is coded via chain-medial clauses. *Backgroundedness/out-of-sequence* is coded in the chain-initial topic clauses. Most conspicuous by its absence, on the surface, is the *perfect/anterior* aspect. This is a reflection of the fact that out-of-sequence clauses cannot be interspersed *in the middle* of the sequential material in the thematic paragraph. They can only be placed *at the beginning* of a thematic paragraph, i.e. between paragraphs.

As uncommon as the Chuave strategy of sequencing information seems at first, on further examination it turns out to be not so different from English and its use of the perfect. In illustration of this, consider the following English example:

(80) a. ...he stepped into the room, looked around, carefully studied the display on the wall, took a chair and sat down...

b. ...he stepped into the room and looked around. **He had already studied the display on the wall on previous occasions**. He took a chair and sat down...

c. ...he stepped into the room and looked around. **Having studied the display on the wall(carefully)**, he took a chair and sat down...

In (80a) all clauses are presented in natural sequential order, and a *comma* conjunction with *zero* — most continuous — subject marking[57] is used. In (80b) one clause is presented **out of sequence**, marked by the perfect/anterior. Automatically a more major **continuity break** occurs on both sides of that clause. A comma cannot be used there, only a *period*. And the subject must be marked by a *pronoun* at both boundaries of the out-of-sequence interjection, never by zero. Finally, in (80c) the backgrounded clause is actually not at all out-of-sequence, but only backgrounded. A more major (period) break is still required before it, and the use of the pronoun — rather than zero — in the subsequent clause. What this demonstrates is that in English too, the introduction of out-of-sequence or backgrounded material creates a break in the thematic paragraph, at least in cases echoing the perfect/anterior itself. Chuave is still different in its insistence on the chain-initial placement of REL-clauses and V-complements — which in English can be interspersed within sequential discourse as *subordinate clauses* without breaking the thematic paragraph. Further discussion of inter-clausal connectivity may be found in Chapter 21, Volume II.[58]

8.4. TENSE-ASPECT-MODAL CATEGORIES IN SUBORDINATE CLAUSES

8.4.1. Preliminaries

In the discussion so far, we have treated primarily tense-aspect-modal categories appearing in simple (main-declarative-affirmative-active) clauses. But the discussion throughout has suggested implicity that TAM markers also appear in complex and/or subordinate clauses, and in fact some of them (cf. (35) above) are more likely to appear in *backgrounded* or subordinate clauses. As a rule of thumb, the general array of TAM categories in complex clauses tends to be more *limited*, as compared with their wider freedom of distribution in simple clauses. One may consider this another reflection of the higher *mar-*

---

57) See discussion in Chapter 22, Volume II, as well as in Givón (1983a, b, c).

58) But also see discussion in Longacre (1976 and forthcoming).

kedness of complex clauses. However, in many if not most cases, more specific functional explanations exist that may have little if anything to do with markedness per se. In this section we will discuss, in general terms, the more likely distribution of TAM categories in subordinate clauses.

8.4.2. Syntax vs. discourse-pragmatics in subordinate clauses

The major categories of subordinate clauses we will survey in this book — most of them in greater detail in Volume II — are:

(a)   Verb complements
(b)   Relative clauses
(c)   Adverbial clauses

They have different semantic and pragmatic *functions*, they vary in their degree of semantic *dependency* on their corresponding main clauses and the manner of such dependency (or "binding"[59]), and they also vary in the corresponding degree of structural/syntactic *integration* they exhibit vis-à-vis their main clauses. In general, one may make the following prediction concerning the coding of TAM categories in subordinate clauses:

(81)   *TAM in subordinate clauses*:
"The more dependent the SUB-clause is semantically/pragmatically on the MAIN-clause, the less likely are independently-expressed TAM markers to appear in the SUB-clause".

The uncoded TAM categories of the SUB-clause may then be inferred, in some systematic fashion, from semantic or pragmatic information given in the main clause or in the discourse context.

8.4.3. TAM categories in topical/backgrounded/presupposed clauses

We have already noted above the preponderance of the *perfect/anterior* in backgrounded REL-clauses, ADV-clauses and complements of cognition verbs. But in many languages all these presuppositional clauses may be completely *nominalized* — i.e. made structurally into nouns — and then most commonly be totally unmarked for TAM categories, except perhaps for some aspectuals. The Chuave chain-initial topic clauses, section 8.3.9., above, represent a similar *neutralization* of TAM categories in backgrounded clauses, but without formal nominalization. Reduced variants of ADV-clauses are also possible in English. Thus consider:

---

59) "Binding", as a general dimension of *semantic dependency* between V-complements and their main-clause verbs, is discussed in Givón (1980b). Greater semantic dependency usually leads to structural/syntactic dependency and *integration* between the two clauses, a process that clearly reflects an *iconic* relation.

(82) a. When he arrived, she left. (unreduced)
      b. Upon *his arrival*, she left. (nominalized/reduced)
      c. When she arrived, she sat down to eat. (unreduced)
      d. Upon *arriving*, she sat down to eat. (nominalized/reduced)
      e. When he finished, he left. (unreduced)
      f. *Having finished*, he left. (nominalized/reduced)[60]

Complements of cognition verbs ('think', 'know' etc.) often exhibit tense-aspect restrictions vis-à-vis their main verbs, such as the so-called tense-agreement in English, as in:

(83) a. John **told** Mary that he **loved** her.
      b. ?John **told** Mary that he **loves** her.
      c. Mary **wished** that John **would** love her.
      d. ?Mary **wished** that John **will** love her.

In many languages such complements must be completely nominalized/reduced, thus displaying no TAM marking at all. As an example of this consider Sherpa, as in:[61]

(84) ti-la   ŋyee   wa-up-ti   ca-no
      he-DAT I-GEN come-INF-DEF know-PERF
      { 'He knew that I came'   }
      { 'He knew of my coming' }

REL-clauses may display strong TAM restrictions, and they may also be further reduced via nominalization, as in Turkish:[62]

(85) a. *Subject REL-clause*:
          gel-**en**   adam
          come-*SUBJ/REL* man
          'the man who came'

---

60) In English, nominalizing a *past tense* clause results in a *perfect-participle* nominalization.

61) For further discussion on nominalized verb complements, see Chapter 13, Volume II, as well as Givón (1980b). The Sherpa data are from my own field notes and originally due to Koncchok J. Lama (in personal communication).

62) From Slobin (1982).

b. *Object REL-clause*:

Ali-nin gör-**düğ**-ü adam
Ali-GEN see-*OBJ/REL*-his man
'the man whom Ali saw' (Lit.: 'The man of Ali's(his)seeing')

The past tense in both (85a, b) is unmarked and only inferred, and the subject is marked as the genitive/possessor of the verb.[63]

8.4.4. Modality in verb complements

With the exception of complements of *presuppositional* verbs, discussed above, verb complements usually form part of the *assertion* in the complex clause. When we further exclude the complements of *implicative* verbs (see Chapter 4, above, as well as Chapter 13, Volume II), we are left with a largely *irrealis* modal space. The irrealis space may be further sub-divided in a way that parallels our three classes of complement-taking verbs:

(86)

verb type	modality type	most likely sub-types
(a) *Modality verbs*:	intentional	'wish', 'intent', 'ability', 'self-imposed obligation'
(b) *Manipulative verbs*:	manipulative	'command', 'manipulation', 'other-imposed need/ obligation/necessity'
(c) *Cognition verbs*:	epistemic, affective	'probability', 'possibility', 'uncertainty', 'doubt', 'hope', 'fear'

The entire modal space of asserted irrealis in language may be then divided, somewhat schematically, as follows:[64]

---

63) In English such a nominalized pattern is possible in sentential subjects, as in "*His* discovery *of* the gold surprised us", or in sentential objects, as in "He told us of *his* discovery *of* the gold".

64) A compatible division, albeit with different terminology, may be found in Palmer (1979). A less compatible one may be found in Chung and Timberlake (forthcoming).

(87)

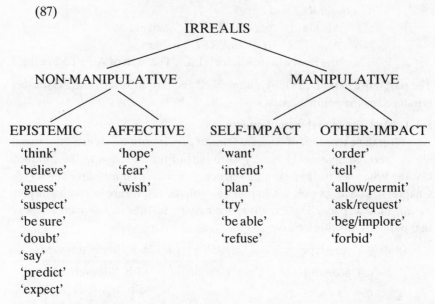

EPISTEMIC	AFFECTIVE	SELF-IMPACT	OTHER-IMPACT
'think'	'hope'	'want'	'order'
'believe'	'fear'	'intend'	'tell'
'guess'	'wish'	'plan'	'allow/permit'
'suspect'		'try'	'ask/request'
'be sure'		'be able'	'beg/implore'
'doubt'		'refuse'	'forbid'
'say'			
'predict'			
'expect'			

The common denominator of all these sub-categories — *qua* irrealis — is that of *future* or *uncertainty*. The epistemic category may also be coded, in some languages, by epistemic adverbs ('probably', 'possibly', 'likely', 'maybe' etc.). And historically, members of each of the four sub-categories may start as lexical verbs — commanding the irrealis modality in their complement scope — and may then *grammaticalize* to become, most commonly, verb affixes imparting the irrealis modality to a seeming main clause. But in some fundamental way these irrealis sub-modalities are most characteristic of the complement scope of *non-presuppositional* cognition verbs and *non-implicative* modality and manipulative verbs.

8.4.5. Subjunctives

Directly related to the irrealis modalities of verb complements are the so-called *subjunctive* modes. They are typically found in the complements of uncertainty *epistemic* verbs and non-implicative *manipulation* verbs, and may be thus divided into "subjunctive of uncertainty" and "subjunctive of manipulation". In some languages the same TAM marker codes both types. Thus, consider the following examples from Spanish:

(88) a. *Manipulation*:

le   dijo a Juán que se   **fuera** (past indic. **se fué**)
him   told to John that REFL go-SUBJUNC
{ 'He told John **to leave**'   }
{ 'He told John that **he (John) must leave**' }

b. *Uncertainty*:

me   dudo   si María se   **fuera** (past indic. **se fué**)
REFL doubt-I if Mary REFL go-SUBJUNC
'I doubt that **Mary left**'

espero que no **venga**   (indic. **viene**)
hope-I that NEG come-SUBJUNC
'I hope that **he won't come**'

But the subjunctive may also appear without the command of main verbs, to impart modalities that are rather compatible with those of verb complements. Thus, the subjunctive of manipulation may be used as a polite command, as in:

(89) vaya   te!
go-SUBJUNC REFL
'Do go on and leave!'

And the subjunctive of uncertainty may be used in compatible expressions *without* the uncertainty verb, as in:

(90) ojala que no   venga!
EXCL that NEG come-SUBJUNC
'May he not come!'

Some languages code the two subjunctive categories differently. Thus, consider the following from Bemba (Bantu):[65]

(91) a. *Manipulation*:

n-déé-mu-ebela   a-boomb-**e**
I-DUR-him-tell   he-work-SUBJUNC
'I am ordering him that **he must/should work**'

b. *Uncertainty*:

n-déé-twiishika a-**inga**-isa
I-DUR-doubt   he-SUBJUNC-come
'I doubt that he **would/will come**'

65) See details in Givón (1972, Chapter 4).

Further discussion of the TAM marking of various subordinate clauses
will be deferred to the specific chapters where these clause-types are discussed
(Chapters 13, 16 and 21 of Volume II).

9 | NEGATION

9.1. INTRODUCTION: NEGATION AS A PROPOSITIONAL MODALITY

As noted in Chapter 8, above, negation is one member of the set of propositional modalities. Within the context of **propositional semantics**, one may place negation at one extreme point on the scale of "truth":

(1)　PRESUPPOSITION　>　REALIS-ASSERTION　>
　　　　(taken for　　　　　　(strongly asser-
　　　　granted as true)　　　ted as true)
　　　　IRREALIS-ASSERTION　>　NEG-ASSERTION
　　　　(weakly asserted　　　　(asserted as
　　　　as true)　　　　　　　　false)

Further, in this logic-based domain, neither presupposition nor irrealis-assertion has asserted **truth value**, so that the scale may be further collapsed to the binary contrast between "true" (realis-assertion) and "false" (NEG-assertion). And within such a reduced system the axiom disallowing contradiction indeed is operative:

(2)　"If P is true, then NEG-P is false"

While axiom (2) may be viewed as part of a formal system, it clearly reflects something about human belief systems, whereby in their capacity of orderly, rational thinkers humans do their best to avoid holding contradictory beliefs.[1]

---

1) Unlike formal systems, humans are capable of compartmentalization, whereby contradictory beliefs held at the same time are rigidly segregated in subparts of the cognitive system, under different *personae*, etc. Further, humans are also capable of *change* or *faulty memory*, whereby they can hold contradictory beliefs in temporal succession. Finally, they are also capable of *contextualizing* parts of or their entire belief system, thus making the truth of some propositions vary with the change of internal or external context.

In terms of the psychological dimension of **subjective certainty** or strength of belief, scale (1) is clearly misleading, and must be replaced by (3) where realis-assertion and NEG-assertion are on a par:

(3) PRESUPPOSITION > $\left\{ \begin{array}{l} \text{REALIS-ASSERTION} \\ \text{NEG-ASSERTION} \end{array} \right\}$ > IRREALIS-ASSERTION

Scale (3) thus expresses the degree of the speaker's certainty vis-à-vis the uttered proposition. And this dimension of subjective certainty is already part of what must be taken into consideration in the communicative contract between speakers and hearers (see Chapter 7, section 7.4.3., above).

Finally, in terms of **discourse-pragmatics**, i.e. the use of negation in communication between speaker and hearer, negation seems to share some interesting properties of **presupposition**, as we shall see shortly. This then yields one more possible scale:

(4) $\left\{ \begin{array}{l} \text{PRESUPPOSITION} \\ \text{NEG-ASSERTION} \end{array} \right\}$ > REALIS-ASSERTION   > IRREALIS-ASSERTION

Scale (4) is motivated by assumptions the speaker makes about what the hearer already knows as **background**, what requires or does not require **evidentiary support**, and what is open to or even invites **challenge** (see Chapter 7, section 7.4.3.).

The three scales of propositional modalities — (1), (3) and (4) — do not represent competing hypotheses about the place of negation within the cognitive epistemic space. Rather, they reflect the fact that in natural language — unlike formal logic — negation is a complex functional domain, drawing on three distinct though partially inter-dependent components:

(a)   *Propositional semantics*: The reversal of the proposition's *truth-value*;

(b)   *Subjective certainty*: A mid-level of *certainty* a speaker may assign to his assertion that an event/state did *not* take place;

(c)   *Discourse-pragmatics*: The speech-act of *denial*, performed under well-defined sub-clauses of the communicative contract.

Of these three aspects of negation in human language, (a) has been sufficiently elaborated in the traditional logic-bound literature,[2] and we will have

---

2) Cf. Russell (1905, 1919) or Carnap (1947, 1959), *inter alia*.

relatively little to add to it. It pertains to a universe of propositions in an idealized system disembodied of speakers, hearers, discourse context, communicative intent or communicative function. Aspect (b) of negation involves the speaker's egocentric assessment of states/events and thus clearly represents a facet of real *behavior*. That behavior is subsumed in aspect (c), which involves the speaker's assessment of the hearer's views and his projected likely behavior vis-à-vis propositions about which the speaker already holds a certain subjective certainty, i.e. (b).

As in the preceding chapters, we will discuss first the functional-semantic aspects of negation, then proceed to construct a typology of the various ways in which languages code negation syntactically and morphologically.

9.2. NEGATION AS A SPEECH-ACT: DENIAL AND ITS DISCOURSE CONTEXT

As noted earlier, the major function of declarative sentences in discourse is to convey new information. Further, within the declarative sentence one can always identify parts ('chunks') that carry no new information but rather are presupposed or *backgrounded*, and parts that are indeed asserted new information. This description must now be further refined, by first noting that in declarative sentences the negative variant is used to convey new information of a very different sort than the corresponding affirmative. In fact, NEG-declaratives may be rightly considered a distinct speech-act, that of **denial** or **contradiction**. In illustration of this, consider first the following example:[3]

(5)   a. *Context*:   -What's new?
      b. *AFF-reply*:   -Oh, my wife is pregnant.
      c. *NEG-reply*:   -Oh, my wife is **not** pregnant.

The query (5a) is of wide scope, not restricting the type or range of information requested in any specific way. Nonetheless, (5b) is a natural reply to (5a) and (5c) is distinctly odd. In fact, a natural rejoinder to (5c) could have been:

(6)   Wait-a-minute, I didn't know she was **supposed to be pregnant**!

Such a rejoinder makes it clear that the negative response (5c) could have been felicitous — if the information concerning the possible, imminent or contemplated pregnancy of the wife had previously become part of the background information shared with the hearer, by whatever means. Put another way:

---

3) This discussion is based on Givón (1975c, 1979a, Ch. 3).

(7)   "The AFF-declarative speech-act is used to inform the hearer of P against the background of the hearer's *ignorance* of P. The NEG-declarative speech-act is used to *deny* P against the background of the hearer's presumed inclination to *believe* in P, believe in the likelihood of P or be *familiar* with P".

When the speaker transacts a NEG-declarative sentence then, the general informational content of the proposition in question is already *shared* between speaker and hearer. Further, the speaker assumes that the hearer tends to believe in the corresponding affirmative, and the NEG-declarative speech act is then a *denial* or *contradiction* of that assumed belief. Put another way, in the affirmative-declarative speech act, two implicit assumptions are made.[4]

(a)   The hearer *does not* know; and
(b)   The speaker *knows*.

In the NEG-declarative speech act, the two *explicit* assumptions are:

(c)   The hearer knows *wrong*; and
(d)   The speaker knows *better*.[5]

A NEG-declarative speech act thus, normally, does not add new information about the verb, subject, object(s) or other participants in the state/event. Rather, it puts the hearer on notice that the speaker does not share his/her belief in the corresponding affirmative.

9.3. PRESUPPOSITION AND THE SCOPE OF NEGATION

As noted in Chapter 7, above, most declarative sentences used in connected, multi-propositional discourse have presupposed/backgrounded portions and asserted/foregrounded portions. Most commonly, the *subject* does not fall under the scope of asserted new information, but the predicate — or at least part of it — does. Further, in our discussion of the speaker-hearer communicative contract (Chapter 7, section 7.4.3.) we noted that asserted new information was open to *challenge*, while presupposed/background information

---

4) See Grice (1968/1975) or Gordon and Lakoff (1971), *inter alia*.

5) The socio-cultural implications of these explicit assumptions can be seen in all cultures, where negatives are considered *less polite*, *contentious*, *unpleasant* or downright *threatening*. It is one thing to tacitly add to a person's knowledge on the implicit background of *non-knowledge*. It is another thing altogether to *challenge* a person's already existing, strongly-held (and oft strongly asserted) *belief*.

was not (or at least much less so). One consequence of these facts concerning the normal distribution of information in sentences in discourse is that in the common use of negation in natural language, only the *asserted* portion of the corresponding affirmative is denied, while the *presupposition* remains outside the negative scope. Let us illustrate this first with a few simple examples:

(8)   a. She saw the man **who came yesterday**
        b. She didn't see the man **who came yesterday**
        c. Mary regretted that **Joe left her**
        d. Mary didn't regret that **Joe left her**

The REL-clause in (b) and the V-complement in (8d) remain shielded from the scope of negation. The main-clause predications in (8b, d) — "saw the man", "regretted something", respectively — are indeed negated. But the presupposed subordinate clauses remain intact since they were not asserted to begin with in (8a) and (8c).

A long philosophical tradition[6] holds that negative sentences such as (9) below are *ambiguous* as to their scope, so that under one reading the subject is indeed excluded from the scope of negation, while under another reading the very *existence* ('referentiality') of the subject is also challenged:

(9)   The King of France is not bald
        (i) There is a King of France, but he's **not bald**.
        (ii) There's **no King of France**, so it is nonsensical to assert that 'He is bald'.

To the linguist, the claim that (9ii) is indeed a legitimate interpretation of negative sentences such as (9) has always been odd, since among other things it would entail that in the corresponding affirmative (10) the existence ('referentiality') of the subject ('the King of France') is being *asserted*. But in human communication definite subjects are *not* used to assert their existence. Rather their existence (and shared knowledge of their *identity*) is *presupposed*, it is part of the background information and thus does not fall under the scope of assertion to begin with. Thus, (10_i) is the normal interpretation of (10), while (10_{ii}) is odd:

---

6) See eg. Russell (1905, 1919) *inter alia*. A similar view in Linguistics was presented in Keenan (1969), where the two types of negation were labeled "strong" ('internal') vs. "weak" ('external') negation.

(10)   The King of France is bald
     (i)   You and I share the knowledge that there is a King of France and who exactly he is, at least for the purpose of this universe of discourse. In addition, I am asserting that he "is bald".
     (ii) "There exists a King of France", and he "is bald".

Even philosophers who take for granted that definite subjects are presupposed[7] nonetheless persist in the belief that the external (9_{ii}) interpretation of (9) is indeed a felicitous interpretation. And it may indeed be that such an interpretation may be *forced* upon speakers/hearers, although in actual use of human language it is exceedingly rare. To illustrate this fact, consider the following text-counts from English narrative fiction. Twenty-two pages of a detective novel were counted, and all negative sentences in main, declarative clauses were tabulated. The results are presented in Table I, below.[8]

TABLE I: THE DISTRIBUTION OF NEGATIVE FORMS IN WRITTEN ENGLISH NARRATIVE

DEF-subject excluded from scope of negation		DEF-subject included under scope of negation		special Subject-negative form		total	
N	%	N	%	N	%	N	%
60	0.89	0	0.00	7	0.11	67	1.00

The results are rather striking. Out of the total of 67 negatives in main, declarative clauses, 89 % were with definite subjects, i.e. of the structural negation type in (9) above. Not a single one of those involved the negation of the referentiality of the subject, i.e. the interpretation (9_{ii}) suggested as possible by the logicians. Rather, the negation of the referentiality of the subject was coded in the text by two other forms of negation, as in:

(11)   a. *Word-negation*: "...**nobody** will take a cash deposit on a car any more..." [p. 49]
     b. *Existential negation*: "...**there was no expression** on her face..." [p. 51]

---

7) See eg. Strawson (1950).

8) The text was from MacDonald (1974, pp. 49-70).

Two of the seven instances using these special forms were of type (11a), and five of type (11b). In addition, one instance of the 60 negatives with definite subjects involved lexical negation of the *object*, thus again leaving the subject outside the negative scope:

(12)   "...she paid **no attention** to him..." [p. 51]

While the forms in (11a, b) indeed deny the referentiality of the subject, they still involve denial of some implicit affirmative proposition held in the hearer's supposed belief. However, that corresponding affirmative proposition involves a **non-referential** NP. Thus, the affirmative likely to have been negated in (11a) is:

(13)   **People** used to take a cash deposit on cars in the past.

The one corresponding to (11b) may have been:

(14)   Under normal circumstances there is **some expression** on a person's face.

And the one corresponding to (12) could have been:

(15)   One would have expected her to pay **some attention** to him.

The source of **generic** information that forms the background upon which the lexical/existential negation is transacted may vary. It may be derived from habits established — and exposed overtly — during the preceding discourse. It may characterize only the particular interlocutor whose peculiar propensities and beliefs are well known to the speaker. Or it may be part of the culturally-shared belief system of a larger group. But whether explicit or implicit, it is that generic information that is negated.

The examples in (11) and (12) above involve denial of some generic information with non-referential subjects or objects. But the very same forms can also be used as an **emphatic** denial of specific information with referential, definite or indefinite arguments. As examples consider:

(16)   a.   *Context*: -**A man** is waiting outside.   (REF, INDEF subject)
       b.   *Response*: -No, there's **nobody** outside (let alone a man).
       c.   *Context*: -You saw **Joe** yesterday, didn't you? (REF, DEF object)
       d.   *Response*: -I saw **nobody** yesterday (let alone Joe).

What the respondent does in (16b, d) is use **generic** negation as a way of responding emphatically to specific assertions about **referential** individuals. The negation of the philosopher's example (10) would thus not be (9) itself, but rather the actual existential-NEG form in (9ii).

This asymmetrical relation between *specific* negation and *generic* negation is of course natural, given the inclusion relation ('type-token relation') between the generic and specific. Thus, if one asserts:

(17) **Joe** is not bald.   (specific-NEG)

one leaves open the possibility that someone else may be bald. But if one asserts:

(18) **Nobody** is bald.   (generic-NEG)

one also denies that Joe could be bald.

9.4. DISCOURSE PRESUPPOSITIONALITY AND NEGATION

In the preceding sections we have established that the corresponding affirmative of a NEG-asserted proposition in connected discourse forms the background, the shared knowledge, with respect to which the NEG-assertion can be interpreted felicitously. But this sense of background is obviously not the normal sense of **logical presupposition**, otherwise the speaker uttering a NEG-assertion would be holding two contradictory beliefs, one in the truth of not-P that he is asserting, the other in the truth of P that he is presupposing. What is involved here is the fact that discourse backgroundedness or **discourse presupposition** may not involve the logician's condition of *truth*, nor even the philosophical pragmaticist's condition of the speaker's *belief* in truth. What is involved here is the condition of **familiarity**, of knowledge **about** the possibility of P (which does not entail truth), rather than knowledge of P (which does). This notion of discourse presuppositionality or discourse backgroundedness is obviously a *weaker* and more general condition, the *unmarked* case. On the other hand, logical presupposition is a stronger, further specification, the *marked* sub-case of discourse backgroundedness. The expected one-way implication relation holds between the two, so that "knowing P" implies "being familiar with P", but not vice versa. That is:

(19) logical presupposition $\supset$ discourse presupposition

One must note that NEG-assertions are not the only type of declarative propositions which necessitate a concept of discourse backgroundedness that is considerably weaker than strict logical presupposition. The same is also true for IF-clauses (see Chapter 21, Volume II). There is some evidence[9] to suggest

---

9) See Haiman (1978) as well as some discussion in Givón (1982c). Much of Haiman's argument centers on a New Guinea language, Hua, a clause-chaining language with roughly the same constraints on placing adverbial clauses — including IRREALIS conditionals — only in chain-initial positions as one finds in Chuave (see Chapter 8, section 8.3.9., above).

that when IF-clauses precede their main clause, they are in some sense dis-
course-presupposed or **background** information in the same sense that the affirmative is the discourse background to the NEG-assertion. In illustration of
this possibility consider the following example:

(20)   a.   ...She said she'd come,
       b.   but she's never on time,
       c.   and besides she often skips her appointments;
       d.   but I'm waiting here anyway,
       e.   and **if she comes**, then I think I'll...

In the discourse chunk in (20), the background status of the IF-clause in (20e)
is underscored by the earlier appearance of (20a), which covers roughly the
same propositional contents. But the If-clause in (20e) is in the **irrealis** mode
and thus, technically speaking, has no truth value by itself. It could not therefore be logically presupposed. Rather, the propositional frame of (20e) is already familiar to the hearer from (20a), where it is presented under an irrealis
modal scope in the complement of the non-factive verb 'say' (see discussion in
Chapter 8, sections 8.2.6.3. and 8.4.4., above).

9.5. NARROWING THE SCOPE OF SPECIFIC NEGATION

As noted above, negation tends to apply to the asserted portions of sentences, leaving presupposed/backgrounded portions outside its scope. In addition, some components of sentences have the explicit ability to further narrow down the scope of what is negated. One of these, as seen in Chapter 7,
above, involves the use of optional adverbials, which even in the affirmative
tend to 'attract' the scope of assertion to them alone. This is echoed in negation, as may be seen in the following examples:[10]

(21)   a.   John didn't kick the ball
       b.   John didn't kick the ball **on purpose**
            ($\supset$ He kicked the ball but **not on purpose**)
       c.   John didn't kicked the ball **that time**
            ($\supset$ He kicked the ball but **not that time**)
       d.   John didn't kick the ball **with enough force**
            ($\supset$ He kicked the ball but **not with enough force**)

10) For further discussion see Horn (1978) and Givón (1979a, Ch. 3).

e. John didn't kick the ball **out of the park**
   ($\supset$ He kicked the ball, but **not out of the park**)
f. John didn't kick the ball **for fun**
   ($\supset$ He kicked it but **not for fun**)
g. John didn't kick the ball **with his toe**
   ($\supset$ He kicked the ball but **not with his toe**)

Under the most normal reading, none of the sentences (21b-g) imply sentence (21a). Rather, implicit in all of them is the truth of the corresponding affirmative of (21a), i.e. 'John kicked the ball'. The only thing they leave under the scope of negation is the optional constituent.

A similar effect of narrowing the scope of negation can be achieved even when the sentence has only obligatory constituents. In English this is easily done with emphatic intonation ('stress') as in:[11]

(22) a. **John** didn't kick the ball — it was **Bill**.
      b. John didn't **kick** the ball — he **threw** it.
      c. John didn't kick the **ball** — he kicked the **dog**.

Note, further, that in English the sentences in (22) have a marked contrastive intonation, while sentence (21a) — without any emphatic stress on any of the three major constituents — probably corresponds to none of (22a, b, c). Rather, sentence (21a) may be a general denial that any event had occurred, without necessarily specifying a single "missing component". Whether this is tantamount to "having a multiply-ambiguous negative sense"[12] is indeed open to question. As we shall see later, other languages may use morphology or word-order, rather than intonation, to express the same narrowed sense of the specific negation in (22a, b, c).

The examples in (21) and (22) above further illustrate our earlier suggestion that the corresponding affirmative — or at least its general propositional contents or "frame" — is a necessary component of the background information that the speaker assumes the hearer is familiar with in transacting the negative speech-act. But that background information may have a wider or a

---

11) See further detail in Atlas (1974) and Horn (1978). Horn goes on to suggest that a negative sentence has $n+1$ possible senses, with n standing for the number of constituents in the sentence, and the extra possibility accommodates a 'neutral' interpretation of negation. As we shall see later, this allowance for the maximal potential ambiguity in negation may be an over-statement of actual language facts.

12) This is a claim specifically made in Horn (1978), cf. footnote 11, above.

narrower scope. And in negation, the speaker denies whatever is assumed to be under the relevant scope of the hearer's belief. In the use of negation, thus, the speaker may, at least sometimes, be attempting to achieve two overlapping goals:

(a) Denial of the hearer's belief; and
(b) Further specification of the grounds for that denial.

While goal (a) is an obligatory ingredient of negation, goal (b) is an option that may or may not be exercised. It is thus probably an overstatement to contend that all negatives are multiply ambiguous (rather than vague/unspecified) in the fashion of (22), and thus that (22a, b, c) are all legitimate interpretations of the non-emphatic negative (21a).

9.6. DEFINITENESS AND REFERENTIALITY OF NOUNS UNDER THE SCOPE OF NEGATION

In Chapter 8, section 8.2.6., we noted that under the scope of the irrealis modality, NP's may receive a **non-referential** interpretation. This opacity-producing property of irrealis is shared by the modality of negation. This suggests that for the purpose of predicting referentiality of nouns, negation may be grouped with *irrealis*, rather than with *realis* as is the case in the scale (3) or presupposition as in scale (4), above (see further discussion in Chapter 11, below). To recapitulate the effect of irrealis on NP referentiality, consider the possible three-way contrast under irrealis scope:

(23) a. *REF, DEF*:   Mary was looking for **the book**.
      b. *REF, INDEF*:   Mary was looking for **a book** she lost yesterday.
      c. *NON-REF*:   Mary was looking for **a book** to read.

The three sentences in (23) may be paraphrased, respectively, as follows:

(24) a. *REF, DEF*:   A book exists, the speaker assumes the hearer already knows its identity; Mary was looking for that book.

      b. *REF, INDEF*:   A book exists, the speaker does *not* assume that the hearer knows its identity; Mary was looking for that book;

      c. *NON-REF*:   The speaker does not refer to any particular book; Mary was looking for some unspecified member of the genus "book".

Of the three variants of the object NP in (23/24), one — the non-referential — cannot appear under the scope of *realis*. Thus consider:[13]

(25) a. *REF, DEF*:   Mary found **the book**.
      b. *REF, INDEF*:   Mary found **a book**.
      (i)   There exists a book, and the speaker does not assume the
            hearer is familiar with its identity; Mary found that book.
      *(ii) The speaker has no particular book in mind; Mary found
            some unspecified member of the genus "book".

When the sentences under the scope of either irrealis (23/24) or realis
(25) are negated, the difference between realis and irrealis disappears, and
only a two-way contrast can be obtained either way, between

(a)   REF, DEF; and
(b)   NON-REF

As an example consider:[14]

(26) a. Mary was not looking for **the book**. (NEG-IRREALIS, REF-DEF)
      b. Mary was not looking for **a/any book**. (NEG-IRREALIS, NON-REF)
      c. Mary did not find **the book**.   (NEG-REALIS, REF-DEF)
      d. Mary did not find **a/any book**.   (NEG-REALIS, NON-REF)

The effect of NEG is thus:

(i)   Eliminate the REF-INDEF interpretation that was possible under
      both modalities; and
(ii) Make possible a NON-REF interpretation under REALIS.

The second effect is not surprising, since negation creates an explicitly **nonexistent** world, a feature it shares with irrealis which creates a **potential** but not
yet existing one. Restriction (i), however, is not as easy to explain. To begin
with, in most languages it is an absolute grammatical restriction, but in some
languages — English among them — one could in fact force the proscribed
REF-INDEF interpretation on a noun by means which describe the NP in
question in some detail, such as a restrictive REL-clause. Thus consider:

---

13) As we shall see in Chapter 11, below, sentence (25b), with a referential interpretation, may
still be vague as to the degree of *exact identifiability* of the referent, i.e. the extent to which the
speaker knows all its properties *exhaustively*. But this is not the issue with the non-referentiality discussed here.

14) For the original observation, much supporting data and the subsequent explanation, see
Givón (1975c, 1979a, Ch. 3).

(27) Mary didn't find **a book** that her mother had told her to bring back, so her mother became real angry.

While expressions such as (27) may be "grammatical" in English, they are exceedingly hard to find in actual discourse, where the alternative below seems to be invariably preferred:[15]

(28) **There was a book** that Mary's mother wanted her to bring back, but Mary didn't find **it**, so her mother got real angry.

The preferred strategy of introducing a referential noun into the discourse for the first time is thus the one in (28), namely:

(a)   Introduce it as a REF-INDEF noun in an affirmative clause (as either subject, as in (28) or as object); and

(b)   Refer to it, when need be, in NEG-clauses only as *definite*.

There is nothing logically necessary about this strategy, but the fact that it is adhered to so consistently cross-linguistically needs an explanation. And it turns out that the explanation is predictable not from the logic of negation, but rather from its pragmatics, namely from the fact (see section 9.2., above) that the negative speech-act is used in discourse in the context when the corresponding affirmative has been discussed, contemplated or is otherwise familiar to the hearer. If a proposition is familiar to someone, so is the identity of its referential arguments. Against such a background, referential arguments appearing in negative clauses should be coded as definite, since the speaker can rightly assume that the hearer is familiar with them (see Chapter 11, below). Negative clauses are thus not used to introduce new propositional information into the discourse, but to deny the truth of already-introduced propositions; nor are they used to introduce new referential participants into the discourse "file" (see ch. 7, above and ch. 11, below).

9.7.   SCALARITY, RELEVANCE AND THE INTERPRETATION OF NEGATION[16]

Other properties associated with the usage and interpretation of negation in human language stem from discourse-pragmatics properties of language rather than from logic. In this section we will briefly consider some is-

15) See text counts in Givón (1979a, Ch. 3) in support of this observation.

16) Much of the material in this section is due to Horn (1978).

sues that involve scalarity and relevance in the use of the speech-act of denial. In purely logical terms, first, the following inference is indeed sound:

(29)   Joe has four mules ⊃ Joe has three mules

But in human language the following denial is fairly typical:

(30)   a.   *Speaker A*:   Does Joe have three mules?
       b.   *Speaker B*:   **No**, he's got four.

If judged by strictly logical criteria, the denial in (30b) is surely false, given the logical soundness of the inference in (29). What makes (30b) felicitous is of course the assumption which speaker B makes that speaker A really meant to ask:

(31)   Does Joe have **exactly** three/**only** three mules?

Speaker B in (30b) thus has to interpret the *purpose* of the query (30a) and its exact *scope*, then make the response — in that case a negative — *relevant* to that purpose and scope. And given the same knowledge of the facts by speaker B in (30) and the same scope/purpose interpretation, the logically felicitous affirmative response (32) would have been disingenuous:

(32)   **Yes**, he's got three mules. [When in fact he's got four]

But the purpose/scope of the question could easily change — and thus demand a different truthful answer. Thus consider:

(33)   a.   *Speaker A*:   Does Joe **have** three mules?
       b.   *Speaker B*:   **Yes**. In fact, he's got four.

Reply (33b) is felicitous under the following interpretation of the scope/purpose of the question:

(34)   Does Joe have **at least** three mules?

Different purposes and scopes of information, query or negation, as in (31) vs. (34), are of course correlated to different **pragmatic reasons** for requesting the information. Thus, in (30/31) a typical request could be grounded in the requirements of an exact census of all stock animals. While in (33/34) it could be grounded in the absolute need for at least a minimal number of mules in order to perform a task that cannot be performed by less.

Horn (1978) has noted that in expressions involving quantity and/or extent of individuals (nouns), qualities (adjectives) or actions (verbs), information may be *scaled*. And the speaker is then bound by the speaker-hearer contract to reveal the maximal amount of information *relevant* to the purpose/

scope of the particular communication. Revealing *more* information than is relevant may be just as damaging or disruptive to the communication as revealing *less* than what is relevant.[17]

There are, finally, some contexts in which either a *yes* or *no* response would be considered inappropriate. As an example consider:

(35) *Context*: [Someone died on the operating table; fact known to B]
Speaker A: -Is he up and about?
Speaker B: (i) -Yes.
(ii) -No.

Technically, response (ii) by B is truthful. However it still disregards the purpose of speaker A, namely to ascertain the condition of the patient. It also disregards the background knowledge of speaker A, i.e. that he is inclined to believe that the patient is still alive and seeks further specification *within those limits*. A somewhat similar situation exists with disguised/indirect speech acts, as in:[18]

(36) *Context*: [Speaker A wants to know what time it is]
Speaker A: -Do you know what time it is?
Speaker B: (i) -Yes.
(ii) -No.

Here it is the affirmative response (i) that is inappropriate, given that speaker B knows that the indirect request by speaker A is not a yes/no question but rather a disguised WH-question/request, such as:

(37) What time is it?

These and related questions will be further discussed in Chapter 20, Volume II. Their relevance here was to show how the appropriate scope of negation — as well as of affirmative assertions — may be governed by conventions, expectations and inferences that are pragmatic in nature and not always well-coded in the visible discourse context.

9.8. THE MORPHO-SYNTAX OF NEGATION

9.8.1. Morpho-syntax of neutral negation

As noted above, the scope of negation may be narrower or wider, de-

---

17) Horn (1978) in this regard follows Grice's (1968/1975) maxim of relevance. We have earlier discussed other facets of the communicative contract (Chapter 7, section 7.4.3.).

18) See extensive discussions in Cole and Morgan (eds, 1975).

pending on a variety of discourse-pragmatic and real-world pragmatic assumptions that the speaker makes about the beliefs and communicative intent
of the hearer. For the purpose of the discussion here, we will consider **neutral
negation** — the least-marked variety — to be one which:

(a)   Takes under its scope only the assertions but not the presupposi-
      tion(s) associated with the corresponding affirmative;
(b)   Leaves the subject of the corresponding affirmative outside the
      scope of negation; and
(c)   Otherwise does not specify the exact grounds for denying the
      corresponding affirmative.

Morpho-syntactically, NEG-markers tend to attach themselves — as
morphemic operators — almost always to the *verb*. In V-first languages
(VSO, VOS) this may most commonly make them at least trivially sentence-
initial operators, and in V-last languages (SOV) sentence-final operators. But
verb-medial languages (SVO) supply overwhelmingly consistent evidence for
the NEG-marker being a verbal (or VP) operator rather than a *sentential*
one.[19] As an example of V-prefix and thus S-initial NEG-marker in a V-first
language consider the following from Bikol (Philippine):[20]

(38) a. *Affirmative*:   nag-gadán 'ang-laláke ning-kandíng
                          AGT-kill   TOP-man   ACC-goat
                          'The man killed a goat'
      b. *Negative*:   **da'í** nag-gadán 'ang-laláke ning-kandíng
                        NEG AGT-kill   TOP-man   ACC-goat
                        'The man didn't kill a goat'

As an example of V-suffix and thus potentially S-final NEG-marker in a V-
final language consider the following from Japanese:[21]

(39) a. *Affirmative*:   otoko-wa bin-o   kowasi-dalo
                          man-TOP   bottle-ACC   break-FUT
                          'The man will break the bottle'

19) Logicians have traditionally considered negation — like all propositional modalities — a
sentential operator. But as we have seen above, the most common form(s) of negation in human
language systematically exclude parts of the proposition from negative scope.

20) From my own field notes, with the data originally due to Manuel Factora (in personal communication).

21) From Yuko Yanagida (in personal communication).

   b. *Negative*: otoko-wa bin-o   kowasa-**nai**-dalo
              man-TOP bottle-ACC break-NEG-FUT
              'The man will not break the bottle'

Finally, for a V-prefix NEG-marker in a V-medial language consider the following from Israeli Hebrew:

  (40) a. *Affirmative*: Yoáv axál   et   ha-léxem
                     Y.   ate   ACC the-bread
                     'Yoav ate the bread'
      b. *Negative*: Yoáv **ló**-axál   et   ha-léxem
                     Y.   NEG-ate ACC the-bread
                     'Yoav didn't eat the bread'

9.8.2. Negative intensifiers, double negation and diachronic change

    As noted in Chapter 6, section 6.8.4., above, negative markers may be derived from main verbs (such as 'miss', 'lack', 'avoid', 'reject', 'fail' etc.), and in such a case Greenberg's (1966) typological correlation holds, so that VO languages tend to have *prefixal* NEG-markers, and OV languages *suffixal* ones. The examples cited in section 9.8.1. above illustrate this situation. We also noted in Chapter 6 that another source of NEG-markers, derived from NEG-intensifiers which are most commonly *object nouns* such as 'thing', 'person' etc., yields exactly the opposite typological prediction, since it gives rise to verbal NEG-prefixes in an OV language and verbal NEG-suffixes in a VO language. When both the old NEG-marker and the intensifier are present, one may speak of so-called "double negation". To illustrate this, consider again the French data from Chapter 6 (examples (85), (86)). In the more conservative, 'official' grammar of French, one finds:

  (41) a. Je **ne**   sais   **pas**   [**pas** = 'step']
         I   NEG know NEG
         'I don't know'
      b. Je **ne**   connais **personne**   [**personne** = 'person']
         I   NEG know   NEG
         'I don't know anybody'
      c. Je **ne**   sais   **rien**   [**rien/ren** = '*thing']
         I   NEG know NEG
         'I don't know anything'

The three NEG-intensifiers in French, *pas*, *personne* and *rien* have by now become grammaticalized, with *pas* taking the more generalized function of specific negation with either referential-definite or non-referential objects:

(42) a. Je **ne**   vois **pas**   le   chien   [REF, DEF]
         I   NEG   see   NEG   the   dog
         'I don't see the dog'

     b. Je **ne**   vois **pas**   des   chiens [NON-REF]
         I   NEG   see   NEG   PART   dogs
         'I don't see (any) dogs'

The non-referential sense (42b) may be intensified further by replacing the rather neutral *pas* with *aucun* 'any' [historically *al-quis-unus* 'to-which-one'], as in:

(43) Je **ne**   vois **aucuns**   chiens [NON-REF, emphatic]
       I NEG   see   NEG-INTENS-PL   dogs
       'I don't see **any** dogs'

And *aucun* itself may be used as a manner adverb to mean further NEG-intensification, akin to 'at all', as in:

(44) Je **ne**   le   connais **aucunement**
       I   NEG   him know   NEG-INTENS-MANNER
       'I don't know him **at all**'

As noted earlier (Chapter 6, section 6.8.4.), in informal/colloquial French as well as in the history of many languages (English included), the older and more neutral NEG-marker tends to drop out, leaving the intensifier as the only NEG-marker. This most commonly results in de-marking (de-emphasizing) the intensifier, as in:

(45) a. Je sais **pas**
         I   know NEG
         'I don't know'

     b. Je vois **pas**   le   chien
         I   see   NEG   the   dog
         'I don't see the dog'

     c. Je vois **rien**
         I   see   NEG
         'I don't see anything'

     d. Je vois **aucune** personne
         I   see   NEG-F person
         'I don't see anybody at all'

9.8.3. Syntactic coding of negative scope

As noted earlier, negation may be either neutral — a denial of the state/event without specifying the grounds — or more specific and narrow in its scope, denying only specific aspects (verb, subject, object etc.) of the event and thus tacitly allowing that some event of that kind did indeed take place. One way of accomplishing this syntactically is by the use of stress/intonation alone, as in English:

(46) a. John didn't kick the ball   [neutral]
     b. **John** didn't kick the ball   [SUBJ-negation]
        [⊃ Someone else did]
     c. John didn't kick the **ball**   [OBJ-negation]
        [⊃ He kicked something else]
     d. John didn't **kick** the ball   [V-negation]
        [⊃ He did something else with it]

A more explicit means of achieving the same end is by using cleft-focusing (see Chapter 17, Volume II), as in:

(47) a. It was not **John** who kicked the ball [but someone else]
     b. It was not the **ball** that John kicked [but something else]
     c. It was not **kicking** that John did to the ball [but something else][22]

In other languages, constituent negation under a narrow scope, as in (46b, c, d) above, requires word-order change. Thus, in Bikol (Philippine) the specific constituent within NEG-scope must be fronted, as in:[23]

(48) a. nag-gadán 'ang-laláke ning-kandíng   (affirmative)
        AGT-kill   TOP-man   ACC-goat
        'The man killed a goat'
     b. **da'í** nag-gadán 'ang-laláke ning-kandíng (neutral negation)
        NEG AGT-kill   TOP-man   ACC-goat
        'The man didn't kill a goat'

---

22) In general, most languages have severe restrictions on clefting the verb, and many cannot do it at all. English requires here the nominalization of the verb and its recapitulation with the pro-verb *do*.

23) From my own field notes, with the data originally due to Manuel Factora (in personal communication)

c. **da'í** 'ang-laláke nag-gadán ning-kandíng (SUBJ-negation)
   NEG TOP-man AGT-kill ACC-goat
   'The **man** didn't kill a goat'

d. **da'í** 'ang-kandíng g-in-adán kang-laláke (OBJ-negation)[24]
   NEG TOP-goat ACC-kill AGT-man
   'The man didn't kill the **goat**'

A more explicit cleft-focus negation can also be made in Bikol, using the cleft-NEG prefix with the same fronting of the focused constituent, plus an overt REL-clause structure (which again requires the fronted constituent to be the topic). Thus consider:

(49) a. **bakú** 'ang-laláke 'ang-nag-gadán ning-kandíng (SUBJ-
         NEG TOP-man TOP-AGT-kill ACC-goat NEG-cleft)
         'It's not the **man** who killed a goat' [but someone else]

     b. **bakú** 'ang-kandíng 'ang-g-in-adán kang-laláke (OBJ-
         NEG TOP-goat TOP-ACC-kill AGT-man NEG-cleft)
         'It is not the **goat** that the man killed' [but something else]

In Ute (Uto-Aztecan), the scope of negation is again marked by a combination of morphology and word-order. For neutral negation, the NEG-markers are both on the verb:[25]

(50) a. ta'wá-**ci** siváₐtu-ci paxá-qa (affirmative)
         man-SUBJ goat-OBJ kill-ANT
         'The man killed the goat'

     b. ta'wá-**ci** siváₐtu-ci **ká**-paxá-**na** (neutral negation)
         man-SUBJ goat-OBJ NEG-kill-ANT/NEG
         'The man didn't kill the goat'

To narrow the scope of negation to a particular constituent, the negative prefix — a more recent intensifier — is moved to the beginning of the clause, and is augmented by an emphatic particle (etymologically the verb 'be'). The negated constituent must then directly follow it. Thus consider:

---

24) The emphatic fronting of a non-agent obligatorily requires it to become the clausal *topic* in Bikol. The same holds for clefting (see below) and definitization of the direct object.

25) For further detail see Givón (1980a, Chapter 4).

(51) a. **kác-**'urá ta'wá-**ci**   sivą́ątu-ci pax̂á-**na** (SUBJ-negation)
          NEG-be man-SUBJ goat-OBJ kill-ANT/NEG
          'The **man** didn't kill the goat'

      b. **kác-**'urá sivą́ątu-ci ta'wá-**ci**   pax̂á-**na**   (OBJ-negation)
          NEG-be goat-OBJ man-SUBJ kill-ANT/NEG
          'The man didn't kill the **goat**'

The same narrowed focus can also be expressed by a more explicit cleft-focus construction, with the verb then assuming a REL-clause form, as in:

(52) a. **kác-**'urá ta'wá-**ci**   sivą́ątu-ci pax̂á-qa-tŭ (SUBJ-NEG-cleft)
          NEG-be man-SUBJ goat-OBJ kill-ANT-REL
          'It was not the **man** who killed the goat' (but someone else)

      b. **kác-**'urá sivą́ątu-ci ta'wá-**ci**   pax̂á-qa-ną (OBJ-NEG-cleft)
          NEG-be goat-OBJ man-GEN kill-ANT-REL
          'It was not the **goat** that the man killed' (but something else)

Unlike the non-cleft NEG-focus constructions (51a, b), in the NEG-cleft construction only the clefted constituent is morphologically marked by negation (the prefix *kác-'urá*), but the verb is not. Further, in the OBJECT-cleft, as in object REL-clauses in Ute, the subject must appear in the *genitive* form, which is most commonly identical to the *object* form of the noun.

Finally, in Russian, word-order is also used to signal the scope of narrower negation, but the position to which the negated constituent is moved is the clause final position (rather than clause initial, as in Bikol or Ute).

Thus consider:[26]

(53) a. Ivan jego ubil   (affirmative)
          I.   him killed
          'Ivan killed him'

      b. Ivan jego **ne**   ubil   (neutral negation)
          I.   him NEG killed
          'Ivan didn't kill him'

      c. jego ubil **ne** Ivan   (SUBJ-negation)
          him killed NEG I.
          '**Ivan** didn't kill him' (someone else did)

      d. Ivan ubil **ne** jego   (OBJ-negation)
          I.   killed NEG him
          'Ivan didn't kill **him**' (but someone else)

26) From Dreizin (1980); the interpretation is my own.

9.9. FURTHER ISSUES IN THE GRAMMAR AND FUNCTION OF NEGATION

9.9.1. Embedded negation, NEG-transport and scalarity

When a main verb takes a sentential/verbal complement, there arises the theoretical possibility of the negation applying either to the main verb or to the complement verb — or at both levels. In logic, the double appearance of the NEG-marker in the same proposition simply cancels the negation out:

(54) $\sim \sim P = P$

But such simple cancellation does not hold for natural language in quite the same way. Consider first negation at the *lexical* level — when combined with the normal syntactic negation:[27]

(55)   a. You are welcome   (affirmative)
       b. You are *not* welcome   (syntactic NEG)
       c. You are *un*welcome   (lexical NEG)
       d. You are *not un*welcome   (syntactic and lexical NEG)

First, (55b) and (55c) are not exactly equivalent in their strength, with the syntactic NEG (55b) seeming stronger somehow. And second, (55d) is not completely an equivalent of (55a), as the logical rule (54) would have it. Rather, a person welcomed by (55d) is considerably less welcome than one welcomed by (55a).

Consider next the appearance of negation in embedded V-complements. Linguists have noted for a long time that sentences such as (56a) below are ambiguous, with their two possible meanings corresponding either to (56b) or (56c):

(56)   a. I **don't** think he came
       b. I think that he **didn't** come
       c. It is **not true** that I think he came

This possible — and partial — meaning equivalence of (56b) to (56a) has been labeled **NEG-transport**. And Bolinger (1968) has observed that in some sense the force of the speaker's certainty in (56a) is weaker than in (56b) — vis-à-vis the complement proposition "He came". In the same vein, Horn (1978) notes that the less embedded — and thus more overt or *up front* — the NEG marker is, the weaker is the certainty force of the main verb 'think' in examples such as:

---

27) This section broadly follows Horn (1978), with considerable deletions.

(57) a. I think she's **sad**   (strongest claim)
    b. I think she's **un**happy
    c. I think she's **not** happy
    d. I think she **isn't** happy
    e. I **doubt** she's happy
    f. I do **not** think she's happy
    g. I **don't** think she's happy (weakest claim)

Such differences in the strength of assertions almost always involve some socio-linguistic correlate of *politeness*. Thus, for example, in Swahili the more external ('main clause') negative in (58a) is considered more polite than the more internal ('embedded clause') negative (58b):

(58) a. **si**-dhani   (kama) ni   kweli
       NEG-I-think (that) be true
       'I **don't** think that it is true'
    b. n-a-dhani   (kama) **si**   kweli
       I-PRES-think (that) NEG-be true
       'I think that it is **not** true'

The phenomena associated with "NEG-transport" typically involve verbs such as 'think', 'believe', 'suppose', 'imagine' or 'expect' when their sense is "hold an opinion that". These verbs have been characterized by Horn (1978) as **mid-strength** on a scale of the speaker's subjective certainty. A verb that is stronger on that scale, such as 'claim', produces two very distinct readings of the lower-clause and upper-clause negation, without any possible — even partial — overlap between them. Thus consider:

(59) a. I claim that he **didn't** come
    b. I **don't** claim that he came

And a verb with a subjective certainty (in the truth of the embedded clause) *lower* than 'think' also does not produce the overlap or NEG-transport. Thus consider:

(60) a. I hope that he **didn't** come
    b. I **don't** hope that he came

The same scale is noted in the negation of manipulative verbs or their complements. Thus the **mid-scale** 'want' and 'expect'[28] allow partial overlap

---

28) For the scalar strength of "binding" of complement-taking verbs, see extensive discussion in Chapter 13, Volume II, as well as in Givón (1980b).

of the meanings of the two levels of negation, characteristic of NEG-transport, as in:

(61) a. I **didn't** want him to come
      b. I wanted him **not** to come
      c. I **didn't** expect him to come
      d. I expected him **not** to come

On the other hand, verbs of stronger manipulation, even non-implicatives such as 'tell', do not exhibit NEG-transport. That is:

(62) a. I told him **not** to come   ≠   I **didn't** tell him to come
      b. I caused him **not** to come ≠   I **didn't** cause him to come

And the same is also true for verbs lower on the scale than 'want' or 'expect', such as 'wish' or 'hope' in:

(63) a. I wished that he **wouldn't** come ≠ I **didn't** wish that he would come
      b. I hoped that he **wouldn't** come ≠ I **didn't** hope that he'd come

Finally, the same division up and down the scale also holds true for modality verbs. Thus consider:

(64) a. I managed to **not** go ≠ I **didn't** manage to go
                                      (STRONGER, implicative)
      b. I wanted **not** to go   = I **didn't** want to go
                                      (MID-SCALE, non-implicative)
      c. I am able to **not** go ≠ I am **not** able to go
                                      (WEAKER, non-implicative)

The scalarity shown above and its effect on sense-overlap and NEG-transport may be shown not only for verbs, but also for adverbial epistemic operators. Thus, compare (65) below to (64)

(65) a. It is *certain* that he **won't** come (STRONGER, no NEG-transport)
             ≠ It is **not** certain that he'll come
      b. It is *likely* that he'll **not** come (MID-SCALE; NEG-transport)
             = It is **not** likely that he'll come
      c. It is *possible* that he **won't** come (WEAKER; no NEG-transport)
             ≠ It is **not** possible that he'll come

The same scalarity may be shown for *affective* modal adverbials, as in:

(66) a. It is *imperative* that he **not** come [STRONGER; no NEG-transport]
             ≠ It is **not** necessary that he come

b. It would be *nice* if he **didn't** come [MID-SCALE; NEG-transport]
   = It **wouldn't** be nice if he came

c. It would be *fine* if he **didn't** come [WEAKER; no NEG-transport]
   ≠ It **wouldn't** be fine if he came

Horn (1978) suggests a seemingly natural explanation for the differential behavior of the two extremes on the scale vis-à-vis the middle with respect to NEG-transport, noting that when negation — either lexical or syntactic — is applied to the strong extreme, it yields the weak one. And negation of the weak extreme yields the strong one. That is:

(67) a. certain [strong] – – –> uncertain [weak]
      b. sure [strong] – – –> unsure [weak]
      c. possible [weak] – – –> impossible [strong]
      d. able [weak] – – –> unable [strong]

On the other hand, negation of mid-scale operators or verbs still yields a mid-scale operator/verb:

(68) a. be likely [mid-scale] – – –> be unlikely [mid-scale]
      b. be advisable [mid-scale] – – –> be inadvisable [mid-scale]
      c. be nice [mid-scale] – – –> not be nice [mid-scale]

It is thus the fact that the mid-scale expressions do not change their position on the scale radically through negation that allows the phenomenon of seeming NEG-transport and partial meaning overlap between lower-case and upper-case negation. And it is the radical valuation change which top-scale and bottom-scale expressions undergo in negation which makes NEG-transport in their case impossible.

9.9.2. Lexical or incorporated negation

Certain words may be, by their very meaning, contrary or **antonym** to other words, and in that sense incorporate the NEG operator into their lexical structure. Thus, in some sense 'bad' is 'not good', 'short' is 'not long'/'not tall' etc.[29] Such incorporated or lexical negation may sometimes be "raised" in terms of its meaning description. That is, it may arise from a deeper embedded source in the semantic structure of the word. As examples of this consider:

---

29) See discussion of the semantic structure of paired adjectives in Chapter 3, above, as well as Givón (1970a).

(69) a. '*forbid* her to dance' = 'tell her **not to dance**'
      b. '*prevent* him from singing' = 'cause him **not to sing**'
      c. '*unbutton* the shirt' = 'cause the shirt to **not be buttoned**'
      d. '*destroy* the structure' = 'cause the structure to **not be whole**'
      e. '*disclaim* responsibility' = 'claim to **not be responsible**'

Further, in each one of the examples in (69) above, at least historically, negation is marked on the word by a prefix, thus representing **affixal** negation, as distinct from both **lexical** and **syntactic** negation.

In terms of the scale of strength of negation suggested in section 9.9.1. above, there is some difference between these three types of negation:[30]

(70) He is not happy > He is unhappy > He is sad

In terms of speech-act value, first, syntactic negation is the strongest act of denial, affixal negation much weaker, and lexical negation the weakest. In terms of subjective certainty ('strength of conviction') however, that order is reversed.

The non-equivalency of syntactic and affixal negation may also be shown via various syntactic tests that are sensitive to such a difference, as in:[31]

(71) a. Mary isn't happy and Jack isn't happy $\left\{ \begin{array}{c} either \\ *too \end{array} \right\}$

      b. Mary is unhappy and Jack is unhappy $\left\{ \begin{array}{c} too \\ *either \end{array} \right\}$

      c. It was not possible to come, $\left\{ \begin{array}{c} not\ even\ at\ night \\ *even\ at\ night \end{array} \right\}$

      d. It was impossible to come, $\left\{ \begin{array}{c} even\ at\ night \\ ?not\ even\ at\ night \end{array} \right\}$

      e. He isn't able to come, $\left\{ \begin{array}{c} is\ he? \\ *isn't\ he? \end{array} \right\}$

      f. He is unable to come, $\left\{ \begin{array}{c} isn't\ he? \\ *is\ he? \end{array} \right\}$

Thus, some constructions that are sensitive to overt, syntactic negation treat affixal negation the same as they do the affirmative.

---

30) For further discussion of affixal negation cross-language, see Zimmer (1964).

31) Following Horn (1978).

One can also illustrate how, in terms of the negative speech-act of denial, affixal negatives function as affirmative speech-acts. Thus consider:

(72) a. *Context*: -What is your marital status?
      b. *Responses*: -I am ⎧ married. ⎫
                             ⎪ unmarried. ⎪
                             ⎨ divorced. ⎬
                             ⎪ widowed. ⎪
                             ⎩ a bachelor. ⎭
      c. *Less-felicitous response*: -I am not married.
      d. *Context*: -Are you married?
      e. *Response*: -No (I'm not married).
      f. *Less-likely-response*: -I am unmarried.

The context (72a) is the broader one, eliciting information on the background of ignorance. The context (72d) is a narrower one, eliciting denial against the background of having considered the corresponding affirmative. Lexical and affixal negation ('a bachelor' and 'unmarried', respectively) are compatible with context (72a), less so with (72d); and the opposite is true of syntactic negation.

9.9.3. Distributional restrictions, foreground-background and the ontology of negation

We have so far discussed logical/semantic features of negation, i.e. the reversal of truth value. We have discussed more syntactic properties, involving the depth of syntactic embedding of the NEG operator. We have also discussed discourse-pragmatic properties of negation as a speech-act of denial, and the characteristic context/background against which such a speech-act is transacted. In this section we will deal briefly with a number of restrictions on the distribution of negatives which seem to point toward an ontological-cognitive basis underlying our concept of **negative events** or **negative states**.[32]

When one counts the frequency of negative sentences in narrative discourse, especially in the foreground portions which carry the bulk of new, sequential, main-line information, one finds that it is much much lower than that of affirmatives, in the order of less than 5 percent. This skewed distribution should be expected, given what we said earlier about negation being not a speech-act of adding new information, but rather of denial or contradiction.

---

32) The discussion is based on Givón (1979a, Ch. 3).

To this one may also add that — all other things being equal — negative events are less informative than positive ones. But such an assertion is only warranted if accompanied by the following gestalt-pragmatic observation:

(73) "Events are *changes* in an otherwise inert universe. The event is informatively *salient* only if the background inertia of the universe — that of non-eventness — is the more frequent, normal, routine case".

The relation between pragmatic *infrequency* and cognitive *saliency* is thus a fundamental underlying factor in understanding both perception and cognition. Negative propositions are less-frequent in discourse only because, against the background of the inertia of the universe, positive events constitute a more salient break in the routine/background. And as we have seen above, when negative propositions do occur, a reversal of the figure-ground relation must first take place, so that the corresponding affirmative somehow becomes the expected, unsurprising background. Against such a background, the negative proposition then becomes salient or informative.

Many restrictions on the distribution of negatives in the grammar may be viewed in the context of this pragmatic explanation. Thus, consider for example:

(74) a. When John comes, I'll leave.
      b. ?When John **doesn't** come, I'll leave.

(74b) is odd because WHEN-ADV-clauses are normally used to establish a specific point in time by coding that point with an event that did occur then. But how could a non-event designate a point in time? Indeed, ordinarily it cannot, since it did *not occur* at any nor at all times. However, if one tampers with the background of expectations, by designating the end-point of the time during which no event occurred as a salient point, as in:

(75) ...I waited and waited. Finally, when John **didn't** come I left.

the negative WHEN-clause becomes salient and acceptable.

Another context where negatives seem odd is in **presentative** constructions, which are used to open thematic paragraphs or stories, or to introduce important participants for the first time into the discourse (see Chapter 19, Volume II). Thus consider:

(76) a. A man came into my office yesterday and...
      b. ?A man **didn't** come into my office yesterday and...

Here the oddity of (76b) arises from the need to introduce new participants into the discourse in some salient fashion. Introducing them as subjects of events that did occur indeed endows them with salient attributes. Introducing them as subjects of non-events deprives them of saliency — unless the non-event itself is salient against the background of some other prior expectations, as in:

(77) ... It was a holiday, and I was the only one in the building. Suddenly a man who **didn't** know everybody had the day off came in and asked for Joe, so I told him...

The importance of saliency in understanding restrictions on negation is not limited to negative events, but may also be shown vis-à-vis negative *states*. Consider in this connection:

(78) a. A man **with no head on his shoulders** came into my office yesterday and...
　　 b. ?A man **with a head on his shoulders** came into my office yesterday and...

The reason why the negative (78a) is salient and informative while the affirmative (78b) is not is because the *normal case* is (78b), and against that background (78a) is informative, much like "a man with two heads" would have been.

Consider next the oddity of negative restrictive REL-clauses, as in:

(79) a. The man you met yesterday is a crook.
　　 b. ?The man you **didn't** meet yesterday is a crook.

Restrictive REL-clauses are normally used to identify referents uniquely by their participation in some salient event/state already known to the hearer. But normally a non-event is much less likely to serve this purpose — unless the background of expectation changes, as in:

(80) *Context*: You were supposed to meet three men yesterday, but one of them — who turned out to be the most important one, cancelled out at the last minute.

On the background of expectation of (80), (79b) is indeed salient and informative.

Consider next the oddity of negative WH-questions, as in:

(81) a. Where did you leave the keys?
　　 b. ?Where **didn't** you leave the keys?

Question (81b) is odd because normally locative objects are used to designate where things are, not where they are not. This may be understood in terms of the vastness of the universe vis-à-vis the compactness of an individual object within that universe, and thus the following figure/ground or frequency relation:

(82)   "While an object may occupy only *one chunk* of space in the total space of the universe, the number of places where the object *is not* is infinitely large and not enumerable".

But again, this normative expectation may be manipulated to yield the converse situation, as in:

(83)   ... I've searched everywhere, in maybe ten different places, so I know only too well where my keys **are not**, though I still don't know where they are...

Consider next the oddity of NEG-comparatives, as in:

(84)   a.   She ran as fast as he did.
        b.   She didn't run as fast as he did.
        c.   ?She ran as fast as he **didn't**.
        d.   ?She didn't run as fast as he **didn't**.

Comparatives are used to match *degrees* of the presence of certain properties. But the total absence of a property is absolute, and thus could not serve as a standard of comparison at all. In other words, it makes no sense to say "Horse A runs faster than horse B" if horse B does not run at all.

Lastly, one should note that there is evidence to support the view that in paired adjectival properties where one member of the antonymic pair is designated the negative and the other the affirmative, this assignment is not simply a matter of reversal of the truth value (i.e. logical negation), but rather involves a systematic bias in **perceptual saliency**, whereby the member designated as positive is consistently the more salient one. Thus consider:[33]

---

33) See further discussion in Givón (1979a, Ch. 3). H. Clark (1969) has shown that positive members of these pairs are easier to process cognitively, and E. Clark (1971) has shown that children acquire them earlier than the negative members.

(85)

positive	negative	perceptual property
big	small	ease of visual perception
long	short	„ „ „ „
tall	short	„ „ „ „
wide	narrow	„ „ „ „
fat/thick	thin	„ „ „ „
high	low	„ „ „ „
light	dark	„ „ „ „
fast	slow	ease of visual perception of rate of change
loud	quiet	ease of auditory perception
sharp	dull	ease of tactile perception
heavy	light	ease of tactile/weight perception
rough	smooth	ease of tactile perception
spicy	bland	ease of olfactory perception

As we suggested earlier (Chapter 3, section 3.7.1.), the positive members of these antonymic pairs are considered, in human language, to be the **unmarked** members designating the generic name for the property. In addition, they also represent the **presence** (rather than absence) of that property on the scale. The fact that they line up as being consistently the more salient ones for human perception underscores our view of the ontology of negation — and of negative properties — as being founded upon the gestalt principle of figure/ground. What is less common is thus salient and informative. What is the normal case is non-salient and uninformative. On the basis of the general inertia of the universe, change — movement, an event — is salient. Against the background of non-saliency and commonness of the absence of properties, their presence is salient and informative. But in the relatively infrequent instances when the normative figure-ground relations are reversed, and where the affirmative is established as the background expectation in discourse, negative propositions become salient and informative.

10 | PRONOUNS AND GRAMMATICAL AGREEMENT

10.1. INTRODUCTION

In this chapter, we will discuss pronominal systems primarily with regard to the semantic features that underlie them. The discourse function of pronouns will be treated informally, since the subject will be dealt with formally and explicitly in Chapter 22, Volume II.[1] There are cogent reasons for deferring a comprehensive discussion of the discourse function of pronouns until later. Together with other grammatical devices, such as zero anaphora, articles, demonstratives, restrictive modifiers, dislocations and word-order devices, pronouns are part of the large functional domain of **topic identification** or **topic continuity** in discourse. The various constructions which together code this domain may be studied first, from a more restricted point of view of their semantic and syntactic properties. Only when enough background has been established concerning these narrow-scoped properties can one proceed to elucidate their role within a wider functional domain.

One fundamental assumption we will adopt throughout the discussion is that stressed **independent pronouns**, **unstressed/clitic pronouns** and **verb agreement** constitute both a functional-synchronic and diachronic cline. Diachronically, independent pronouns may become de-stressed and cliticized, and unstressed/clitic pronouns eventually become agreement inflections on the verb. Eventually it is common for grammatical agreement to become jointly-coded morphologically (*'portmanteau'*) with other inflectional categories of the verb, in particular tense-aspect-modality. This general diachronic process may be summarized as:[2]

(1)   independent PRO > unstressed PRO > clitic PRO > verb agreement

---

1) But see also Givón (1983a ed., 1983c) for discussion and details.

2) For the original argument for the functional and diachronic connection between pronouns and grammatical agreement, see Givón (1976b).

Diachronic change along this cline is coupled with changes in the discourse function of the pronouns, from the more emphatic, contrastive or **discontinuative** function of independent pronouns toward the anaphoric, **continuative** function of unstressed pronouns and verb agreement. As we shall see later, obligatory verb agreement may develop a number of other functions that are not as directly predictable from its erstwhile anaphoric function.

Cliticization does not only change the discourse function of erstwhile independent pronouns and shrink them in terms of phonological size, but often also reduces the number of semantic distinctions made in a pronominal sub-system. For this reason, the sub-system of stressed independent pronouns in most languages may show a slightly different cluster of underlying semantic features, most commonly a larger cluster than is observed in the clitic or agreement sub-systems. We will survey below some examples of such disparity.

10.2   THE SEMANTIC BASIS OF PRONOMINAL SYSTEMS

Semantic features involved in defining pronominal systems may be lexical or inherent noun features, or propositional-semantic features, or discourse-pragmatic features. The most common ones attested cross-linguistically are:

(a)   *Participant deixis ('person')*: 'Speaker' (1st person), 'hearer' (2nd person) or 'non-participant' (3rd person);

(b)   *Number*: 'Singular', 'dual' or 'plural';

(c)   *Inclusion/exclusion*: This feature pertains to the hearer's inclusion in, or exclusion from, the referential scope of 'we', either dual or plural. 'We-INCL' is thus "we, including you", and 'we-EXCL' is thus "we, excluding you";

(d)   *Class/gender*: This is the inherent-lexical cluster of noun features, applicable most typically to third-person referents; the classification here may correspond closely to semantic-lexical classes, or it may correspond only to erstwhile semantic but currently morphological classes;

(e)   *Spatial deixis*: This cluster pertains again only to third-persons, referring to their spatial position — proximity, distance, visibility — vis-à-vis the speaker or hearer. Spatial deixis may in time be extended to *temporal deixis*, involving proximity to the time of speech or the time-axis associated with the prior mention of the referent in discourse;

(f)   *Case-role*: This pertains either to semantic case-roles, such as agent, patient, dative etc., or — more commonly — to pragmatic/

grammatical case-roles such as subject, direct object, indirect object, genitive, ergative or absolutive.

As one can see from the short description above, there is a strong tendency in human language to make a clear distinction between the two active participants in the communication — speaker ('I', 'we') and hearer ('you', 'y'all') — and non-participants or 3rd persons ('he', 'she', 'it', 'they'). There are a number of reasons why this is a natural division.

(i)   The speaker and hearer are presumably human and presumably in face-to-face contact, so that their spatial deixis and class-gender are well established from the communicative context, and need not be overtly marked. They are themselves the point-of-reference for all spatial and temporal deixis.[3]

(ii) On the other hand, number and inclusion/exclusion are not directly predictable from the speaker and hearer, they are potentially ambiguous in the speech situation, and it is thus only natural that they may require overt specification ('marking').

(iii) Similarly, the case-role of the speaker or hearer when they are also participants in events/states which are reported (and are not necessarily occurring at the time and place of communication) is not predictable from the communicative situation, and must thus be specified just as it is specified for other referents.

So far, the discussion of pronouns above has pertained only to **definite ('anaphoric') pronouns**. One may as well note that there is also another pronoun category, that of **indefinite pronouns**. To contrast the two, consider the following example from English:

(2)   a. John was looking for a book,   (DEF/anaphoric pronoun)
          and he found **it**
      b. John was looking for a book,   (INDEF pronoun)
          and he found **one**

In (2a), 'a book' is *referential* (see Chapter 9, section 9.6., above, as well as Chapter 11, below), and the pronoun referring to it is definite or anaphoric. That means that it refers to an argument already identified in the preceding discourse context. In (2b), on the other hand, 'a book' is *non-referential* and the pronoun 'one' referring to it is indefinite. That means that the pronoun

---

3) In the most primitive form of human deixis, namely pointing toward a referent with one's eyes, face or finger, it is only that point-of-reference — the eyes, face or finger attached to the speaker/pointer — that makes the deixis/reference at all possible.

there introduces a referential argument into the discourse for the first time. In this chapter we will deal primarily with definite pronouns.

One must finally note that third-person definite pronouns are often in the same category — synchronically or diachronically — as either demonstratives ('demonstrative pronouns') or definite articles. For this reason we will also describe demonstratives below. The use of demonstratives as articles — i.e. noun modifiers rather than noun substitutes — will be discussed in Chapter 11, below, as well as in Chapter 22, Volume II.

10.3   SPECIFIC ORGANIZATION OF PRONOMINAL SYSTEMS

In this section we will illustrate what has been discussed above by citing the specific pronominal systems of a number of typologically-different languages.

10.3.1. Ute (Uto-Aztecan)[4]

In this section many of the semantic distinctions outlined above will be illustrated through the pronominal system of Ute. We will begin with independent pronouns, by definition all animate.

(3)   **independent subject pronouns**

person	singular		dual		plural	
1ST	nṹ'	'I'	támi	'we-INCL'	táwi	'we-INCL'
			nṹmụ	'we-EXCL'		
2ND	'ṹmụ	'you'	mṹni	'you'		
3RD-VISIBLE	máas	'he/she'	mamṹs	'they'		
3RD-INVIS	'uwás	'he/she'	'umṹs	'they'		

As one can see, the *dual* category is found only in the inclusive-we. Otherwise all other non-singular pronouns cover both dual and plural.

Independent non-subject (mostly object and genitive/possessive) pronouns are almost predictable, phonologicaly, from the subject forms, given a general rule in Ute that (a) the last vowel of subject nouns is silenced/devoiced, and (b) when that vowel is resurrected in non-subject forms, the stress is often 'attracted' to it, especially in bi-syllabic words.[5]

---

4) For details see Givón (1980a).

5) From a purely phonological perspective, the subject form is predictable from the object form by (a) vowel deletion/silencing and (b) stress shifting forward. For further detail see Givón (1980a, Ch. 1).

(4)   **independent non-subject pronouns**

person	singular		dual		plural	
1ST	nųnąy	'me/my'	tamí 'us/our-INCL'		tawí 'us/our-INCL'	
			nųmų́y		'we/our-EXCL'	
2ND	'ųmų́y	'you/your'	mųní		'you/your'	
3RD-VISIBLE	máayas	'him/his/her'	mamų́as		'them/their'	
3RD-INVIS	'uwáyas	'him/his/her'	'umų́as		'them/their'	

Next, the demonstrative series displays the gender contrast of animate vs. inanimate, and pertains only to third persons. Three degrees of deixis are marked, two of which have already appeared in third person pronouns above — remote-visible and remote-invisible. The SG/PL distinction applies only to animates, a characteristic situation with American Indian languages. The inherent identity of the 3rd-person pronouns in (3), (4) above with the remote animate demonstrative in (5) below is obvious.[6]

(5)   **demonstrative articles/pronouns**

class	near SUBJ/NON-SUBJ	remote-visible SUBJ/NON-SUBJ	remote-invisible SUBJ/NON-SUBJ
inanimate	'íca/'icą́y	márų/marų́	'úrų/'urú
animate-SG	'ína/'iną́y	má(a)/máay	'úwa/'uwá(y)
animate-PL	'ímų/'imų́	mámų/mamú	'úmų/'umų́

Clitic pronouns in Ute must be suffixed to some word in the clause, regardless of word-type. Most commonly that word is first in the clause. These pronouns thus do not constitute, strictly speaking, *verb* agreement (see below). Rather, they are **second position clitics**,[7] where the first word in the clause may or may not be a verb. In terms of case-role, clitic pronouns can refer to either subject, object or possessive/genitive nouns. This is a reduction ('neutralization') of one distinction that is marked more fully in independent pronouns. As can be seen in (6) below, a number of other distinctions are also neutralized.

6) The "pronouns" add the suffix -s (-sų) to the demonstrative stem. This suffix is historically a conjunction (see Givón, 1980a, Ch.17).

7) For a general discussion of second-position clitics see Steele (1977). There are grounds for believing that second position clitics may eventually lead to the development of verb-suffixal grammatical agreement. The possibility hinges on the potential high frequency of verbs as clause-initial words in connected discourse, where both subject and object anaphora — or anaphoric pronominalization — are of high frequency.

(6) **clitic/suffix pronouns**

person	singular	dual	plural
1ST	-n(ŋ)	-*rami* (INCL)	-rawi (INCL)
			-nŋmŋ (EXCL)
2ND	-m(ŋ)		-amŋ
3RD-VISIBLE	-'a		-amŋ
3RD-INVIS	-'u		-umŋ
3RD-VIS-INANIM	-ax̂		/
3RD-INVIS-INANIM	-ux		/

10.3.2. Samoan (Austronesian)[8]

The Samoan pronoun paradigm is interesting for two features, one being the more complete plural-dual distinction, the other the more complete inclusive-exclusive distinction. Cited are only the absolutive/subject independent pronouns.

(7) **absolutive/subject independent pronouns**

person	singular	dual		plural	
		INCL	EXCL	INCL	EXCL
1ST	o-a'u	o-tsaa-'ua	o-maa-'ua	o-tsaa-tsuo	o-maa-tsou
2ND	o-'oe	o-'ou-lua		o-laa-'ua	
3RD	o-iya	o-laa-'ua		o-laa-tsou	

The prefix *o-* in all pronoun forms above is the absolutive case prefix. The morpheme *-tsaa-* marks 'inclusive', the morpheme *-maa-* 'exclusive', *-'ua* marks 'dual' (except in one form where it is *-lua*) and *-tsou* marks 'plural' (except in one form where it is *-'ua*). The rest of the rather transparent morphemes are less predictable, displaying most likely the footprints of diachronic reanalysis within the system.[9]

10.3.3. Bemba (Bantu)[10]

The independent subject personal pronoun system in Bemba excludes 3rd persons, which are formally part of the demonstrative series.

---

8) From my own field notes, with the Western-Samoan data originally from Sivai Teofilo (in personal communication).

9) For a similar re-analysis in other languages and some discussion, see Chafe (1977).

10) For further detail see Givón (1972, Ch. 1, 2).

(8)   **independent subject personal pronouns**

person	singular	plural
1ST	ine 'I'	ifwe 'we'
2ND	iwe 'you'	imwe 'y'all'

Third person independent pronouns, used as emphatic subject or object pronouns (with a tonal difference between subject and object use), are simply the demonstrative pronoun/article series. Their tonal pattern is again different when used as pronouns (without the noun) than as articles (with the noun). The demonstratives are inflected for gender, number and four spatial deictic postions.

(9)   **demonstrative independent pronouns**

class	number	near speaker	near hearer	near both	remote from both
1/2	SG	uyu	uyo	uno	ulya
	PL	aba	abo	bano	balya
3/4	SG	uu	uo	uno	ulya
	PL	ii	io	ino	ilya
5/6	SG	ili	ilyo	lino	lilya
	PL	aya	ayo	yano	yalya
7/8	SG	ici	icyo	cino	cilya
	PL	ifi	ifyo	fino	filya
9/10	SG	ii	io	ino	ilya
	PL	ishi	ishyo	shino	shilya
11/9	SG	ulu	ulo	luno	lulya
	PL	ishi	ishyo	shino	shilya
12/13	SG	aka	ako	kano	kalya
	PL	utu	uto	tuno	tulya
14	(mass)	ubu	ubo	buno	bulya
15	(mass)	uku	uko	kuno	kulya

Clitic anaphoric pronouns divide into subject and object pronouns, both prefixed on the verb, with the subject clitic pronoun preceding the TAM marker and the object pronoun following it. They are also marked for singular/plural and class/gender, along the same lines as in (9) above, with the human class (1/2) functioning as the 'he'/'she' and 'they' pronouns.

(10)   **clitic subject pronouns** (with **-li** 'be')

category	singular		plural	
1ST person	n-di	'I am'	tu-li	'we are'
2ND person	u-li	'you are'	mu-li	'y'all are'
class 1/2	a-li	'he/she is'	ba-li	'they are'
class 3/4	u-li	'it is'	i-li	'they are'
class 5/6	li-li	'it is'	ya-li	'they are'
class 7/8	ci-li	'it is'	fi-li	'they are'
class 9/10	i-li	'it is'	shi-li	'they are'
class 11/10	lu-li	'it is'	shi-li	'they are'
class 12/13	ka-li	'it is'	tu-li	'they are'
class 14		bu-li	'it is'	
class 15		ku-li	'it is'	

(11)   **clitic object pronouns**   (with-**mona** 'see')

category	singular		plural	
1ST	a-à-**m**-mona	'he saw me'	a-à-**tu**-mona	'he saw us'
2NP	a-à-**ku**-mona	'he saw you'	a-à-**mu**-mona	'he saw y'all'
class 1/2	a-à-**mu**-mona	'he saw him/her'	a-à-**ba**-mona	'he saw them'
class 3/4	a-à-**u**-mona	'he saw it'	a-à-**i**-mona	'he saw them'
class 5/6	a-à-**li**-mona	'he saw it'	a-à-**ya**-mona	'he saw them'
class 7/8	a-à-**ci**-mona	'he saw it'	a-à-**fi**-mona	'he saw them'
class 9/10	a-à-**i**-mona	'he saw it'	a-à-**shi**-mona	'he saw them'
class 11/10	a-à-**lu**-mona	'he saw it'	a-à-**shi**-mona	'he saw them'
class 12/13	a-à-**ka**-mona	'he saw it'	a-à-**tu**-mona	'he saw them'
class 14		a-à-**bu**-mona	'he saw it'	
class 15		a-à-**ku**-mona	'he saw it'	

10.4   GRAMMATICAL AGREEMENT

10.4.1. Pronouns and agreement

Diachronically, what begins as an independent, stressed and phonologi-cally large independent pronoun eventually becomes de-stressed and cliticized or bound to larger, stressed lexical words. The fact that this process also involves changes in the discourse-pragmatic function of the NP, along the functional continuum of **topic continuity/predictability**, will be discussed in greater detail in Chapter 22, Volume II.[11] At this point it will be enough to say that independent/stressed pronouns tend to be emphatic or contrastive, while unstressed, clitic or 'agreement' pronouns tend to be non-emphatic, continuative or **anaphoric**.

The nouns that pronouns "refer to" or "stand for" may perform different case-roles within the clause. And case-role differences often participate in determining a number of properties of clitic pronouns:

(a)   The manner of their cliticization;
(b)   The word-type on which they will cliticize;
(c)   Their morphotactic position relative to that word, i.e. where they will cliticize (i.e. prefix or suffix);
(d)   The likelihood that the clitic pronoun will become an obligatory component of the word on which it cliticizes — and thus become obligatory "grammatical agreement".

Most commonly, pronouns co-referential to the subject or object will cliticize on the verbal word, while those co-referential to the possessor ('genitive') will cliticize on the possessed noun.[12]

As mentioned in section 10.1., above, there is no formal difference between clitic pronouns, de-stressed pronouns and grammatical agreement. Older generations of clitic pronouns display phonological/assimilatory erosion and often merge with other verb-inflectional categories, to the point where it may be difficult to distinguish them morphologically even if the semantic categories underlying them persist in the ensuing "grammatical agreement". And conservative writing systems tend to preserve the illusion of word-status of de-stressed pronouns long after simple phonological criteria point to the fact that they are already cliticized. Diachronic as well as functional analysis points to the inherent identity of pronouns and "agreement".[13]

11) See details also in Givón (1980a, Ch. 17, 1983a, 1983b, 1983c).

12) For some tentative generalizations concerning factors which determine the morphotactics of cliticization, see Givón (1977a, 1979a, Ch. 6).

13) See discussion in Givón (1976b). Phonological attrition eventually plays havoc with the code-efficiency of pronouns, so that a depleted system of grammatical agreement is eventually replaced by a new generation of de-stressed independent pronouns which soon again cliticize. A good example of this occurring right now is colloquial English or colloquial French.

As a brief illustration of the semantic similarity of verb-agreement and pronouns, consider the following from Spanish:

(12)   trabaj-é 'I worked'   trabaj-**amos** 'we worked'
       trabaj-**aste** 'you worked'   trabaj-**aron** 'y'all/they worked'
       trabaj-**ó** 'he/she worked'

And similarly in Israeli Hebrew:

(13)

avád-**ti**	'I worked'	**a**-avód	'I will work'
avád-**ta**	'you worked'(m.)	**ta**-avód	'you will work'(m.)
avád-**t**	'you worked'(f.)	**ta**-avd-**í**	'you will work'(f.)
avád	'he worked'	**ya**-avód	'he will work'
avd-**á**	'she worked'	**ta**-avód	'she will work'
avád-**nu**	'we worked'	**na**-avód	'we will work'
avád-**tem**	'y'all worked'(m.)	**ta**-avd-ú	'y'all will work'(m.)
avád-**ten**	'y'all worked'(f.)	(**ta**-avód-**na**	'y'all will work' (f.))
avd-**ú**	'they worked'	**ya**-avd-**ú**	'they will work'(m.)
		(**ta**-avód-**na**	'they will work'(f.))

10.4.2. Obligatory grammatical agreement

Pronouns — and unstressed anaphoric pronouns — may be used as "noun substitutes" under conditions of co-reference. When they cliticize, however, the probability increases that they may be interpreted by subsequent generations of speakers as *obligatory* parts of the verbal word, not only as substitutes for the co-referent NP but also when the co-referent NP is present. Under such conditions, one may say that the verb "agrees with an NP", and one then observes the phenomenon of **grammatical agreement**.

Schematically, the diachronic development from anaphoric unstressed pronouns to cliticized grammatical agreement may be described as:[14]

(14)   John, **he** went home $\implies$ John **he**-went home

Most commonly, grammatical agreement continues — at least for a while — to perform the old anaphoric function of the unstressed pronoun. But when it is obligatory, it also appears when the noun itself is present in the clause, i.e. when no anaphoric function is required. As illustration, consider the following examples from Swahili:[15]

---

14) For the original argument and supporting evidence, see Givón (1976b).

15) See also Ashton (1944).

(15) a. *Obligatory grammatical agreement*

    (i) ṁtoto **a**-na-kula   ṁkate
        child *he*-PROG-eat bread
        'The child is eating bread'

    (ii) watoto **wa**-na-kula   ṁkate
        children *they*-PROG-eat bread
        'The children are eating bread'

    (iii) ṁti **u**-me-vunjika
        tree *it*-PERF-break
        'The tree broke'

    (iv) miti   **i**-me-vunjika
        trees *they*-PERF-break
        'The trees broke'

  b. *Anaphoric pronominalization*

    (i) **a**-na-kula ṁkate
        '*He/she* is eating bread'

    (ii) **wa**-na-kula ṁkate
        '*They* are eating bread'

    (iii) **u**-me-vunjika
        '*It* broke'

    (iv) **i**-me-vunjika
        '*They* broke'

In (15a) above, the clitic/prefixed pronouns refer to the subject, a fact that is recapitulated in their anaphoric use in (15b). But grammatical agreement may — less often — also involve the direct object. This is the case with definite human objects in Spanish, as in:

(16) a. **le**-ví   a   Juán ayer   (obligatory agreement)
      him-saw-I DAT John yesterday
      'I saw John yesterday'

    b. **le**-ví   ayer   (anaphoric pronominali-
      him-saw-I yesterday   zation)
      'I saw him yesterday'

    c. *ví a Juán ayer   (*no agreement)

10.4.3. Grammatical agreement and the topic hierarchy

10.4.3.1. Preliminaries

In Chapter 5, above, we discussed the hierarchy of case-roles in terms of

(a)   the likelihood that they become primary or secondary **clausal topic**, and

(b)   the correlated likelihood that they become the grammaticalized **subject** or **direct object** of the sentence.

In this section we will see how grammatical agreement is also fundamentally a topic-related feature of the grammar, and how the same topic hierarchy — or topic hierarchies — may predict many features of grammatical agreement. This is of course not surprising if one considers the diachronic origin of grammatical agreement, arising from anaphoric pronouns, which are themselves definite and refer to *highly topical* NP's.[16]

The role of topicality in grammatical agreement is evident from the following implicational hierarchies which predict what type of NP is more likely to develop — or display — grammatical agreement with the verb.
The hierarchies are:

(17)   a. *Semantic case-role*:   AGT > DAT/BEN > PAT > OTHERS

         b. *Pragmatic case-roles*: SUBJ > D-OBJ > OTHERS

         c. *Humanity/animacy*:   HUMAN/ANIMATE > NON-HUMAN/INANIMATE

         d. *Definiteness*:   DEF > INDEF

The relevance of scales (17b) and (17d) to topicality is direct. The "subject" case is that of the primary/most-continuous argument in the clause and the "direct object" case is that of the secondary/next-to-most continuous argument. Definites are NP's already familiar to the hearer from the preceding discourse context, while indefinites are introduced into the discourse for the first time and are thus unfamiliar and less predictable/continuous. Scales (17a) and (17c) relate to topicality indirectly, via universals of either **cognition** and/or human **culture**, predicting:

(a)   that humans/animates are more likely to talk about themselves;

(b)   that humans/animates are more likely to construe themselves as causes; and

---

16) By "highly topical" we mean here, informally, "highly continuous", "predictable" or "recurrent" in the discourse. The more formal discussion of this is found in Chapter 22, Volume II, as well as in Givón (1983a, b, c,).

(c) that humans/animates are likely to pay more attention to salient changes than to inert states.

The typological predictions concerning the likelihood of grammatical agreement may be divided into two related kinds:

(i) *Synchronically*: A language is more likely to display obligatory grammatical agreement with an NP type higher on the scales in (17) than with one lower on these scales.

(ii) *Diachronically*: Grammatical agreement is likely to develop first in NP types higher on the scales in (17) than in ones lower on these scales.

We will discuss each of the hierarchic scales in (17).

10.4.3.2. Semantic case-roles and agreement

The hierarchy (17a) is the same one discussed in Chapter 5 above and from which the likelihood of becoming primary topic ("subject") or secondary topic ("direct object") was predicted. Due to the fact that in simple clauses agents are most likely to be the subjects and datives are most likely to be the direct objects, much of the data supporting hierarchy (17a) also supports hierarchy (17b). Let us consider first Hebrew, where subject agreement is obligatory while object agreement is impossible, either in the Biblical style or in the Israeli style:[17]

(18) a. *SUBJ agreement*: ha-yéled ra'á 'et ha-kélev
the-boy saw-*he* ACC the-dog
'The boy saw the dog'

b. *OBJ clitic PRO (Biblical)*: ha-yéled ra'á-**hu**
the-boy saw-*he*-**him**
'The boy saw him'

c. *OBJ agreement (Biblical)*: *ha-yéled ra'á-**hu** 'et ha-kélev
the-boy saw-*he*-**him** ACC the-dog

d. *OBJ anaphoric PRO (Israeli)*: ha-yéled ra'á 'ot-**o**
the-boy saw-*he* ACC-**him**
'The boy saw him'

---

17) The pervasive *diglossia* of Israeli Hebrew speakers makes them consider the Biblical clitic pronouns, as in (18b), grammatical. At the rock-bottom basilect level of informal, colloquial style they are clearly "strange", "awkward" or "inappropriate".

e. *OBJ agreement (Israeli)*:* ha-yéled ra'á   'ot-ó   'et
                    the-boy saw-*he* ACC-**him** ACC
                    ha-kélev
                    the-dog

In Spanish, next, if one combines the two facts, (a) that human-definite objects display obligatory agreement, and (b) that DAT/BEN objects are overwhelmingly human and definite in discourse (while PAT objects are prototypically inanimate, though of course not obligatorily so), one can see how agreement is obligatory for AGT/SUBJ NP's and DAT/BEN objects but impossible for human PAT objects. Thus consider:

(19) a. Juán **le**-dió   el libro a   María   (SUBJ/AGT and
        J.   **her**-gave-*he* the book DAT M.   DAT agreement)
        'John gave the book to Mary'

     b. *Juán dió el libro a María   (lack of DAT agreement)

     c. *Juán **lo**-dió el libro a María   (*PAT object agreement)
        it-gave-*he*

Further, the human object in Spanish — dative or direct — requires agreement only if it is a **conscious participant**, i.e. a protoypical dative. This may be illustrated by the following contrast:

(20) a. Juán **le**-vió   a   María en la   calle
                             (María construed as DAT object)
        J.   **her**-saw-he DAT M.   in the street
        'John **saw/met** Mary in the street' [⊃ She saw him too, i.e. was
                                      conscious of the event]

     b. Juán vió   a   María en la   calle
                             (María construed as PAT object)
        J.   saw-he DAT M.   in the street
        'John **saw** Mary in the street' [⊃ She didn't see him, i.e. she
                                 wasn't conscious of the event]

Beyond the DAT object, obligatory agreement of PAT object (or of objects lower on the scale (17a)) is hard to find. One example which evolved from such agreement of PAT objects into another function in the New Guinea Pidgin Tok Pisin will be discussed in section 10.6.2., below.

10.4.3.3. Pragmatic/grammatical case-roles and agreement

The same data given above in support of the primacy of AGT over PAT-object also supports the primacy of SUBJ over direct object in grammatical agreement. This is due to the common conflation, in nominative-accusative languages, of AGT with SUBJ and of PAT with DO.[18]

The data supporting the primacy of the direct object over the indirect object in grammatical agreement again sometimes overlaps with the data seen above on the primacy of the DAT/BEN over other objects. This is so because the DAT/BEN object has the highest claim to the DO position (see Chapter 5, above). As first illustration, consider the following situation in KinyaRwanda (Bantu), where object agreement is not obligatory. When two objects are present, the DO may display object agreement, but a "demoted" ('dative-shifted') object may not:[19]

(21) a. umugabo ya-bwiiye   ibinyoma   (PAT = DO)
        man   he-PAST-tell lies
        'The man told lies'

     b. umugabo ya-bwiiye   abaana ibinyoma   (DAT = DO)
        man   he-PAST-tell children lies
        'The man told the children lies'

     c. DAT = DO; DAT agreement:
        umugabo ya-**ba**-bwiiye   abaana ibinyoma
        man   he-PAST-**them**-tell children lies   ['them' =
        'The man told the children lies'   'children']

     d. DAT = DO; PAT agreement impossible:
        *umugabo ya-**bi**-bwiiye   abaana ibinyoma
        man   he-PAST-**them**-tell children lies   ['them' =
                                                                'lies']

The same is seen in KinyaRwanda when an oblique case is promoted to DO optionally. When it is unpromoted, the PAT-DO controls the optional agreement. When the oblique is promoted to DO, it controls the agreement:[20]

18) For some discussion of the agreement situation in ergative languages, see further below.

19) From Kimenyi (1980).

20) From Kimenyi (1980).

(22) a. PAT = DO:
      umuana ya-nyooye   amata n-umuhehe
      boy   he-PAST-drink milk with-straw
      'The boy drank the milk with a straw'

     b. PAT = DO, PAT agreement:
      umuana ya-**ya**-nyooye   amata n-umuhehe
      boy   he-PAST-**it**-drink milk with-straw
      'The boy drank the milk with a straw'

     c. PAT = DO, INST agreement impossible:
      *umuana ya-**u**-nyooye   amata n-umuhehe
      boy   he-PAST-**it**-drink milk with-straw
                                 ['it' = 'straw']

     d. INSTR = DO:
      umuana ya-nyw-**eesh**-eje   umuhehe amata
      boy   he-PAST-drink-INSTR straw   milk
      'The boy used the straw to drink milk'

     e. INSTR = DO, INSTR agreement:
      umuana ya-**u**-nyw-**eesh**-eje   umuhehe amata
      boy   he-PAST-**it**-drink-INSTR straw   milk
      'The boy used the straw to drink milk'

     f. INSTR = DO, PAT agreement impossible:
      *umuana ya-**ya**-nyw-**eesh**-eje   umuhehe amata
      boy   he-PAST-**it**-drink-INSTR straw milk
                                   ['it = 'milk']

Even in languages where promotion to DO or topic involves no noun morphology but only a change in word-order, the primacy of DO over IO in grammatical agreement can be demonstrated. Thus, consider the following from Amharic:[21]

(23) a. AGT/SUBJ topic, SUBJ agreement:
      Almaz bet-u-n   bä-mäträgiya-w   tärrägä-**čč**
      A.   house-DEF-OBJ with-broom-DEF swept-*she*
      'Almaz swept the house with a broom'

     b. PAT topic, SUBJ & PAT agreement:
      bet-u-n   Almaz bä-mäträgiya-w   tärrägä-čč-**iw**
      house-DEF-OBJ A.   with-broom-DEF swept-she-*it*
      'The house Almaz swept with the broom'   ['it' = 'house']

21) The data is originally from Haile (1970) and Fulas (1974).

c. PAT topic, no INSTR agreement:
*bet-u-n   Almaz bä-mäträgiya-w   tärrägä-čč-bb-**at**
house-DEF-OBJ A.   with-broom-DEF swept-she-with-**it**
                                          ['it' = 'broom']

d. INSTR topic, SUBJ & INSTR agreement:
bä-mäträgiya-w   Almaz bet-u-n   tärrägä-čč-bb-**at**
with-broom-DEF A.   house-DEF-OBJ swept-she-with-**it**
'With the broom Almaz swept the house'   ['it' = broom']

e. INSTR topic, no PAT agreement:
*bä-mäträgiya-w   Almaz bet-u-n   tärrägä-čč-**iw**
with-broom-DEF A.   house-DEF-OBJ swept-she-**it**
                                          ['it' = 'house']

In Amharic, the left-most constituent is more topical, and the left-movement of objects — in the absence of morphological promotion to DO — serves as its functional equivalent.

10.4.3.4. Subject and object agreement in ergative languages

The predictive hierarchies in (17) pertain primarily to nominative languages. In Ergative languages a great variety of possibilities exist. In some, verb agreement is controlled by the subject/topic regardless of the ERG/ABS distinction, i.e. much as in nominative languages. As an example, consider the following from the surface-ergative language Kâte (New Guinea):[22]

(24) a. ...be' guy   fo-ve'...   (intransitive; ABS subject)
        pig sleep lie-**3-sg**-PAST
        '...the pig lay down to sleep...'

b. ...be'-ko   nana na-ve'...   (transitive; ERG subject)
        pig-ERG taro eat-**3-sg**-PAST
        '...the pig ate taro...'

In other surface-ergative languages, verb agreement is controlled only by the ergative NP and never by the absolutive — even when the absolutive is the subject. As an example consider the following from Jacaltec:[23]

22) From Anderson (1976).

23) For further details see Craig (1977). The absolutive most commonly has *zero* pronominal reflection on the verb. However, absolutive-referring pronouns may appear on the pre-verbal auxiliary. These tend to represent another—diachronically younger—pronominal series. As seen in Chapter 5, above, in Jacaltec the ERG/ABS morphological contrast is found only in clitic pronouns but not in full NP's.

(25) a. *Intransitive*: x-Ø-'ayc'ay hej te' te'
ASP-ABS/3-fall PL the tree
'The trees fell down'

b. *Transitive*: x-Ø-**s**-watx'e naj te' ñah
ASP-ABS/3-**ERG/3**-make he the house
'He made the house'

In the intransitive (25a), the absolutive subject agreement on the verb is *zero*. In the transitive (25b) the absolutive object agreement remains *zero*, while the ergative subject agreement is a marked morpheme (*-s-*).

Next, in other surface-ergative languages it is the absolutive rather than the ergative that controls grammatical agreement on the verb, in both intransitive and transitive clauses. Thus, consider the following from Avar'(Caucasian):[24]

(26) a. vas **v**-eker-ula (intransitive, SG-MS subject)
boy-ABS **m**-run-PRES
'The boy runs'

b. jas **j**-eker-ula (intransitive, SG-F subject)
girl-ABS **f**-run-PRES
'The girl runs'

c. ins:u-c:a jas **j**-ec:-ula (transitive, SG-F object)
father-ERG girl-ABS **f**-praise-PRES
'The father praises the daughter'

d. vas-as: šiša **b**-ek-ana (transitive,
boy-ERG bottle-ABS **sg**-break-PAST SG-INAN object)
'The boy broke the bottle'

The most likely origin of absolutive-only verb agreement pattern must involve the fact that the ergative clause probably arose from re-analysis of a passive clause. Within the passive clause, the patient is the grammatical subject, and therefore controls verb agreement in accordance with our hierarchy (17b) above.[25]

---

24) From Anderson (1976).

25) Re-analysis of passive to ergative is one major pathway for developing ergative constructions, and is normally supported by an etymological connection between the ERG-marker and the AGT-of-passive marker. The other major pathway involves re-analysis of nominalized/participial transitive clauses, with their subject marked by the *genitive*. In both Jacaltec and Sherpa, for example, the ERG-marker is etymologically related to/derived from the *genitive*, and only the ERG-subject controls verb agreement. For further discussion see Givón (1980c).

Finally, one must also note that it is possible for an ergative language to have both ergative and absolutive verb agreement. Thus consider the following from Abaza (Caucasian):[26]

(27) a. intransitive, ABS agreement:
a-ph°ɨs   **d**-qa-cᵒ'a-d
the-woman ABS-up-sit-PAST/ACT
'The woman sat up'

b. transitive, ABS and ERG agreement:
a-ph°ɨs   a-qac'a   **d-l-ši-d**
the-woman the-man   ABS-ERG-kill-PAST/ACT
'The woman killed the man'

In (27b), -*d*- agrees with the absolutive 3rd-person object, while -*l*- agrees with the feminine, third-person ergative subject.

10.4.3.5. The humanness/animacy hierarchy and agreement

The primacy of subject agreement over object agreement by itself also supports the primacy of human/animate agreement over non-human/inanimate, since as we have seen in Chapter 5, above, the agent has the strongest claim to subjecthood and the agent is overwhelmingly human or animate. In the same vein, the primacy of the dative/benefactive over other object types in both direct-objectization (Chapter 5) and agreement (see previous sections) also supports the primacy of human/animate in agreement, since (a) the dative/benefactive is a human/animate argument, and (b) the direct object has a higher claim to verb agreement than indirect objects. In addition, one could also cite direct evidence in support of the primacy of human/animate over non-human/inanimate in object agreement. Consider first the following data from Swahili, where verb agreement with human objects is obligatory regardless of definiteness and referentiality, though with non-human objects it is obligatory only for definite objects (see further below):[27]

(28) a. ni-li-**mw**-ona   ṁtoto   (human, REF-INDEF)
I-PAST-**him**-see child
'I saw a child'

b. ni-li-**mw**-ona   yule ṁtoto   (human, DEF)
I-PAST-**him**-see the child
'I saw the child'

---

26) From Anderson (1976).

27) For further detail see Ashton (1944).

   c. *ni-li-ona   (yule) ṁtoto
      I-PAST-see (the) child

   d. si-ku-**mw**-ona   ṁtoto yeyote   (human, NON-
      I-NEG/PAST-**him**-see child any   REF)
      'I didn't see any child'

   e. ni-li-ona   kikapu   (inanimate, REF-INDEF)
      I-PAST-see basket
      'I saw a basket

   f. ni-li-**ki**-ona   kikapu   (inanimate, DEF)
      I-PAST-**it**-see basket
      'I saw **the** basket'

A reminiscent situation is also found in Spanish, where human direct objects, marked by the dative preposition, require obligatory grammatical agreement if they are definite. Non-human definite objects, on the other hand, do not display object agreement:

  (29) a. **le**-ví   a   Juán en la   calle   (human, DEF)
          him-saw-I DAT J.   in the street
          'I saw John in the street'

       b. *ví   a   Juán en la   calle
          saw-I DAT J.   in the street

       c. ví   el   árbol en la   calle   (inanimate, DEF)
          saw-I the tree in the street
          'I saw the tree in the street'

       d. ? **lo**-ví   el   árbol en la   calle
          it-saw-I the tree in the street

10.4.3.6. The definiteness hierarchy and agreement

Swahili may also serve as an illustration for the primacy of definite over indefinite in grammatical agreement. In this language, for inanimate/non-human objects, agreement is obligatory when they are definite (indeed, it marks definiteness in such objects), but impossible if they are indefinite. This is demonstrated by the contrast between sentences (28e) and (28f) above.

10.5. GRAMMATICAL AGREEMENT OF MODIFIERS WITH THE HEAD NOUN IN THE NP

So far, we have discussed only grammatical agreement of subjects and various objects with the verb. This is indeed the more prevalent agreement pattern. But a less-common one also exists, whereby modifiers "agree with" the head noun they modify within the noun phrase. The features most commonly involved in such agreement are:

(a)   Singularity/plurality
(b)   Noun class/gender
(c)   Case-role of the NP
(d)   Definiteness/indefiniteness of the NP

Such features in agreement do not always vary independently but often co-vary. For example, gender/class and number are often signaled by a *portmanteau* ('joint') morpheme. To illustrate gender/class -cum- number agreement within the NP, consider the following from Swahili (Bantu):[28]

(30) a. **ki**-le **ki**-kapu **ch**-angu **ki**-dogo amba-**cho ki**-me-vunjika...
         the   basket   mine   small   REL   *it*-PERF-break
         'that small basket of mine that broke...'

      b. **vi**-le **vi**-kapu **vy**-angu **vi**-dogo amba-**vyo vi**-me-vunjika...
         the   baskets   mine   small   REL   *they*-PERF-break
         'those small baskets of mine that broke...'

      c. **yu**-le **m̂**-toto **y**-angu **m̂**-dogo amba-**ye u**-me-kufa...
         the   child   mine   small   REL   *he*-PERF-die
         'that small child of mine who died...'

      d. **wa**-le **wa**-toto **wa**-ngu **wa**-dogo amba-**wo wa**-me-kufa...
         those children mine   small   REL   *they*-PERF-die
         'those small children of mine who died...'

The next example, from Israeli Hebrew, illustrates gender and number agreement together with the agreement (or 'spreading') of the definite morpheme:

(31) a. ísh   gadól   exád
         man   big-MS/SG   one-MS/SG
         'one big man'

28) For further detail see Ashton (1944).

b. ishá   gdolá   axát
   woman big-FM/SG   one-FM/SG
   'one big woman'

c. anashím gdolím   axadím
   man-PL   big-MS/PL   one-MS/PL
   'several big men'

d. nashím   gdolót   axadót
   woman-PL   big-FM/PL   one-FM/PL
   'several big women'

e. ha-ísh   ha-gadól   ha-zé
   the-man   the-big   the-this-MS/SG
   'this big man'

f. ha-ishá   ha-gdolá   ha-zót
   the-woman the-big   the-this-FM/SG
   'this big woman'

As an example of case-agreement, consider the following from Bemba (Bantu):[29]

(32) a. **in**-gaanda **ií**   **y**-aandi **i**-kulu
        house   this mine   big
        'this big house of mine'

    b. **mu**-n-gaanda **umú** **mw**-aandi **mu**-kulu
       in-house   this   mine   big
       'in this big house of mine'

In (32a), it is the gender/number of 'house' which controls the grammatical agreement of the three modifiers following 'house'. In (32b) it is the prepositional locative case *mu*- ('inside') which controls the grammatical agreement. The NP in (32a) could either be a subject or direct object, both of which are morphologically unmarked, so that the gender/number of the head noun controls grammatical agreement.

In Bantu languages, this case-agreement across the NP is limited to only one contrast, between the marked locative-prepositional case and the unmarked subject/object case. In other languages the phenomenon may be more extensive. Thus, consider the following from Latin, where every case-

---

29) From Givón (1972, Chapter 1).

30) For details see Palmer (1954).

role displays such agreement between head nouns and their modifiers:[30]

(33) vir   bonus   puerō   bono   librum
     man-NOM good-NOM boy-DAT good-DAT book-ACC
     bonum   dedit
     good-ACC gave
     'The good man gave the good boy a good book'

Both synchronically and diachronically, verb agreement with the subject (or to a lesser extent the object) is more likely than head-noun agreement with modifiers, and there are some grounds for believing that the second arises diachronically from the first.[31]

10.6. THE FUNCTIONS OF GRAMMATICAL AGREEMENT

In this section we will survey briefly a range of functions that may be performed by grammatical agreement. Some of these are related, closely or less closely, to the original function of anaphoric pronominalization from which agreement presumably arose. Others are less predictable from that function and have their own peculiar histories.

10.6.1. The anaphoric-pronoun function

We have already discussed this function above. We may illustrate it again for subject and object agreement, by considering the following examples from Swahili:[32]

(34) a. baba yangu **a-li-kufa**   (subject present; obligatory
      father mine **he**-PAST-die   agreement)
      'My father died'

    b. **a-li-kufa**   (subject absent; anaphoric
      he/she-PAST-die   pronominalization)
      'He/she died'

---

31) The diachronic process via which head-modifier agreement arises has not yet been investigated in any depth. In the clearer cases, such as Bantu languages [cf. the Swahili examples in (30) above], the entire noun-prefix system is of a demonstrative-pronoun origin (Greenberg, 1977). Since the adjectives in Bantu are of a nominal origin (Givón, 1979a, Chapter 6) the nominal prefix has been carried into the adjectival paradigm via the re-analysis of adjectives as nouns. Further, subject-verb agreement is clearly of pronominal origin in Bantu, as elsewhere. And the pronominal verb-agreement is transferred into a pronominal modifier agreement when a verb becomes a REL-clause modifier. The spread of such modifier agreement into other modifier categories then presumably proceeds via analogy. Whether this process can be generalized to other languages displaying head-modifier agreement remains to be seen.

32) See details in Ashton (1944).

   c. ni-li-**ki**-soma   kitabu   (object present; obligatory
       I-PAST-**it**-read book   DEF-OBJ agreement)
       'I read **the** book'

   d. ni-li-**ki**-soma   (object absent; anaphoric
       I-PAST-**it**-read   pronominalization)
       'I read **it**'

A similar anaphoric function may be seen for noun-modifier agreement:[33]

  (35) a. baba **y**-angu   a-li-kufa   (head present; obligatory
         father AG-mine he-PAST-die   agreement)
         'My father died'

       b. **y**-angu   a-li-kufa   (head absent; anaphoric
         PRO-mine he-PAST-die   pronominalization)
         '**Mine** died'

       c. mw-ana **m̂**-kubwa a-li-kufa   (head present; obligatory
         child   AG-big   he-PAST-die agreement)
         'The big child died'

       d. **m̂**-kubwa a-li-kufa   (head absent; anaphoric
          PRO-big he-PAST-die   pronominalization)
         '**The big one** died'

       e. m̂tu a-li-**ye**-fika   ni hapa (head present;
         man he-PAST-AG/REL-come be here   obligatory
         'The man who came is here'   agreement)

       f. a-li-**ye**-fika   ni hapa (head absent;
         he-PAST-PRO/REL-come be here   anaphoric
         '**The one who came** is here'   pronominalization)

As one can see from the examples above, performing the same anaphoric function within the NP — marking co-reference with the deleted head — in a language such as English, in which no head-modifier agreement exists, requires the use of an explicit pronoun such as 'one' (see below).

---

33) See Ashton (1944).

10.6.2. Marking verb-type and transitivity

This function develops as a rare but nonetheless predictable offshoot of obligatory object-verb pronominal agreement. In Tok Pisin (a New Guinea Neo-Melanesian Pidgin) the erstwhile obligatory agreement was eventually re-interpreted as part of the verbal stem, signaling transitive verbs (i.e. verbs which take direct objects which erstwhile precipitated obligatory agreement). As examples consider:[34]

(36) har-*im* 'to hear'
pait-*im* 'to fight' [vs. pait 'to be in a fight']
pam-*im* 'to pump'
bruk-*im* 'to break' [vs. bruk 'to get broken']
tan-*im* 'to turn (something)' [vs. tan 'to turn', intr.]
liptap-*im* 'to raise', 'to lift up'

10.6.3. Supplemental case-marking function

In many languages, some object case-functions are either impossible to mark on the noun, or impossible to mark if the object is promoted to DO, or cannot be marked by word-order alone. When such an object controls obligatory verb-object agreement, however, that agreement can serve to supplement the less-than-explicit case-marking morphology. This is typical of Bantu languages when both a benefactive and definite patient-object are present. The obligatory human-class agreement of the benefactive may then be considered an augmentation of the case-marking morphology. As an example consider the following from Swahili:[35]

(37) a. ni-li-**ki**-vunja   chupa
I-PAST-**it**-break bottle
'I broke the bottle'

b. ni-li-**m̂**-vunja   m̂toto chupa
I-PAST-**him**-break child   bottle
'I broke the bottle **to the child's detriment**'

A similar use of the difference between human and non-human object pronouns appears in Spanish, to signal the difference between the dative and accusative case when the verb alllows both:

---

34) From Mühlhäusler (1973); see also discussion in Givón (1976b).

35) See Ashton (1944). As we have seen in Chapter 3, section 3.6.2.4, case-markers may be associated with the verbal inflectional morphology without necessarily arising via pronominal/grammatical agreement. These are most commonly of verbal origin.

(38) a. **le**-ví   a   Juán en la   calle
          him-saw-I DAT John in the street
          'I saw John in the street' [⊃ 'and he was aware of me']

      b. **lo**-ví   a   Juán en la   calle
          it-saw-I DAT John in the street
          'I saw John in the street' [⊃ 'and he was unaware of me']

10.6.4. Differentiation between main and subordinate clause

It has been suggested that in many non-standard dialects of American English, the use of unstressed subject pronouns approaches the status of obligatory grammatical agreement.[36] But the same dialects do not impose obligatory subject agreement in subject REL-clauses. Since these are also the same dialects that dispense with the standard English relative pronouns, one may conceivably argue that the presence of subject-agreement in main clauses becomes an important — though not necessarily the only — [37] signal in distinguishing the main clause from the REL-clause. Schematically, this may be illustrated as:

(39) a. *Main clause*: the man **he**-came to dinner
                          'The man came to dinner'

      b. *REL-clause*: the man came to dinner is my friend
                         'The man who came to dinner is my friend'

In many core-Bantu languages, this very same distinction is made by either using a different subject-agreement pronoun in main clauses than in subject REL-clauses, and/or by a tonal difference between the two. Thus consider the following from Bemba:[38]

(40) a. umukashi **á-à-īshìlè**   (main clause)
          woman   **she**-PAST-come
          'The woman came'

---

36) See Dillard (1972) and Tyson (1974).

37) Intonation obviously plays an important role in coding this difference, especially in sub-dialects that drop the REL-pronoun but do not display obligatory (or 'near-obligatory') subject agreement in main clauses.

38) From Givón (1972). The tonal difference is not confined to the pronominal agreement morpheme in (40), but creates a *tonal displacement* through the entire verbal word, and that displacement may be considered an *intonational* phenomenon in Bemba.

b. umukashi ù-à-ìshīlē...   (subject REL-clause)
   woman   **who**-PAST-came
   'The woman who came...'

c. abakashi **bá**-à-īshìlè   (main clause)
   women   **they**-PAST-came
   'The women came'

d. abakashi **bà**-à-īshīlē   (subject REL-clause)
   women   **who/PL**-PAST-came
   'The women who came...'

10.6.5. Marking existential-presentative constructions

Subjects of simple clauses are protoypically referential and definite (see discussion in Chapter 11, below), and these are the ones which most commonly display subject-agreement of the type discussed throughout this chapter. A much less common sentence pattern in languages is that found with **referential-indefinite** subjects (see Chapter 19, Volume II). Such sentences tend to display uncommon characteristics vis-à-vis simple sentences with definite subjects, such as for example verb-subject (VS) word order in a language with the normal SV order for definite subjects (see Chapter 6, section 6.5., above). Another way in which such sentences may be distinguished from those with definite subjects is by a different agreement pattern. Thus, for example, in Kinya-Rwanda (Bantu) existential-presentative sentences display **locative** subject agreement and suppress the normal gender/number agreement. Thus consider:[39]

(41) a. umugabo **ya**-riho   ku-nzu   (DEF subject)
        man   **he**-PAST-be in-house
        'The man is in the house'

     b. abagabo **ba**-riho   ku-nzu   (DEF subject, plural)
        men   **they**-PAST-be in-house
        'The men were in the house'

     c. INDEF subject:
        kyeera **ha**-riho   umugabo a-ka-kira   abaana
        past   **there**-PAST-be man   **who**-SEQ-have children
        batatu
        three
        'Once upon a time there was a man who had three children...'

39) From Kimanyi (1976, 1980); see also discussion in Givón (1976b).

    d. kyeera **ha**-riho   abagabo batatu...   (INDEF subject,
        past   **there**-PAST-be men   three   plural)
        'There were once three men...'

While in official English the subject agreement distinction between 'was' (41c) and 'were' (41d) is presumably observed in existential clauses, in colloquial English neutralizations of such a distinction are common in such clauses, as in:

(42)   a. There's many things I need to tell you...
        b. There's lots of them who came over yesterday and...

Such a neutralization is grammatically coded in Israeli Hebrew via the neutral 'be' particle *yesh* which requires no subject agreement. Thus consider:

(43)   a. ha-ísh   hay-**á**   ba-báyit   (DEF subject,
          the-man   was-**he**   in-the-house   SG-MS)
          'The man was in the house'

        b. ha-ishá   hay-**tá**   ba-báyit   (DEF subject,
          the-woman   was-**she**   in-the-house   SG-FM)
          'The woman was in the house'

        c. ha-anashím   hay-**ú**   ba-báyit   (DEF subject, PL)
          the-men   were-**they**   in-the-house
          'The men were in the house'

        d. **yesh** ba-báyit   ísh-xad...   (INDEF SUBJ,
          be   in-the-house   man-one   SG-MS)
          'There's a man in the house...'

        e. **yesh** ba-báyit   harbé anashím...   (INDEF SUBJ,
          be   in-the-house   many   men   PL)
          'There're many men in the house...'

        f. **yesh** ba-báyit   ishá-axat...   (INDEF SUBJ,
          be   in-the-house   woman-one   SG-FM)
          'There's a woman in the house...'

The neutralization of grammatical agreement in existential-presentative constructions parallels the fact that the grammatical subject of 'be' in such constructions is *much less topical* than the more common definite subject.[40]

---

     40) It has been suggested above that agreement is a topic-based phenomenon. For further discussion see Givón (1976b).

10.7. INDEFINITE PRONOUNS

The phenomenon of indefinite pronouns is fundamentally rather different from that of definite/anaphoric pronouns discussed so far. While definite pronouns refer to NP's already introduced in prior discourse context as **referential**, indefinite pronouns seem to follow **non-referential** NP's. The sense in which indefinite pronouns "refer" to an antecedent NP is of course problematic, since while the indefinite pronoun itself may be referential, its antecedent NP is not. As illustration of this general situation, consider the following examples from English:

(44) a. John was looking for **the woman**, and he found **her**.
                               DEF-REF   DEF-REF

b. John was looking for **a woman**, and he found **her**.
                               INDEF-REF   DEF-REF

c. John was looking for **a woman**, and he found **one**.
                               NON-REF   REF-INDEF

In both (44a) and (44b) above the antecedent NP is referential, and in both it is referred to subsequently with a definite/anaphoric pronoun. In (44c), on the other hand, the antecedent NP is non-referential and its subsequent reference is via an indefinite pronoun — which nonetheless is referential. The problem of what the co-reference relation is in (44c) above will be further discussed in Chapter 11, below.

The use of the numeral 'one' in (44c) as an indefinite-referential pronoun does not necessarily tag 'one' as inherently either a referential or indefinite entity. As an illustration of this, consider the following examples from English:

(45) a. I don't know about **this one**.   **The one** I saw earlier was different.
              REF-DEF   REF-DEF

b. I don't know if **anyone** came. I saw **no one**.
              NON-REF   NON-REF

In (45a) 'one' is associated with definite/anaphoric pronominal expressions, while in (45b) it is associated with non-referential pronominal expressions.

While the use of 'one' as a pronoun — indefinite or anaphoric — is subject to a great deal of cross-linguistic, diachronically-derived variation, it is nonetheless a common usage. However, other grammatical devices may be used to code the very same function. For example, in languages which allow *zero* anaphoric pronouns, the zero may be also interpreted as indefinite or non-referential. For illustration we may consider the following from Israeli Hebrew, where zero object anaphora is common:

(46) a. *Question*: raíta   **oto**?   [DEF-REF antecedent]
          saw-you *ACC*-**him**
          'Did you see him?'

     b. *Response*: kén, raíti.   [zero anaphoric/definite
          yes   saw-I Ø   pronoun]
          'Yes, I saw (him)'

     c. *Question*: raíta   míshehu sham?   [NON-REF ante-
          saw-you anyone   there   cedent]
          'Did you see anyone there?'

     d. *Response*: kén, raíti.   [zero REF-INDEF pronoun]
          yes   saw-I Ø
          'Yes, I saw (someone)'

     e. *Response*: ló, lo-raíti.   [zero NON-REF pronoun]
          no   NEG-saw-I
          'No, I didn't see (anyone)'

Such zero anaphora is not unrestricted. For example, if the discourse context is not interrogative, but rather a declarative clause with a referential NP as the antecedent (either definite or indefinite) definite/anaphoric pronouns must be used subsequently, as in:

(47) a. **Hu** bá   le-shám, ve-axréy-xen **hu** azáv.
          he came-he to-there and-after-that **he** left-he
          'He came there, and later he left'

     b. bá   le-shám **ísh-xad**, ve-axréy-xen **hu** azáv
          came-he to-there **man-one** and-after-that **he** left
          'A man came over there, and later he left'

Indefinite pronouns seldom if ever cliticize onto the verbal word, since they are by definition discontinuous and low in topicality.[41] Depending on their diachronic origin, they may or may not display some of the features which underlie pronominal systems (cf. section 10.2, above). Being indefinite, they can never refer to speaker or hearer (which have definite refer-

---

41) See Chapter 22, Volume II, as well as Givón (1983a, b, c).

ence), but only to third persons. Nor can they display spatial deixis, which again involves definite reference. Number distinctions are possible in indefinite pronouns, as in English:

(48)   a.   I have *one*.
       b.   I have *some*.

In some languages both anaphoric and indefinite pronouns may combine some pronominal element plus a **classifier**, and in such a case the pronoun displays class/gender distinctions. As an illustration consider the following from Mandarin Chinese:[42]

(49)   a.   *Context*:   nǐ   xǐhuān nèi-běn shū   ma?   [DEF-REF
                         you like   that-CL book Q   antecedent]
                         'Do you like **that/the** book?'

       b.   *Response*: (wǒ) xǐhuān nèi-běn   [DEF pronoun
                         (I)   like   that-CL   with classifier]
                         'I like **thát one**'

       c.   *Context*:   nǐ   xiǎng-yào shū   ma?   [INDEF, NON-REF
                         you want   book Q   antecedent]
                         'Would you like **a/any** book?'

       d.   *Response*: (wǒ) xiǎng-yào yi-běn   [INDEF, NON-REF
                         (I)   want   one-CL   pronoun with classifier]
                         'I'd like **one**'

       e.   *Context*:   Did he buy **a hat**? [INDEF, NON-REF antecedent]

       f.   *Response*: (tā) mǎi-le   yi-ge   [INDEF, REF
                         (he) buy-ASP one-CL   pronoun with classifier]
                         'He bought **one**'

In Mandarin, there exists a whole set of noun classifiers, used most commonly in quantifying expressions.[43] In (49a) such a classifier combines with the demonstrative/article 'that', and in (49b) that combination is used as an emphatic definite pronoun. In (49d) the combination of 'one' and the classifier is used as a non-referential (indefinite) pronoun, and in (49f) the same combination is used as a referential-indefinite pronoun.

---

42) From C.N. Li (in personal communication), but see also Li and Thompson (1981).

43) The subject of numeral classifiers will be discussed in Chapter 12, Volume II. For a comprehensive discussion elsewhere, see Greenberg (1978).

10.8. NOUN CLASSIFIERS AND PRONOUNS

In section 10.7., above, we have seen an example from Mandarin
Chinese where class/gender morphemes existing in the language quite independently of the pronominal system have begun to invade the pronominal system, so that in combination with either definite demonstrative or the indefinite numeral 'one', the classifiers in fact form the basis of a class/gender distinction in the emergent pronominal system. The use of noun classifiers as
pronouns — with or without other augments — is also found elsewhere. Thus,
for example, Greenberg (1977) points out that the Bantu and Niger-Congo
noun-classifying morphemes, which appear as either prefixes, suffixes or
both are diachronically, of deictic-pronominal origin. A very early stage of
such a development is seen in Jacaltec (Mayan), where the classifiers are
transparently derived from noun stems and — without further augmentation
— are used as definite pronouns and definite articles. Thus consider:[44]

> (50) a. *Classifiers used as definite articles*:
>
> (i) xul   **naj** Pel   [**naj** = 'person']
>   came CL Peter
>   'Peter came'
>
> (ii) xpotx **ix**   Malin **no7** txitam   [**ix** = 'woman';
>   killed CL Mary CL pig   **no7** = 'animal']
>   'Mary killed the pig'
>
> b. *Classifiers used as definite pronouns*:
>
> (i) xul   **naj**
>   came CL
>   'He came'
>
> (ii) xpotx **ix**   **no7**
>   killed CL CL
>   'She killed it'

It is thus likely that noun classifiers are the diachronic source of all class/gen-
der features of pronouns, and that when the latter combine with deictic elements they yield class/gender inflected demonstrative pronouns. And either
one of the last two categories can give rise to definite articles. Schematically
these potentials may be summed up as:

---

44) See Craig (1982ms, 1977).

(51) CLASSIFIER → PRONOUN → DEF-ARTICLE
                      ↓
          DEICTIC-PRONOUN → DEF-ARTICLE

11 | DEFINITENESS AND REFERENTIALITY

11.1. INTRODUCTION

In a number of preceding chapters both definiteness and referentiality of nouns (or NP's) were discussed informally, in connection with related functional domains, such as topicality, modality or pronouns. In this chapter we will treat these two related topics more systematically. At least one of them, definiteness, must await full treatment later (Chapter 22, Volume II), since it is a member of a larger functional domain, that of **topic identification** ('topic continuity').[1] The discussion below will thus remain, to some extent, incomplete.

The treatment of both referentiality and definiteness in Linguistics has certain antecedents in philosophy and logic, ones which will be mentioned below, though not in full detail. There are sufficient grounds for believing that the philosophical tradition of treating both referentiality and definiteness is too restrictive to render a full account of the facts of human language, and some discussion of these issues will be found further below. Since referentiality is a narrower-scope phenomenon than definiteness, and since it can be described — at least under one reading — within the scope of sentential modality ('propositional modality'), it makes sense to deal with it first. Definiteness is clearly a discourse-scope phenomenon. To understand it, one must first understand the sentence-scoped phenomenon of referentiality. As we shall see later, eventually referentiality also exhibits some wide-scoped, discourse-dependent features.

11.2. REFERENTIALITY

11.2.1. Existence and reference: The logical tradition

In the logico-philosophical tradition, the modalities of propositions are

---

1) See details in Givón (ed. 1983a).

either "true", "false" or "possible", and these modalities map propositions onto The Real World, where the events or states expressed by those propositions either did take place at some particular time or did not. In a somewhat parallel fashion the nominal **arguments** ('participants', 'topics') in the proposition — be they subject, object etc. — are marked in various ways for their **referential scope** ('denotation') in The Real World. The so-called **existential quantifier** is used to indicate that an argument refers to a real, existing entity in The Real World. The so-called **universal quantifier** is used to indicate that an argument refers to all members/tokens of the group/type covered by the term. And under some conditions, the use of no quantifier may indicate lack of existence/reference in The Real World. Such a formulation is consistent with the logic-based view of language as a set of propositions about some world. It disregards the existence and role of both speaker and hearer in the communication. More narrowly, it also disregards the modal and referential *intent* of speakers vis-à-vis propositions and referents, respectively. As an illustration of a clean example of the use of the two quantifiers in logic, consider:

(1) a. 'Socrates is bald' = $\exists\,x, Sx, Bx = $ There exists an x;
$$\text{that x is Socrates;}$$
$$\text{that x is bald.}$$

 b. 'All Greeks are bald' = $\forall x, Gx \supset Bx = $ For all x,
$$\text{if x is Greek,}$$
$$\text{then x is bald}$$

There are a number of reasons why this logic-based traditional approach to referentiality cannot adequately describe the facts of natural language.[2]

(a) "The Real World" vs. the universe of discourse

The study of human language(s) suggests that reference relations are not a mapping of propositions or terms in a language onto The Real World, but rather a mapping from the language to some **Universe of Discourse**. This universe of discourse is constructed or negotiated between speaker and hearer, and communication then refers to states, events or individuals within that constructed world. It is of course true that this contingent universe of discourse often — and perhaps most commonly — coincides or overlaps with the logician's "Real World". But such overlap may be only partial, and at any rate

---

2) It is outside the scope of this chapter to discuss all the inadequacies of the logical tradition of reference. It is a huge subject that is yet to be confronted in full. For some suggestions, see Givón (1973b, 1982c).

it is not necessary in order for language to carry on its referential functions —
those pertaining to propositions as well as those pertaining to arguments.
Thus consider:

(2)   a. There was once **a white unicorn** *who* lived in the forest.
          He lived all by *him*self and Ø was rather lonely.
          One day *he* met a frog...

      b. There was once **a black horse** *who* lived in the forest.
          He lived all by *him*self and Ø was rather lonely.
          One day *he* met a frog...

The fact that in The Real World white unicorns presumably do not exist but
black horses do, makes little difference to the way natural languages construct
their grammar of propositional and nominal reference. Once a universe of discourse has been set up, reference proceeds in the same fashion regardless of
whether *nothing* in that universe ever existed in The Real World, *everything* in
it existed in The Real World, or of any other degree of overlap existing
between the two.

(b) The universal quantifier vs. non-referentiality

The only explicit way to mark arguments as non-referential in the logical
tradition is to "bind" them with the universal quantifier, thus making them
refer to *all* nouns covered by the term. But in human language non-referentiality may also involve **individuals** rather than the entire group. Further, non-
referentiality may also involve reference to neither individuals nor the entire
group, but rather the **attributive** use of a nominal argument.[3] As examples
consider:

(3)   a. *Generic non-referential*: **All teachers** are bald.
      b. *Individual non-referential*: I am looking for **a teacher**.
      c. *Attributive non-referential*: Joe is **a teacher**.

(c) Degrees of non-referentiality

In deductive logic, an argument either has or doesn't have reference in
The Real World. But human language has a number of peculiar expressions in
which the property of reference seems to be *graded*. Thus consider:[4]

---

3) For considering this problem within the logical tradition itself, without necessarily challeng-
ing the adequacy of the entire tradition, see Donellan (1966).

4) For more discussion see further below, as well as Givón (1982c).

(4)   a. If you see **the man** with a green hat there, tell him...
       b. If you see **a man** with a green hat there, tell him...
           (i) *Referential*: I have such a man in mind, and if you see **him**...
           (ii) *Non-referential*: I don't have any particular man in mind, so
                     if you see **one**...
       c. If you see **someone** with a green hat there, tell **him/them**...
       d. If you see **anybody** with a green hat there, tell **them**...

There is a clear gradation from (4a) through (4d), so that (4a) is clearly referential, (4b) may or may not be, (4c) is less likely but still could, and (4d) is
least likely to refer to any specific individual.

(d) **Speaker's referential intent**
     In the logical tradition of reference, the relation of reference involves no
consideration of the speaker's **referential intent**. But the examples in (4)
above already suggest that the speaker's "intent to refer to some individual" is
an important component in understanding referentiality in human language.
This facet of referentiality in language is related to the fact that reference involves the universe of discourse (rather than the real world). Unlike in logic,
in human language speakers and hearers **negotiate** the scope of the particular
universe they talk about, and also establish the identities of individuals ('arguments') they **intend** to take for granted as existing within that universe. Thus,
the ambiguity — in human language — of (4b) above is not a matter of
whether "a man with a green hat" exists in some Real World, but rather
whether the speaker *has in mind* some particular individual answering to that
description, whether he "intends that individual as referential".

(e) **Individual reference and propositional modalities**
     The logical tradition of reference is silent on the systematic connection
between **referential modalities** of arguments and **truth modalities** of propositions. But as we shall see below, such systematic connection does indeed exist
in human language.

(f) **Discourse-pragmatics of referentiality**
     In the logical tradition of reference, referentiality is a purely **semantic**
property, not transcending the scope of individual propositions. But as we
shall see later, in human language referentiality shades in a systematic way
into discourse-pragmatics, where notions such as "importance" and "relevance" pervade the grammar of reference in ways that are, in principle, im-
penetrable to traditional logical analysis.

11.2.2. Fact, non-fact and reference

In Chapters 8 (section 8.2.6.) and 9 (section 9.1.), as well as in Chapter 7 (section 7.4.) above, we discussed propositional modalities in natural language, outlining four major modalities:

(a) Presupposition
(b) Realis-assertion
(c) NEG-assertion
(d) Irrealis-assertion

For the purpose of defining the relation between propositional modalities and the referential modes of nominal arguments, it is possible — and in some contexts also desirable — to collapse the four propositional modalities into two larger modal categories:

(i)   *FACT*: Presupposition, realis-assertion
(ii) *NON-FACT*: Irrealis-assertion, NEG-assertion

The necessary relation between propositional and nominal modalities can now be expressed as follows:

(5)   "Under the scope of the propositional modality FACT, nominal arguments can only be **referential**. On the other hand, under the scope of the propositional modality NON-FACT, nominal arguments can be also **non-referential**".[5]

Let us illustrate this necessary relation between propositional and nominal modalities with clear, prototypical instances of FACT and NON-FACT:

(6)   a. *FACT, presupposition*:
        Mary regretted that she saw **an eagle**
        [⊃ Mary saw a *particular* eagle, one that the speaker
        is committed to assert: "it did exist"]

      b. *FACT, realis-assertion*:
        Mary saw **an eagle**
        [⊃ Mary saw a *particular* eagle, one that the speaker
        is committed to assert: "it did exist"]

---

5) In chapter 9, section 9.6., we have already seen that under the scope of NEG-assertion indefinite nominal arguments can *only* be non-referential, while under the scope of irrealis-assertion they can be either referential or non-referential.

 c. *NON-FACT, irrealis-assertion*:
  Mary will see **an eagle**
  (i) [⊃ Mary will see a *particular* eagle, one that the speaker
   is committed to assert: "it does exist"]
  (ii)[⊃ The speaker is *not* committed to assert that Mary
   will see a *particular* eagle, but only that she may see
   some member of the type 'eagle']

 d. *NON-FACT, NEG-assertion*:
  Mary did not see **an eagle**
   [⊃ There was no particular eagle such that "Mary saw
   it"]

There are grounds for believing that in human language the modality of
FACT is the **unmarked**, neutral propositional modality, the one taken for
granted. In contrast, the modality of NON-FACT is the **marked** one, the one
that requires explicit specification. We have, in fact, already dealt with the
basis for such an assumption at two distinct points earlier. First, we noted in
Chapter 8, above, arguments based on both discourse-pragmatics and percep-
tion/cognition that IRREALIS-assertion is the marked case in human language, while REALIS-assertion is the neutral, unmarked case. And second,
we noted in Chapter 9, above, that for reasons of both discourse pragmatics
and cognitive saliency, NEG-assertions are the marked case in human language while the affirmative assertions are the neutral, unmarked case. Once
these assumptions concerning the markedness of propositional modalities are
granted, they have three important consequences:

(7) a. *Markedness of nominal modalities*: The modality **referential** is
  the general, unmarked case for nominal arguments; while the
  modality **non-referential** is the restricted, marked case.

 b. *Order of specification of propositional modalities*: It should be
  easier — more economical, more natural — to specify explicitly
  the various **non-fact** propositional modalities in human language, and then assume that the modality **fact** prevails
  elsewhere.

 c. *Order of specification of nominal modalities*: Similarly, it
  should be more economical and more natural to specify
  explicitly the array of linguistic ('grammatical', 'pragmatic') environments where the nominal modality **non-referential** may
  appear, and then assume that the modality **referential** will appear elsewhere.

Consequence (7a) arises directly from the necessary interrelation between propositional and nominal modalities, as expressed in (5), (6) above. Consequence (7b) is a practical outcome of the marked status of *non-fact* vis-à-vis *fact* in both grammar and discourse. And consequence (7c) is the outcome of (7a) and (7b) when taken together.

11.2.3. Non-fact modalities and non-referential nominals

11.2.3.1 Tense-aspects

Of the four major tenses — past, present, future and habitual — two behave like non-fact modalities vis-à-vis the referentiality of nominal arguments under their scope — *future* and *habitual*. Thus consider:

(8) *Future*: a. John will read **the book**   (REF, DEF)
             b. John will read **a book**   (INDEF)
                 (i) There's a book, and John will read **it** (REF, INDEF)
                 (ii) John'll read **some** book,   (NON-REF, INDEF)
                     no matter which

(9) *Habitual*: a. John always reads **the same book**   (REF, DEF)
               b. John always carries with him **a book**   (INDEF)
                 (i) ...that his mother gave him   (REF, INDEF)
                 (ii) ...of some sort or another (NON-REF, INDEF)

11.2.3.2. The scope of non-implicative verbs

Most transitive verbs, when not under the explicit scope of a non-fact modality, imply the existence of their objects. For example:

(10) John found **a book** ⊃ There's a specific book that John found

A small group of verbs, such as 'want', 'look for', 'imagine' or 'dream', do not imply the existence of a specific object. These are the so-called "world-creating" verbs, and they behave just like an irrealis/non-fact modality with respect to the reference properties of object nominals under their scope. Thus consider:

(11) a. John is looking for **the book**   (REF, DEF)
      b. John is looking for **a book**...   (INDEF)
          (i) ...that his mother gave him   (REF, INDEF)
          (ii) ...on physics; any physics book will do (NON-REF, INDEF)

11.2.3.3. The scope of complements of non-implicative verbs

As we have seen in Chapter 4 above, both modality and manipulation verbs may be either implicative or non-implicative with respect to the truth mode of their sentential complements. When a modality verb is **implicative**, it imposes the **fact** modality on its complement, and within that complement then nominals can only be referential (unless another non-fact modality intervenes). Thus consider:

    (12)   a.   John managed to eat a hamburger ⊃ John ate a hamburger
            b.   John managed to eat **the hamburger**   (REF, DEF)
            c.   John managed to eat **a hamburger**   (INDEF)
               (i)   John ate a *specific* hamburger   (REF, INDEF)
              (ii) *John ate some *non-specific*   (*NON-REF, INDEF)
                   hamburger

Under the scope of a **non-implicative** modality verb, however, a non-referential argument in the complement is possible. Thus consider:

    (13)   a.   John wanted to eat a hamburger ≠ John ate a hamburger
            b.   John wanted to eat **the hamburger**   (REF, DEF)
             c.   John wanted to eat **a hamburger**   (INDEF)
               (i)   ...that his wife packed for him   (REF, INDEF)
              (ii) ...any one, so long as it was big   (NON-REF, INDEF)

The same holds for the complements of manipulative verbs. When the verb is **implicative**, it imposes a **fact** modality on its complement, and within that complement one cannot then get a non-referential nominal (unless another non-fact modality intervenes). As illustration consider:

    (14)   a.   Mary made John eat a hamburger ⊃ John ate a hamburger
            b.   Mary made John eat **the hamburger**   (REF, DEF)
             c.   Mary made John eat **a hamburger**   (INDEF)
               (i)   There was a *specific* hamburger that John ate (REF, INDEF)
              (ii) *John ate some *non-specific*   (*NON-REF, INDEF)
                   hamburger

Under the scope of **non-implicative** manipulation verbs, on the other hand, non-referential arguments in the complement are possible, as in:

    (15)   a.   Mary told John to eat a hamburger ≠ John ate a hamburger
            b.   Mary told John to eat **the hamburger**   (REF, DEF)
             c.   Mary told John to eat **a hamburger**...   (INDEF)
               (i)   ...that she cooked for him   (REF, INDEF)
               (ii) ...a big one, if he could find one (NON-REF, INDEF)

11.2.3.4. The scope of complements of non-factive verbs

Factive verbs impose the **fact** modality on their sentential complements, and thus bar non-referential nominals from the complement. As an example consider:

(16) a. She regretted that he read a letter ⊃ He read a letter

     b. She regretted that he read **the letter** (REF, DEF)

     c. She regretted that he read **a letter** ... (INDEF)

        (i) ...she sent him a year before (REF, INDEF)

        (ii) *...be it any letter (*NON-REF, INDEF)

Non-factive verbs, on the other hand, impose the **non-fact** modality on their complements, and under that scope non-referential nominals may indeed appear, as in:

(17) a. She thought that he read a letter ⊅ He read a letter

     b. She thought that he read **the letter** (REF, DEF)

     c. She thought that he read **a letter**... (INDEF)

        (i) ...that she sent him (REF, INDEF)

        (ii) ...,though it was a book (NON-REF, INDEF)

11.2.3.5. The scope of modal operators

Probabilistic modal operators such as 'can', 'may', 'must', 'should', 'might', 'would' etc. and their adverbial counterparts such as 'maybe', 'possibly', 'probably', 'surely', 'likely', 'supposedly' etc. all impose the non-fact ('irrealis') modality on the entire proposition they operate on, so that nominals within that proposition may be non-referential. Thus consider:

(18) a. John may have read **the book** (REF, DEF)

     b. John may have read **a book**...

        (i) ...that Sally gave him last year (REF, INDEF)

        (ii) ...or two in his life (NON-REF, INDEF)

(19) a. Maybe John read **the book** (REF, DEF)

     b. Maybe John read **a book**...

        (i) ...that Sally gave him last year (REF, INDEF)

        (ii) ...or two in his life (NON-REF, INDEF)

11.2.3.6. The scope of negation

As we have seen in Chapter 9, above, negation as a **non-fact** modality allows non-referential nominals under its scope — but disallows referential-indefinite nominals. As an illustration of this again, consider:

(20) a. She didn't read **the book**   (REF, DEF)
    b. She didn't read **a book**   (INDEF)
      *(i) A book existed but she didn't read **it**   (*REF, INDEF)
      (ii) There was no book that she read   (NON-REF, INDEF)

11.2.3.7. The scope of irrealis adverbial clauses

Simple conditional clauses, being future oriented, constitute a **non-fact** modality and thus allow non-referential nominals under their scope, as in:

(21) a. If John finds **the book**,...   (REF, DEF)
    b. If John finds **a book** ...   (INDEF)
      (i) ..., even if it is long, ...   (NON-REF, INDEF)
    ?(ii) ...that he's been looking for all day long,... (?REF, INDEF)

While non-referential nominals are admissible in conditional clauses, it is not clear whether referential-indefinite ones are, and it may well be that irrealis conditional clauses impose the same pragmatic-based restriction — i.e. by barring referential-indefinites — as does negation.[6]

11.2.3.8. Nominal predicates

Nominal predicates (cf. Chapter 4, section 4.2.2., above) may be either referential or non-referential. As illustration consider:

(22) a. John is **the teacher** I told you about   (REF, DEF)
    b. John is **a teacher** I met last year   (REF, INDEF)
    c. John is a **teacher** (by profession)   (NON-REF, INDEF)

The non-referential usage in (22c) is sometimes called "attributive".[7]

11.2.3.9. Non-declarative speech-acts

Both **imperative** and **interrogative** speech acts are manipulative in nature, and this means, among other things, that they are "future projecting" with respect to the expected response from the manipulee. This "future projection" amounts, in fact, to an **irrealis** modality, and thus a **non-fact** modality under which the relevant proposition falls. Let us illustrate this first with imperative constructions and their more subtle variants. For the prototypical im-

---

6) If correct, this restriction is due to the discourse-pragmatic *topical* status of conditionals (and perhaps other adverbial clauses), see Haiman (1978).

7) See Donellan (1966).

perative, consider:[8]

(23) a. Go get me **the book** at the bottom of the stack   (REF, DEF)
   b. Go get me **a book** about physics that Mary   (REF, INDEF)[9]
    left for me at the desk downstairs
   c. Go get me **a book** on physics,   (NON-REF, INDEF)
    a good one please

More polite, toned-down or indirect manipulations exhibit the same distribution of nominal modalities:

(24) a. Would you please get me **the book**   (REF, DEF)
   b. Would you please get me **a book** that Mary left
    for me downstairs at the desk   (REF, INDEF)
   c. Would you please get me **a book** on physics,
    a good one if possible   (NON-REF, INDEF)

In yes-no questions one finds a similar distribution:

(25) a. Have you seen **that movie**?   (REF, DEF)
   b. Have you seen **a movie** called "Inserts"?   (REF, INDEF)
   c. Have you seen **a good movie** lately?   (NON-REF, INDEF)

Finally, the same situation holds for WH-questions, as in:

(26) a. Who saw **that movie**?   (REF, DEF)
   b. Who here has seen **a movie** called "Inserts"? (REF, INDEF)
   c. Who here has seen **a good movie** lately? (NON-REF, INDEF)

11.3. DEFINITENESS

11.3.1. Preliminaries

We have been dealing so far with definite NP's and definiteness infor-

---

8) For a discussion of non-declarative speech acts and prototypical imperatives, see Chapter 20, Volume II, as well as Givón (1983e).

9) It is not clear whether the referential-indefinite option in imperatives is ever exercised, and it is likely that the same restriction seen under the scope of negation (see 11.2.3.6. above as well as Chapter 9) is also evident here. That is, that a referential nominal under the scope of IMPERA-TIVE could only be definite. In other words, a sentence such as (23b) is highly unlikely to occur in text, but rather its equivalent is more likely to occur: "There's *a book* about physics that Mary left for me at the desk downstairs; go get *it* for me". Thus, referential-indefinite nouns are first introduced into the discourse under a normal *declarative* scope, then referred to in the imperative as *definite* (anaphoric pronoun).

mally, in earlier discussions of reference, anaphoric pronouns, demonstratives and so on. It would be easy now to give a first approximation of a more explicit treatment. As will become obvious later, such a first approximation must remain incomplete until definiteness is discussed in its proper — wider — context, i.e. in the context of its larger functional domain of **topic continuity in discourse** (cf. Chapter 22, Volume II). Such further elaboration on the subject will not detract from the inherent correctness of the more restricted treatment here, but simply will expand and amplify the details.

11.3.2. Shared knowledge, exact reference and definite description

In earlier logic-bound philosophical treatments (cf. Russell, 1905, 1919; Carnap, 1947, 1959, *inter alia*), there was no clear separation between "definite" and "having exact reference". This was due to the fact that the formalization of language did not allow for notions such as "speaker", "hearer", "communicative intent" or "discourse context". The referential reading of a definite nominal was freely translated by the existential quantifier, as in the celebrated example:

(27)   **The king** of France is bald = There is **a king** in France, (REF, INDEF)
            and **he** is bald   (REF, DEF)

As we noted in Chapter 7, above, this concept of definiteness is plainly incompatible with the facts of natural language, where (27) never **asserts** the existence of the king of France, but only **presupposes** that the speaker already shares the knowledge of that existence. And in fact, later versions of logic-based approaches to natural language (cf. Strawson, 1951) did recognize this problem and attempted to deal with it within the general framework of presupposition. As we also suggested in Chapter 7, the framework of presupposition by itself, so long as it remained within purely semantic bounds (that is, pertaining to relations between propositions or to the speaker's own modal or referential intent regardless of the hearer), is incapable of dealing with the facts of natural language and its use in communication. To replace that framework, we suggested one involving the **communicative contract**, through which speakers can assume that hearers either know or are unwilling to challenge, for whatever reason, a certain proposition. It is within this framework that we will treat **definiteness** as a sub-species of referentiality. One seeming exception to this, involving definite-marked **generic nominals**, will be discussed under a separate heading later.

11.3.3. Grounds for assuming the assignment of unique reference

In section 11.2., above, we made an informal distinction between two kinds of referential nominals: **Definite** and **indefinite**. The two may now be defined a bit more rigorously in terms of the communicative contract:

(28) *Indefinite*: "Speakers code a referential nominal as indefinite if they think that they are *not* entitled to assume that the hearer can — by whatever means — assign it unique referential identity".

   Definite: "Speakers code a referential nominal as definite if they think that they are entitled to assume that the hearer can — by whatever means — assign it unique reference".

There are a number of grounds on which the speaker may assume that the hearer is capable of assigning unique reference to nominals mentioned in the discourse by the speaker. We will deal first with those that are relatively independent of the specific discourse.

11.3.3.1. Definiteness arising from the permanent file

(a) Referentially unique physical or cultural entities

Presumably entities like "the sun", "the moon", "the earth", "the world", "Venus" etc. are uniquely identifiable to members of all human cultures. In the same vein, geographic entities may be permanently filed by members of smaller communities, entities such as "the mountain", "the pine tree", "the lake", "the spring", "city hall" etc. In principle, the size of the group is an irrelevant consideration, and could go as low as two individuals.

Permanently-filed referents may be culturally-shared non-physical items, be they of a spiritual nature ("The Great Spirit"), political ("The Senate", "The President", "The Flag"), artistic ("The Met", "Willie Nelson"), festive ("Walpurgisnacht") etc. Again, the size of the group is immaterial so long as both speaker and hearer share its conventions. As long as the group is relatively stable,[10] the assumption of **referential accessibility** via the permanent file holds.

(b) Proper names

Names of persons, locations etc. may be viewed as entries in the perma-

---

10) Relative stability of a group may be expressed in terms of stable *membership* or, more relevant here, in terms of stable *concepts* and conceptual networks.

nent file, again with various degrees of generality vis-à-vis the group which shares them as unique referents.

11.3.3.2. Definites arising from immediate deictic availability

(a) Absolute deictic availability

In any communication ('discourse') the referential uniqueness of two participating entities is taken for granted:

(a) "I", the speaker; and
(b) "you", the hearer.

In addition, various other entities may acquire referential uniqueness via their association with the speaker or hearer. Such an association may be purely *contingent*, as in the use of spatial deictic demonstrative ("this", "that", "here", "there"). But it may also involve various shades of permanence due to a mix of either physical or cultural considerations. Thus for example, "my head", "my arms", "my heart" etc. are uniquely referential because

(a) "I" is uniquely referential; and
(b) Physically a human has only one head, one heart, two arms etc.

The same blend of considerations also accounts for the unique reference of "my mother", "my father", "my ex-wife" etc.

Less biological/objective and more culturally-dependent are uniquely referring expressions such as "my house", "my job", "my reputation" etc. But again their uniqueness derives from the same joint sources described above.

(b) Relative or contingent deictic availability

Once a nominal has been mentioned in ('entered into') the discourse, i.e. one that refers to neither the speaker nor the hearer, referents associated with it, such as body parts, kin relations or culturally-based possessions, acquire the same kind of unique reference as referents associated with "I" or "you". Thus, "his mother", "her head", "their house" etc. are uniquely referential due to the same blend of sources.

A similar uniqueness is conferred upon unique **parts of wholes**, once the whole has been entered into the discourse. Thus, once *a house* has been mentioned, "the door", "the kitchen", "the living-room", "the dining-room" etc. gain unique reference through the same blend of sources. Similarly, once *a car* has been mentioned, "the trunk", "the wheel", "the brakes" etc. are uniquely referential through the same conventions.

11.3.3.3. Definites arising from the specific discourse file

So far we have dealt with establishing unique reference on grounds that are relatively independent of the *contents* of a specific discourse. Such discourse-independent unique reference sprang either from what is obvious/accessible in the immediate **deictic context**, or what is available/accessible from the **permanent file** subscribed to by all members of the culture. Claiming the existence of such a permanent file presupposes some cognitive-based assumptions about **permanent memory** and data-base organization in the brain, assumptions we will not discuss here in any detail. Having cleared the ground of deictic and generic availability of unique reference, we now turn to deal with the most interesting — and grammatically/structurally most relevant — source of unique reference, the one emanating from the contents of specific communications, that is, from the actual information passed from speaker to hearer.

11.3.4. Definites, indefinites and the active discourse file

11.3.4.1. Permanent vs. active file

As suggested above, the permanent file stores shared background knowledge held by all members of the culture/group. Its bulk is **generic**, containing the shared **lexicon**. But it also stores some permanently-filed **specific** referents.

In contrast, the **active file** (also called 'the discourse file' or 'the discourse register') is the knowledge file maintained by speakers/hearers for the purpose of producing and interpreting a *particular* discourse as it is being transacted. It again contains both propositional and referential information. And it overlaps with the permanent file in two obvious ways:

(a)   Specific information communicated in the discourse may eventually find its way into the permanent file (cf. Chapter 7, section 7.8., above); and

(b)   Within the reference-related portion of the active file, terms from the permanent file referring to unique individuals have the same status — in terms of assumptions speakers may make about what hearers know — as terms referring to unique individuals entered into the file through the specific discourse.

Clause (b) above allows for **automatic access** between the two files, so far as their reference-related portions are concerned. Once such a provision of cross-file access is made, the foundations of the phenomenon of definiteness in human language have been laid, whereby the unifying principle is that of assumed **referential accessibility**.

11.3.4.2. Referential accessibility: Entering and re-entering the discourse

When the speaker mentions a referential entity ('topic', 'argument') for the *first* time in a particular discourse, he can make one of two assumptions about the hearer's ability to uniquely identify that referent (see (28) above):

(a)   The hearer *can* assign unique identity to the referent, due either to referential accessibility from the permanent file or deictic accessibility given the immediate discourse context (cf. the various clauses of section 11.3.3., above). Under such an assumption, the speaker will code the referent as **definite**; or

(b)   The hearer *cannot* assign unique identity to the referent. Under such an assumption the speaker will code the referent as **referential indefinite**.

Once the indefinite referent has been entered into the active file, the speaker can then go on and assume — at least for a certain time span during the same discourse — that it is uniquely identifiable to the hearer. And during that period, in all subsequent mentions, the speaker may code the referent as **definite**.

While morpho-syntactically **referential-indefinite topics** tend to be uniformly coded — by *one* grammatical device — whenever they enter into the active file, **definite topics** are coded in all languages by a wide variety of means. This is due to the fact that the grammar of all languages systematically clues the hearer not only about whether he is expected to identify the topic, but also about the *extent* of that **topic's accessibility**, the *source* of that accessibility and often the rough *location* within the specific discourse where the topic may be accessed. Thus, for example, a *name* clues the speaker to search for the identity of a definite within the permanent file. A *spatial deictic* ('this') would clue a search in the immediate environment, a *deictic pronoun* ('I', 'you') would clue identification of either speaker or hearer, etc. But if the clue indicates access neither in the permanent file nor in the immediate deictic environment, the chances are that it supplies clues to the accessibility of the information within the specific discourse — i.e. a search through the **active file**.

As an illustration of some of the definite grammatical devices used to mark a topic re-entering the discourse from the active file, consider the following simple example, in which the first entry and then various re-entries of one referent are traced:

(29) a. Once there was **a king**; (REF-INDEF, subject)
    b. **he** lived in a big castle (DEF, anaphoric pronoun, subject)
    c. and **Ø** loved to fish for trout. (DEF, zero anaphora, subject)
    d. **He** had a queen, (DEF, anaphoric pronoun, subject)
    e. and she bore **him** two sons. (DEF, anaphoric pronoun, object)
    f. She also bore **him** a daughter, (DEF, anaphoric pronoun, object)
    g. but otherwise stayed in the kitchen, (absence)
    h. supervised the cooks, (absence)
    i. scolded the maids (absence)
    j. and watched the children grow. (absence)
    k. One day **the king** decided... (DEF, full NP)

The decision as to which definite device to use hinges on considerations of topical or thematic **continuity** ('predictability'). The full details of this complex functional domain in the grammar will be described in Chapter 22, Volume II.[11] But even a cursory look at (29) could reveal some apparent generalizations. Thus, for example, the assignment of subject vs. object role has something to do with the **importance** of the topic. Zero anaphora requires the shortest referential distance to the left — one clause — plus most commonly subjecthood. Pronouns are used over short referential distances — much like zero anaphora — but when the **thematic continuity** is not quite as high. And full definite NP's (cf. (29k)) are used after a considerable gap of absence.

11.3.4.3. Time-span of the active file

We have already noted above that referential entities entered in the permanent file, as well as those which are deictically available from the immediate environment, are in some sense permanent members of *any* **active discourse file**. In addition, one must note that it is likely that other referents entered into the active files via a *particular* discourse may vary in terms of the degree of their **time stability** within the file. While much research needs to be done yet in this area, most of it psycho-linguistic in nature, a number of factors can be singled out:

    (a) *File size or discourse size*: If the discourse ('communication') is very short, and if therefore the number of topics/referents in it is rather small, then presumably none of them undergo appreciable **decay** during the short life-span of the particular file. On the other hand,

---

11) For further details, already available in print, see Givón (1983a, b, c).

if the discourse is long and the total number of referents/topics in it is large, more of them are likely to get lost — in time — from the memory capacity charged with maintaining the active file. Due to that loss, they will be treated — upon re-entry into the discourse — as new *indefinites* entering into the file for the first time.

(b) *Degree of structural specificity of the file*: All other things being equal, the more well-structured an active file is — most likely in terms of the **thematic structure** of the discourse — the longer individual referents are likely to persist in the memory capacity charged with maintaining the file. This suggestion has much empirical support from the study of discourse comprehension and episodic memory of *propositions*, although so far not of referents.[12]

(c) *Degree of importance/centrality of a referent in the discourse*: Some topics/referents are more important or central to the discourse, either in terms of their *relevance* to the major theme(s) or in terms of their frequency of appearance ('continuity', 'persistence') in the discourse. These two aspects — thematic importance and discourse frequency — are obviously related but can be discussed independently.[13] One would then expect that more central topics will remain in the active file longer than less central ones.

11.3.4.4. Integrated flow-diagram of referential accessibility

Given what has been said above concerning the permanent file, the deictic source of unique reference and the active discourse file, one can now summarize the relation between the referentially-relevant portions of the three sources for establishing unique reference in the following flow-diagram:

---

12) See in particular Mandler and Johnson (1977), Mandler (1978), Johnson and Mandler (1980), Mandler and Goodman (1982), Kintsch and van Dijk (1978), *inter alia*.

13) For example, throughout the play "Waiting for Godot", Godot — clearly in some sense a central character - never appears on stage, nor does he persist or recur much in the discourse. Nonetheless, his survival in the active file is assured.

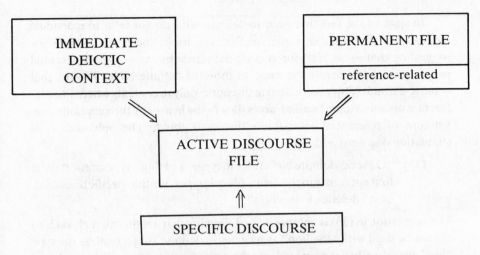

The three sources of information — both referential and propositional — feeding into the active discourse file can be viewed as the three **contexts** for communication.

11.3.5. Generic definites

There is a certain tradition in linguistics — which has most likely arisen because of the relative paucity of quantifiers in logic and thus the lack of distinction in logic between "non-referential" and "generic" — which assumes that **definite generic** nominals are non-referential in the same sense discussed in section 11.2. above. As an illustration of generic-definites, consider:

(30)	a.	**The lion** is dangerous	(GEN-DEF, SUBJ)
	b.	All animals fear **the lion**	(GEN-DEF, OBJ)

There are, obviously, reasons for treating GEN-DEF nominals as non-referential, mostly the fact that they do not refer to any particular individual, but rather to *all members* of the type — or to the *type* itself. Before going further, note that a similar meaning may be coded either with **generic-plurals**, as in:

(31)	a.	**Lions** are dangerous	(GEN-PL, SUBJ)
	b.	All animals fear **lions**	(GEN-PL, OBJ)

or with the **universal quantifier:**[14]

(32)	a.	**All lions** are dangerous	(QUANT-PL, SUBJ)
	b.	Animals fear **all lions**	(QUANT-PL, OBJ)

---

14) The use of "all" as the quantifier creates additional problems of potential ambiguity with which we will not concern ourselves at this point.

In spite of the fact that generic-definite NP's do not refer to individual members of the type but rather to the type itself, there are grounds for suggesting that — at least for generic-definite subjects — their referential properties are inherently the same as those of definite NP's. That is, that generic-definite subjects are used in discourse only in contexts where their referent is assumed to be **familiar/accessible to the hearer** by the very same conventions of referential accessibility discussed above. The only additional stipulation one must add is this:

(33)   "Generic-definite NP's refer to *types*, and those types must thus be first entered into the active file *qua types*, via the specific discourse, or via deictic obviousness".[15]

The suggestion in (33) is another way of claiming that a sentence such as (30a) cannot be used with "the lion" as its generic-definite subject unless the type "lion" had already been entered into the active file. In other words, we do not make generic statements such as (30a) unless the topic "lions" has already been pre-established — by whatever means. Dictionary definitions are not pronounced in the abstract, but rather in the context of searching for a particular *type* to be defined.

The confusion arises through a mix-up in meta-levels. The most common reference — and definite description — in human language indeed pertains to members of the **universe of tokens**. But reference and definite description may on occasion pertain also to members of the **universe of types**, within which each type behaves, referentially, like tokens do within their universe of tokens. As we shall see later, many languages mark generic subjects systematically as definite, and in others it is one coding option. And this option is too widespread cross-linguistically to be a mere accident.

11.4. MORPHO-SYNTACTIC CODING OF DEFINITENESS AND REFERENTIALITY

11.4.1. Preliminaries

In the preceding sections we treated referentiality and definiteness as two separate issues, one essentially semantic, the other discourse-pragmatic. Such

---

15) Whether the third venue of access to the active file, from the permanent file, is relevant in this case remains to be seen. For one thing, *all* types are stored in the permanent file, as items in the lexicon. For another, it is not clear under what condition one lexical item would be more accessible/ retrievable from the lexicon than another, except via specific instances of priming, which would then presumably constitute entry via a specific discourse.

a clear separation is to some extent over-simplified, a subject to which we will return later. When one looks at the morpho-syntactic coding of definiteness and referentiality, the somewhat arbitrary nature of an absolute separation between the two becomes even clearer. This is because at the coding level one most commonly finds a shaded gradation from one sub-system into the other. This gradation may be described on a linear scale, as in:

(34)   DEFINITE > REF-INDEFINITE > NON-REFERENTIAL > GENERIC

The morpho-syntactic evidence supporting this scale has to do with the fact that in many languages, regardless of the coding-density they employ along this continuum/scale, coding devices are used to code *contiguous sections* of the scale. Very seldom do they leap over sections or create gaps. Thus, one language may code DEF and REF-INDEF with the same marker. Another may code REF-INDEF and NON-REF INDEF with the same marker. Another may code NON-REF INDEF and GENERIC with the same marker. And finally (cf. section 11.3.5., above), a language may also code GENERIC and DEF the same way. This last fact raises the possibility of re-formulating the linear scale in (34) as a helical *hoop*:[16]

(35)

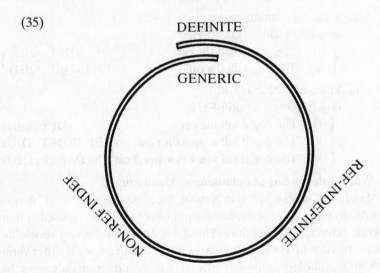

16) The hoop — or wheel — formulation wa. developed jointly with Derek Bickerton (in personal communication), and was presented first in Givón (1978). The discussion in section 11.3.5. above makes it clear, however, that the closure of the hoop — i.e. the overlap of *generic* and *definite* — is not on the same meta-level ('plane') but rather on two adjacent meta-levels. That is, REF-DEF pertains to the universe of tokens, while GEN-DEF pertains to the universe of types, one meta-level above. Such helix-like looping is of course reminiscent of Hegelian dialectics, where synthesis is presumably on a "higher level".

While it is perhaps premature to suggest a firm typology of coding definiteness and referentiality, one can distinguish between major and minor typological themes. We will begin by discussing the major themes and languages that exemplify them.

11.4.2. Morphologically undifferentiated coding: Newari

In Newari (Sino-Tibetan) the demonstratives "this" and "that" may be optionally used to code definites, and the numeral "one" may be occasionally used to code referential indefinites. But it is quite possible to dispense with such morphology altogether and use the bare forms of the nouns — with their case-markers — for definites, ref-indefinites, non-referentials and generics. As an example consider:[17]

(36) a. tebul-e   kạp du   (REF-INDEF, SUBJ)
          table-LOC   cup be
          'There's **a cup** on the table'

      b. kạp tebul-e   du   (DEF, SUBJ)
          cup table-LOC   be
          '**The cup** is on the table'

      c. khica-nạ   bhatu syat-ạ
          dog-ERG   cat   kill-PERF
          $\Big\{$ (i) 'The dog killed **the cat**'   (DEF, OBJ) $\Big\}$
          $\Big\{$ (ii) 'The dog killed **a cat**'   (REF-INDEF, OBJ) $\Big\}$

      d. khica-nạ   bhatu syat-i
          dog-ERG   cat   kill-FUT
          $\Big\{$ (i)   'The dog'll kill **the cat**'   (DEF, OBJ) $\Big\}$
          $\Big\{$ (ii)   'The dog'll kill **a (specific) cat**'   (REF-INDEF, OBJ) $\Big\}$
          $\Big\{$ (iii) 'The dog'll kill **some (unspec.) cat**' (NON-REF, OBJ) $\Big\}$

11.4.3. Word-order coding of definiteness: Mandarin

In Mandarin Chinese, just as in Newari, the demonstrative "that" may be used optionally to code definites, and the numeral "one" may be used optionally to code referential-indefinites. These constitute a relatively recent development. In a diachronically-older layer of the language, word-order variation without morphology is used to differentiate definite from indefinite. No further means are provided for differentiating referential from non-referen-

---

17) From my own field notes, originally due to Harsha Dhaubhadel (in personal communication).

tial indefinites. As illustration consider:[18]

(37) a. kèrén lái   le   (SV, DEF, SUBJ)
        guest come ASP
        'The guest(s) arrived'

     b. lái   kèrén le   (VS, REF-INDEF, SUBJ)
        come guest(s) ASP
        'A guest/some guests arrived'

     c. wǒ yīnyuè tīng le   (OV, DEF, OBJ)
        I   music listen ASP
        'I listened to the music'

     d. wǒ tīng le   yīnyuè   (VO, REF-INDEF, OBJ)
        I listen ASP music
        'I listened to (some) music'

     e. wǒ yào tā dǎ-pò   zh'uāngzi
        I   want he hit-broken window

$$\left\{\begin{array}{l}\text{(i) 'I want him to break \textbf{a (specific) window}'} \\ \qquad\qquad\qquad\qquad\text{(VO, REF-INDEF, OBJ)} \\ \text{(ii) 'I want him to break \textbf{some (unspec.) window}'} \\ \qquad\qquad\qquad\qquad\text{(VO, NON-REF, OBJ)}\end{array}\right.$$

11.4.4. Word-order coding of topicality: Ute

Definiteness and topicality are of course closely related, since, all other things being equal, a definite NP is a more **continuous** topic, one already entered in the active file. An indefinite-referential NP is a more **unpredictable** topic, one being entered into the active file for the first time. As noted in Chapter 6, section 6.5., above, discontinuous nominal topics in Ute — be they either referential-indefinite or definites re-entering the discourse after a certain gap of absence — occupy a pre-verbal position (SV, OV). On the other hand, more continuous topics occupy a post-verbal position (VS, VO). This marking system is by itself sensitive to neither referentiality nor definiteness. It is supplemented by the use of the remote-invisible deictic "that"/"those" (in a post-nominal position) to explicitly mark definites. And by the use of object incorporation, at least in some cases, to explicitly mark non-referential ob-

---

18) From C.N. Li (in personal communication), but see also Li and Thompson (1975, 1981) and an earlier discussion in Givón (1978).

jects. As an illustration of this system once more consider:[19]

(38) a. ... yoĝóbų-ci págakwa-pųgá... (SV, DISCONT-SUBJ)
          coyote-SUBJ leave-REM
          { (i) '...so then **the coyote** left...' (DEF)   }
          { (ii) '...so then **a coyote** left...' (REF-INDEF) }

      b. ... págakwa-pųgá yoĝóvų-ci (VS, CONT-SUBJ, DEF)
          leave-REM coyote-SUBJ
          '...and **the coyote** left...'

      c. ... x'urá yoĝóvų-ci pųníkya-pųgá (OV, DISCONT-OBJ)
          then coyote-OBJ see-REM
          { (i) '...so then he saw **the coyote**...' (DEF)   }
          { (ii) '...so then he saw **a coyote**...' (REF-INDEF) }

      d. ... pųníkya-pųgá yoĝóvų-ci... (VO, CONT-OBJ, DEF)
          see-REM coyote-OBJ
          '...and he saw **the coyote**...'

      e. ... yoĝóvų-'ǫ́ą́-mi... (NON-REF, INCORP, OBJ)
          coyote-trap-HAB
          '...he always traps **coyotes**...'

11.4.5. The Creole prototype: Hawaii English Creole

In all Creole languages, as well as in many non-Creoles, one finds a morphological system marking definiteness and referentiality that is based on a three-way distinction between definite, referential-indefinite and non-referential, with generic subjects going either with the non-referential or with definite subjects. In Hawaii English Creole, the three markers are:[20]

(a) *da* ('the') = DEF
(b) *wan* ('one') = REF-INDEF
(c) Ø (zero) = NON-REF

As an illustration of this, consider:

(39) a. ge wan-man he no like potato... (REF-INDEF, SUBJ)
         have one-man he NEG like potato
         'There was **a man** who didn't like potatoes...'

---

19) For details see Givón (1980a, Ch. 17, 1983d).

20) The description is based on Bickerton (1975, 1977b, 1981).

b. da-man   no   like   potato   (DEF, SUBJ)
   the-man   NEG   like   potato
   'The man didn't like potatoes'

c. he   read   da-book   (DEF, OBJ)
   he   read   the-book
   'He read the book'

d. he   read   wan-book   (REF-INDEF, OBJ)
   he   read   one-book
   'He read a book'

e. he   no   read   book   (NON-REF, OBJ)
   he   NEG   read   book
   'He didn't read any book(s)'

f. Joe   he   teacher   (NON-REF, PRED)
   Joe   he   teacher
   'Joe is a teacher'

g. Joe   he   wan-teacher   I   bin-see...   (REF-INDEF, PRED)
   Joe   he   one-teacher   I   PERF-see
   'Joe is a teacher that I saw...'

h. (da)   elephant   he   big   animal   (GEN-SUBJ)
   (the)   elephant   he   big   animal
   { 'The elephant is a big animal' }
   { 'Elephants are big animals' }

The use of the contrast between the numeral 'one' and zero to code the referential-indefinite vs. non-referential contrast is also found in Israeli Hebrew,
Turkish, Mandarin Chinese, Persian, Sherpa, Romance, Germanic and
others, and will be discussed again later.[21] So far as one can tell, the Creole
coding system is the most consistent one attested, in terms of unifying the
marking system for subjects , objects and predicates, and in terms of abiding
by the predictions of the scale (34) and the hoop (35).

11.4.6. Definite vs. Indefinite: English

Although in English there are some more specialized devices for coding
non-referentiality, most commonly the major morphological contrast is between definite ('the') and indefinite ('a') article. The latter — in the appropri-

21) For further discussion, see Givón (1978, 1981c).

ate modal environment — can mark either a referential or non-referential nominal. Many illustrative examples have already been given in section 11.2., above. The diachronic development of such a system, via extending the scope of the referential-indefinite marker 'one' eventually to cover also non-referential indefinites, will be discussed further below.

11.4.7. Referential vs. non-referential: Bemba

In Bemba (Bantu), the major morphological distinction marked on nouns in the area of definiteness and referentiality is the referential/non-referential distinction. The VCV-form of the nominal prefix marks REF, and the CV- form marks NON-REF. The use of pre-nominal demonstratives to reinforce the referential *definite* interpretation is optional. As an illustration consider:[22]

(40) a. **umu**-ana   a-à-ish-ile   (REF-DEF, SUBJ)
         REF-child he-PAST-come-ASP
         '**The child** came'

      b. ku-à-ish-ile   **umu**-ana   (REF-INDEF, SUBJ)
         LOC-PAST-come-ASP   REF-child
         '...there came **a child**...'

      c. a-à-som-ene   **ici**-tabo   (REF, OBJ)
         he-PAST-read-ASP REF-book
         $\left\{\begin{array}{l}\text{(i) 'He read \textbf{the book}'} \\ \text{(ii) 'He read \textbf{a book}'}\end{array}\right.$ (DEF) ⎱
                                                                                   (INDEF) ⎰

      d. a-à-fwaaya   **ici**-tabo   (REF, OBJ)
         he-PAST-want REF-book
         $\left\{\begin{array}{l}\text{(i) 'He wanted \textbf{the book}'} \\ \text{(ii) 'He wanted \textbf{a (specific) book}'}\end{array}\right.$ (DEF) ⎱
                                                                                   (INDEF) ⎰

      e. a-à-fwaaya   **ci**-tabo   (NON-REF)
         he-PAST-want NREF-book
         'He wanted **some (nonspec.) book**'

      f. umu-ana   **umu**-puupu   (REF, PRED)
         REF-child REF-thief
         $\left\{\begin{array}{l}\text{(i) 'The child is \textbf{the thief}'} \\ \text{(ii) 'The child is \textbf{a thief}...}\end{array}\right.$ (DEF) ⎱
                                                                                   (INDEF) ⎰
                           ...that someone saw and...'

22) For further details see Givón (1972, 1973b).

g. umu-ana   **muu**-puupu   (NON-REF, PRED)
    REF-child   NREF-thief
    'The child is **a thief**'

11.4.8. The marking of generic nominals

As we have noted earlier above (section 11.3.5.), generic nominals occupy a peculiar position on the continuum of definiteness and referentiality (cf. (34), (35)). On the one hand, they clearly do not refer to specific individuals within the universe of tokens, and thus share some of the properties of **non-referentials**. On the other hand, they may be — particularly when used as subjects — highly topical and continuous, and thus likely to have been entered into the active discourse file. And in this sense they share many properties of **definites**. This intermediate status of generics is reflected in their morpho-syntactic coding, where on some occasions they may be — in the very same language — coded as referential definites, and on others as non-referentials. What one suspects, then, is that most languages may have at least two distinct ways of coding generic nominals. In discourse contexts where they are highly **topical**, the language may opt to code them as definite; while in discourse contexts where they are of low topicality, the language may opt to code them as non-referential. In the following sub-sections we will illustrate such options in a number of languages.

11.4.8.1. Definiteness, subjecthood, plurality and incorporation: English

A highly-topical generic noun is likely to be coded as subject in English, and then it may be coded as definite, indefinite or plural, as in:

(41) a. **The elephant** is a big animal
      b. **An elephant** is a big animal that...
      c. **Elephants** are big animals

While in all three cases above the scope of the expression surely includes *all* elephants, it is likely that further research will establish discourse-pragmatic differences between the three. One would predict, for example, that the definite in (41a) will be used when 'elephant' is more topical/continuous in the discourse than either the indefinite (41b) or the plural (41c). Plurality is thus not only a *semantic* feature increasing the number. It also decreases referentiality. And decreased referentiality leads to the *discourse-pragmatic* decrease of topicality. The relationship between these semantic and pragmatic facts may be summed up as:[23]

(42) a. "A plural or group is less likely to be used when unique referential identity is important in communication. Singulars are more
likely to be referential".

b. "A non-referential nominal is less likely to be an important discourse topic. Referential nominals are more likely to be important topics".

The facts summarized in (42) are not logically necessary, but rather reflect
deep cognitive constraints on **saliency**. Single individuals *stand out* perceptually more than groups. Their referential identity is more important since they
must be differentiated from other members of the group — who share their
type properties. Further, it is likely that both human *egocentricity* and the *size*
of the human hand — relative to objects that need to be handled — dictate the
assigning of a higher **world-pragmatic importance** — and higher frequency of
interaction and **attention** — to individual entities than to groups. And higher
frequency of interaction and attention must be at the root of higher discourse
topicality in communication.

English also illustrates another device in coding generic nominals,
namely, one specific to objects — their **incorporation** into the verbal word. In
English this is limited to nominalized verb-phrase (VP) compounds. Thus
consider:

(43) a. He hunted **the deer/a deer**   (unincorporated, REF)
b. He did some **deer**-hunting   (incorporated, GEN/NON-REF)

While in (43a) a specific, referentially unique deer must be involved, in (43b)
the subject is most likely to have hunted *many* deer, or to have spent a considerable amount of time hunting for *any* deer he could find. We will return to
consider the iconicity of object incorporation later on.

11.4.8.2. Referentiality and subjecthood: Bemba

As noted in section 11.4.6. above, the main morphologically-marked distinction in Bemba is between referential and non-referential, with both the
REF-indefinite and definite marked the same way, with the VCV- noun prefix. Generic subjects are marked by the VCV- prefix which characterizes defi-

---

23) The connections between plurality and non-topicality have been noted earlier by Timberlake (1975), Givón (1976b), Silverstein (1976), Hopper and Thompson (1980), *inter alia*. Some earlier discussion of this may be found in Chapter 5, section 5.4.4.2.2., above.

nites, never by the non-referential CV- prefix. Thus consider:[24]

(44) **aba**-ntu   baa-suma
      REF-people   NREF-good
          (i) '**The people** are good'   (REF, DEF)
          (ii) '**People** are good'   (GEN)

11.4.8.3. Demonstratives and object incorporation: Ute

As seen in section 11.4.4. above, generic objects may be expressed in Ute via incorporation into the verbal word. Thus consider:[25]

(45) a. 'uwás-'urá   yoǧóvу̣-ci   'ǫą́-pу̣gá..   (REF-OBJ)
          he-be   coyote-OBJ trap-REM
          '...so then he trapped **a/the** coyote..'

      b. 'uwás-'urá   yoǧóvу̣-'ǫą́-na-pу̣gá-vaci...   (GENERIC-OBJ)
          he-be   coyote-trap-HAB-REM-BKGR
          '...in those days, he used to trap **coyotes**...'

      c. 'uwás-'urá   yoǧóvу̣-'ǫą́-mi-tу̣   'urá-ąy (GENERIC-OBJ)
          he-be   coyote-trap-HAB-NOM be-IMM
          'He is a **coyote**-trapper'

Generic subjects are expressed either as normal unmarked subjects or with the use of a demonstrative—most commonly the *visible* one. This demonstrative grade is not commonly used in definitization away from the immediate scene. Thus:

(46) a. kwaná-**ci**   'u   páǧakwa-pу̣gá   (DEF-SUBJ)
          eagle-SUBJ   that-INVIS leave-REM
          'So **the eagle** took off'

      b. kwaná-**ci**   pу̣ká-yу̣cí-mi
          eagle-SUBJ   fast-fly-HAB
          (i) '**The (particular) eagle** flies fast'   (DEF-SUBJ)
          (ii) ⎰'**An eagle** flies fast' ⎱   (GEN)
               ⎱'**Eagles** fly fast'   ⎰
               ⎰'**The eagle** flies fast'⎰

      c. máa   kwaná-**ci**   pу̣ká-yу̣cí-mi   (GEN)
          that-VIS   eagle-SUBJ   fast-fly-HAB
          '**The eagle** flies fast'

---

24) See Givón (1972, 1973b).

25) See further detail in Givón (1980a).

11.4.8.4. Object incorporation: Coptic

In Coptic both definite and REF-indefinite objects are marked by the object prefix. The non-referential object is unmarked and is almost always incorporated into the verbal word. Thus consider:[26]

(47) a. a-f-muut   m-p-esou   (DEF, OBJ)
          ASP-he-kill   OBJ-DEF-sheep
          'He killed **the sheep**'

     b. a-f-muut   n-u-esou   (REF-INDEF, OBJ)
          ASP-he-kill   OBJ-INDEF-sheep
          'He killed **a sheep**'

     c. a-f-meut-esou   (GENERIC, OBJ)
          ASP-he-kill-sheep
          'He did some **sheep**-killing'

There are two striking features which characterize the incorporation of generic objects into the Coptic verb:

(a)   The object becomes part of the verbal word and thus loses its separate word status; and

(b)   The object loses its direct-object prefix, one which marks both definite and indefinite direct/accusative objects.

Both features in fact point to the incorporation process (47c) as being an object **removal** or object **demotion** process, via which the construction is rendered **intransitive** ("objectless"). Both must be considered iconic expressions of decreased referentiality, reflecting the following coding principle:

(48)   "The less referential and/or individuated an entity is, the less it is likely to be given *independent coding expression* in the grammar".[27]

Removal of independent word-status is a direct iconic expression of decreasing referential importance of an entity. Removal of the direct-object marker — as we shall see below — is for an object loss of higher topical status (cf. Chapter 5, above).

---

26) Reconstruction due to Stephen Emmel (in personal communication).

27) The iconic use of independent word status to code independence and importance in language may be seen in other areas of the grammar. Thus, for example, noun-modifier compounds such as "black-bird" etc. in effect remove the independence of the adjective (or noun) modifier, since some black-birds may be brown (the females). Similarly, in the syntax of verb complements it has been shown (Givón 1980b) that the less independent a complement verb is semantically from the main verb, the more likely it is to co-lexicalize with the main verb.

11.4.8.5. The antipassive in an ergative language: Nez Perce

As noted in Chapter 5, section 5.4.4.2.3.3., above, the antipassive construction in ergative languages is used when objects are either indefinite or low in referentiality. Thus Kalmár (1979, 1980) notes that in Eskimo the antipassive is used only when topic objects are introduced into the narrative for the first time. And Cooreman (1982, 1983) has shown that in Chamorro (a) objects in the antipassive constructions are the *lowest* in topicality of all constructions that can code transitive clauses, and (b) the majority of objects in the antipassive construction are non-referential.

In an ergative language, the antipassive clearly has the effect of removing the direct object via *demotion*, since the entire construction then becomes intransitive, both in terms of verb morphology as well as in terms of loss of the ergative morphology on the subject. This is best illustrated by data from Nez Perce, which has a peculiar twist on the ergative theme:

(a)   Ergative subjects are morphologically marked;
(b)   Absolutive subjects are morphologically *unmarked*; but
(c)   Absolutive direct objects are morphologically *marked*.

Morphologically, then, the absolutive is not a unified category in Nez Perce as it is in most ergative languages. And the antipassive in Nez Perce then involves three morphological adjustments toward the intransitive prototype:

(i)   Removal of the ERG marker from the subject;
(ii)   A switch from ERG-transitive to ABS-intransitive subject agreement on the verb; and
(iii) Removal of the DO marker from the object.

As illustration, consider:[28]

(49) a. 'ipí   hi-kuu-ye   (intransitive)
         he (ABS) he/ABS-go-ASP
         'He went'

      b. 'ip-ním   páa-sapiik-a   walás-na   (ERG-transitive,
         he-ERG   he/ERG-sharpen-ASP knife-OBJ   REF-object)
         'He sharpened **a/the** knife'

---

28) From Rude (1982, 1983).

    c. 'ipí   hi-sapíik-a   wálc   (ANTIPASS-

        he (ABS) he/ABS-sharpen-ASP knife   intransitive,

        'He sharpened **some** knife/knives'   NON-REF object)

In **nominative** languages such as English, Uto or Coptic, above, where generic objects may be expressed via pluralization or incorporation, the effect of such demotion on the marking system of the rest of the clause is small, since a nominative coding system is by definition less sensitive to transitivity. **Ergative** languages, as suggested in Chapter 5, possess a morphology that is sensitive neither to the semantic extreme of **agentivity** nor to the pragmatic extreme of **topicality**. Rather, ergative morphology is sensitive to **transitivity**. And one of the main features of the transitive prototype is the existence of a salient, visibly-changing direct object. The downgrading of referentiality and topicality of the object makes it a less prototypical object. And in an ergative language this is enough to undermine the transitivity of semantically transitive clauses. The antipassive construction is a major grammatical device for coding lowered referentiality or topicality of direct objects, and its morphological effect on the clause as a whole is to bring it closer to the intransitive prototype.

11.4.9. Other means of coding definiteness

11.4.9.1. The use of demonstratives as articles

One of the most common ways for a language to diachronically develop a DEF-marker is through the de-marking of a deictic/demonstrative modifier. Most commonly, it is the *distant* demonstrative that undergoes such a development, but it is possible to develop not only definite but also indefinite articles via this channel. Such a process has been reported for Dutch (Kirsner, 1979) but may also be seen in colloquial English. Thus consider:[29]

(50) a. I saw **this** girl yesterday, and...   [⊃ hearer is not expected to know the girl's identity = INDEF]

      b. I saw **that** girl yesterday, and...   [⊃ hearer is assumed to know the girl's identity; = DEF]

The demonstratives used in (50) are unstressed, and their erstwhile *spatial* deixis is *bleached out*. Nonetheless, their development from the proximate

---

29) Kirsner's explanation of this process is of a radically different sort, choosing instead to argue that the underlying semantics of the spatial deictics is of a different kind.

(INDEF) and distal (DEF) demonstratives can be related to their original deictic values via the following probabilistic/pragmatic/abductive inferences:

(51) a. "What is near the speaker and away from the hearer must be *less well known to the hearer*, thus indefinite".

b. "What is away from the speaker and thus near the hearer must be *better known to the hearer*, thus definite".

It is thus not the entire deictic value of the erstwhile demonstrative that is bleached out, but only its **speaker-related** value. But this is only to be expected, since definiteness/indefiniteness is a **hearer-related** pragmatic feature.

The same process, as applying only to the distal ('that') demonstrative, has occurred in Romance languages, Germanic, Sherpa, Mandarin and others. Quite often two word-orders are used, one for stressed deictic modifiers, the other for unstressed, bleached articles. As an example consider the following from Swahili:[30]

(52) a. m̂tóto **yúle**
child that
'**thát** child'

b. **yule** m̂tóto
that child
'**the** child'

The same may be shown in Ute, but with the opposite word-order variation:[31]

(53) a. ta'wáci 'u
man that
'**the** man'

b. 'ú ta'wáci
that man
'**thát** man'

11.4.9.2. Definite accusative

One fairly common way of handling definitization of objects is via a case-marker that codes only definite direct objects, or definite accusative ('patient') objects. As an example consider the following from Israeli Hebrew:

---

30) See Ashton (1944).

31) See Givón (1980a, Chapter 17).

(54) a. raíti   séfer-**xad**   sham   (REF-INDEF)
   saw-I   book-one   there
   'I saw **a book** there'

  b. lo   raíti   áf   séfer   sham   (NON-REF)
   NEG   saw-I   EMPH   book   there
   'I didn't see **any book** there'

  c. raíti **et**   ha-séfer   sham   (DEF)
   saw   ACC   the-book   there
   'I saw **the book** there'

The naturalness of this process may first be viewed diachronically, by noting two likely sources of the definite-accusative marker. First, it may come from a former serial-verb, as in Mandarin, where this usage is not obligatory. Thus consider:[32]

(55) a. wǒ dǎ-pò   le   zh'uāngzi   (REF-INDEF)
   I   hit-broken ASP   window
   'I broke **a window**'

  b. wǒ **bǎ**   zh'uāngzi dǎ-pò   le   (DEF)
   I   ACC   window   hit-broken ASP
   'I broke **the window**'

The DEF-ACC marker *bǎ* in Mandarin is historically the serial verb 'seize', 'hold' (see discussion in Chapter 5, section 5.5.4.6.). The definitizing effect of the use of serial verbs can be illustrated for other object case-roles which are often indefinite, such as the instrumental. Thus, consider the following example from Nupe:[33]

(56) a. kúta **lá**   foma   wā   nyikǎ   (DEF)
   K.   took   handnet caught fish
   { 'Kuta used **the handnet** to catch a/the fish' }
   { 'Kuta caught a/the fish with **the handnet**' }

  b. kúta wā   nyikǎ   **be-foma-nyi**   (INDEF)
   K.   caught fish   *with*-handnet-*with*
   'Kuta caught the fish with **a handnet**'

---

32) From C.N. Li (in personal communication), but see also Li and Thompson (1975, 1981) as well as discussion in Givón (1978).

33) See Madugu (1978).

In (56a) the serial-verb 'take' is used as an instrumental marker; the instrument is thus the direct object — i.e. more topical — and obligatorily definite; but the accusative may be indefinite. In (56b), on the other hand, the direct object precedes and is more likely to be definite, while the instrument follows with a pre/postposition (*be-....-nyi*) and is more likely to be indefinite. The definitizing power of a serial verb — and of the DEF-ACC marker derived from it — thus comes from the more topical status of the direct object (vis-à-vis the indirect object; see discussion in Chapter 5, section 5.5.3.).

The other likely source of definite accusatives is from re-analysis of dative case-markers. Since dative objects are overwhelmingly human and definite, they often spread on to mark *human definite* objects and may then spread further to *definite* objects in general.[34]

A more synchronic explanation of the prevalence of definite-accusative markers may point out that, of the major case roles, those of **subject**, **dative-benefactive** and **locative** are overwhelmingly definite in discourse, and thus require little or no marking for definiteness. In contrast, **instrumentals** and **manner adverbs** are overwhelmingly indefinite and non-referential. The only major argument with unpredictable definiteness is the **patient**. It is thus a case-role where marking definiteness explicitly is communicatively important.[35]

11.4.9.3. Definite object agreement

As noted in Chapter 10, above, verb pronominal agreement with definite objects is more likely than with indefinites, and as a result object agreement may serve to mark definite objects. As an illustration of this, consider again the following from Swahili:[36]

(57) a. ni-li-soma   kitabu   (INDEF object)
          I-PAST-read   book
          'I read **a book**'

---

34) An intermediate stage of this development may be seen in Spanish, where the erstwhile directional-locative and then dative preposition *a* is already used for human accusatives. For further discussion see Givón (1976b).

35) For text-counts of the definiteness of major arguments in text, see Givón (1979a, Ch. 2). See there also the argument noting the important role of the accusative case-role in introducing new referential-indefinite arguments into the discourse. For a similar synchronic argument, see Comrie (1975, ms.).

36) See Ashton (1944).

    b.   ni-li-**ki**-soma   kitabu   (DEF object)
        I-PAST-*it*-read   book
        'I read **the book**'

11.4.10. Definitization and case-roles

Given the varied ways languages may code definiteness, one may as well ask why languages such as Newari (section 11.4.2. above) exist, where neither definiteness nor referentiality is morphologically coded, and how such languages can perform their communicative function. The answer is in part general, i.e. that linguistic communication can always rely on the thematic, pragmatic and semantic **redundancies** available from the context. One such redundancy, however, is almost entirely predictable from what we know about semantic and pragmatic case roles. Some of them tend to involve more **topical** (and thus referential and definite) nominals, while others tend to involve less topical, indefinite or non-referential nominals. These are not grammatical restrictions, but rather **text-frequency** facts; but they make it possible to leave definiteness and referentiality morpho-syntactically unmarked in almost all case-role positions without a major loss of communicative resolution. The most common generalizations may be summed up as follows:[37]

(a)   *Subjects*: Overwhelmingly definite in discourse;

(b)   *Dative/benefactive*: Overwhelmingly definite in discourse;

(c)   *Time and place*: Overwhelmingly definite in discourse;

(d)   *Instrument*: Overwhelmingly indefinite and pragmatically non-referential (see discussion below) in discourse;

(e)   *Manner*: Overwhelmingly non-referential in discourse;

(f)   *Patient*: Overwhelmingly referential in discourse, but may be either definite or indefinite.

This summary suggests that the only position where predictability is low, and where high indeterminancy may arise as a result of lack of explicit marking, is that of the **patient/accusative** object. It is thus not altogether an accident (cf. section 11.4.9.2., above) that special provisions for marking definiteness are most commonly made for the patient or direct object. In addition, most languages have a special construction — existential presentative — for coding referential-indefinite subjects. While rare in discourse, such a construction serves to mark *important* topics entering into the discourse for the first time. It

---

37) For text counts and further discussion see Chapter 5, above as well as Givón (1976b, 1979a, Chapter 2).

thus contrasts with the patient or direct-object position, where most referen-tial-indefinites enter the discourse as *less-important* topics.[38]

11.5.   SCALES AND CONTINUA IN DEFINITENESS AND REFERENTIALITY

11.5.1. The pragmatics of referentiality

So far, we have treated the contrast between referential and non-referen-tial as a **semantic** one, involving the **referential intent** of the speaker regardless of the communicative context. This treatment, although divergent from the logical tradition, nonetheless preserves one feature of that tradition, namely the approach to referentiality as inherently a feature of propositional seman-tics. In this section we shall see that semantic referentiality is merely a special ('marked') case of a wider, discourse-pragmatic phenomenon, and that in human language referentiality is a matter of **communicative importance**, rather than pure referential uniqueness, of nominals.

The argument is rather simple. We have seen above how a number of lan-guages use special morphemes to mark referential-indefinite nominals as dis-tinct from non-referential ones. Many languages use the numeral 'one' for such a purpose (cf. Creoles, Israeli Hebrew, Mandarin Chinese, Persian, Sherpa, Romance languages, Germanic languages etc.). Others, such as Bemba, use the morphology of the nominal prefix for that purpose. Others yet, such as Ute, use object incorporation into the verb to effect this function for object nominals. In all these languages, the *semantically* non-referential noun always gets marked by these special devices. In addition, however, nouns that are semantically referential (i.e. "assumed by the speaker to exist as unique individuals") but whose exact referential identity is **communica-tively unimportant** in the particular discourse, are just as consistently marked by the same devices which code non-referentiality. As an illustration of this, consider the following from Israeli Hebrew:[39]

(58) a. kaníti   et-ha-séfer   etmól   (DEF)
          bought-I ACC-the-book yesterday
          'I bought **the book** yesterday'

---

38) Existential-presentative constructions will be discussed in Chapter 19, Volume II.

39) For the initial discussion, see Givón (1978, 1981c and, in particular, 1982c).

   b. kaníti   séfer-**xad** etmól   (REF-INDEF)
       bought-I book-*one* yesterday
       'I bought **a book** yesterday'

   c. ló   kaníti (af)   séfer etmol   (NON-REF)
       NEG bought-I (even) book yesterday
       'I didn't buy **a/any book** yesterday'

The contrast between semantically referential (58b) and semantically non-referential (58c) indefinite nouns is thus marked by the numeral 'one' as suffix (*-xad*) vs. the unmarked noun form, respectively. Consider now the following two examples from a wider discourse:

  (59) a. …az yatsáti la-rexóv
            so exited-I to-the-street
          '… so I went out into the street

      b. ve-haláxti ktsát
         and-went-I little
         and moved on a bit

      c. ve-axárkax nixnásti   le-xanút   sfarím
         and-later   entered-I to-shop-of books
         and then entered a bookstore

      d. ve-kaníti   séfer-**xad** she-ishtí   ratstá   **oto**
         and-bought-I book-*one* that-wife-my wanted-she *it*
         mizman;
         long-time
         and bought **a book** that my wife had wanted for a long time;

      e. ve-az   xazárti   ha-báyta   ve-natáti   la   **oto**,
         and-then returned-I to-the-house and-gave-I to-her *it*
         and then I went back home and gave **it** to her,

      f. ve-hi   samxá meód, ki   **ze** hayá séfer she-…
         and-she glad-she very   because *it* was-it book that
         and she was very happy, because **it** was a book that…'

  (60) a. …az yatsáti la-rexóv
            so exited-I to-the-street
          '… so I went out into the street

b. ve-haláxti   ktsat
   and-walked-I   little
   and moved on a bit

c. ve-axárkax   nixnásti   le-xanút   sfarím
   and-later   entered-I   to-shop-of   books
   and then entered a bookstore

d. ve-kaníti   séfer
   and-bought-I book
   and bought **a book**

e. ve-bilíti   sham ktsat zman   ve-histakálti   be-itoním,
   and-spent-I   there little time and-looked-I   at-magazines
   and spent some time there looking at magazines,

f. ve-az   aláxti   ha-báyta   ve-hitraxátsti ve-axálti....
   and-then   went-I   to-the-home   and-washed-I   and-ate-I
   and then I went home and washed up and ate...'

In both (59) and (60) "a book" is equally semantically/logically referential, being under the same FACT scope of past tense and an implicative verb. However, in (59) the referential identity of the book *mattered* in the subsequent discourse. It is not only semantically but also **pragmatically referential**. In (60), on the other hand, the referential identity of the book does not matter, the subject did some "book buying", the book is not an important topic in the discourse. The referentiality marker — the numeral 'one' — is used to mark the pragmatically-referential book in (59) but not the pragmatically non-referential book in (60). In other words, the REF/NON-REF distinction that matters in actual text is not the semantic one, but the discourse-pragmatic one.

The same situation exists in all other languages using 'one' as the referential-indefinite marker. It exists in Bemba with the use of the VCV-/CV- contrast in the nominal prefix, as in:

(61) a. ...na-o   a-à-somene   **ifi**-tabo...
        and-he   he-PAST-read   REF-books
        '...and then he read **the/some** books...' [⊃ whose exact identity
                                                              mattered]

     b. ...na-o   a-à-somene   **fi**-tabo...
        and-he   he-PAST-read   NREF-books
     { '...and then he read **books**...'   [⊃ whose exact identity
     { '...and then he did some **book**-reading...'   didn't matter]

The same is true in Ute and Coptic where non-referential objects can be incorporated into the verb. Thus consider the following from Coptic:[40]

(62) a. a-f-muut   n-u-esou
       ASP-he-killed   OBJ-INDEF-sheep
       'He killed **a sheep**'   [⊃ whose exact identity mattered]

    b. a-f-meut-esou
       ASP-he-killed-sheep
       'He did some **sheep**-killing'   [⊃ whose exact identity
                                                      didn't matter]

Finally, in ergative languages such as Chamorro (Cooreman, 1982, 1983) and Nez Perce (Rude, 1982, 1983), the objects in the **antipassive** construction display a high proportion of semantically non-referential nouns, and all of them — including the semantically referential ones — exhibit the *lowest topicality* on the average as compared with the objects in the ergative or passive constructions.

The facts concerning the semantic and pragmatic referentiality of definites and indefinites may now be summarized as follows, using two measures related to topicality and **topic importance** — **topic continuity** in the *preceding discourse* and **topic persistence** in the *subsequent* discourse:[41]

(63)

measure	DEFINITE	INDEFINITE		
		PRAG-REF	PRAG-NON-REF	SEM-NON-REF
continuity in the preceding discourse [being in the active file]	high	low	low	low
persistence in the subsequent discourse [remaining in the active file]	high	high	low	low
morpho-syntactic marking	DEF	REF-INDEF	NON-REF	NON-REF

40) Reconstruction due to Stephen Emmel (in personal communication).

41) For these measures and their theoretical and cross-language justification, see Givón (1983a).

The facts summarized in (63) make it now possible to re-define definiteness and referentiality in natural language in a more realistic fashion.

(64) (a) **Definiteness** is correlated with high topical continuity vis-à-vis the preceding discourse, i.e. having been entered in the active file;

(b) **Pragmatic referentiality** is correlated with high topical persistence vis-à-vis the subsequent discourse, i.e. persisting in the active file;

(c) **The morpho-syntactic** marking systems in natural languages are sensitive to pragmatic referentiality rather than to semantic referentiality. Thus nominals that are semantically referential but pragmatically non-referential are coded the same way as nominals that are semantically non-referential.

(d) **Semantic non-referentiality** is thus a special, more marked case of the more general feature of pragmatic non-referentiality;

(e) **The continuum space** of definiteness and referentiality may be given as:

DEF > PRAG-REF > SEM-REF

whereby having the feature DEF implies also having PRAG-REF, but not vice versa; and having the feature PRAG-REF implies also having SEM-REF, but not vice versa.

11.5.2. Semi-referentiality

Consider the following set of English yes-no questions:

(65) a. Did you see **any man** there?
b. Did you see **some man** there?
c. Did you see **a man** there?
d. Did you see **a bald man** there?
e. Did you see **a bald man** there wearing a blue tie with green polka dots and twirling a silver baton on his left toe?

So far, in the discussion above, we have represented the REF/NON-REF contrast — be it semantic or pragmatic — as a *discrete* feature. But the data in (65) are subtly graded so that (65a) represents a situation where the speaker is less likely to have any particular individual in mind, and then that likelihood slowly increases toward (65e). The last example displays the highest likelihood of a referential interpretation of the noun, given the extreme detail.

A related phenomenon may be seen in Spanish, one which may be labeled "degree of genericity". Thus consider:[42]

(66) a. María siempre habla con **brujos**
     Mary always   speaks with *sorcerers*
     'Mary always talks to sorcerers'

 b. María siempre habla con **los brujos**
     Mary always   talks with *the sorcerers*
     (i) 'Mary always talks to the sorcerers (not fully identified)'
     (ii) 'Mary always talks to the sorcerers (previously identified)'

While (66a) is the prototypical generic interpretation of "sorcerers", (66b(i)) is an intermediate grade, where perhaps the **subject** of sorcerers had been previously mentioned but still no **specific group** of sorcerers has been singled out in full detail.

Next, in the grammar of WH-questions in Ute, a major distinction is made between referential and non-referential WH-questions. The referential WH-question aims to solicit a full **definite description** of the queried constituent, such as 'Mary', 'the tall man', 'this horse' etc. The non-referential WH-question, on the other hand, aims to solicit a **type** response, such as 'a man', 'a tall woman', 'horses' etc. The semantic structure of the interrogative pronouns, further, makes it impossible to elicit a completely non-specified type response, since it requires specifying *animacy* and *plurality* of the queried nominal (in addition to the *case*-role distinction between subject and object). In both referential and non-referential WH-questions, then, a contrast between English and Ute reveals intermediate categories of both definiteness and referentiality. Thus consider first referential WH-questions:[43]

(67) a. 'áa wúy̨ka-x̂a?
     WH work-ANT
     'Who exactly worked [AN, SG]?'

 b. 'áa-my̨ wúy̨ka-ŝa-qa?
     WH-PL work-PL-ANT
     'Who exactly worked [AN, PL]?'

---

42) Sandy Thompson (in personal communication) also suggests that a similar distinction exists in Mandarin, coded by the contrast between "be" and "exist".

43) See details in Givón (1980a, Ch. 12).

c. 'aĝá-rʉ   yáxi-kya?
WH-NOM break-ANT
'Which one exactly broke [INAN]?'

The degree of specificity of the referential WH-question in Ute is thus higher than in English. But in both one could point to shades and gradations. Thus, in English one may contrast 'who' and 'which one' in two different ways. First, 'which one' queries a much more specific definite description than 'who', i.e.:

(68)   a.   Who did it?

               (i)   The butler
               (ii) Mary
               (iii) A man in a top hat who sneaked in and out undetected
               (iv) A blind man
               (v)   A woman

          b.   Which one did it?

                (i)   The butler
                (ii) Mary
              *(iii) A man in a top hat who...
              *(iv) A blind man
              *(v)   A woman

Further, the range of responses appropriate to 'who' is split in Ute between the referential WH-question, which would cover responses (68a(i), (ii)), and the non-referential WH-question, which would cover responses (68a (iii), (iv), (v)).

Non-referential WH-questions in Ute display the same semantic features as the referential ones. That is, the WH-pronouns are marked for *animacy* and *number* (in addition to case-role). Thus consider:[44]

(69)   a.   'íni wúyka-x̂a?
               WH work-ANT
               'What kind of person/animal worked [AN, SG]?'

          b.   'iní-u   wúyka-x̂a-qa?
               WH-PL work-PL-ANT
               'What kind of persons/animals worked [AN, PL]?'

c. 'ípu yáxi-kya?
   WH break-ANT
   'What kind of a thing broke [INAN]?'

As stated above, non-referential WH-questions of this kind would elicit responses of the type (68a(iii), (iv), (v)) — but these are graded on a continuum of degree of specificity/referentiality.

Further, non-referential WH-questions may be further divided into those of "greater certainty" and "lesser certainty" — by the speaker — about the possibility of a type-description being available. Thus consider:

(70) a. 'íni 'ará-'ay, 'ína?
        WH be-IMM this-SUBJ
        '**What kind** of a person/animate is this [AN, SG]?'

     b. 'ính-kway 'ará-'ay, 'ína?
        WH-MOD be-IMM this-SUBJ
        '**What kind** of a person/animate **could this possibly** be [AN, SG]?'

Questions such as (70a), without the modal suffix -*kway*, are used when the speaker assumes that an easy answer exists for the type question, i.e. that the description is one of the normal set of readily-identifiable types. On the other hand, (70b) will be used when the speaker expects type identification to be problematic, when the entity to be described does not exhibit — *prima facie* — enough of the properties used for easy classification into one of the more normal types. But this sense of "normality" has to do with the gradation of type descriptions: "Normal" types already exhibit some criterial properties used for making decisions about membership. In other words, they are already **partially described**. On the other hand, "less normal" types exhibit fewer criterial properties. In other words, they are **less described**.

The modal suffix -*kway* is also used to decrease referentiality in declarative sentences, in conjunction with a systematic use of non-referential WH-pronouns. Thus consider:

(71) a. wíitus-'urá 'uwás-'u yoĝóvu-ci   'urá-pugá...
        past-be   he-that coyote-SUBJ be-REM
        'Long time ago there was **that coyote**...'   [DEF]

     b. wíitus-'urá yoĝóvu-ci   'urá-pugá...
        past-be   coyote-SUBJ   be-REM
        'Long time ago there was **a coyote**...'   [REF, INDEF]

c. wíitʉs-'urá 'uwás... 'íni-kway 'urá-pʉgá...
   past-be   he   WH-MOD
   'Long time ago there was **that...what's his name**?'

[SEMI-DEF]

d. wíitʉs-'urá 'íni-kway 'urá-pʉgá...
   past-be   WH-MOD be-REM
   'Long time ago there was **a-what-cha-ma-call-it**...'

[SEMI-REF]

Thus, while (71c) decreases the degree of definiteness as compared with (71a), (71d) decreases the degree of referentiality as compared with (71b).

11.5.3. Semi-definiteness

We have already seen above some facts suggesting that not only referentiality but also definiteness can be a matter of degree, not merely of categorial presence or absence. This has to do with the completeness of the description. Thus, consider the following example from English:

(72) a. The man who killed Smith was insane.
        (i) 'I know exactly who killed Smith, and he was insane'.
        (ii)'Someone killed Smith; I don't know his full identity; but one thing I know about him — he was insane'.
     b. The man who killed Smith was an insane escaped prisoner...
     c. The man who killed Smith was an insane escaped prisoner who had spent ten years at Mayhem before being transferred...
     d. The man who killed Smith was a good friend of mine.
     e. The man who killed Smith was my good friend Archie.

In each case in (72), "Someone killed Smith" is presupposed. However, each one of the descriptions (72a) through (72d) can be used either as a fully specified definite description, or as a partially-specified one. And further, the **degree of specification** — and with it the likelihood that the expression will be used as a fully-specified description — increases. The interpretation (72a(ii)) is **attributive**, while the interpretation (72a(i)) is **referential**. What the data strongly suggest is that a graded continuum exists from non-referentiality through referentiality and on to definiteness. Along this continuum, languages tend to mark the most salient and/or pragmatically/communicatively useful categories or **prototypes**. And the most common prototypes cross-linguistically are "definite", "pragmatically referential" and "pragmatically non-referential". Still, an individual language may, on occasion, display a richer array of marked distinctions.[45]

11.5.4. Indefiniteness, referentiality and the numeral 'one'

As we have seen in section 11.4.5, above, perhaps the most common way of marking indefinites explicitly is by the use of the numeral 'one' to mark **referential-indefinites**. This contrasts normally with the use of the unmarked ('zero') form of the noun to mark non-referentials. Over time, however, the numeral 'one' marking referential-indefinites tends to be extended to cover *all* indefinites, including **non-referentials**. English provides of course a good example of this, as in:

(73) a. He bought **a book**   (REF, INDEF)
     b. He didn't buy **a book**   (NON-REF)
     c. Joe is **a teacher**   (NON-REF, ATTRIBUTIVE)
     d. Joe is **a teacher** I met last year   (REF, INDEF)

There are still surviving vestiges in English of the non-referential use of the zero/unmarked noun, as in:

(74) a. They elected him **president**
     b. He is **king** of the mountain
     c. She was **governess** to the prince

The same process of extension over time, from REF-INDEF to unrestricted INDEF, has also occurred in French (Price, 1971).

Spanish may be shown to occupy an intermediate position along the continuum of extending the scope of 'one' from REF-INDEF to unrestricted INDEF. Thus in predicate nominals, one observes a distinction already neutralized in English (cf. (73c, d)):[46]

(75) a. Es   profesor de Inglés   (NON-REF; unmarked)
        is-he professor of English
        'He is **an English professor**'

     b. Es   **un** profesor de Inglés   (REF-INDEF; 'one')
        is-he *one* professor of English
        que encontré...
        that met-I
        'He is **an English professor** that I met...'

---

45) Thus, for example, Keenan and Ebert (1973) report that in both Malagasy and Frisian, the degree-of-definiteness distinction in (71a) is morphologically marked.

46) For more details and further discussion, see Givón (1981c).

But in the complements of non-implicative verbs one finds 'one' used in both referentials and non-referentials, as in:

(76) a. estamos buscando   a   **una** criada   (NON-REF)
        are-we looking-for DAT *one* maid
        que sea   buena
        that be-SUBJUNC   good
        'We are looking for **a good maid**'

    b. estamos buscando   a   **una** criada   (REF-INDEF)
        are-we looking-for DAT *one* maid
        que nos está   esperando aquí
        that us is-she   waiting   here
        'We are looking for **a maid** that is waiting for us here'

Similarly, it is already possible to use the numeral 'one' in generic subjects in Spanish, as in:

(77) a. **un** amigo es alguien   que te   (GENERIC; 'one')
        one friend is someone that you
        quiere   mucho
        loves-he much
        '**A friend** is someone who loves you a lot'

    b. *amigo es alguien que te quiere mucho   (*unmarked)

Since both the use of 'one' (or other quantifiers) to mark REF-INDEF nouns and the diachronic spreading from REF-INDEF to unrestricted (thus also NON-REF) INDEF is so widespread, one must conclude that — as is the normal case in gradual diachronic change — the spreading proceeds along a functional/semantic continuum by small inferential steps. The major steps along this continuum may be given as:

(78) quantification > $\left\{ \begin{matrix} \text{referentiality} \\ \text{denotation} \end{matrix} \right\}$ > $\left\{ \begin{matrix} \text{genericity} \\ \text{connotation} \end{matrix} \right\}$

This continuum is obviously an **implicational/inclusion hierarchy**, whereby **type membership** (genericity, having connotation) is the most general case, **referentiality** (being an individual token, having denotation) is a more restricted case, and **having quantity** is the most restricted case. The evolution of the numeral 'one' along this continuum is thus another case of **semantic bleaching**, via which lexical words become grammatical/inflectional morphemes. And the set-inclusion relation of the three properties may be given as:

(79)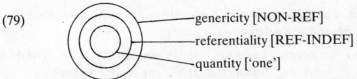

genericity [NON-REF]

referentiality [REF-INDEF]

quantity ['one']

Three questions must now be answered regarding the naturalness of this process — and thus the naturalness of the proposed continuum along which the numeral 'one' slowly develops into a grammatical marker:

(a) *Why start with a quantifier to mark REF-INDEF?*
     The answer to this is two-fold:
     (i)   A quantifier implies referentiality (cf. (77), (78)); and
     (ii)   Unlike most other modifiers, such as deictics, possessives/genitives, REL-clauses or other restrictive modifiers, it does not subsume definiteness;

'One' is thus a natural marker for introducing a referential topic into the discourse for the first time.

(b) *Why referential?*
     In the universe of discourse, existence or having unique identity is a precondition for participation, action or statehood. In other words, human communication is by and large — or "prototypically" — about real events [realis] and referential individuals (see discussion in Chapter 8, sections 8.2.6., 8.2.7.).

(c) *Why indefinite and why 'one'?*
     When a new referential argument is introduced into the discourse for the first time, the speaker obviously does not expect the hearer to identify it by any **referential** properties, since by definition that argument had not been entered into the active file before. He must then be expecting the hearer to "connect" or "cohere" the new argument by some other means, and the only means available are its **connotational** or **generic** properties. It is thus identified as being *one member out of many within the type*. This is obviously a peculiar and complex task, since the speaker must (a) imbue the new topic with referentiality, but (b) at the same time suggest its type membership as "one of the

type". The numeral 'one' (for singulars) or 'some' (for plurals) is certainly a prime candidate for coding such a conflicting message.[47]

47) Other means are also available though seemingly less frequent cross-language. Thus, for example, a reflex of *de* 'of', 'from' — *des* — marks plural indefinites in French. *De* 'of' itself marks the "partitive" — pragmatically non-referential — case in many grammatical environments in French, particularly with reference to mass nouns, as in:

Il boit **du** vin   'He drinks **some wine/of the wine**'
je ne bois pas **de** vin   'I don't drink **any wine**'

The last mentioned, however, are non-referential uses and thus do not compare with the inherently referential quantifier 'some'.

BIBLIOGRAPHICAL REFERENCES

Aissen, J. (1978) "Direct object advancement in Tsotsil", in D. Perlmutter (ed.) *Studies in Relational Grammar* [to appear].

Aissen, J. (1979) "Possessor ascension in Tsotsil", *Papers in Mayan Linguistics*, Columbia, Mo.: Lucas Brothers.

Anderson, L. (1982) "The 'perfect' as a universal and as a language-particular category", in P. Hopper (ed., 1982).

Anderson, S. (1970) "A little light on the role of deep structure in semantic interpretation", *NSF Report* no. 26, Cambridge: Harvard Computational Lab.

Anderson, S. (1976) "On the notion of subject in ergative languages", in C. Li (ed., 1976).

Antilla, R. (1977) *Analogy, State of the Art Report* no. 10, The Hague: Mouton.

Ashton, E. (1944) *Swahili Grammar*, London: Longmans.

Arnauld, A. (1662) *La Logique, ou l'Art de Penser*.

Atlas, J. (1974) "Presupposition, ambiguity and generality", Claremont, CA: Pomona College (ms.).

Austin, J.L. (1962) *How to Do Things with Words*, Cambridge: Harvard University Press.

Bach, E. (1970) "Is Amharic an SOV language?", *Journal of Ethiopian Studies*, 8.1.

Bateson, G. (1979) *Mind and Nature*, New York: Bantam.

Beauzée, N. (1767) *Grammaire Générale, ou Exposition Raisonnée des Eléments Nécessaires du Langage*.

Bennett, P. (1975) "Tone and the Nilotic case system", *BSOAS*, 36.1.

Bentivoglio, P. (1983) "Topic continuity and discontinuity in discourse: A study of spoken Latin-American Spanish", in T. Givón (ed., 1983a).

Benveniste, E. (1968) "Mutations of linguistic categories", in W.P. Lehmann and Y. Malkiel (eds), *Directions for Historical Linguistics*, Austin: University of Texas Press.

Berlin, B. and P. Kay (1969) *Basic Color Terms: Their Universality and Evolution*, Berkeley: U.C. Press.

Bickerton, D. (1975) "Creolization, linguistic universals, natural semantax and the brain", Honolulu: University of Hawaii (ms.).

Bickerton, D. (1976) "Creole tense-aspect systems and universal grammar", paper read at the *International Conference on Pidgins and Creoles*, Georgetown, Guyana, August 1976 (ms.).

Bickerton, D. (1977a) "Creoles and natural semantax", Honolulu: University of Hawaii (ms.).

Bickerton, D. (1977b) *Change and Variation in Hawaii English*, vol. II, *NSF Report*, Honolulu: University of Hawaii (ms.).

Bickerton, D. (1981) *Roots of Language*, Ann Arbor: Karoma Publishers.

Bickerton, D. and T. Givón (1976) "Pidginization and syntactic change: From SOV and VSO to SVO", *Parasession on Diachronic Syntax*, Chicago: *Chicago Linguistics Society*, University of Chicago.

Bickerton, D. and C. Odo (1976) *Change and Variation in Hawaii English*, vo. I, *NSF Report*, Honolulu: University of Hawaii (ms.).

Bloomfield, L. (1922) "Review of E. Sapir's *Language*", *The Classical Weekly*, 18.

Bloomfield, L. (1924) "Review of F. de Saussure's Course in General Linguistics", *The Modern Language Journal*, 8.

Bloomfield, L. (1926) "A set of postulates for the science of language", *Language*, 2.

Bloomfield, L. (1933) *Language*, New York: Holt, Rinehart and Winston.

Bolinger, D. (1948) "The information of accosting questions", *English Studies*, 29.

Bolinger, D. (1952) "Linear modification", in his *Forms of English*, Cambridge: Harvard University Press [1965].

Bolinger, D. (1954) "Meaningful word order in Spanish", *Boletín de Filología de la Univeridad de Chile*, vol. 8.

Bolinger, D. (1958) "Intonation and grammar", *Language Learning*, 8.1.

Bolinger, D. (1964) "Intonation as a universal", *Proceedings of the 9th International Congress of Linguists*, H.G. Lunt (ed.), The Hague: Mouton.

Bolinger, D. (1968) "Postposed main phrases: An English rule for Romance subjunctives", *Canadian Journal of Linguistics*, 14.

Bolinger, D. (1978) "Intonation across languages", in J. Greenberg et al (eds, 1978, vol. I).

Bolinger, D. (1982) "Intonation and its parts", *Language*, 58.3.

Bopp, F. (1833) *Vergleichende Grammatik des Sanskrit, Zend, Griechischen, Lateinischen, Litauischen, Gothischen und Deutschen*, Berlin.

Brugmann, K. (1902/1904) *Kurze Vergleichende Grammatik der Indogermanischen Sprachen*, Strassburg.

Bucelatti, G. (1970) A Grammar of Babylonian, Los Angeles: University of California (ms.).

Bull, W. (1968) *Time, Tense and the Verb*, Berkeley: U.C. Press.

Carnap, R. (1947) *Meaning and Necessity*, Chicago: University of Chicago Press.

Carnap, R. (1959) *The Logical Syntax of Language*, Patterson, N.J.: Littlefield, Adams and Co..

Chafe, W. (1977) "The evolution of the 3rd person verb agreement in Iroquois languages", in C. Li (ed., 1977).

Chafe, W. and J. Nichols (eds, forthcoming) *Evidentiality: The Coding of Epistemology in Language*, Ablex.

Chang, B.S. and K. Chang (1980) "Ergativity in Spoken Tibetan", *The Bulletin of the Institute of History and Philology*, Academia Sinica, 51.1 (Taipei).

Chomsky, N. (1957) *Syntactic Structures*, The Hague: Mouton.

Chomsky, N. (1961) "On the notion "rule of grammar"", in R. Jacobson (ed.) *Proceedings of the 12th Symposium on Applied Mathematics*, Providence: American Mathematical Society.

Chomsky, N. (1965) *Aspects of the Theory of Syntax*, Cambridge: MIT Press.

Chomsky, N. (1966) *Cartesian Linguistics*, New York: Harper and Row.

Chomsky, N. (1968) *Language and Mind*, New York: Harcourt, Brace and World.

Chung, S. (1975) "Dative and grammatical relations in Indonesian", U.C. San Diego (ms.).

Chung, S. (1976a) *Case Marking and Grammatical Relations in Polynesian*, Ph.D. dissertation, Harvard University (ms.).

Chung, S. (1976b) "On the subject of two passives in Indonesian", in C. Li (ed., 1976).

Chung, S. (1981) "Transitivity and surface filters in Chamorro", in J. Hollyman and A. Pawley (eds.), *Studies in Pacific Languages and Cultures in Honor of Bruce Biggs*, Auckland: Linguistic Society of New Zealand.

Chung, S. and A. Timberlake (forthcoming) "Tense, aspect and mode", in T. Shopen (ed., forthcoming).

Clark, E. (1971) "What's in a word?", in T. Moore (ed.) *Cognitive Development and the Acquisition of Language*, New York: Academic Press.

Clark, H. (1969) "Linguistic processes in deductive reasoning", *Psychological Review*, 76.4.

Clark, H. (1971) "The primitive nature of children's relational concepts", in J. Hayes (ed.) *Cognition and the Development of Language*, New York: Wiley and Son.

Cole, P. and J. Morgan (eds, 1975) *Speech Acts, Syntax and Semantics*, vol. 3, New York: Academic Press.

Coleman, L. and P. Kay (1981) "Prototype semantics and the English word *lie*", *Language*, 57.1.

Comrie, B. (1975) "Definite direct object and referent identifiability", Los Angeles: University of Southern California (ms.).

Comrie, B. (1976) *Aspect*, Cambridge: Cambridge University Press.

Comrie, B. (1978) "Ergativity", in W.P. Lehmann (ed., 1978).

Comrie, B. (1979) "Definite and animate direct objects: A natural class", *Linguistica Silesiana*, 3.

Comrie, B. (1983) "Discussion", in W. Chisholm (ed.) *Interrogativity*, *Typological Studies in Language*, vol. 4, Amsterdam: J. Benjamins.

Cooper, W. and J.R. Ross (1975) "World order", *Parasession on Functionalism*, Chicago: *Chicago Linguistics Society*, University of Chicago.

Cooreman, A. (1982a) "Transitivity, ergativity and topicality in Chamorro Narrative discourse", *Berkeley Linguistic Society*, no. 8, Berkeley: University of California.

Cooreman, A. (1982b) "Topicality, ergativity and transitivity in narrative discourse: Evidence from Chamorro", *Studies in Language*, 6.3.

Cooreman, A., B. Fox and T. Givón (1984) "The discourse definition of ergativity", *Studies in Language*, 8.1.

Cordemoy, G. de (1666) *Discourse Physique de la Parole*.

Craig, C. (1976) "Properties of basic and derived subjects in Jacaltec", in C. Li (ed., 1976).

Craig, C. (1977) *The Structure of Jacaltec*, Austin: University of Texas Press.

Craig, C. (1982) "Noun classifiers in Jacaltec", Eugene: University of Oregon (ms.).

Creamer, M.H. (1974) "Ranking in Navajo nouns", *Diné Bizaad Nanil'įįh* [*Navajo Language Review*], 1.

Creider, C. (1975) "Thematization and word-order", LSA Winter (ms.).

Creider, C. (1976) "Functional sentence perspective in verb-initial languages", paper read at the *7th Conference on African Linguistics*, Gainsville: University of Florida (ms.).

Creider, C. (1977) "A syntactic sketch of Nandi", London: University of Western Ontario (ms.).

Crouch, J.E. (1978) *Functional Human Anatomy*, [3rd edition], Philadelphia: Lea and Febiger.

Daneš, F. (ed., 1974) *Papers on Functional Sentence Perspective*, The Hague: Mouton.

DeLancey, S. (1981) "An interpretation of split ergativity and related patterns", *Language*, 57.3.

DeLancey, S. (1982) "Agentivity and causation: Data from Hare (Athabascan)", LSA Winter, San Diego, December 1982 (ms.).

Delbrück, B. (1901) *Grundfragen der Sprachforschung*, Strassburg.

Denny, J.P. and C.A. Creider (1976) "The semantics of noun classes in Proto-Bantu", *Studies in African Linguistics*, 7.1.

Derbyshire, D. (1977) "Word order universals and the existence of OVS languages", *Linguistic Inquiry*, 8.

Derbyshire, D. (1979a) *Hixkaryana*, *Lingua Descriptive Studies*, no. 1, Amsterdam: North Holland.

Derbyshire, D. (1979b) *Hixkaryana Syntax*, Ph.D. dissertation, University of London (ms.).

Derbyshire, D. (1981) "A diachronic explanation for the origin of OVS languages", SIL Summer Institute, Missoula, Montana (ms.).

Derbyshire, D. and G.K. Pullum (1981) "Object initial languages", *IJAL*, 47.3.

Dik, S.C. (1978) *Functional Grammar*, Amsterdam: North Holland.

Dillard, J. (1972) *Black English: Its History and usage in the United States*, New York: Vintage Press.

Dixon, R.M.W. (1972a) "Where have all the adjectives gone?", Canberra: Australian National University (ms.).

Dixon, R.M.W. (1972b) *The Dyirbal Language of North Queensland*, Cambridge: Cambridge University Press.

Dixon, R.M.W. (ed., 1976) *Grammatical Categories in Australian Languages*, Canberra: Australian Institute of Aboriginal Studies.

Dixon, R.M.W. (1977) "The syntactic development of Australian languages", in C. Li (ed., 1977).

Dixon, R.M.W. (1979a) "Ergativity", *Language*, 55.1.

Dixon, R.M.W. (1979b) "Corrections and comments concerning Heath's "Is Dyirbal ergative?"", *Linguistics*, 17.

Donellan, K. (1966) "Reference and definite description", *The Philosophical Review*, 75.3.

Dreizin, F. (1980) "The flavour of Russian negation: Some notes on and around", Haifa: University of Haifa (ms.).

Dryer, M. (1982) "Tlingit: An object-initial language?", paper read at the *Western Conference on Linguistics*, Edmonton: University of Alberta (ms.).

Du Bois, J. (1981) "Self-evident", in W. Chafe and J. Nichols (eds, forthcoming).

Du Marsais, C.C. (1729) *Véritables Principes de la Grammaire*.

Eastman, C.M. and E.A. Edwards (1981) "The influence of pragmatic function on linear order in Haida", paper read at the *Western Conference on Linguistics*, Seattle: University of Washington (ms.).

Egerod, S. (1975) "Typology of Chinese sentence structure", paper read at the *8th Conference on Sino-Tibetan Languages and Linguistics*, Berkeley: University of California (ms.).

Firbas, J. (1966a) "On defining the theme in functional sentence perspective", *Travaux Linguistiques de Prague*, 1.

Firbas, J. (1966b) "Non-thematic subjects in contemporary English", *Travaux Linguistiques de Prague*, 2.

Fodor, J.A. and M.F. Garrett (1967) "Some syntactic determinants of sentential complexity", *Perception and Psycholinguistics*, vol. 2.

Fox, A. (1983) "Topic continuity in Biblical Hebrew Narrative", in T. Givón (ed., 1983a).

Fox, B. (forthcoming) untitled Ph.D dissertation, Los Angeles: University of California (ms.).

Fulas, H. (1974) "Pseudo object constructions in Amharic", *Proceedings of the IV Congresso Internazionale di Studi Etiopici*, Rome: Academia Nazionale dei Lincei.

García, E. (1975) *The Role of Theory in Linguistic Analysis: The Spanish Pronoun System*, Amsterdam: North Holland.

Gary, N. (1974) "A discourse analysis of certain root transformations in English", Los Angeles: University of California (ms.).

Givón, T. (1970a) "Notes on the semantic structure of English adjectives", *Language*, 46.4.

Givón, T. (1970b) "The resolution of gender conflicts in Bantu conjunction: Where syntax and semantics clash", *CLS* no 6, Chicago: *Chicago Linguistics Society*, University of Chicago.

Givón, T. (1971a) "Historical syntax and synchronic morphology: An archaeologist's field trip", *CLS* no 7, Chicago: *Chicago Linguistics Society*, University of Chicago.

Givón, T. (1971b) "Some historical changes in the noun-class system of Bantu, their possible causes and wider implications", in W.-C. Kim and H. Stahlke (eds) *Papers in African Linguistics*, Edmonton: Linguistic Research.

Givón, T. (1972) *Studies in ChiBemba and Bantu Grammar*, Supplement no. 3, *Studies in African Linguistics*.

Givón, T. (1973a) "The time-axis phenomenon", *Language*, 49.4.

Givón, T. (1973b) "Opacity and reference in language: An inquiry into the role of modalities", in J. Kimball (ed.) *Syntax and Semantics*, vol. 2, New York: Academic Press.

Givón, T. (1975a) "Serial verbs and syntactic change: Niger-Congo", in C. Li (ed., 1975).

Givón, T. (1975b) "Focus and the scope of assertion: Some Bantu evidence", *Studies in African Linguistics*, 6.2.

Givón, T. (1975c) "Negation in language: Function, pragmatics, ontology", *Working Papers in Language Universals*, vol. 18, Stanford: Stanford University.

Givón, T. (1976a) "On the SOV reconstruction of So. Nilotic: Internal evidence from Toposa", *Supplement no. 6, Studies in African Linguistics* [papers in honor of W. Welmers on the occasion of his 60th birthday].

Givón, T. (1976b) "Topic, pronoun and grammatical agreement", in C. Li (ed., 1976).

Givón, T. (1976c) "On the VS word-order in Israeli Hebrew: Pragmatics and typological change", in P. Cole (ed.) *Studies in Modern Hebrew Syntax and Semantics*, Amsterdam: North Holland.

Givón, T. (1977a) "On the SOV origin of the suffixal agreement conjugation in Indo-European and Semitic", in A. Juilland (ed.), *Linguistic Studies Offered to Joseph Greenberg on the Occasion of his 60th Birthday*, Stanford: Anma Libri.

Givón, T. (1977b) "The drift from VSO to SVO in Biblical Hebrew: The pragmatics of tense-aspect", in C. Li (ed., 1977).

Givón, T. (1978) "Definiteness and referentiality", in J. Greenberg, C. Ferguson and E. Moravcsik (eds, 1978).

Givón, T. (1979a) *On Understanding Grammar*, New York: Academic Press.

Givón, T. (1979b) "Language typology in Africa: A critical review", *Journal of African Languages and Linguistics*, 1.2.

Givón, T. (1979c/1973) "Prolegomena to any sane Creology", in I. Hancock et al (eds), *Readings in Creole Studies*, Ghent: Story-Scientia.

Givón, T. (ed., 1979d) *Discourse and Syntax, Syntax and Semantics*, vol. 12, New York: Academic Press.

Givón, T. (1980a) *Ute Reference Grammar*, Ignacio: Ute Press.

Givón, T. (1980b) "The binding hierarchy and the typology of complements", *Studies in Language*, 4.3.

Givón, T. (1980c) "The drift away from ergativity: Diachronic potentials in Sherpa", *Folia Linguistica Historica*, 1.1.

Givón, T. (1981a) "Direct object and dative shifting: Semantics and pragmatics of case", in F. Plank (ed.) *Objects*, New York: Academic Press.

Givón, T. (1981b) "Typology and functional domains", *Studies in Language*, 5.2.

Givón, T. (1981c) "On the development of the numeral 'one' as an indefinite marker", *Folia Linguistica Historica*, 2.1.

Givón, T. (1982a) "Tense-aspect-modality: The Creole prototype and beyond", in P. Hopper (ed.) *Tense and Aspect: Between Semantics and Pragmatics, Typological Studies in Language*, vol. 1, Amsterdam: J. Benjamins.

Givón, T. (1982b) "Evidentiality and epistemic space", *Studies in Language*, 6.1.

Givón, T. (1982c) "Logic vs. pragmatics, with human language as the referee: Toward an empirically viable epistemology", *Journal of Pragmatics*, 6.1.

Givón, T. (ed., 1983a) *Topic Continuity in Discourse: Quantitative Cross-Language Studies, Typological Studies in Language*, vol. 3, Amsterdam: J. Benjamins.

Givón, T. (1983b) "Topic continuity in discourse: The functional domain of switch-reference", in J. Haiman and P. Munro (eds, 1983).

Givón, T. (1983c) "Universals of discourse structure and second language acquisition", in W. Rutherford and R. Scarcella (eds) *Language Universals and Second Language Acquisition, Typological Studies in Language*, vol. 5, Amsterdam: J. Benjamins.

Givón, T. (1983d) "Topic continuity and word-order pragmatics in Ute", in T. Givón (ed., 1983a).

Givón, T. (1983e) "The speech-act continuum", in W. Chisholm (ed.), *Interrogativity, Typological Studies in Language*, vol. 4, Amsterdam: J. Benjamins.

Givón, T. (forthcoming) "Iconicity, isomorphism and non-arbitrary coding in syntax", in J. Haiman (ed., 1984).

Goral, D. (forthcoming) untitled Ph.D. dissertation, Berkeley: University of California (ms).

Gordon, D. and G. Lakoff (1971) "Conversational postulates", *CLS* no 7, Chicago: *Chicago Linguistics Society*, University of Chicago.

Greenberg, J. (1966) "Some universals of grammar with particular reference to the order of meaningful elements", in J. Greenberg (ed.) *Universals of Language*, Cambridge: MIT Press.

Greenberg, J. (1977) "Niger-Congo noun-class markers: Prefixes, suffixes, both or neither", in M. Mould and T. Hinnebusch (eds) *Papers from the 8th Conference on African Linguistics*, Supplement no. 7, *Studies in African Linguistics*.

Greenberg, J. (1978) "How does a language acquire gender markers", in J. Greenberg et al (eds, 1978, vol. 3).

Greenberg, J., C. Ferguson and E. Moravcsik (eds, 1978) *Universals of Human Language*, 4 volumes, Stanford: Stanford University Press.

Grice, H.P. (1968/1975) "Logic and conversation", in P. Cole and J. Morgan (eds, 1975).

Grimm, J. (1819-1837) *Deutsche Grammatik*, Göttingen.

Haile, G. (1970) "The suffix pronoun in Amharic", in W.-C. Kim and H. Stahlke (eds) *Papers in African Linguistics*, Edmonton: Linguistic Research.

Haiman, J. (1978) "Conditionals are topics", *Language*, 54.3.

Haiman, J. (1980) "The iconicity of grammar: Isomorphism and motivation", *Language*, 56.3.

Haiman, J. (ed., 1984) *Iconicity in Syntax, Typological Studies in Language*, vol. 6, Amsterdam: J. Benjamins.

Haiman, J. (forthcoming) *Natural Syntax*, Cambridge: Cambridge University Press.

Haiman, J. and P. Munro (1983) *Switch Reference, Typological Studies in Language*, vol. 2, Amsterdam: J. Benjamins.

Hale, K. (1977) *A Grammatical Sketch of Walbiri*, in T. Shopen (ed., forthcoming) (ms.).

Hale, K. (1980/1981) "On the position of Walbiri in a typology of the base", Bloomington: Indiana Linguistics Club (ms.).

Halliday, M.A.K. (1967) "Notes on transitivity and theme in English", *Journal of Linguistics*, 3.

Harris, A.C. (1982) *Diachronic Syntax: The Kartvelian Case* (ms.).

Harris, A.C. (1983) "Questions in Georgian Languages", in W. Chisholm (ed.) *Interrogativity, Typological Studies in Language*, vol. 4 Amsterdam: J. Benjamins.

Harris, Z. (1956) "Co-occurrence and transformation in linguistic structure", *Language*, 33.

Hawkins, J. (1980) "On implicational and distributional universals of word-order", *Journal of Linguistics*, 16.

Hawkinson, A. and L. Hyman (1974) "Natural topic hierarchies in Shona", *Studies in African Linguistics*, 5.2.

Heath, J. (1977) "Choctaw cases", Berkeley: *Berkeley Linguistic Society*, vol. 3 University of California.

Heath, J. (1979) "Is Dyirbal ergative?", *Linguistics*, 17.

Heath, J. (1980) "Dyirbal ergativity: Counter-rejoinder to Dixon", *Linguistics*, 18.

Henry, D.P. (1964) *The De Grammatico of St. Anselm*, Notre Dame: Notre Dame University Press.

Herzberger, H. (1971) "Setting Russel free", paper read at the *Philosophy Colloquium*, London: University of Western Ontario (ms.).

Hetzron, R. (1971) "Presentative function and presentative movement", *Studies in African Linguistics*, Supplement no. 2.

Hinds, J. (1979) "Properties of discourse structure", in T. Givón (ed., 1979d).

Hook, P.E. (1974) *The Compound Verb in Hindi, Michigan Series in South and Southeast Asian Languages*, vol. 7, Ann Arbor: Center for South and Southeast Asian Studies, University of Michigan.

Hopper, P. (1979) "Aspect and foregrounding in discourse", in T. Givón (ed., 1979d).

Hopper, P. (ed., 1982) *Tense and Aspect: Between Semantics and Pragmatics, Typological Studies in Language*, vol. 1, Amsterdam: J. Benjamins.

Hopper, P. and S. Thompson (1980) "Transitivity in Grammar and Discourse", *Language*, 56.

Hopper, P. and S. Thompson (1983) "The communicative basis for lexical categories", to appear in *Language*.

Horn, L. (1972) *On the semantic Properties of Logical Operators in English*, Ph. D. dissertation, Los Angeles: University of California (ms.).

Horn, L. (1978) "Some aspects of negation", in J. Greenberg et al (eds, 1978, vol. 4).

Humboldt, W. von (1836-1839) *Über die Kawisprache*, Berlin.

Humboldt, W. von (1836/1971) *Linguistic Variability and Intellectual Development*, trans. by G.C. Bruck & F.A. Raven, Coral Gables: University of Miami Press.

Hwang, M.-O. (1982) "Topic continuity/discontinuity in Korean narrative", Los Angeles: University of California (ms.).

Hyman, L. (1975) "The change from SOV to SVO: Evidence from Niger-Congo", in C. Li (ed., 1975).

Janda, R. (1978) "A case of liberation from morphology to syntax: The fate of the English genitive marker -(e)s", Los Angeles: University of California (ms.).

Jespersen, O. (1909) A Modern English Grammar on Historical Principles, Heidelberg.

Jespersen, O. (1924) The Philosophy of Grammar, London.

Johnson, D. (1974) Relational Constraints on Grammars, Yorktown Heights: IBM T.J. Watson Research Center.

Johnson, N. and J. Mandler (1980) "A tale of two structures: Underlying and surface forms of stories", Poetics, 9.

Judson, H.F. (1978) "Annals of science", The New Yorker, November 27, December 4, December 11, 1978.

Justus, C. (1976) "Relativization and topicalization in Hittite", in C. Li (ed., 1976).

Justus, C. (1978) "Syntactic change: Evidence for restructuring among coexistent variants", Journal of Indo-European Studies, 6.

Kalmár, I. (1979) Case and Context in Inuktitut (Eskimo), Ottawa: National Museum of Man, Mercury Series, no. 49.

Kalmár, I. (1980) "The anti-passive and grammatical relations in Eskimo", in F. Plank (ed.) Ergativity: Toward a Theory of Grammatical Relations, New York: Academic Press.

Karttunen, L. (1971) "Some observations on factivity", Papers in Linguistics, 4.

Karttunen, L. (1974) "Presupposition and linguistic context", Theoretical Linguistics, 1.2.

Katz, J.J. and J.A. Fodor (1963) "The structure of a semantic theory", Language, 39.

Kay, P. and C.D. McDaniel (1978) "The linguistic significance of the meaning of basic color terms", Language, 54.

Keenan, E.L. (1969) A Logical Base for a Transformational Grammar of English, Ph. D. dissertation, Philadelphia: University of Pennsylvania.

Keenan, E.L. (1972) "Two types of presupposition in natural language", in C.J. Fillmore and D.T. Langendoen (eds) Studies in Linguistic Semantics, New York: Holt, Rinehart and Winston.

Keenan, E.L. (1975) "Some universals of passive in Relational Grammar", CLS no. 11, Chicago: Chicago Linguistics Society, University of Chicago.

Keenan, E.L. (1976a) "Towards a universal definition of "subject"", in C. Li (ed., 1976).

Keenan, E.L. (1976b) "Remarkable subjects in Malagasy", in C. Li (ed., 1976).

Keenan, E.L. and B. Comrie (1972/1977) "Noun Phrase accessibility and universal grammar", *Linguistic Inquiry*, 8.

Keenan, E.L. and K. Ebert (1973) "A note on marking transparency and opacity", *Linguistic Inquiry*, 4.3.

Kimenyi, A. (1976) *A Relational Grammar of KinyaRwanda*, Ph.D. dissertation, Los Angeles: University of California (ms.).

Kimenyi, A. (1980) *A Relational Grammar of KinyaRwanda,* Berkeley: U.C. Press, *Linguistics Series*, no. 91.

Kintsch, W. and T. van Dijk (1978) "Toward a model of text comprehension and production", *Psychological Review*, 85.

Kirsner, R. (1979) "Deixis in discourse: An exploratory quantitative study of the modern Dutch demonstrative adjectives", in T. Givón (ed., 1979d).

Kiparsky, P. and C. Kiparsky (1968) "Fact", in M. Bierwisch and K. E. Heidolph (eds) *Progress in Linguistics*, The Hague: Mouton.

Kuno, S. (1981) *The Structure of the Japanese Language*, Cambridge: MIT Press.

Lakoff, G. (1973) "Hedges: A study in meaning criteria and the logic of fuzzy concepts", *Journal of Philosophical Logic*, 2.

Lakoff, G. (1977) "Linguistics gestalt", *CLS no. 13*, Chicago: *Chicago Linguistics Society*, University of Chicago.

Lakoff, G. (1982) "Categories and cognitive models", *Berkeley Cognitive Science Report no. 2*, Berkeley: Institute for Human Learning, University of California.

Lakoff, G. and M. Johnson (1980) *Metaphores we Live By*, Chicago: University of Chicago Press.

Lancelot, C. and A. Arnauld (1660) *Grammaire Générale et Raisonnée*.

Langdon, M. (1977) "Syntactic change and SOV structure: The Yuman case", in C. Li (ed., 1977).

Lehmann, W.P. (1973) "A structural principle for language and its implications", *Language*, 49.

Lehmann, W.P. (ed., 1978) *Syntactic Typology*, Austin: University of Texas Press.

Li, C.N. (ed., 1975) *Word Order and Word Order Change*, Austin: University of Texas Press.

Li, C.N. (ed., 1976) *Subject and topic*, New York: Academic Press.

Li, C.N. (ed., 1977) *Mechanisms for Syntactic Change*, Austin: University of Texas Press.

Li, C.N. and S. Thompson (1973) "Historical change in word-order: A case-study in Chinese and its implications", in J. Anderson (ed.) *Proceedings of the 1st International Conference on Historical Linguistics*, Edinburgh: University of Edinburgh (ms.).

Li, C.N. and S. Thompson (1975) "The semantic function of word-order: A case study in Mandarin", in C. Li (ed., 1975).

Li, C.N. and S. Thompson (1976) "Subject and topic: A new typology for language", in C. Li (ed., 1976).

Li, C.N. and S. Thompson (1981) *Mandarin Chinese: A Functional Reference Grammar*, Berkeley: U.C. Press.

Lieberman, A.M., F.S. Cooper, D.P. Shankweiler and M. Studdert-Kennedy (1967) "Perception of the speech code", *Psychological Review*, 74.6.

Lightfoot, D. (1976a) "Syntactic change and the autonomy thesis", paper read at the *Symposium on Syntacitic Change*, U.C. Santa Barbara, May, 1976 (ms.).

Lightfoot, D. (1976b) "The base component as a locus for syntactic change", *Proceedings of the 2nd International Conference on Historical Linguistics*, Amsterdam: North Holland.

Longacre, R. (1972) *Hierarchy and Universality of Discourse Constituents in New Guinea Languages*, Washington: Georgetown University Press.

Longacre, R. (1976) *Anatomy of Speech Notions*, Lisse: Peter de Ridder Press.

Longacre, R. (1979) "The paragraph as a grammatical unit", in T. Givón (ed., 1979d).

Longacre, R. (forthcoming) "Interclausal connections", in T. Shopen (ed., forthcoming).

MacDonald, J.D. (1974) *The Dreadful Lemon Sky,* Greenwich: Fawcet.

MacDonald, R. (1951/1971) *The Way Some People Die*, New York: Bantam .

McCawley, J. (1970) "English as a VSO language", *Language*, 46.

Maddieson, I., T. Shopen and T. Okello (1973) "Longo tonology, supra-segmentality and paradigms", paper read at the *4th Conference on African Linguistics*, New York: Queens College, C.U.N.Y. (ms.).

Madugu, I.G. (1978) "The Nupe verb and syntactic change", Ibadan: University of Ibadan (ms.).

Mallinson, G. and B. Blake (1981) *Language Typology*, Amsterdam: North Holland.

Mandler, J. (1978) "A code in the node: The use of a story schema", *Discourse Processes*, 1.

Mandler, J. and M. Goodman (1982) "On the psychological validity of story structure", *JVLVB*, 21.

Mandler, J. and N. Johnson (1977) "Remembrance of things parsed: Story structure and recall", *Cognitive Psychology*, 9.

Medin, D.L. and M.M. Schaffer (1978) "Context theory of classification and learning", *Psychological Review*, 85.3.

Miller, G.A. and W.G. Taylor (1948) "The perception of repeated bursts of noise", *Journal of the Acoustic Society of America*, 20.

Mühlhäusler, P. (1973) "Reduplication and repetition in New Guinea Pidgin", Canberra: Australian National University (ms.).

Munro, P. (1974) *Topics in Mojave Syntax*, Ph.D. dissertation, San Diego: University of California (ms.).

Munro, P. (ed., 1980) *Studies in Switch Reference*, *UCLA Papers in Syntax*, no. 8, Los Angeles: University of California.

Munro, P. and L. Gordon (1982) "Syntactic relations in Western Muskogean: A typological perspective", *Language*, 58.2.

Noback, C.R. and M. Moscowitz (1963) "The primate nervous system: Functional and structural aspects in phylogeny" in J. Buettner-Janusch (ed.) *Evolutionary and Genetic Biology of Primates*, vol. 1, New York: Academic Press.

Noback, C.R. and W. Montagna (eds, 1970) *The Primate Brain*, New York: Appleton.

Oh, C.-K. and D.A. Dinneen (eds, 1979) *Presupposition, Syntax and Semantics*, vol. 11, New York: Academic Press.

Orr, D.B., H.L. Friedman and J.C.C. Williams (1956) "Trainability of listening comprehension of speeded discourse", *Educational Psychology*, 56.

Palmer, F.R. (1979) *Modality and the English Modals*, London/New York: Longmans.

Palmer, L.R. (1954) *The Latin Language*, London: Faber and Faber.

Paul, H. (1880) *Prinzipien der Sprachgeschichte*, Halle.

Paul, H. (1916-1920) *Deutsche Grammatik*,.

Payne, T. (1982) "Role and reference related subject properties and ergativity in Yup'ik Eskimo and Tagalog", *Studies in Language*, 6.1.

Peirce, C.S. (1955) *Philosophical Writings*, edited by J. Buchler, New York: Dover.

Perlmutter, D. and P. Postal (1974) *Relational Grammar*, lecture notes, LSA Summer (ms.).

Piattelli-Palmarini, M. (ed., 1980) *Language and Learning: The Debate Between Jean Piaget and Noam Chomsky*, Cambridge: Harvard University Press.

Pike, K. (1954) *Language in Relation to a Unified Theory of the Stucture of Human Behavior*, The Hague: Mouton.

Posner, M. and S. Keele (1968) "On the genesis of abstract ideas", *Journal of Experimental Psychology*, 77.

Price, g. (1971) *The French Language*, London: Arnold.

Quine, W. van O. (1953) *From a Logical Point of View*, Cambridge: Harvard University Press.

Rosch, E. (1973) "Natural categories", *Cognitive Psychology*, 4.

Rosch, E. (1975) "Human categorization", in N. Warren (ed.) *Advances in Cross-Cultural Psychology*, London: Academic Press [1977].

Rosch, E. and B.B. Lloyd (eds., 1978) *Cognition and Categorization*, Hillsdale, NJ: Erlbaum.

Ross, J.R. (1970) "Gapping and the order of constituents", in M. Bierwisch and K.E. Heidolph (eds) *Progress in Linguistics*, The Hague: Mouton.

Ross, J.R. (1972) "The category squish: Endstation Hauptwort", *CLS no 8*, Chicago: *Chicago Linguistics Society*, University of Chicago.

Ross, J.R. (1973) "Nouniness", in D. Fujimura (ed.) *Three Dimensions of Linguistics*, Tokyo: TEC Corp..

Ross, J.R. (1974) "Clausematiness", in E.L. Keenan (ed.) *Semantics for Natural Languages*, Cambridge: Cambridge University Press.

Rude, N. (1982) "Promotion and topicality of Nez Perce objects", *BLS no. 8*, Berkeley: *Berkeley Linguistic Society*, University of California.

Rude, N. (1983) untitled Ph.D. dissertation, Eugene: University of Oregon (ms).

Russell, B. (1905) "On defining", *Mind*, 14.

Russell, B. (1919) *Introduction to Mathematical Philosophy*, London: Allen and Unwin.

Sanders, J. and J. Thai (1972) "Immediate dominance and identity deletion", *Foundations of Language*, 8.

Sapir, E. (1921) *Language*, NY: Harcourt Brace.

Saussure, F. de (1915) *Course in General Linguistics*, trans. by C. Bally and A. Feidlinger, New York: Philosophical Library [1959].

Schleicher, A. (1861) *Compendium der Vergleichenden Grammatik der Indogermanischen Sprachen*, Weimar.

Schuhardt, H. (1900) *Über die Klassifikation der Romanischen Mundarten*, Graz.

Schuhardt, H. (1914) *Die Sprache der Saramakkanger in Surinam*, Amsterdam.

Searle, J.R. (1970) *Speech Acts*, Cambridge: Cambridge University Press.

Shopen, T. (ed., forthcoming) "Syntactic Typology and Linguistic Field Work" (ms).

Silva-Corvalán, C. (1977) *A Discourse Study of Some Aspects of Word-Order in the Spanish Spoken by Mexican-Americans in West Los Angeles*, M.A. Thesis, Los Angeles: University of California (ms.).

Silverstein, M. (1976) "Hierarchy of features and ergativity", in R.M.W. Dixon (ed., 1976).

Slobin, D. (1977) "Language change in childhood and history", in J. MacNamara (ed.) *Language Learning and Thought*, New York: Academic Press.

Slobin, D. (1982) "The acquisition and use of relative clauses in Turkic and Indo-European languages", Berkeley. University of California (ms.).

Soemarmo (1970) *Subject-Predicate, Focus-Presupposition and Topic-Comment in Bhasa Indonesian and Javanese*, Ph.D. dissertation, Los Angeles: University of California (ms.).

Sridhar, S.N. (1976) "Dative subjects, rule government and relational grammar", *Studies in the Linguistic Sciences*, 6.1.

Steele, S. (1977) "Clisis and diachrony", in C. Li (ed., 1977).

Strawson, P.F. (1950) "On referring", *Mind*, 59.

Talmy, L. (1972) *Semantic Structures in English and Atzugewi*, Ph. D. dissertation, Berkeley: University of California (ms.).

Tanz, C. (1971) "Sound symbolism in words related to proximity and distance", *Language and Speech*, 14.

Thurman, R. (1978) *Interclausal Relations in Chuave*, M.A. Thesis, Los Angeles: University of California (ms.).

Timberlake, A. (1975) "Hierarchies in the genitive of negation", *Slavic and Eastern European Journal*, 19.

Traugott, E. (1974) "Spatial expressions of tense and temporal sequencing: A contribution to the study of semantic fields", Stanford: Stanford University (ms.).

Tyson, A. (1974) "Pleonastic Pronouns in Black English", Los Angeles: University of Southern California (ms.).

Vachek, J. (ed., 1966) *A Prague School Reader in Linguistics*, Bloomington: Indiana University Press.

van Dijk, T. (1972) *Some Aspects of Text Grammar*, The Hague: Mouton .

Vennemann, T. (1973a) "Explanations in linguistics", in J. Kimball (ed.) *Syntax and Semantics*, vol. 2, New York: Academic Press.

Verhaar, J. (1982a) "Ergativity, accusativity and hierarchy", *Sophia Linguistica*, 11 [1983].

Verhaar, J. (1982b) "Two aspects of pragmatics: Topicality and iconicity" in *Proceedings of the 13th International Congress of Linguists*, Section no. 14, *Pragmatics*, Tokyo, August, 1982 [1983].

Verhaar, J. (1983) "Syntactic ergativity in contemporary Indonesian", *Proceedings of the Third Eastern Conference on Austronesian Linguistics*, Ohio University, Athens (ms.).

Wachowicz, C. (1976) "Double WH questions", Stanford: Stanford University (ms).

Wald, B. (1973) *Variation in the Tense Markers of Mombasa Swahili*, Ph.D. dissertation, New York: Columbia University (ms.).

Weiss, A.P. (1929) *A Theoretical Basis of Human Behavior*, [2nd edition], Columbus.

Whitney, W.D. (1867) *Language and the Study of Language*, New York.

Whitney, W.D. (1874) *The Life and Growth of Language*, New York.

Whorf, B.L. (1956) *Language, Thought and Reality*, Cambridge: MIT Press.

Wierzbicka, A. (1981) "Case marking and human nature", *Australian Journal of Linguistics*, 1.

Wilkins, W. and A. Kimenyi (1975) "Strategies in constructing a definite description: Some evidence from KinyaRwanda", *Studies in African Linguistics*, 6.2.

Williamson, K. (1965) *A Grammar of the Kolokuma Dialect of Ịjọ*, Cambridge: Cambridge University Press.

Witherspoon, G. (1977) *Language and Art in the Navajo Universe*, Ann Arbor: University of Michigan Press [Ch. 3: "Classification of the world through language"].

Wittgenstein, L. (1918) *Tractatus Logico Philosophicus*, trans. by D.F. Pears and B.F. McGuinness, New York: The Humanities Press [1961].

Wittgenstein, L. (1953) *Philosophical Investigations*, trans. by G.E.M. Anscombe, New York: Macmillan.

Woodbury, A. (1975) *Ergativity of Grammatical Processes: A Study of Greenlandic Eskimo*, M.A. Thesis, Chicago: University of Chicago (ms.).

Zimmer, K. (1964) *Affixal Negation in English and Other Languages, Word Monograph no. 5*, New York.

INDEX OF SUBJECTS